'This is an important and scholarly book for all those interested in children's welfare, wellbeing and successful learning. It offers new insights about creating truly inclusive school communities and offers hope to marginalised young people.'

Emerita Professor Pamela Munn, *Former Dean, Moray House School of Education, University of Edinburgh, Scotland*

'This book offers a compelling alternative perspective to the traditional views of behaviour management in schools. The proposed alternative, focusing on humanistic and relational approaches, is deep and refreshing, a much needed analysis to move towards more inclusive schooling.'

Professor Sulochini Pather, *Institute of Childhood and Education, Leeds Trinity University, UK*

'With current policy and guidance in England veering towards zero-tolerance approaches, isolation rooms and punishment in schools, this book offers an empathetic alternative based on social justice, equity and compassion. Never mind Tom Bennett – Joan Mowat should be advising the DFE.'

Dr David Colley, *Associate Lecturer, Oxford Brookes University*

'In questioning the nature and purposes that education should serve, Joan Mowat's focus on meeting the needs of all young people, in and with their communities, gives new insight, hope and courage to all educators that schools can be equitable, inclusive and compassionate, and that authentic and lasting change is possible through strengthening relationships, creating empowering cultures and environments and building community.'

Margery McMahon, *Professor of Educational Leadership & Head of the School of Education, University of Glasgow*

Building Community to Create Equitable, Inclusive and Compassionate Schools through Relational Approaches

This book draws on an extensive international literature and policy context, from a wide range of fields of enquiry, to challenge the orthodoxies and systemic issues that serve to marginalise children and young people and lead the way for schools to become more equitable, inclusive and compassionate in their practice.

With a particular focus on children with social, emotional and behavioural/mental health needs, it critiques policy and practice as they pertain to behaviour management and school discipline in the UK and the USA, and offers alternative perspectives based on collaborative and relational approaches to promoting positive behaviour and building community. Each chapter features reflection points to provoke discussion as well as offering additional suggested reading, culminating in a discussion of the role of school leaders in leading for social justice.

Ultimately, this book will be of benefit to scholars, researchers and students working in the fields of behaviour management, inclusion and special needs education, and education, policy and politics more broadly. It will also offer substantial appeal to education professionals, school leaders and those with a locus in the mental health and wellbeing of children and young people.

Dr. Joan G Mowat is a senior lecturer in the School of Education at the University of Strathclyde and author of 'Using Support Groups to Improve Behaviour,' published by SAGE. She leads the 'Into Headship' programme for prospective headteachers. She has extensive experience in the classroom, latterly as Depute Head at Vale of Leven Academy. She undertook a short secondment as a national development officer for 'Better Behaviour-Better Learning.' Her principal research interests are the inclusion of children with social, emotional and behavioural needs, leadership for social justice and the relationship between poverty, attainment and wellbeing. Joan co-led a highly successful Scottish Universities Insight Seminar Series on this topic.

Routledge Research in Special Educational Needs

This series provides a forum for established and emerging scholars to discuss the latest debates, research and practice in the evolving field of Special Educational Needs.

Books in the series include:

Inclusive Teamwork for Pupils with Speech, Language and Communication Needs
Rosalind Merrick

Social and Dialogic Thinking and Learning in Special Education
Radical Insights from a Post-Critical Ethnography in a Special School
Karen A. Erickson, Charna D'Ardenne, Nitasha M. Clark, David A. Koppenhaver, and George W. Noblit

Policy, Provision and Practice for Special Educational Needs and Disability
Perspectives Across Countries
Edited by Peter Wood

Technology Use by Adults with Learning Disabilities
Past, Present and Future Design and Support Practices
Jane Seale

International Issues in SEND and Inclusion
Perspectives Across Six Continents
Edited by Alan Hodkinson and Zeta Williams-Brown

Building Community to Create Equitable, Inclusive and Compassionate Schools through Relational Approaches
Joan G Mowat

For more information about this series, please visit: www.routledge.com/Routledge-Research-in-Special-Educational-Needs/book-series/RRSEN

Building Community to Create Equitable, Inclusive and Compassionate Schools through Relational Approaches

Joan G Mowat

LONDON AND NEW YORK

First published 2023
by Routledge
4 Park Square, Milton Park, Abingdon, Oxon OX14 4RN

and by Routledge
605 Third Avenue, New York, NY 10158

Routledge is an imprint of the Taylor & Francis Group, an informa business

© 2023 Joan G Mowat

The right of Joan G Mowat to be identified as author of this work has been asserted in accordance with sections 77 and 78 of the Copyright, Designs and Patents Act 1988.

All rights reserved. No part of this book may be reprinted or reproduced or utilised in any form or by any electronic, mechanical, or other means, now known or hereafter invented, including photocopying and recording, or in any information storage or retrieval system, without permission in writing from the publishers.

Trademark notice: Product or corporate names may be trademarks or registered trademarks, and are used only for identification and explanation without intent to infringe.

British Library Cataloguing-in-Publication Data
A catalogue record for this book is available from the British Library

Library of Congress Cataloging-in-Publication Data
Names: Mowat, Joan G, author.
Title: Building community to create equitable, inclusive and compassionate schools through relational approaches / Joan G Mowat.
Description: New York : Routledge, 2023. | Series: Routledge research in special educational needs | Includes bibliographical references and index. |
Identifiers: LCCN 2022025867 (print) | LCCN 2022025868 (ebook) | ISBN 9781138607606 (Hardback) | ISBN 9781032372969 (Paperback) | ISBN 9780429467110 (eBook)
Subjects: LCSH: Students with disabilities--Education--Cross-cultural studies. | Inclusive education. | Educational equalization. | School management and organization. | Home and school. | Community and school. | Special education teachers--Training of.
Classification: LCC LC4031 .M69 2023 (print) | LCC LC4031 (ebook) | DDC 371.9/046--dc23/eng/20221007
LC record available at https://lccn.loc.gov/2022025867
LC ebook record available at https://lccn.loc.gov/2022025868

ISBN: 978-1-138-60760-6 (hbk)
ISBN: 978-1-032-37296-9 (pbk)
ISBN: 978-0-429-46711-0 (ebk)

DOI: 10.4324/9780429467110

Typeset in Galliard
by KnowledgeWorks Global Ltd.

This research monograph is dedicated to my husband, Gordon, my daughter, Alison and in loving memory of Emma and Fraser. It is also dedicated to Emeritus Professor John MacBeath, Emerita Professor Pamela Munn and Professor Roger Slee, all of whose work has been a great inspiration to me and for whose support and encouragement I have been very grateful.

Contents

List of Figures	xi
List of Tables	xiii
List of Charts and Boxes	xv
Foreword	xvi
Acknowledgements	xix
List of Acronyms	xxi

Introduction: Making a Difference to the Lives of Children and Young People	1

PART I
Understanding the Drivers for Change within the System: The Policy Context — 7

1 Understanding the Policy Context: The Macrosystem — 9

2 Inclusive Education: Challenges, Tensions and Dilemmas — 25

PART II
Exploring and Understanding the Problem — 43

3 Marginalisation, Social Exclusion and the Impact of Poverty on Children and Young People — 45

4 Schools as Places of Belonging or Exclusion: School Disaffection — 65

x *Contents*

5 Understanding Social, Emotional and Behavioural
   Needs (SEBN)/Mental Health Needs (SEMHN)   81

6 Looking through the Lens of Developmental Theory
   to Understand Social, Emotional and Behavioural
   Needs (SEBN)/Mental Health Needs (SEMHN)   96

PART III
Towards New Understandings: Challenging
Orthodoxies and Building Community through
Relational Approaches   113

7 Challenging the Orthodoxies of Behaviour
   Management through an Examination
   of Power, Influence and Authority   115

8 Challenging the Orthodoxies of Behaviour
   Management through a Focus on Policy
   and Practice   132

9 Building Community through Nurture
   and Trauma-Informed Practice   154

10 Building Community through Restorative
    Justice/Practice   173

PART IV
Empowering the School Community   189

11 Working Collaboratively Together to Empower
    the School Community through Pupil Participation
    and Parental Engagement   191

12 Empowering the School Community through Socially
    Just and Culturally Responsive Leadership   213

   References   234
   Index   271

Figures

i.1	Illustration of the structure of the book.	4
2.1	A representation of Ainscow, Booth, and Dyson's (2006a) typology of inclusion.	27
2.2	A summary of key points.	32
2.3	A representation of the 'looping effect'.	39
3.1	Illustration of levels of structural inequality.	48
3.2	Representation of Messiou's (2019) conceptualisation of marginalisation.	50
3.3	How marginalisation may manifest itself in relation to what is valued by the child and what is valued by society, if lacking.	53
3.4	An ecological representation of resilience building upon Olsson et al. (2003) and other theorists.	54
3.5	Word Art illustration of the executive summary to the 4th interim report of the Scottish attainment fund.	63
6.1	Representation of *classical conditioning* as described by Newman and Newman (2016).	103
8.1	Word Art representation of *Behaviour and Discipline in Schools*.	142
8.2	Illustration from *Included, Engaged and Involved* (Part 2).	148
9.1	Modification of MacKay's (2015) research agenda for nurture in education.	161
10.1	Model of transfer.	175
10.2	Framework to guide implementation of *restorative practice* for school leaders.	186
11.1	Illustration of community.	192
11.2	A visualisation of the relationship between control and agency/autonomy.	195
11.3	A representation of Hart's ladder of participation.	204
11.4	Continuum of parental engagement in children's learning.	207
11.5	The shifting of the locus of *agency* from school to parent along the continuum towards *parental engagement*.	207

xii *Figures*

11.6 An interpretation of Tett and Macleod (2020, pp. 457–8).   209
12.1 Representation of the role of school leaders in leading
      for social justice.   215
12.2 A model of cultural responsiveness of school leaders.   228
12.3 A representation of the relationship between wellbeing,
      learning and behaviour.   230

Tables

1.1	Key themes to emerge from analysis of international educational policy	15
2.1	The three levels of inclusion	40
3.1	Components of oppression	47
5.1	Four key concerns associated with the categorisation of children and young people with EBD	84
6.1	The characteristics of adult responses to the adult attachment interview	99
6.2	The key mechanisms of operant conditioning	104
7.1	A summary of the key philosophical positions of Kant, Durkheim, Dewey, MacMurray, Wilson, Peters and Hirst on (school) discipline	121
7.2	A brief synopsis of forms of power	124
7.3	The production of the 'hidden injuries of schooling'	129
9.1	Features of secondary nurture which make it distinctive	160
9.2	Impact of nurture groups classified according to level	162
9.3	The Scottish government's staged intervention model	168
9.4	Facilitators and barriers to interagency collaboration	170
10.1	A synthesis of two models of transfer	175
10.2	Synthesis of discussion of the concept of coherence, deriving from a range of literature as cited by K. Reimer (2020)	181
10.3	Comparison between *RJ* as enacted in a Canadian elementary/primary school and in a Scottish comprehensive secondary school	183
11.1	The four types of extrinsic motivation	194
11.2	The relationship between the continuums of control/agency and autonomy and self-determination	195
11.3	The relationship between the continuums of control/agency and autonomy and the degree to which approaches to school discipline and promoting positive behaviour are pro-active	197

xiv   *Tables*

11.4 The foci of enquiry for Riley (2017), Messiou (2012b)
      and Florian et al. (2017)   200
11.5 A comparison between Riley's *Framework for Belonging*
      and Meesiou's *Framework for Promoting Inclusion*   201
11.6 The *framework for participation*   202
12.1 Modification of Table 1.2   218
12.2 The five principles of courageous leadership   218

Charts and Boxes

Charts

3.1 Illustration of trends in attainment between the most
and least deprived quintiles of the Scottish Index of Multiple
Deprivation.   61

8.1 Content analysis of *Better Behaviour – Better Learning*
(Scottish Executive Education Department, 2001).   149

8.2 Content analysis of *Positive Behaviour in the Early Years*
(Dunlop et al., 2008).   150

8.3 Content analysis of *Better Relationships, Better Learning,
Better Behaviour* (Scottish Government, 2013).   150

8.4 Content analysis of Included, *Engaged and Involved*
(Scottish Government, 2017d).   151

8.5 Content analysis of *Developing a Positive Whole-School Ethos
and Culture: Relationships, Learning and Behaviour*
(Scottish Government, 2018a).   151

Boxes

6.1 Support groups: philosophical underpinnings   108
7.1 Extract from TESS   116
9.1 Case study   166
9.2 Exemplification of level 3   169

Foreword

I came to my reading of Building Community to Create Equitable, Inclusive and Compassionate Schools through Relational Approaches with elevated anticipation. Here was a manuscript engaging with challenges that have framed my own professional and intellectual life. Without diverting your attention away from Dr Mowat's challenging and inspiring work, let me briefly explain.

As a young teacher in metropolitan Melbourne, Australia, I had been placed in a position of responsibility for junior high school students. This effectively meant that I was a point of referral for difficult and disruptive students and was expected to dispense sanctions to promote discipline. The unremitting traffic of disengaged and defiant young people in their middle high school years soon taught me that my interventions were pretty useless. It was apparent that these young people were not in the favoured streams. I used to quip that there were three streams with euphemistic but abundantly apparent names: Kangaroos, Koalas and Roadkill. Cynical nomenclatures are an educational tradition in Australia. When I went to primary school, there was the 'opportunity grade' for the stragglers and strugglers. The occupants knew that all of their opportunities evaporated with the closing of the opportunity grade door. Today it would most likely be called the inclusion class.

With more instinct than theory, I was easily convinced that school wasn't meeting the needs of this cohort of young people. Placing them in an alternative setting, which with heightened optimism we called Teaching Units (echoes of the opportunity grade) wherein there would be a small number of students and teachers working closely together on an experientially based learning programme, seemed a reasonable proposition. As their mastery of skills and their behaviour improved through individual guidance, we would be able to successfully choreograph their return to school. That was the plan. We would have known better had we read Her Majesty's Inspector's (HMI, 1978) report on the shortcomings of the off-site solution in England. I suspect you know where this story leads us. The schools were very supportive of the creation of Teaching Units and predictably the pathway from the referring school to the Teaching Unit was smoother than the return journey.

At the time, Australian state education jurisdictions were in the process of abolishing corporal punishment and revising the regulations governing the use of suspension and exclusion from school. The popular media reported, in gendered language, an emasculation of teachers and a rising crisis in school discipline reflected in the growing volume of suspensions. It was also interesting to note that, in the 1980s and 1990s, there was a discernible shift in the discourse applied to describing many of the children being caught in the disciplinary gaze. Formerly difficult and disruptive students were increasingly being described as disordered and pathologically defective. Schools were not suitable for these students: they required expert ministering of other professionals. Accordingly, an admixture of behaviourism in its more punitive forms and interventions to fix defective kids and their families dominated the field of school discipline and student behaviour.

Despairing the intransigence of schooling, I embarked on doctoral studies to try to understand the forces at work. Reading a range of theorists, I suggested that discipline in its common application was the default vocabulary for control and that control was to be achieved through a range of strategies. Mine was an attempt to recast discipline as an educational concept with connection (relationships) being a key-connection between the student, what they were learning, how they were learning, where they were learning and where it was leading them.

Achieving discipline implied bringing schools into the diagnostic gaze. It seemed to this observer that many of the students who were disturbed, defiant, defective and disruptive were educational fringe-dwellers and that, rather than being brought into the centre of school life, all of the discipline strategies were pushing them irrevocably further away. As Professor Furlong (1992) would have predicted, my work quickly was thrown onto the pile of largely sociological studies that failed to satisfy those clamouring for seductive quick fixes to get 'the buggers to behave' (Cowley, 2014).

In this third decade of another century, I continue to observe the hubris of behaviour gurus, growing numbers of young people being excluded from schools, the growth of strategies for the relocation and containment of defective students and the constant pirouetting of discourse around care and control.

I recently read a compelling article by Stephen Ball and Jordi Collet-Sabe (2021) entitled Against School: an epistemological critique. At the risk of reductionism, Ball and Collet-Sabe apply Tim Rogan's (2017) observation that '... the critique of capitalism in the twentieth century shifted away from a fundamental demolition of its "moral and spiritual desolation" to a single-minded focus on the calculation of the relative advantages and disadvantages it generates – a shift from "Is it morally wrong?" to "Does it have bad outcomes?" – "Who wins and who loses?" Describing a school as an "intolerable institution," they invite us to consider whether we have in fact allowed similar "displacement or avoidance of moral argumentation by calculative evaluation." After years of pressing for school reform, their argument is compelling.'

With greater resilience, Joan G Mowat takes up this challenge to reform schools in what you are about to read. My elevated anticipation was not simply motivated by my interest in the subject of this book. It was equally summoned

xviii *Foreword*

by having attended presentations by Joan G Mowat. They were remarkable for their assiduous preparation, clear and precise articulation and considerable conceptual challenge. This then is what you are about to receive through Building Community to Create Equitable, Inclusive and Compassionate Schools through Relational Approaches, which – put simply – is a wonderful book.

Far from giving up on the project of schooling, Dr Mowat helps us to better grasp policy and evidentiary contexts, theoretical challenges to longstanding orthodoxies and the requirements for building nurturing relationships that foster inclusion, engagement and learning.

Professor Roger Slee,
Diamond Jubilee Chair in Disability and Inclusion,
University of Leeds

References

Adams, M., & Bell, L. A. (Eds.). (2016). *Teaching for diversity and social justice.* London: Routledge.

Adams, M., Hopkins, L. E., & Shlasko, D. (2016). Classism. In M. Adams, & L. A. Bell (Eds.), *Teaching for diversity and social justice* (pp. 213–253). London: Routledge.

Adams, M., & Zúñiga, X. (2016). Core concepts for social justice education. In M. Adams, & L. A. Bell (Eds.), *Teaching for diversity and social justice* (3rd ed., pp. 95–129). London: Routledge.

Addison, D., Casimir, A. E., Mims, L. C., Kaler-Jones, C., & Simmons, D. (2021). Beyond deep breathing: A new vision for equitable, culturally responsive, and trauma-informed mindfulness practice. *Middle School Journal, 52*(3), 4–14.

Ainscow, M., Booth, T., & Dyson, A. (2006a). *Improving schools, developing inclusion.* London: Routledge.

Acknowledgements

I would like to thank the following people for their support of this research monograph:

Emerita Professor Pamela Munn, former Dean of Moray House School of Education, University of Edinburgh.

Professor Roger Slee, Centre for Disability Studies, University of Leeds.

Emeritus Professor John MacBeath, University of Cambridge.

Professor Gillean McCluskey and Dr Gale Macleod, Moray House School of Education and Sport, University of Edinburgh.

Professor Brahm Norwich, Graduate School of Education, University of Exeter.

My long-suffering friend and former colleague, Mrs Alicia Tindal.

Gordon McKinlay, former Head of Schools, Renfrewshire Council.

Mrs Tracey Henderson, Improvement Officer, Stirlingshire Council.

Dr Alison Marmont, in a personal capacity.

Henry Hepburn, News Editor of the *Times Educational Supplement Scotland*.

Professor Kathryn Riley, Professor of Urban Education, University College London.

I would like to acknowledge and thank the following organisations and individuals that granted permission for the use of material within this research monograph:

Taylor and Francis for the use of material from the journals *Cambridge Journal of Education* and *Emotional and Behavioural Difficulties* and for the modification of figure 7.3 from *Creating Capacity for Learning and Equity*, Edn. 1 by Mary A. Hooper and Victoria L. Bernhardt, Copyright © 2016 by Routledge. Reproduced by permission of Taylor and Francis Group.

SAGE publications for the use of material from the journals *European Educational Research Journal (EERJ)* and *Improving Schools*.

PBJ Management and Tim Minchin for the use of material from the song 'Prejudice' from the album 'Ready for This' recorded in the Queen Elizabeth Hall, London in 2008.

Wall to Wall Media, Warner Bros TV Production UK, for the reproduction of material from the BBC 2 documentary *Blitz: The Bombs That Changed Britain*, Series 1, Episode 3, produced by Tim Kirby and broadcast on 18.08.18.

xx *Acknowledgements*

The Scottish Government for the adaptation of a table and text from the *Additional support for learning: statutory guidance 2017* and the use of an image from *Included, Engaged and Involved* (Part 2).

I would also like to thank the team at Routledge who have supported me through the process.

List of Acronyms

ASN	Additional Support Needs
APA	American Psychiatric Association
ADHD	Attention Deficit Hyperactivity Disorder
BESD	Behavioural, Emotional and Social Difficulties
C&YP	Children and Young People
CD	Conduct Disorder
CfE	Curriculum for Excellence
DfE	Department for Education
EBD	Emotional and Behavioural Difficulties
GCSE	General Certificate of Secondary Education
GTCS	General Teaching Council for Scotland
ICEA	International Council of Education Advisors
NIF	National Improvement Framework
ODD	Oppositional Defiance Disorder
OECD	Organisation for Economic Cooperation and Development
OOSCI	Out-of-School Children Initiative
PISA	Programme for International Student Assessment
RICs	Regional Improvement Collaboratives
SAC	Scottish Attainment Challenge
SNSA	Scottish National Standardised Assessments
SEAL	Social and Emotional Aspects of Learning
SEL	Social and Emotional Learning
SEBD	Social, Emotional and Behavioural Difficulties
SEBN	Social, Emotional and Behavioural Needs
SEMHD	Social, Emotional and Mental Health Difficulties
SEMHN	Social, Emotional and Mental Health Needs
SEND	Special Educational Needs and Disabilities
SDGs	Sustainable Development Goals
UK	United Kingdom
UNICEF	United Nations Children's Fund
USA	United States of America

Introduction
Making a Difference to the Lives of Children and Young People

Why equitable, inclusive and compassionate schools? Schools are a microcosm of wider society and reflect the cultural values and norms of society in time and place, but they also play a significant role in shaping that same society and the people we become. If we wish to create and live in a world where people are caring and compassionate towards each other; have a sense of belonging to their communities and of being valued; where all have an equal chance of being able to contribute meaningfully to society and have access to the resources which enable them to live healthy and worthwhile lives; and where people are not discriminated against in terms of age, gender, disability, race, sex, sexual orientation, and religion or belief (amongst other human rights), then this has to be reflected in our schools. As such, the essence of this research monograph (from this point onwards referred to as book) is about the nature and purposes that education should serve and the role that schools should play within this.

This book has been written during a tumultuous period as COVID-19 swept the world, leaving a devastating trail behind it. But what it has highlighted is the importance of human values, bringing a realisation to many as to what really matters in life – the value of family and friendships. It has also highlighted global inequalities, which have impacted on families, children and young people. This brings to the fore the need for compassionate and relational approaches in working with children and families and in building community, founded on collaboration and trusting relationships.

Who this book is for

Whilst it is intended that this book should be of value to masters- and doctoral-level students and academics in the field of education, its scope extends far beyond this. If it is to make an impact and a genuine difference in the lives of children and young people, then it needs to speak to a wide range of policy-makers, academics and professionals from a range of academic disciplines and professional backgrounds who have a vested interest in the welfare and education of children and young people. Its reach needs to extend from government-level

DOI: 10.4324/9780429467110-1

2 *Introduction*

policymakers to school leaders and teachers in the classroom; from academics and professionals in the field of education to clinical and educational psychologists and other related disciplines and professions.

My own professional journey

As someone who has spent 27 years in the classroom working in a range of Scottish schools in the central belt, I have seen first-hand the impact of poverty on the lives of communities, families and children. As a Depute Head Teacher in a Secondary school (serving children aged 11–17), located in an area of multiple deprivation, I have also witnessed the stresses and strains that this puts on the school system, on school leaders and class teachers on a day-to-day basis. It is the sense of impotence which arose in dealing daily with incidences of, sometimes serious, indiscipline and the frustration, anger and despair which this generated in teachers, parents and the pupils themselves which drew me towards the need to work collaboratively with others to support pupils who were presenting with *Social, Emotional and Behavioural Needs* (SEBN) through a group work intervention (Mowat, 2007) and took me down the path which has led to the successful completion of my PhD and the authorship of this book.

I have also experienced first-hand the impact of a range of educational policies on the system; the changing nature of Scottish education over time; and the increasing pressures of accountability, which are part of a wider, global trend. More recently, as a senior lecturer in the School of Education at the University of Strathclyde, leading leadership programmes for aspiring headteachers over an eleven-year period has been invaluable in keeping me grounded regarding the issues facing schools and their leadership teams.

The focus of the book

What this book is not

Schools are highly complex organisations and each has its own history, culture and constraints. There can often be a disjunction between policy rhetoric and reality on the ground with schools caught in the middle of competing imperatives. There is no one-size-fits-all solution or magic bullet to the problems posed by inequality, exclusion and marginalisation, poverty, school disaffection and indiscipline (despite the multiplicity of books which purport to do so), mental health problems and the multitude of other issues which beset schools (never mind the impact of the pandemic) but the starting point has to be to raise awareness, develop and deepen understanding and to challenge the orthodoxies which can act as an impediment to progress. This book, therefore, does not set out to offer definitive answers but to explore the nature of the problem and to offer alternative perspectives and potential avenues of exploration for policymakers, educators and those invested in the wellbeing of children and young people.

Introduction 3

What this book is

Whilst the focus of this book is primarily the group of children who would be considered to have *SEBN* (Scotland)/*Social, Emotional and Mental Health Needs* (SEMHN) (England) and the policies and practices adopted by schools to promote positive behaviour, this discussion is placed within a much broader narrative which focusses on inclusion and its alter-ego, marginalisation, more generally and on the global policy context which acts as a catalyst for exclusionary practices in the first instance and shapes responses at the national and local level. As such, the book focusses on the needs of *all* children and young people. Recognising that a child may be marginalised or excluded on the basis of more than one characteristic alone – it is how a range of variables interact and intersect in the life of the child that will determine this outcome – the book examines the problem holistically, from a wide range of perspectives and fields of enquiry.

The book seeks to disrupt and challenge the orthodoxies that prevail within society and schools that frame our understanding of these issues, bringing into question the utility and value of concepts such as behaviour management and examining how schools can sometimes, inadvertently, disenfranchise and disengage from communities, families and children, becoming places of exclusion rather than places of inclusion and belonging. It offers an alternative perspective to the focus on high-stakes, accountability régimes and zero-tolerance approaches to school discipline (more recently advocated as a means to greater social mobility), offering instead a perspective that focusses on a sense of belonging, unconditional positive regard, relational approaches to promoting positive behaviour, building a sense of community and building capacity for change through empowering the school community.

The book commences with a broad focus on all children before gradually honing in more specifically on children presenting with SEBN/SEMHN and the approaches adopted by schools to support them and promote positive discipline. Whilst many of the themes covered in this book are not new, it is the integration of these themes across what may appear to be disparate fields of enquiry and the narrative thread that runs through the book that I believe makes this a unique contribution to the field which, I hope, will help the reader to come to an understanding of the complexity of the issues which the book seeks to address.

It should be noted that, across the jurisdictions of the United Kingdom and beyond, there is a range of terminology used to describe children presenting with SEBN/SEMHN and various other concepts and the use of Anglicised/Americanised spelling. Each chapter will set out the approach to be adopted and the justification for this, but it should be noted that, in general, the terminology adopted reflects the source material.

Features of the book

Each chapter of the book is underpinned by a set of *goals for understanding*, expressed in the form of a set of questions. This emanates from the work of Emeritus Professor David Perkins and his colleagues at the Harvard Graduate School of Education on *Teaching for Understanding* – a four-part framework

4 *Introduction*

designed to foster deeper learning. The reflection points are designed to foster deeper thinking around the issues within the text and additional suggested reading allows for further engagement with ideas.

A road map

The book is in four parts, illustrated in Figure i.1.

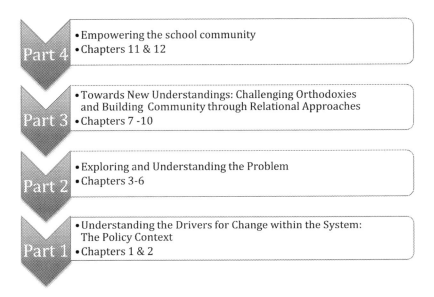

Figure i.1 Illustration of the structure of the book.

> ***Part I: Understanding the drivers for change within the system: the policy context***
>
> *Chapter 1: Understanding the policy context: the macrosystem*
>
> Illustrated through the USA and the UK (English and Scottish) policy contexts, this chapter explores key international drivers of global policy and how these shape policy at the national level and create the context for schools, exploring the inherent tensions therein. Key themes within the chapter are globalisation and the role of organisations such as the *Organisation for Economic Cooperation and Development* (OECD) and the *United Nations Children's Fund* (UNICEF); neo-liberalism; policy borrowing; and the tension between autonomy and accountability, themes expanded upon in subsequent chapters.
>
> *Chapter 2: Inclusive education: challenges, tensions and dilemmas*
>
> Building on the previous chapter, this chapter critiques the multiple ways in which inclusion and inclusive education are understood, portrayed in public policy and enacted in practice, tracing this through global policy from a rights perspective. It explores the dialectic relationship between inclusion and exclusion and the tensions between policy rhetoric and reality.

Introduction 5

Part II: Exploring and understanding the problem

Chapter 3: Marginalisation, social exclusion and the impact of poverty on children and young people

This chapter examines the concept of marginalisation from an ecological perspective, understood through the lens of resilience. The chapter then focusses on the wellbeing and education of children living in poverty, exploring the relationship between poverty and *Adverse Childhood Experiences*, illustrated through the Scottish policy context.

Chapter 4: Schools as places of belonging or exclusion: school disaffection

Building on previous themes, the focus of this chapter is the role that schools play in either creating a sense of belonging or exclusion and how they may, inadvertently, disengage from communities, families and students through their systems, structures, curriculum, pedagogy and ethos, leading to student disaffection, a central argument in this book. The chapter forwards a perspective based on the centrality of a sense of belonging to school and unconditional positive regard as underpinning relationships within the school.

Chapter 5: Understanding Social, Emotional and Behavioural Needs (SEBN)/ Mental Health Needs (SEMHN)

This chapter looks more specifically at how *SEBN/SEMHN* are understood and the controversy around disorders such as *Attention Deficit Hyperactivity Disorder* (ADHD). It also looks at alternative *biopsychosocial* explanations to account for children's behaviour.

Chapter 6: Looking through the lens of developmental theory to understand Social, Emotional and Behavioural Needs (SEBN)/Mental Health Needs (SEMHN)

How adults respond to children is framed by their understanding of the nature of children and childhood and of childhood development. This chapter explains and critiques a range of developmental theories arguing that some of these theories are entirely incompatible with each other yet they sit side-by-side as bedfellows, manifest in school discipline policies.

Part III: Towards new understandings: challenging orthodoxies and building community through relational approaches

Chapter 7: Challenging the orthodoxies of behaviour management through an examination of power, influence and authority

This chapter draws on theories of power, influence and authority to examine where agency lies and to make the argument that behaviour management, premised on the notion that children will only behave if their behaviour is controlled and manipulated by adults, is no longer a construct of value, drawing on the work of Foucault, Wrong and Furlong, the last of whom talks about the 'hidden injuries of schooling.'

(Continued)

6 Introduction

Chapter 8: Challenging the orthodoxies of behaviour management through a focus on policy and practice

This chapter critiques national policy on school discipline in England and Scotland, examining how power, authority, agency and autonomy are represented within the policy rhetoric and tracing this back to zero-tolerance and authoritarian approaches in the USA.

Chapter 9: Building community through nurture and trauma-informed practice

Offering an alternative to authoritarian approaches to behaviour management, this chapter focusses on humanistic and relational approaches that have at their heart the holistic needs of children – nurture and trauma-informed practice. The chapter highlights the importance of a positive school ethos and climate and discusses collaborative approaches to supporting children and young people – integrated children's services, staged intervention and multi-agency and inter-professional working.

Chapter 10: Building community through restorative justice/practice

Following a discussion of universal versus targeted approaches to intervention, the focus of this chapter is restorative justice/practice, exploring some of the tensions and dilemmas in enactment.

Part IV: Empowering the school community

Chapter 11: Working collaboratively together to empower the school community through pupil participation and parental engagement

This chapter compares and contrasts three frameworks – Messiou (2012b), Florian, Black-Hawkins, and Rouse (2017) and Riley (2017) – to cast light on how to build participative, inclusive and collaborative school cultures through enquiry approaches which promote pupil voice and participation and parental engagement, embedded within a more general discussion of these imperatives and the climate for learning within the school.

Chapter 12: Empowering the school community through socially just and culturally responsive leadership

The driving force within this chapter is building capacity for change through leadership for social justice (illustrated through a case study) and culturally responsive schooling; building social and cultural capital; exploring the relationship between the school and its wider community; and teacher professionalism.

Part I

Understanding the Drivers for Change within the System

The Policy Context

The first two chapters focus on key underlying forces that shape education policy globally – neo-liberalism, children's rights and the goals for sustainable development, and inclusion – and the role that international organisations play within this.

DOI: 10.4324/9780429467110-2

1 Understanding the Policy Context
The Macrosystem

> **Goals for Understanding**
>   I. What are the international drivers for change within educational systems across the world and what influences this?
> II. How does this impact at the national and more local level and what are the tensions within the system?

We live in a volatile and unpredictable world with many contradictions. At the time of initially writing this statement (pre-pandemic), I was entirely unaware of how prophetic it would prove to be. The challenge that this book seeks to address – how we can create equitable, inclusive and compassionate schools which have the potential to empower the school community and where all children are equally valued and can achieve – is highly complex. It cannot be understood by focussing on education alone or in isolation of the wider global policy context. Within a neo-liberal agenda, and in an age of globalisation in which international imperatives drive the school system and nations compete to 'be the best' (never better exemplified than through the OECD league tables), it is imperative to understand the forces on schools which shape our understanding and actions and create the contexts in which schools (and their leaders) operate.

This chapter will therefore draw from the international literature and policy context to highlight key drivers for change and trace these through to national policy with a particular focus on the USA and the UK, specifically, England and Scotland, highlighting the tensions within the system. The chapter commences with an examination of the insidious impact of neo-liberal ideology on international and national policy.

The impact of globalisation on educational policy

Globalisation, promoted through organisations with global reach and channelled through a neo-liberal agenda of marketisation, competition and the commodification of public services, has had a profound impact on educational policy, leading to a convergence in educational policy-making worldwide (d'Agnese,

DOI: 10.4324/9780429467110-3

10 *Understanding the Drivers for Change within the System*

2018; Mowat, 2020a; Sellar & Lingard, 2018). The *Organisation for Economic Cooperation and Development* (OECD) is one of many world players exerting influence on the direction of education policy at a global level. One might ask (in the vernacular), 'What's not to like? After all, surely it's a good thing for policy to "travel" across the world, for us to learn from the "best practice" of other nations and to "up our game" in the international league that constitutes global comparisons?' The response to this is to state that it depends on the nature of the game we are playing.

The relentless and insidious march of neo-liberalism

There is undoubtedly value in the work generated by organisations such as the OECD and UNICEF (United Nations Children's Fund) in informing education systems and the research community across the world and through the investment of resources in addressing problems of global significance. However, there is a darker side to this body of work. The problems are so insidious and so integrated into our ways of thinking and being (Holloway & Brass, 2018) that it is very difficult for policymakers, school leaders and teachers to stand back from the findings and recommendations of the reports emanating from organisations such as the OECD objectively. The discourse surrounding them is so pervasive (and also so seemingly persuasive) that it would take a very discerning and brave individual, institution, state or, indeed, nation to 'stand up and be counted.'

At a time when education systems are driven by 'big data' and by a 'what works' agenda, it would appear counter-intuitive to argue against this mantra and go against the flow. However, an extensive range of commentators has critiqued the neo-liberal agenda that underpins much of the thinking that informs the reports: the focus on marketisation and managerialism, and the performativity and commodification of education leading from it (Ball, 2003, 2015; d'Agnese, 2018; Mowat, 2015b).

Neo-liberalism, according to Connell (2013), is on the ascendancy. It seeks through the free market and the institutional arrangements which make this possible to extend and create new markets at a global level (p. 100). It blurs the boundaries between the state and private sector, leading to the privatisation and commodification of public services (Ball, 2003; Mowat, 2015b). This transformation takes place through three mechanisms – the *market* (related to competition, survival and income maximisation), *managerialism* (efficiency, effectiveness and corporate culture) and *performativity* (productivity, targets, achievement and comparison) (Ball, 2003), leading to a new discourse around education and its practices.

Under this régime, the norms of collaboration and care for others are replaced by what Slee (2018b) describes as a culture of collective individualism in which 'students are reduced to the bearers of results,' which, when aggregated, are used to judge performance at all levels of the system from the individual teacher to the state (p. 16). The ethics of professional judgement and cooperation are replaced by those of competition, performance and a pursuit of 'excellence' (Ball, 2003).

Students become commodities who 'add value' or not to the school (Ainscow, Booth, & Dyson, 2006b) or pose an 'opportunity' or 'risk' to it (Slee, 2018b) (an issue to be explored further in Chapter 2).

The accountability that this agenda engenders brings with it an emotional toll on teachers and directs them away from their core purpose to serve the needs of their students (Ball, 2003). In the process, it reconstitutes the relationship between teachers and schools and the identity of teachers individually and collectively (Ball, 2003): 'What it means to teach and what it means to be a teacher ... are subtly but decisively changed in the processes of reform' (Ball, 2003, p. 218). This is compounded for teachers who find themselves in conflict with the underlying values associated with neo-liberalism and the cultures and practices associated with performativity (A. Moore & Clarke, 2016).

The impact of this reform agenda can be seen very clearly in England in which a plethora of post-Primary school provision has emerged, competing for the 'spoils,' most clearly evidenced in the *Academies* programme introduced by New Labour and the *Free Schools* programme by the following Coalition government. However, Dumay and Dupriez (2014), in commenting on the 'quasi-market' which has emerged, have found no evidence that market competition leads to school effectiveness and, indeed, it strengthens the association between the social composition of the school and student achievement, heightening social inequalities.

The role of the OECD in forwarding this agenda

The OECD, through the *Programme for International Student Assessment* (PISA), plays a significant role in taking this agenda forward. Sellar and Lingard (2013) account for this through two mechanisms – *infrastructural* governance (a product of the systems and networks through which it gathers data) and *epistemological* governance (its capacity to shape educational thinking globally). The key paradigm of the OECD is that differences in educational outcomes can be accounted for by national educational policies and structures. The implication of this is that 'less successful' education systems should learn from the world's best-performing school systems by imitating their policies and practices (Feniger & Lefstein, 2014).

Whilst the above may appear to be a rational line of argument, what it conceals is a project of such great scope that it brings into question the whole nature of schooling and the purposes that education should serve (d'Agnese, 2018). To return to our sporting analogy, it changes the nature of the game: 'Numbers define our worth, measure our effectiveness and, in a myriad of other ways, work to inform or construct what we are today' (Ball, 2015, editorial, p. 299), guiding the decisions about where to invest our efforts (Ball, 2003).

Within this arena, there is an unquestioned rhetoric positioning education as primarily concerned with serving the economy and creating a skilled workforce (d'Agnese, 2018); a denial of the role of history, culture and society in shaping educational policy and structures and what counts as knowledge (Feniger &

12 *Understanding the Drivers for Change within the System*

Lefstein, 2014); and a totalitarian agenda which provides little space for dissension (Ball, 2003). According to d'Agnese (2018), it risks the erosion of a diversity of perspectives and 'even educational plurality worldwide' (p. 2). Writing in the Guardian, Ball and Noddings (2014) question the mandate which the OECD has to exercise such powers, becoming the 'global arbiter of the means and ends of education around the world' but with no accountability in this regard (cited in J. Bates, Lewis, & Pickard, 2019, p. 74).

Within this paradigm, reductionist understandings of education prevail (Ball, 2003; A. Bates, 2013; Coffield, 2012; d'Agnese, 2018): 'Education is identified with learning, learning with assessment, assessment with PISA's tests' (d'Agnese, 2018, p. 4). Teachers are conceived as technicists (A. Bates, 2013), 'delivering' a restricted and often prescribed (and proscribed) curriculum, leading to an erosion of educational quality and an impoverished educational landscape in which a holistic focus on the child and the moral obligation to care for and nurture children are lost (p. 39).

The competitiveness that PISA's tests engender and the 'blame culture' which often accompanies a poorer than hoped-for (or expected) outcome creates a powerful force for systems change (J. Bates et al., 2019). Sellar and Lingard (2018) outline how, through the power of the media and creating 'public moods' of concern, governments can create a reform mandate from PISA results to drive forward their own agendas.

The key international drivers for change

What is clearly evident in examining the range of policies and reports emanating from the OECD, UNICEF, the World Bank and other international organisations is that, increasingly, education in general (and schooling in particular) is perceived as the solution to a wide range of economic, social, technological and environmental problems. A narrative of risk emerges from the policy documentation emanating from the OECD as it reflects on the multiple influences shaping educational policy across the world, from changing demographics (e.g., global movements of populations) to the impact of the pandemic (OECD, 2020, 2022).

UNICEF

Every child learns

UNICEF's Education Strategy 2019–2030 – *Every Child Learns* (UNICEF, 2019b) – calls for a radical rethink of global education policy such that it enhances learning outcomes for all children, acknowledging that many children lack the skills to enable them to realise their potential and make a worthwhile contribution to their communities. The strategy therefore focusses on equitable access to learning opportunities; improved learning and skills for all; and improved learning in emergencies and fragile contexts (p. 4), particularly apt when in the throes of a pandemic, with an increased focus on equity, inclusion and early years. It encompasses a strengthening of systems through partnership working; the enhancement of the generation of data and evidence to inform practice; and scalable and sustainable innovation with an aim to finding innovative ways of accelerating learning for vulnerable children and transforming the education system. These goals are to be achieved through collaboration with UNESCO's *Out-of-School Children Initiative* (OOSCI),[1] launched in 2012, and through the pursuit of the *Sustainable Development Goals (SDGs)*, taken forward in partnership with global organisations such as the *Global Partnership for Education*.

The sustainable development goals

Building on the *Convention on the Rights of the Child* (UNICEF, 1989) promoting universal education and *Education For All* (UNESCO, 1990), 17 SDGs were formulated by the United Nations General Assembly in 2015 to be attained by 2030 (UNICEF, 2019a). Of these, SDG4 – *a quality education* (ensure inclusive and equitable quality education and promote lifelong learning opportunities for all), SDG1 – *no poverty*, SDG3 – *good health and wellbeing* and SDG10 – *reduced inequalities* are of particular relevance to children and young people.

The World Bank

The World Bank, the largest financier of education in the developing world (investing US$45 billion in the period 2000–2017), seeks to address the goals for sustainability, in particular SDG4 – *a quality education*. The focus of its efforts is on building human capital and achieving 'Learning for All' in the developing world (The World Bank, 2019). It is clearly informed by neo-liberal ideology and a business model, highlighting the importance of data to inform improvement. Whilst its investment in projects across the world to improve the life chances of children are to be lauded, its work is framed within a discourse of 'productivity,' 'driving economic growth,' 'payoffs from investment,' 'improved management of education systems,' 'rapid accelerated development and prosperity' and a 'what works' agenda. Through its capabilities for investment, it not only has the influence to define the nature of educational policy at a global level but also to impose it through the conditionality attached to such investment (J. Bates et al., 2019), making it a very powerful world player.

The global pandemic

Despite the initial assessment that children would be unlikely to be affected by the pandemic due to their greater immunity from infection (Mowat, in press-a; UNICEF Office of Global Insight & Policy, 2020), it is now generally acknowledged that it has had a significant impact on their education and mental health

14   *Understanding the Drivers for Change within the System*

and wellbeing, amplifying and exacerbating inequalities (Mowat, in press-a; in press-b). There were significant differences in how countries across the world responded to COVID-19. Low-income countries experienced school closures disproportionally (Mowat, in press-a; in press-b; Thorn & Vincent-Lancrin, 2021; UNESCO, UNICEF, & The World Bank, 2020) whilst also having the lowest proportion of children with a fixed internet connection which would have facilitated home schooling (Mowat, in press-b; UNICEF, 2021a). Children living in high-income countries were more likely to have free or subsidised access to the internet and to be in receipt of subsidised or free devices provided by the state (Mowat, in press-b; UNESCO et al., 2020).

The OECD chronicles the range of different approaches adopted to mitigate the impact of the pandemic on learning, including the provision of learning hubs to meet the needs of the most vulnerable and disadvantaged children and the children of those deemed to be essential workers in countries such as the UK (Thorn & Vincent-Lancrin, 2021). Vincent-Lancrin, Cobo Romaní, and Reimers (2022) draw together case studies from across OECD countries/states to identify commonalities in response, such as the reliance on multi-modal solutions, initiatives to promote digital inclusion and the mobilisation of networks and partnerships to quickly design and implement a solution. As countries have emerged from various lockdowns, they have sought to put in place compensatory policies to address the loss of learning, such as increased class time, accelerated learning and catch-up programmes (UNESCO et al., 2020). *Trends Shaping Education 2022* (OECD, 2022) presents the pandemic as an opportunity to reconceptualise and reconfigure education in the service of creating more sustainable environments, raising a series of questions relating to the role of education, accountabilities, who educates and in which conditions, and the organisation and delivery of the service.

The race to the top and the magic bullet – policy borrowing

The increasing prominence of international league tables[2] and the reports emanating from them have put pressure on education systems throughout the world to 'perform' and to be seen to be out-performing other nations (Ball, 2003; 2015; Dumay & Dupriez, 2014; Hodgson & Spours, 2016; Polesel, Rice, & Dulfer, 2014; Ringarp & Rothland, 2010). Allied to the growth of the knowledge economy (Brunila, 2011), these international comparators have become highly influential in shaping educational policy (Bøyum, 2014; Hodgson & Spours, 2016; MacBeath, 2013). Facilitated by strengthening global networks and the marketing of public policy across the world, nations turn towards policy borrowing as a potential solution to perceived problems (Dolowitz & Marsh, 2000; Mowat, 2018a). As such, there is a drive at a global level not only to 'import' policy but also to 'export' it. However, comparative studies demonstrate that a failure to give due consideration to the cultural and political context brings into question the notion of 'transfer' of policy and practice from one context to another (Feniger & Lefstein, 2014; Mowat, 2018a; Steiner-Khamsi, 2014).

A synthesis

In bringing this discussion together, four principal themes emerge from the policy context which, whilst distinctive in their own right, are strongly inter-connected – a drive for excellence, social justice, economic prosperity and sustainability (Mowat, 2020a) (cc. Table 1.1). In the light of the pandemic, a key driver is the need for highly responsive, flexible and collaborative school systems.

As discussed in the introduction to the book, it is important to recognise that schools are part of, and reflect, broader societal goals, aspirations and norms: 'Schools are agents of the dominant society and as such, they reflect the underlying cultural patterns of that society' (Barnhardt, 1981).

Table 1.1 Key themes to emerge from analysis of international educational policy

A drive for social justice	*A drive for excellence*	*A drive for economic prosperity*
Inclusion & diversity	Curricular reform and	The impact of globalisation
Equity	pedagogy	and neo-liberal ideology
Human rights	Teacher professionalism	Building the workforce
Social mobility	High-quality leadership	Active & responsible citizens
Wellbeing	Standards agenda	who contribute to
	Empowerment agenda	economic prosperity
	School governance	Digital technologies
	Highly responsive,	
	flexible and collaborative	
	school systems	
Underpinned by sustainability		

Source: Modification of table 2, Mowat (2020a).

Reflection Point

In reflecting on your experience of the education system in your own country, how do the arguments made to this point resonate with your own experience? Do they ring true? What examples might you offer of policy borrowing within your own national context and what issues does this raise?

Tracing international themes through national policy

The drive for excellence and social justice

Whilst some might argue that the juxtaposition of excellence and social justice is an oxymoron, it is a very clear theme to emerge in OECD policy documentation in which the relationship is made explicit (see Gomendio, 2017; OECD, 2012, 2016, 2017, 2018; Schleicher, 2014). The key argument forwarded within the aforementioned reports is that equity and excellence are not mutually exclusive: 'excellence without equity risks leading to large economic and social disparities;

16 *Understanding the Drivers for Change within the System*

equity at the expense of quality is a meaningless aspiration' (Schleicher, 2014, p. 15). However, both Sellar and Lingard (2013) and Bøyum (2014) observe that PISA largely ignores contextual factors such as structural inequality which impact on these outcomes: 'they do not question whether there should be disadvantaged homes at all' (Bøyum, 2014, p. 868).

The USA: levelling the playing field

The drive for excellence and social justice is articulated through a wide range of national initiatives, such as *No Child Left Behind* and *Race to the Top* in the USA. *No Child Left Behind* was seen by some as a real opportunity to address inequitable education outcomes, going against the paradigm of meritocracy which saw individual talent and grit as being all that is required to overcome life's obstacles (Blankstein, Noguera, & Kelly, 2015). However, the failure to take account of the conditions under which children are educated, together with the narrow focus on standardised tests and outcomes, served to reinforce disadvantage, the assumption being that all children, no matter their developmental stage, should reach the same milestones at the same time.

> The goal of levelling the playing field to enable all students to have access to opportunity has been lost. We have become so obsessed with keeping track – of holding accountable – of comparing and ranking and sorting – that we have little time or appetite left to question what we are keeping track OF … or WHY.
>
> (p. 97)

The authors ask, 'Isn't it time to acknowledge that we need to rethink what we mean by achievement, student success and quality education?' (p. 99). According to L. Darling-Hammond, Cook-Harvey, Flook, Gardner, and Melnick (2018), the legacy of the programme was a focus on 'punishments, competition and comparison,' the marginalisation of children who didn't boost test scores, zero-tolerance discipline policies and teaching to the test, causing well-qualified educators to flee the most disadvantaged schools (pp. 23–4).

Race to the Top,[3] introduced in 2012 by the Obama administration, was a competitive grant to foster innovation in school districts and address under-achievement in disadvantaged areas with a focus on rigorous standards and assessments, 'big data,' support for teachers and school leaders and 'rigorous interventions.' These reforms took place against a backdrop of increasing marketisation, diversity and choice in the school system with charter schools coming to the fore. Despite the avowed intentions of the policy to 'give everyone the best education possible' (President Obama), critics raise concerns about its tendencies for micro-managing and over-surveillance of teachers; the use of incentives ('crunchier carrots') and consequences ('sharper sticks') through mechanisms such as performance pay; and the implementation of strategies which have failed in the past to secure improvement (DuFour & Mattos, 2013).

Understanding the Policy Context 17

Over a decade of reform, teachers in the USA no longer saw this externally imposed agenda as something external to them, becoming both subjected to and the subject of accountability measures which served to 'monitor and discipline their performance and being' (p. 379). They had internalised this neo-liberal agenda (Holloway & Brass, 2018), in the process becoming 'the marketized, managed and performative teacher' (p. 379) rather than the autonomous professional who has the knowledge, skills and relationships with their students to make informed decisions about their teaching (see the discussion of Foucault and Power in Chapter 7).

The United Kingdom

Education policy is a devolved function of each country that constitutes the UK – England, Scotland, Wales and Northern Ireland – each of which has its own distinctive culture, ideology and institutions that frame policy decisions. The discussion to follow explores educational policy as it pertains to England and Scotland. A key distinction lies in Scotland having a fully professional, graduate workforce, registered through the General Teaching Council for Scotland (GTCS).

England – 'upping the game'

The scope of reform within the education system in England is of such magnitude that it is impossible to do justice to it within this discussion (for a fuller discussion see J. Bates et al., 2019). It takes place within a highly complex arena of structural changes to the nature, form and governance of schools, with a plethora of different forms of provision funded by the state, the private sector and partnerships between the state and private sector (see Table 6.1 in J. Bates et al., 2019). What is quite remarkable, despite the differing ideologies of political parties, is the degree to which policies introduced within one government are then built on by another. For example, New Labour (1997–2010) built on the legacy of the Conservative (Thatcher/Major [1979–1997]) government with regard to the diversification of the system and policies promoting parental choice, seeing competition as a route to improving standards (J. Bates et al., 2019). The basic premise of such policies is that the pressures exerted by 'consumers' (families) through mechanisms such as parental choice (forcing schools to compete); autonomy (enabling schools to differentiate their provision); and funding being attached to student enrolments (penalising unattractive schools) (Dumay & Dupriez, 2014) will lead to schools 'upping their game.'

Over the past 30 years, education in the UK has become highly politicised, driven by fears of a lack of competitiveness in economic and technical markets (Smyth & Wrigley, 2013). This is no more in evidence than in the national curriculum introduced by the Conservative (Thatcher [1979–1990]) government through the *Education Reform Act 1988* but built on by successive governments. These, and subsequent policy developments, have taken place against a backdrop of a 'name and shame' culture as schools (largely those in poorer areas) failed to meet the government's targets, leading to a breakdown in trust and the

18 *Understanding the Drivers for Change within the System*

development of acrimonious relationships between teachers, their unions and the government (Bangs, MacBeath, & Galton, 2011; J. Bates et al., 2019; Smyth & Wrigley, 2013).

On what Bangs et al. (2011) describe as 'a wave of euphoria' from the teaching profession, New Labour came sweeping into power in 1997 under the premiership of Tony Blair and a banner of 'education, education, education.' However, the euphoria soon dissipated when it became evident that the anticipated shift in direction was not forthcoming and a narrative of 'bog standard' comprehensives emerged. It was under this panoply that New Labour introduced the *National Literacy and Numeracy strategies* and, for the first time, national targets became part of the landscape of the English educational system.

A key plank of New Labour education policy, *Every Child Matters* (and its American counterpart, *No child Left Behind*), was an explicit admission that schools could not meet the needs of all children (MacBeath et al., 2007). During New Labour's administration, a stronger theme of social justice emerged within the educational policy landscape. This is reflected in an extensive raft of policies, including the *London, City* and *National Challenges* and the targeting of more directed funding towards schools in disadvantaged areas through the *Academies* programme and *Building Schools for the Future* (J. Bates et al., 2019). Whilst the *London Challenge* was hailed as a success (Kidson & Norris, 2014), leading to its roll-out across England, critics make the case that there are alternative explanations to account for the improved student outcomes (Burgess, 2014; Greaves, Macmillan, & Sibieta, 2014, cited in Mowat, 2018a).

Subsequently, under the Coalition and Conservative (Cameron/May [2010–2019]) governments, the *Pupil Premium Grant* was introduced to improve education outcomes for disadvantaged pupils in schools in England. In general, however, there has been a movement away from welfare-orientated policy in education with the emphasis being directed towards reforms of the curriculum and national qualifications, the aim being to make them more challenging (J. Bates et al., 2019).

This has been paralleled with the introduction in 2016 of five new *headlines measures*,[4] part of key stage 4 (aged 14–16, leading up to GCSEs [General Certificate of Secondary Education]) reforms, to evaluate the performance of schools and individual teachers, to be published in performance tables (Gewirtz, Maguire, Neumann, & Towers, 2021). The authors trace this development historically (from the mid-19th century), relating it to the *deliverology* movement, popularised by Michael Barber, Head of Blair's *Delivery Unit*, described as a top-down, 'systematic process for driving progress and delivering results in government and the public sector' (pp. 506–7). They note that the sophistication of the measures lends them a seeming plausibility leading some progressive educators to see them as 'a means of increasing access to high-status knowledge for disadvantaged students' (p. 504). However, drawing from data derived from a *National Union of Teachers* survey conducted in 2016,[5] they conclude that the measures themselves and their means of delivery are incompatible with school improvement.

Whilst the new measures may appear to align more with social justice than previous iterations, in combination with the reforms to the curriculum and assessment, they were seen to have disenfranchised the most disadvantaged and low-attaining students and eroded the professional autonomy of teachers. Opportunities to study subjects, such as the creative arts, diminished; there were fewer opportunities for students to develop higher-order thinking skills; and, in the process, teaching and learning became dehumanised, impacting on the mental health and wellbeing of students.

School governance, autonomous school systems and accountability

Within what has been proclaimed by the UK government as an autonomous school system, through standardisation and a hegemonic discourse of neo-liberalism and accountability (Smyth & Wrigley, 2013), power has shifted to the centre, with schools, such as *Academies* and *Free schools* (including *University Technological Colleges*), being held directly accountable to the Secretary of State for Education. This has led to a concordant reduction in the role of local authorities and a shift in the responsibilities and accountabilities of school governing bodies within a landscape in which the boundaries between the state, private and third sector are becoming increasingly blurred (Earley, 2013, drawing on Ball, 2009). It is no more in evidence than in the highly standardised and pre-scribed national curriculum, providing little scope for autonomy and innovation. It is manifested also in scrutiny through the inspection régime, national targets and performance tables; incentives created through the 'quasi-market' (such as performance-related pay); and scrutiny by the various 'actors' who have a stake in schools, such as Boards of *Multi-Academy Trusts* (Glatter, 2012; Higham, 2013; Mathews & Ehren, 2017).

Whilst *Academies* and other variants within the English system are freed from the shackles of the national curriculum, the reality is that the inspection régime and the pressures to maintain reputations in the face of market competition make these schools just as accountable. Meantime, the *real* irony is that local authorities (which, in reality yield little power and have largely relinquished their traditional developmental roles), schools (and their governing bodies and leadership teams) and individual teachers are held to account for the outcomes of this draconian and inflexible régime.

Scotland: steering a steadier but tumultuous course

Education policy in Scotland is strongly tied to the nation's sense of identity as being distinct from that of England (Arnott, 2017; Lingard & Sellar, 2014; Mowat, 2018b; Riddell, 2016), diverging increasingly from the rest of the UK (Beck, 2019). Rooted in historical and cultural traditions, in social democratic values (Lingard & Sellar, 2014; Mowat, 2018b) and in egalitarian principles (Gatherer, 2013), it builds on the giants of the Scottish Enlightenment and on the notion of competitive meritocracy (Paterson, 2020). In contrast to the

20   *Understanding the Drivers for Change within the System*

plethora of schooling in England, Scotland has embraced the comprehensive secondary school as a 'school for all,' with the phasing out of selection between the mid-1960s and early 80s (Paterson, 2020).

Informed by the deliberations of the *International Council of Education Advisors* (ICEA) appointed by the Scottish Government and commissioned regional reports from the OECD (OECD, 2021; Scottish Government, 2015), Scottish education has ploughed a less contentious path with greater consensus between political parties and between the government and teaching unions. However, the 'close knit' policy community that characterises Scottish education is also its 'Achilles heel.' There is a tendency towards an unquestioning stance relating to policy decisions and the power relations underpinning them, and a lack of transparency in the policy process (often relying on compromises 'behind closed doors'), leading to a form of 'groupthink' (Mowat, 2018b; Murphy & Raffe, 2015). This is clearly evident in the circuitous nature of much educational policy in Scotland with the embedding of OECD discourse becoming more pervasive as its influence grows (Mowat, 2018b; Sellar & Lingard, 2013).

Curriculum for Excellence

The drive for excellence is demonstrated in the national curriculum, *Curriculum for Excellence* (CfE), framed around four capacities. Arising from concerns about an overly crowded curriculum that constrained teacher autonomy, it was introduced in 2004. Whilst secondary teachers generally welcomed the curriculum, a lack of understanding of the underpinning philosophy led to tensions in its enactment (Priestley & Humes, 2010; Priestley & Minty, 2013).

Whilst CfE, in a recent review commissioned by the Scottish Government (OECD, 2021), is described as 'an inspiring and widely supported philosophy of education' (Executive Summary), it was considered to lack in coherence, structure and a long-term perspective, requiring greater ongoing stakeholder development and ownership to mitigate against the 'overwhelming' deluge of over-technical information emanating from *Education Scotland*. The *Muir Review* of the Scottish Education system (Scottish Government, 2022b), arising from the Scottish Government's response to the OECD report (Scottish Government, 2021e), has far-reaching recommendations. Key amongst them are the replacement of current national bodies (such as *Education Scotland*), with a requirement that the newly established organisations work more closely with professional bodies and learners, and a national discussion on establishing a compelling and consensual vision for the future of Scottish education, largely welcomed by the Scottish government in its response to the report (Scottish Government, 2022a).

Equity in Scottish education

Whilst there is a strong commitment to closing the poverty-related attainment gap in Scotland (Education Scotland, 2017b), the policy mechanism for taking this forward – the *National Improvement Framework* (NIF) – is heavily

Understanding the Policy Context   21

informed by neo-liberal ideology, with a discourse of outcomes, standards, 'excellence' and quality, 'robust and consistent evidence' (informed by data to be collected and evidenced by those at the chalk face) and the introduction of *Scottish National Standardised Assessments* administered to children as young as five-years old. What is noticeably lacking is any real focus on inclusion, other than a brief reference to a personalised approach to evaluate progress.

It is realised through the *Scottish Attainment Challenge (SAC)*, modelled on the *London Challenge*. Launched in 2015 and refreshed in 2021, it represents a significant investment by the Scottish Government channelled through a range of income streams directly to local authorities and schools. Like its counterpart south of the border, it is heavily data-driven with direct accountability to the Scottish Government (shifting the locus of power).

An agenda of empowerment

Arising from the recommendations of the OECD, ICEA and the review of governance of Scottish schools (Scottish Government, 2017c), a new tier of governance – *Regional Improvement Collaboratives* (RICs) – has been introduced, bringing together the work of clusters of local authorities with the aim of fostering collaboration amongst professionals and empowering teachers (Swinney, 2019). This, and the introduction of a headteacher charter, was intended to address perceived shortcomings related to structural barriers in closing the poverty-related attainment gap, with the reforms having both centralising and decen-tralising tendencies (Forde, Torrance, Mitchell, McMahon, & Harvie, 2022). The tension between autonomy and accountability was clearly evident within the proposed legislation (ultimately rejected but enacted through agreement with local authorities and teaching unions) as schools and their leaders, whilst having greater freedoms (such as having more control over the appointment of staff), will be held to greater account for their actions (Forde & Torrance, 2017).

An evaluation of the RICs identified a range of positive impacts on students (with the provision of new and blended learning opportunities); teachers (devel-oping pedagogical skills); schools (leadership and development planning skills); and local authorities (building a collaborative culture) (Scottish Government, 2021g). However, the degree to which consciousness of the work of the RICs has filtered down to the grassroots level is questionable.

A synthesis

What is clear from the discussion within this chapter is that 'excellence' is rarely defined or portrayed in policy documentation other than in very reductionist ways, associated with standardised tests in a restricted number of subject areas. Despite the rhetoric in much OECD and national documentation, the bottom line is that it is these narrow outcomes that schools are often judged by and will therefore be the things that schools will invest their efforts in to ensure their survival. The focus on performativity and 'deliverology' almost inevitably leads to a narrowing

22 Understanding the Drivers for Change within the System

of the curriculum and teaching to the test, which, even in the words of the OECD, 'leaves a pupil with a hollowed-out and flimsy understanding' (Sellgren, 2017), making it more likely that schools will invest in short-term 'quick-fixes' and even, as identified by Gewirtz et al. (2021), cheating to boost grades.

The coupling of excellence with equity in an uncritical way within the varied international and national reports is of concern given that the neo-liberal agenda through which much of this policy is both formulated and enacted creates the very conditions under which some children, particularly those who are disabled, living in poverty or are otherwise disadvantaged, become marginalised. Even Scotland, which has tended to resist the more extremes of policy 'south of the border' (Beck, 2019), is not immune to the relentless and insidious march of neo-liberalism. This is not to diminish the value of 'big data' to inform public policy, nor to fail to recognise the imperative of governments to be accountable to their electorates, but the underlying ideologies and systems, structures, policies and practices associated with neo-liberalism serve to distort the very thing that we are attempting to measure in the first instance, in the process diminishing its value and bringing into question the purpose that education serves. Whilst there are distinct differences between the two nations in these regards, there may be greater commonalities than on first appearance.

Reflection Point

Within your own national context, to what degree and in which ways has this neo-liberal agenda impacted on education policy and on you as an educator or leader? What effect has it had on student learning?

Brief conclusion: an alternative paradigm

The tensions that have been identified within the English and Scottish education systems are not confined to the UK and are not new (Hargreaves & Fullan, 2012). For both Hooper and Bernhardt (2016), speaking to the USA context, and Hargreaves and Fullan (2012), school improvement is not about compliance to externally imposed standards or individual accountability but *mutual accountability* and *powerful collective responsibility*, respectively. The former is characterised by high levels of trust, a shared sense of responsibility for the success of each student, but also willingness to 'call out' actions that present as a barrier to achieving this vision (p. 133). With regard to the latter, 'it is about improving as an *individual*, raising the performance of the *team*, and increasing quality across the *whole provision*' (p. 23).

What is at stake is a failure to focus on the holistic needs of children (A. Bates, 2013):

> Education as a public service needs to be recognised by policy-makers and school leaders as a complex phenomenon which cannot be reduced to abstract measures without diminishing the humanness of the children that

Understanding the Policy Context 23

it has a duty to serve. In the everyday life of a school, being of service signifies a moral obligation to care for and nurture children.

(p. 52)

L. Darling-Hammond et al. (2018), drawing from insights gained from the *Comer School Development Program,* argue that a focus on the whole child through relationship building and pedagogy 'grounded in an understanding of the science of learning and development' facilitates 'meaningful, deep learning, and helps students acquire the social-emotional skills, habits, and mindsets necessary to be successful in school and in life beyond school' (p. 24).

It is evident that there needs to be a fundamental shift in thinking and in the paradigms which inform education at an international and national level such that we can create and invest in schools which are equitable, inclusive, compassionate and empowering in their policies and practice, necessitating consideration of the role that Higher Education and the labour market play within this.

Additional Suggested Reading

Education Policy, Practice and the Professional, 2nd ed.

Bloomsbury, 2019. Jane Bates, Sue Lewis and Andy Pickard

This text provides a comprehensive account of the education policy landscape in England, tracing it from developments from the 1980s to the Conservative government of Theresa May.

Reclaiming Education in the Age of PISA: Challenging OECD's Educational Order

Routledge, 2018. Vasco D'Agnese

The title says it all! This text provides a very strong critique of neo-liberalism and the role that the OECD plays on the global stage of education policy.

With the Whole Child in Mind: Insights from the Comer School Development Program

ASCD, 2018. Linda Darling-Hammond and colleagues

This text draws from the experience of implementation of a programme in the USA across a range of states that has particular relevance for disadvantaged children.

Closing the Attainment Gap – A Realistic Proposition or an Elusive Pipe Dream?

Journal of Education Policy, 2018, volume 33, issue 2. Joan G Mowat

This article interrogates the *Scottish Attainment Challenge* through the lens of policy borrowing, using it as a case study to bring out the complexities and challenges of policy borrowing as a process and concept.

Notes

1. Retrieved from https://www.allinschool.org/
2. Such as PISA, TIMSS (Trends in International Mathematics and Science Study) and PIRLS (Progress in International Reading Literacy Study).
3. Derived from the Obama administration White House archives/education.
4. Subsequent modifications were made to these measures in 2019.
5. The authors acknowledge the limitations of the data in terms of a response rate of 2.6% and an acknowledgement of potential bias with regard to respondents.

2 Inclusive Education
Challenges, Tensions and Dilemmas

> **Goals for Understanding**
> I. How are inclusion and inclusive education conceptualised within the literature and policy context and what are the inherent tensions and dilemmas?
> II. What are the tensions between inclusion as 'an ideal' and inclusion as a reality and the challenges facing educators?

The pandemic has brought to the fore and magnified inequalities in the lives of children and young people (from this point onwards, referred to as children): no more so than for those who are disabled (UNICEF, 2020a). The disruption to health and social services (in more than a third and at least a quarter of countries respectively) and learning (at least a half of countries) for disabled children brought about by COVID-19 restrictions may have exacerbated mental health issues for some children and placed them at greater risk of abuse or neglect. This has been compounded by the lack of assistive devices and specialised curricula to support learning in the home as disabled children were shielded or quarantined (Mowat, in press-b). Even prior to the pandemic, and despite the *Education for All* movement, the UNESCO *Global Education and Monitoring Report* (Slee, 2018a), defining the scope of inclusive education, paints a dismal picture of 124 million children and adolescents not in primary or lower secondary education in 2016, with 28 million children homeless and/or displaced due to conflict across the world, posing particular difficulties for education provision.

Building on the previous chapter, which chronicled the insidious march of neo-liberalism and its impact on the globalisation of education policy worldwide, this chapter hones in on the themes of inclusion and inclusive education, the inherent tensions therein and the dichotomy between the ideal and reality, as reflected within the literature and international and national policy.

DOI: 10.4324/9780429467110-4

Conceptualising inclusion

An enigma of 'wicked proportions' (J. Anderson, Boyle, Page, & Mavropoulou, 2020)

Understanding inclusion would appear, at a surface level, to be relatively straightforward – after all, is it not a cornerstone of international and national policy? Yet, Slee (2018a), in keeping with many other commentators (J. Anderson et al., 2020; Corcoran, Claiborne, & Whitburn, 2019), argues that the theory and practice of inclusive education are characterised by ambivalence and confusion, lacking a tight conceptual focus. For some, the problem is located within the contradictory interests and intentions within public policy (Larsen, Holloway, & Hamre, 2019). For others, it lies in the paradigmatic war between the psychological and sociological sciences (Kinsella, 2020).

What might initially appear to be a simple question posed to a group of Masters-level students, 'How do you understand inclusion?,' elicited a wide range of responses. These ranged from those which stressed the importance of access to services, facilities, resources, the curriculum and, more broadly, to education and society through the removal of barriers to participation and learning, to those which stressed the importance of all children feeling accepted, equally valued and able to contribute, regardless of background or characteristics (race, gender, ethnicity, sexual orientation, religious beliefs and socio-economic background). All were clear that it was about the school, working in partnership with parents and external services, adapting and modifying to the needs of the child. For some, it was about the enhancement and achievement of all learners and the realisation of potential through the creation of an inclusive learning environment. Some responses located the quest within a human rights framework, expressed in 'entitlement to,' 'a right to be educated' and 'a commitment to ensure.' However, whilst one response indicated that inclusive practice should be located within 'the same learning environment,' for others, this was stated more equivocally, 'within an environment of equity' and 'an environment suited to the individual.'

In many ways, the students' viewpoints capture some of the many different perspectives forwarded within what has become a highly contested field in which there is a strong polarisation of views. This is no more exemplified than within the debates around the place of special schooling and within critical disability studies (Lang, 2007; Norwich, 2013; Shakespeare, 2014). It is also represented within the phenomenon of researchers, politicians and practitioners talking about very different phenomena when talking about inclusion (Qvortrup & Qvortrup, 2018), assuming a shared understanding.

Slee (2018a) attests that how inclusion is understood globally needs to be located within geopolitical and cultural contexts, highlighting the need to understand inclusion as historically and socioculturally situated (rooted in customs, traditions and practices). Thus, what inclusion means in the developing world (or in places characterised by conflict or displacement of populations) may be entirely different from how it is understood in developed nations (Slee, 2018a). What some might consider to be exclusionary practices (such as separate special educational provision) may, in the context of the developing world, be the only access to education for children who are disabled (Florian, 2019; Mowat, in press-b).

The restricted understanding of concepts such as equity and inclusion, manifest in publications from the Organisation for Economic Cooperation and Development (OECD), compounds the problem (Mowat, 2018b). For example, Schleicher (2014) equates inclusion to 'all students reach(ing) at least a basic minimum level of skills' (p. 17). There is no sense within this definition of inclusion as being a rights issue or of it being related to participation, equity and a sense of belonging. Whilst later reports (Burns & Gottschalk, 2019; OECD, 2018) are more enlightened, even the more recent working paper on the topic (Brussino, 2021) defines inclusion only in relation to what it is not – integration.

Making sense of the 'wicked problem'

A typology of inclusion

A range of theorists has sought to bring clarity to the field. Ainscow, Booth, and Dyson's (2006a) typology of inclusion identifies six principal means by which inclusion is understood, spanning those which pertain to specific groups of learners to a view of inclusion as pertaining to all (see Figure 2.1).

According to the UK Government's *Code of Practice* (DfE & DoH, 2015), *Special Educational Needs and Disabilities* (SEND),[1] as it is now called in England, having previously been referred to solely as SEN, is categorised as

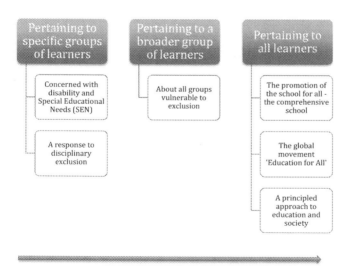

Figure 2.1 A representation of Ainscow, Booth, and Dyson's (2006a) typology of inclusion.

28 *Understanding the Drivers for Change within the System*

relating to sensory or motor difficulties; communication and interaction; cognition and learning; and social, emotional and mental health. It is deemed to apply to children and young people who have 'significantly greater difficulty in learning than the majority of others of the same age' and/or 'a disability which prevents or hinders him or her from making use of facilities of a kind generally provided for others of the same age in mainstream schools or mainstream post-16 institutions' (pp. 16–7). Thus, it is a normative concept in that the difficulties experienced by children so deemed are understood relative to the experience of other children.

The final category of the typology – *a principled approach to education and society* – is captured within the UNESCO guidelines for inclusive education (UNESCO, 2009):

> Inclusion is thus seen as a process of addressing and responding to the diversity of needs of all children, youth and adults through increasing participation in learning, cultures and communities, and reducing and eliminating exclusion within and from education. It involves changes and modifications in content, approaches, structures and strategies, with a common vision that covers all children of the appropriate age range and a conviction that it is the responsibility of the regular system to educate all children.
>
> (pp. 8–9)

However, Norwich (2013), drawing from Cigman (2007), observes that such an understanding distances inclusive education from disability, leading to an over-simplification of the differences between different facets of diversity.

Limitations

Qvortrup and Qvortrup (2018), in keeping with the discussion to follow in Chapter 3, observe that, of the varied definitions of inclusion within the literature, the subjective experience of the child is often overlooked or missing, failing to recognise that a child may be able to participate within a community but may not have a sense of belonging or be recognised by others within that community. These were both features of my own initial definition of inclusion (Mowat, 2008): 'a sense of being included, of feeling valued, and most of all, being able to learn in an environment best suited to the needs of the child' (p. 94). Subsequently, a sense of belonging (Korpershoek, Canrinus, Fokkens-Bruinsma, & de Boer, 2020; Prince & Hadwin, 2013; Riley, 2017; Slee, 2019), or connectedness (Lester, Waters, & Cross, 2013), is increasingly being identified as an important dimension of inclusion and child wellbeing (see Chapters 4 and 11).

Inclusive education

Inclusion can be understood as both a process (including) and the end-point of the process (included), underpinned by varied philosophical and ideological stances and values. Inclusive education is the broad umbrella under which it is to be realised. Norwich (2013), drawing from a range of theorists, observes that the multiple ways in which inclusive education is understood add to the ambiguity around the term. Amongst the examples he offers are: accepting/valuing/extending scope to all; enhancing equal opportunity; giving voice to and empowering those who are not normally heard; a road without end; or not an end in itself, but a means to an inclusive society (Mowat, in press-b).

Loreman (2009), in contrast, argues that inclusive education has distinctive and established characteristics, such as all children attend their neighbourhood school and learn in regular, heterogeneous classrooms with same-age peers (Mowat, in press-b). Whilst Loreman is unequivocal that any form of provision external to the mainstream classroom is not compatible with inclusive education, all commentators do not share this view. Some argue that in order to ensure the long-term goal of inclusion in society (as identified by Norwich, 2013), for some students, such as those with severe or complex needs, on the autistic spectrum or those with *Social, Emotional and Behavioural Needs/Social, Emotional and Mental Health Needs* (SEBN/SEMHN), specialist provision beyond the mainstream classroom, even for short periods of time, may be required (Hornby & Evans, 2014; Mowat, 2015a, in press-b; Shakespeare, 2014).

Brussino (2021) explores the issue from a pedagogical perspective – *inclusive teaching*, which is concerned with the promotion of learning and wellbeing for *all* students (the author's emphasis) in order to meet diverse student needs and learning styles and to be achieved through *inclusive pedagogy* (see the discussion to follow and Chapter 11), *curriculum* and *assessment*.

Slee (2018a) defines inclusive education as being concerned with the rights of children to access and be present, participate and achieve within the neighbourhood school, and the removal of barriers to such to achieve excellent educational experiences and outcomes for all (p. 8). His philosophy is guided by a set of questions concerned with the nature of the world that we want children to live in and the kinds of schools and classrooms and learning needed to achieve this end. His final question gets to the heart of the matter: 'When we look at our schools – who is in, who is out, who decides and what are we going to do about it?' (p. 9).

Inclusive education and children's rights

Understandings of childhood which underpin children's rights

The way in which we as adults and educators respond to children is informed by our understanding of childhood and what it entails, and historical, cultural, economic and social forces shape these understandings (Mayall, 2015). Such an understanding brings into question understandings of children's rights as objective realities, divorced from context (Reynaert, Desmet, Lembrechts, & Vandenhole, 2015). Archard (2014) argues that how a culture thinks about the extent, nature and significance of childhood will vary according to the *boundaries* which distinguish childhood from adulthood; the *dimensions* of childhood – its

30 *Understanding the Drivers for Change within the System*

distinctive features; and *divisions* – the various stages of childhood from infancy to adolescence, 'reflecting prevailing general beliefs, assumptions and priorities' (p. 39) and, presumably, values.

The predominant theory in Western cultures is that of the child as being separate from adulthood and in a state of development: 'lacking the capacities, skills and powers of adulthood' (Ibid, p. 43). It is this understanding which underpins differential rights and responsibilities for children and adults and, therefore, the formulation of specific rights for children, reflected in the *United Nations Convention on the Rights of the Child* (UNCRC) which has been adopted almost universally across the world.

The Salamanca Statement and Framework

The *Salamanca Statement and Framework* (UNESCO, 1994) has undoubtedly been one of the most significant landmarks in the road to achieving inclusion for all and bringing children's rights to the fore. According to Florian (2019), 25 years on, it has heightened consciousness of the concept of inclusive education and challenged the structures of schooling, and the orthodoxy of the time that some children should not be educated in regular[2] or mainstream schools (Mowat, in press-b). For Ainscow, Slee, and Best (2019), it has provided an educational (child-centred pedagogies); a social (the formation of a just and non-discriminatory society); and an economic (more economic provision) justification for change.

Whilst the prime focus of the *Salamanca Statement and Framework* aligns with the first category of Ainscow et al.'s (2006a) typology – *concerned with SEN* – over time, inclusive education has come to be understood much more broadly to encompass all children who could potentially be excluded from education (Florian, 2019), as exemplified in Figure 2.1, with the narrative shifting from special needs to a focus on inclusive schools and learning environments (Qvortrup & Qvortrup, 2018). Subsequently, a range of policy initiatives has taken this agenda forward globally from *Education for All* (UNESCO 1990) to the 2017 UNESCO *Guide for Ensuring Inclusion and Equity in Education* (Ainscow et al., 2019). This occurs against a backdrop of six out of ten children globally not acquiring basic literacy or numeracy skills after several years in attendance at school (UNESCO, 2020). For Ainscow et al. (2019), the pursuit of inclusive education is not just about structural change but about a paradigmatic shift in values and thinking which creates a vision that shapes a culture of inclusion in schools and classrooms, involving the wider community.

It will be evident from the discussion to this point that, despite the efforts to achieve consensus, there is no definitive understanding of inclusion, inclusive pedagogy or inclusive education around which all parties can reach agreement. The discussion to follow explores the inherent tensions and dilemmas that lie at the heart of the quest towards inclusive education.

Reflection Point

Slee asks about the type of world we would want our children to live in and the kinds of schools, classrooms and learning required to achieve this end. He poses the questions, 'Who's in? Who's out? And who determines this?' Set up a conversation with colleagues and consider how you would respond to these questions.

How have children's rights impacted on practice within your professional context in the journey towards achieving inclusion for all?

Tensions and dilemmas

The tension between SEN(D)[3] and inclusion

Whilst the Warnock report (Department for Education and Skills, 1978) in the UK, from which SEN derived, represented a radical departure from previous understandings of children with disabilities being regarded as uneducable, rather than leading to a transformation of schooling for disabled children, it led to the development of parallel, segregated, education systems sustained by determinist perspectives of ability and intelligence (Dorling & Tomlinson, 2016; C. Hart, Drummond, & McIntyre, 2007; Slee, 2018a). Instead of leading to the abandonment of categories, it led to their replacement by seemingly more benign categories (Norwich, 2013). Over time, the term SEN(D) became associated with a growing population of students and to be applied variously to an extensive range of associated provision across the world (Slee, 2018b). Ironically, given Warnock's initial intent, it became synonymous with 'individual student pathology or categories of impairment and disability' (Slee, 2018a) and associated with an ever-expanding 'SEN industry' (Slee, 2018b; Tomlinson, 2015), represented in subsequent government reports and categorisations (Norwich, 2013). C. Hart et al. (2007) draw attention to the impact of such deficit thinking on a range of negative consequences for children's learning, arising from ability labelling and grouping and determinist views of children's ability (see Figure 2.2).

The earlier work of Dweck and Elliot (1983), later popularised as 'Mindsets,' comparing the impact of fixed-ability perspectives on intelligence (an *entity* mindset) with that of more fluid understandings (an *incremental* mindset), clearly resonates with Hart's thinking. Indeed, Korpershoek et al. (2020) reveal a correlation between student achievement and a *mastery-goal orientation* (associated with an *incremental* mindset) which was associated in the minds of students with a sense of belonging and a more favourable classroom climate.

Florian et al. (2017) argue that inclusive education should focus on extending what is 'otherwise available' to children of a similar age (p. 14), rather than offering support that is additional to or different from that on offer to other

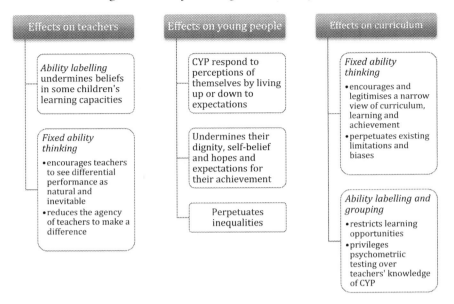

Figure 2.2 A summary of key points.
Source: Derived from C. Hart et al. (2007), figure 38.1.

children (Florian, 2019), the common understanding of SEN(D) provision which relates to an individual, rather than a social, level of analysis (Norwich, 2013). For Florian (2019), in so far as targeted responses to individual needs rely on differentiated forms of provision for some, this represents a 'repetition of exclusion' within schools (p. 695). This has parallels with Norwich's *dilemma of difference* (Norwich, 2013, drawing from Minow, 1990) who asks, 'When does treating people differently emphasise their differences and stigmatise or hinder them on that basis? And when does treating people the same become insensitive to their difference and likely to stigmatise or hinder them on that basis?' (p. 7) (Mowat, in press-b).

Florian et al. (2017) note that there has been a movement back towards categorisation fuelled by concerns that the umbrella term, SEN(D), obscures particular learning difficulties, denies a common vocabulary and prevents the gathering of data on specific groups. Nonetheless, the authors argue that inclusive education should focus on changing school practices rather than on differences between learners (Florian et al., 2017). Both Florian (2019) and Slee (2018a) attest that the language of SEN(D) and inclusion have merged with the distinction between the two concepts becoming blurred. A key issue therefore for Florian (2019) is the degree to which SEN(D) provision can be considered to be part of the problem or part of the solution in creating an equitable education system (Mowat, in press-b).

SEN(D) – a rational concept?

Rix, Sheehy, Fletcher-Campbell, Crisp, and Harper (2013) establish little consistency in how the term is understood and applied across 50 countries (55 administrations) and a lack of international coherence in the provision for children so identified. Likewise, there was no consistent pedagogy associated with SEN(D) provision other than that which would be considered good practice for all children (mirroring a finding in an earlier study of SEN provision conducted by P. Davis & Florian, 2004), although promising practices for sensory and/or physical impairment were identified. For Rix, Nind, Sheehy, Simmons, and Walsh (2010), the only two unifying aspects were that children in all countries 'with' SEN(D) were marginalised (although who and why varied across jurisdictions) and that 'special provision' constituted something that was additional to that which was normally on offer to other children (Mowat, in press-b), the issue that Florian et al. (2017) seek to address.

Hardy and Woodcock (2015), likewise, identify a lack of consistency across nations with regard to how inclusion is understood and portrayed within policy. This is characterised by conflicting stances which could be placed along a continuum from those that embrace diversity to those mired in a discourse of 'mainstreaming' and 'regular classrooms,' the latter operating from a position of deficit, reflecting neo-liberal influences and pressures. The authors pose the question as to how inclusive education can be furthered in a policy context characterised by fragmentation, incoherence, inconsistency or discrimination.

Thus, processes, systems and structures that appear on the surface to be rational and objective may be highly subjective. This reproduces itself at a local level in which different local authorities/councils/regions or even individual schools may interpret and enact national policy differently (Allan, 2013; Squires, 2012), often influenced by budgetary constraints, leading to a 'postcode lottery.'

Disproportionality in special education

Irrespective of setting, in countries which have developed SEN(D) provision, children from ethnic, racial and immigrant populations are over-represented, manifest in under-achievement and diminished educational opportunities, with the explanation often framed in terms of 'cultural' deficiencies in the child, family or community (Dyson & Kozleski, 2008; Slee, 2018b; Tomlinson, 2016). For such groups, inequalities in education and life chances 'are sustained and recreated by structures, policies and policy-makers' (p. 57), underpinned by determinist beliefs (Dorling & Tomlinson, 2016). A relationship has been established between SEN(D), socio-economic status and ethnicity (Strand & Lindorff, 2018) and, likewise, between SEN(D), socio-economic status (SES) and attainment (Ainscow et al., 2010), including children's mental health and wellbeing (Mowat, 2019a, 2020a).

This disproportionality is also reflected in school exclusions. McCluskey, Cole, Daniels, Thompson, and Tawell (2019) note that young people with SEN(D) in the UK experience 'a layering of disadvantage.' They are more likely to be living

34 *Understanding the Drivers for Change within the System*

in conditions of poverty and adversity and experience higher rates of school exclusion than other children, putting them at greater risk of mental health difficulties, contact with the criminal justice system and victimisation (McAra & McVie, 2010; McCluskey, Cole et al., 2019). Armstrong (2018) argues that there is a financial, ethical, legal and educational case for how teachers are supported in their role in meeting the behavioural needs of children with disabilities or mental health difficulties.

For many children growing up in the developing world (specifically Africa, Asia and South America), disability is compounded by poverty (Slee, 2018a) and, as has been well documented, this is not just a problem for the developing world. Parsons (2016) demonstrates that the attainment of children in England is stratified according to ethnicity, gender and deprivation with poverty being the main determinant.

Disability as a social construct and a form of oppression (see further discussion of concepts in Chapter 3)

The distancing of SEN(D) and the discourse surrounding it from the discourse of inclusion/inclusive education has its roots in the ideology of the *social model* (Norwich, 2013; M. Oliver & Barnes, 2012) in which disability is perceived, not as a trait of an individual, but as an interaction between the individual and society (Ostiguy, Peters, & Shalsko, 2016). Within this paradigm, a distinction is made between impairment (the underlying condition) and disability (discriminatory practices within the social environment which prevent people with impairments from participating fully in society) (Giddens, 2006). An impairment (or limitation) becomes a disability when the resources or accommodations for the individual to function as would be expected in society are not available to them (Ostiguy et al., 2016). Thus, a child who is visually impaired would be considered disabled if they have no access to Braille.

As such, advocates of the *social model* argue for a transformation of the environment and, as previously intimated by Ainscow et al. (2019), for a paradigmatic shift in thinking and values, such as represented within the *Index for Inclusion* (Booth & Ainscow, 2011) which focusses on the removal of barriers to participation and learning (physical environment, organisation, culture and policies, relationships, curriculum and pedagogy). It has also manifested itself in a rejection by some commentators of special schools (Norwich, 2013) or extraction from the classroom for additional support, reflected in the arguments of Florian et al. (2017) and Slee (2018b) as previously discussed.

Norwich (2013) observes that what constitutes an impairment is, in itself, a social construction, shaped by societal expectations and values. He cautions that there is no definitive understanding of the *social model* and it is only in the UK that it has taken on associations with oppression and discrimination. Shakespeare (2014) is strongly critical of the view that the '*medical model*' (*Individual, Deficit, Medical* [IDM] model) of disability sums up 'everything which is backward-looking and reactionary' (p. 11) and is a form of oppression, in contrast to the '*social model*' which has become synonymous with progressive approaches to disability. The concept of *disablism* aligns with this understanding of disability as a form of oppression (Shakespeare, 2014). Slee (2018b) argues that societies act to varying degrees to enable or disable individuals, erecting barriers to access and participation according to sets of norms. In contrast, *ableism* is reflected in the reification of 'a standardised or ordained body type' (p. 67). It follows, therefore, that the philosophy underlying the *social model* also derives from normalising discourses as how barriers are understood is relative to social norms, although this is rarely acknowledged.

Ableism is defined by Ostiguy et al. (2016) as 'the pervasive system that oppresses people with disabilities whilst privileging people who do not currently have disabilities' (p. 299). It operates at multi-levels from individual beliefs and behaviours to institutional policy and practice and is represented within cultural norms, which, collectively, act to maintain the status quo and lead to exclusion from society. By this view, disability is seen as a socially constructed category that frames an individual's sense of identity, reinforced through a process of socialisation in which it is viewed as a form of individual tragedy to be met with a form of benevolent humanitarianism (Ostiguy et al., 2016; Slee, 2018b).

Whilst Shakespeare recognises many of the benefits of the *social model* – its focus on social transformation; its liberating effect on the lives of people who are disabled; and the broadening of the focus of research away from more individualistic approaches, for him, its benefits are over-stated. In contrast, its limitations, in terms of failing to truly represent the lives of people who may experience pain, suffering and limitations arising directly from their impairment (which cannot be fully explained by social barriers or discrimination) are under-stated. He argues that the distinction between disability and impairment, central to the *social model*, is over-simplistic and does not hold true: 'disability is a complex interaction of biological, psychological, cultural and socio-political factors, which cannot be extricated without imprecision' (p. 26) (Mowat, in press-b).

These arguments may appear to be over-theoretical to the policymaker or busy practitioner, but how disability is understood has profound consequences for policy and how practice is envisioned and enacted. For example, whilst Shakespeare (2014) recognises that the removal of barriers to learning and inclusive provision may serve the needs of children well, he also argues that, for some, separate or alternative provision may serve their needs more effectively in achieving their ends and goals.

The conflict between performativity and inclusion

As discussed in Chapter 1, one of the greatest tensions lies in the quest for inclusion and the unrelenting pursuit of 'excellence' (rarely defined and equated narrowly to attainment in standardised tests) at a global level, fuelled by the

36 *Understanding the Drivers for Change within the System*

OECD's standardised tests and the competitive drive for ascendancy in the international league tables (Ball, 2015; Ball & Noddings, 2014). An extensive range of theorists raises concerns that these goals are not compatible, particularly within education systems strongly driven by neo-liberal ideology and competition between schools (Razer, Friedman, & Warshofsky, 2013), such as in the USA and England.

Within a social justice agenda which positions inclusive education as inclusion through selective and parentally selected segregation (occurring in multiple ways in England) and in which teachers are simultaneously charged to be inclusive in their practice and are under intense scrutiny to raise standards, teachers are regarded as the barriers to inclusion with little consideration given to resource or workload demands (Done & Andrews, 2020).

Such an emphasis leads to exclusionary teaching practices; a competitive ethos within the school; setting by ability and uniform judgements of the capabilities of individual pupils (as described by C. Hart et al., 2007); a narrowing of the curriculum and teaching to the test (Razer et al., 2013); 'winners and losers' as some children are deemed to add less value to the school (Barton, 2019), restricted access to some schools (Ainscow, Booth, & Dyson, 2006b); and exclusionary disciplinary practices (Cole, McCluskey, Daniels, Thompson, & Tawell, 2019; McCluskey, Cole et al., 2019; Mowat, in press-b). Thomas and Macnab (2019) argue that, if schools are to become truly inclusive, they need to reject 'assessment–competition–and discipline-orientated concerns' (see the discussion of Foucault's critique of discipline in Chapter 7) as they try to wrestle with the competing, performative demands of government and the rhetoric of an inclusive society (p. 14). These issues will be explored in greater depth in Chapter 4.

Transformation of the education system

In reflecting on progress towards achieving inclusive education and the transformation of the education system, Slee (2018a) asks about the degree to which schools have truly transformed themselves and reformed their practices, curriculum, pedagogy and assessment such that all children are valued, or has 'special education relocated itself in the regular school?' (pp. 26–7).

In a later paper (Slee, 2019), he argues that, rather than schools being democratic institutions of community and belonging committed to dismantling the exclusions that marginalise and oppress individuals, belonging has become 'an accoutrement of privilege' (p. 2) with schools being a place 'for some' and not 'for all.' He outlines the many ways in which schools through their culture and structures can disenfranchise children who are displaced, disabled and otherwise disadvantaged. Further, caveats, which are enshrined within enactments of human rights legislation, serve to marginalise the same populations for whom inclusion is conditional (Mowat, in press-b) (see Chapter 4 and the discussion of Kathryn Riley's work on a sense of belonging in Chapter 11).

The disparity between rhetoric and reality as reflected in the policy context

The English policy context

Key legislation for taking forward SEND in England is captured within the *Children and Families Act 2014* and associated regulations, including *The Special Educational Needs and Disability Regulations 2014*, and is supported by the *Code of Practice 2014* (DfE & DoH, 2015) and its more recent updates. The *Code of Practice* is designed to provide a more efficient and less confrontational service for children and families and sets out clearly the duties and obligations of all, including statutory requirements and a *0-25 Education, Health and Care (EHC) Plan* to meet the needs of children with more complex needs.

However, the *National Audit Report* pertaining to SEND in England (National Audit Office, 2019) establishes that there is a lack of consistency in the quality of support (whether in special or in mainstream schools) for children with SEND across the country (accounting for 14.9% of the student population) with those not in receipt of an EHC plan particularly vulnerable in this respect, and to exclusion from school. During the period 2014–2019, there had been a 20.2% increase in children attending Special Schools, leading to unsustainable costs incurred by local authorities.

The Scottish policy context

As outlined in Chapter 1, Scotland, as a devolved nation within the UK, has its own legislature and approach to meeting the needs of children formerly classified as having SEN but now classified as having *Additional Support Needs* (ASN), enshrined initially within the *Education (Additional Support for Learning) (Scotland) Act (2004)* and the subsequent amended Act in 2009 and 2016. The most recent *Education (Scotland) Act 2016* accords to children aged 12 or over (who have the capacity to and wish to do so) the same rights as adults, other than being a party to mediation services and placing requests for schools.

According to the Scottish Government, additional support may arise as a consequence of aspects of the learning environment, health or disability, family circumstances or social and emotional factors, thus aligning with the *social model* in some respects but still maintaining a 'within child' perspective. It is premised on the belief that the need for additional support may potentially apply to any child whether permanent or temporary (e.g., support for bereavement), embracing a wider constituency of students than SEN (Scottish Government, 2020d). A *Co-ordinated Support Plan* (CSP) for children with more complex needs was introduced, supported through *Getting It Right for Every Child (GIRFEC)*, a multi-agency approach to identifying and supporting children's needs in partnership with the school and family (see Chapter 9).

Key developments have been the *National Framework for Inclusion* (Scottish Teacher Education Committee [STEC], 2014 and again in 2022), framed around

38 *Understanding the Drivers for Change within the System*

the revised *Professional Standards* (GTCS, 2012),[4] and *Supporting Children's Learning Code of Practice* (Scottish Government, 2017e), providing statutory guidance for local authorities and schools on matters such as *Co-ordinated Support Plans* and dispute resolution.

The most recent review of the ASL Act (Scottish Government, 2020d) determines that 31.9% of Scottish children have been identified as having an ASN with the conditions identified not being mutually exclusive. For example, for the increasing numbers of children presenting with Autism Spectrum Disorder (ASD) their issues were compounded with social, emotional and behavioural problems associated with poverty and inequality, and more than half of young people entering the Secure Care and Justice Systems had at least one disability. The committee informing the review raised issues about the disparity between the rhetoric in public documentation and reality, the disproportionate rates of exclusion for children with ASN and the use of part-time timetables for these children.

The report identifies a significant disconnect between the stated intentions of the legislation and policy and practice on the ground, relating to the lack of recognition of the demands on senior leadership teams in schools and specialist managers in supporting children with ASN, and strategic and operational factors influencing and symptomatic of the disconnect (e.g., being unable to influence service changes). A lack of value attached to the students themselves and those supporting them, strongly reinforced by the pressures of the focus on attainment, and a concordant lack of agency or a sense of being listened to compound the problem (Scottish Government, 2020d).

Reflection Point

This discussion has honed in on some of the tensions and challenges that face educators in creating inclusive school environments. Where do you stand on some of these issues and what impact do they have on school policy, practice and the lives of children? How might we create more inclusive school environments?

The dialectic and dynamic relationship between inclusion and exclusion[5]

In reconciling the various perspectives under discussion, I would argue that inclusion and exclusion exist within a dialectic and dynamic relationship and should not be considered as dichotomous. Inclusion can only be understood when one identifies what it is that one wishes individuals to be excluded from and vice versa (Mowat, 2008). This relates to Slee's (2018a) final question, 'Who is in, who is out, who decides?,' as this is a matter of values and cultural norms and expectations which are situated in the present and past and also an issue of where power and agency lie (see Chapter 7).

Norwich (2013, 2021) argues for a movement away from dichotomous understandings within the field (e.g., medical vs. *social model* of disability; inclusion vs.

Inclusive Education 39

Figure 2.3 A representation of the 'looping effect'.
Source: Hacking (1999).

integration). Drawing from Zachar (2000) and Hacking (1999), he observes that diagnostic categories (as they apply to psychiatric disorders or learning disabilities or difficulties), rather than being characteristic of natural phenomena (Zachar, 2000), arise from the 'looping effect' (see Figure 2.3) which occurs when individuals interact with the world, in the process, changing them (Hacking, 1999).

The tendency towards an *essentialist bias* (a belief that things have a set of characteristics which make them what they are) leads to a concordant tendency to look for the similarities in children presenting with a specific condition but fails to recognise the many differences in presentation (Zachar, 2015).

Further, as will be expanded upon in Chapter 3 and building on this argument, without risking falling into the trap of marginalising those whom we seek to include by assuming that all members of an identified group will have shared characteristics that are readily identifiable, it is important to recognise the subjective experience of the child or young person and to recognise that marginalisation or exclusion (and the associated aspects related to labelling and stigmatisation [Armstrong & Hallet, 2012; Lauchlan & Boyle, 2007; Mowat, 2015a; Norwich, 2013; Slee, 2013]) may be experienced differentially, therefore it is important to listen to the voices of children (Messiou, 2012a, 2012b, 2019; Mowat, 2015b) (see Chapter 3 and discussion of Messiou's work in Chapter 11).

Whilst some might argue that inclusion should be limitless, this dialectic relationship places boundaries around inclusion – there will always be a point where inclusion, however it is conceptualised, merges into exclusion and vice versa. Further, as previously outlined, how inclusion and exclusion are understood and experienced reside within historical and sociocultural contexts (Tsovoka & Tarr, 2012). This implies that inclusion and exclusion lie on a continuum with fluid and not static boundaries and are experienced differentially and contextually. The imperative then becomes one of understanding the nature of these boundaries, what and who determines them, and how, through such understanding, public policy and practice can promote inclusive education. This understanding aligns most with insights from critical disability studies as described by Shakespeare (2014).

Hansen (2012) came to a similar conclusion arguing that 'inclusion presupposes exclusion' (p. 94). She argues that all communities, in order to secure coherence and stability and, indeed, survival, need to put limits on what constitutes inclusive practice within that setting and therefore have elements of both

40 *Understanding the Drivers for Change within the System*

inclusion and exclusion inherent within them, shaped by the professional identities of teachers and the discourses in which their practice is framed.

> We can identify inclusion neither by defining a normative limit between inclusion and exclusion nor by avoiding limits and making inclusion unambiguous. Thus, it is not possible to put meaning into the concept of inclusion without its otherness, exclusion.
>
> (p. 96)

For her, there is a gap between the 'vision' and rhetoric of inclusion as limitless (or, as described by Norwich, 2013, 'a road without end') and practice on the ground, with perceived inadequacies explained in theories external to the concept itself (e.g., in stigma and marginalisation; normality and divergence; IMD explanations), failing to critique the concept or acknowledge its limitations, a concern raised also by Qvortrup and Qvortrup (2018).

Similarly, Qvortrup and Qvortrup (2018) argue that inclusion implies (and actualises) exclusion. On the basis that a child may participate within multiple communities within the school setting, they observe that the degree to which a child may be excluded (physically, socially and/or psychologically) within the classroom and the wider environs of the school may vary from context to context: 'a child is not either completely included or excluded, but that he/she is included in or excluded from the different communities in different degrees' (p. 803, abstract). Drawing on sociological systems theory, they present a framework which examines the concept of inclusion through three dimensions: *levels* of inclusion; the *types* of social communities/*arenas* of inclusion (in or out of school) from which a child may be excluded; and the *degree* to which a child may be excluded within a specific community (c.c. Table 2.1).

Table 2.1 The three levels of inclusion

Levels of Inclusion	Not just related to physical location but to the child's active social participation and a sense of belonging to the community.
Arenas of Inclusion	Not just related to the classroom but to the multiple social arenas in which the child participates. For example,
	i. In the formal systems and structures of the school, such as the learning community of the classroom
	ii. The complex interactions within the classroom
	iii. Related to, but not part of, the school community (e.g., sports clubs)
	iv. Interpersonal relationships between children
	v. Interpersonal relationships between children and adults.
Degrees of Inclusion	The child may be included/excluded to varying degrees on a continuum, with varying degrees of visibility: a child could be at the centre, the periphery or be entirely excluded from a community.

Source: Derived from Qvortrup and Qvortrup (2018, pp. 810–4).

Inclusive Education 41

Within each arena, social boundaries are created between the excluded and included, concerned with the social practices characteristic of that environment, with success or failure in one environment having an impact on success or failure in another. Thus, a child may participate within the formal structures of the school (e.g., the classroom) but still experience exclusion from the informal community of other children both within and outwith the school (e.g., not being invited for sleepovers), aspects which may assume a greater importance to the child than may be formally recognised in definitions of inclusion. The authors conclude that it is important to understand inclusion holistically and not reduce it to the question of being included or excluded from the formal learning context, recognising the effort required to realise inclusion in practice: 'the ideals, aspirations and settings for inclusion are clear ... it is hard work to realise and implement these ideals in practice' (p. 806).

What this discussion highlights is the disparity between the aspirations set out in international reports (such as the *Global Education and Monitoring Report*) and within much of the international literature set against the reality on the ground: whilst significant progress has been made, there is still a long way to go in terms of realising the vision of inclusive education. Whilst it is crucial to hold on to a vision of, and be passionate about, inclusive education across the world, Norwich (2013) claims that the stance of critical theorists 'may stay "pure" in some ethical sense, but will not engage and change the world' (Chapter 1, electronic source). It is important to recognise that it is through enlightened public policy, the visionary actions of school leaders and the day-to-day interactions within the classroom that the vision will be realised. There may therefore be a need to move away from what Norwich (2013), drawing from Berlin (1978), describes as the 'hedgehog' position (representative of a purist vision of inclusive education) towards the position of the 'fox,' moving beyond critique, seeking to reconcile oppositional stances and seeking resolution to tensions and dilemmas, as argued within this chapter. The next chapter will explore further issues pertaining to the marginalisation of children and young people.

Additional Suggested Reading

Achievement and Inclusion in Schools (2ⁿᵈ ed.)

Routledge 2017. Lani Florian, Kristine Black-Hawkins and Martyn Rouse

This book explores the relationship between inclusion and achievement and provides a framework for participation that could be of great value to practitioners in pursuing their own enquiries. The case studies are insightful and exemplify the work of schools to promote inclusive pedagogy within a range of settings. The book achieves a good balance between theory and practice.

(Continued)

> ### Addressing Tensions and Dilemmas in Inclusive Education: Living with Uncertainty
>
> *Routledge 2013. Brahm Norwich*
>
> This insightful book tussles with the tensions and dilemmas within the field of inclusive education in an engaging way and provides an overview of the key theories and philosophical positions.
>
> ### Disability Rights and Wrongs Revisited (2nd ed.)
>
> *Routledge 2014. Tom Shakespeare*
>
> This is a key text within the field of disability studies, which extends beyond considerations of children and schooling. The author critiques the various approaches towards disability studies and cautions against over-simplistic dichotomies
>
> ### Inclusive Education isn't Dead, it Just Smells Funny
>
> *Routledge 2018. Roger Slee*
>
> This relatively short book packs a fair punch! With elegant prose and a conversational style, it gets to the heart of some of the key issues in inclusive education. It is provocative in style but highly insightful. You may not agree with all of the arguments forwarded, but it will make you reflect deeply on your values and beliefs about inclusion and inclusive practice.

Notes

1. Both Special Needs and Disability and Special Needs and Disabilities are used within policy documentation. For the purposes of this book, the term Special Needs and Disabilities will be used.
2. Whilst, in the UK, the word 'normal' would be used, in the international literature the Americanised 'regular' is more the norm, therefore this term will be used.
3. Whilst, in England, the term SEND is represented in government policy, globally, the term SEN is more prevalent. Therefore, from this point on SEN(D) will be used, other than in contexts where it does not apply, such as Scotland.
4. A revised set of Standards was published in 2021 by the GTCS.
5. Please note that a condensed version of this discussion can be found in Mowat (in press-b).

Part II

Exploring and Understanding the Problem

The initial two chapters in this part of the book focus on marginalisation, social exclusion and school disaffection. The remaining chapters hone in on our understanding of *Social, Emotional and Behavioural Needs/Social, Emotional and Mental Health Needs* and on the developmental theories that shape our understanding of children's behaviour and responses to them.

DOI: 10.4324/9780429467110-5

3 Marginalisation, Social Exclusion and the Impact of Poverty on Children and Young People

---

Goals for Understanding

I. What is marginalisation?

II. How does it relate to social justice, social exclusion, equity, social inequality, socio-economic status and poverty, and the wellbeing and attainment of children and young people?

Building on previous discussions, this chapter explores the nature of marginalisation and how it relates to the concepts of social justice, social exclusion, equity, social inequality, socio-economic status and poverty, and the wellbeing and attainment of children and young people. The initial discussion, drawing principally from Mowat (2015b), addresses two key questions: 'What does it mean to be marginalised?' and 'Marginalised from what?' Whilst many authors discuss issues pertaining to marginalisation (often framed in terms of social exclusion), few address these fundamental questions explicitly. Marginalisation is often considered at the broader, societal level in public policy (Policy First, 2012) and in terms of marginalised populations or groups (Adams & Bell, 2016; Mowat, 2015b) but the questions above can only be fully addressed by giving consideration to the subjective experience of children and young people.

Conceptualising marginalisation

Marginalisation – an enduring, pervasive, global problem

Marginalisation manifests itself in multiple ways in children and young people (Adams & Bell, 2016) and is a global problem that impacts negatively on societies across the world (Caro & Mirazchiyski, 2011; Mowat, 2015b; Ringarp & Rothland, 2010; Slee & Allan, 2001). Within a Eurocentric legacy in which the 'white, able, heterosexual middle class define their cultural capital as superior,' those who fall outwith these parameters are construed as 'inferior others,' leading to stigmatisation, segregation and exclusion (Pihl et al., 2018, p. 33). Yet,

DOI: 10.4324/9780429467110-6

46 *Exploring and Understanding the Problem*

increasingly, societal problems (such as inequality and youth employment) are seen as individual problems (Brunila, 2011; Mowat, 2015b).

It has been well documented that global inequalities, as identified by Wilkinson and Pickett (2010, 2018), have been magnified through the pandemic. An extensive range of commentators highlights the catastrophic global impact of the restrictions and disruption to schooling posed by the pandemic on the mental health and wellbeing of children and on their learning (Lee, 2020; Mowat, in press-a, in press-b; Shum, Skripkauskaite, Pearcey, Waite, & Creswell, 2021; UNESCO et al., 2020; UNICEF, 2021a, 2021b; UNICEF Data, 2020a, 2020b; World Health Organisation, 2020).

In an 11-month period from the spring of 2020, more than 168 million children were not in school, but missed days of schooling were accounted for disproportionally by children living in low-income countries (Mowat, in press-b; UNICEF & UN Women and Plan International, 2020). A digital divide emerged globally (Mowat, in press-a, in press-b; Seymour, Skattebol, & Pook, 2020; UNICEF & International Telecommunication Union, 2020). A substantial number of children in Europe were living in homes that lacked the resources to support home learning and were living in poorly heated homes (Mowat, in press-a; Van Lancker & Parolin, 2020). Even in high-income countries, there were disparities in the quantity and quality of educational provision with divisions emerging between private and state provision and between children from middle-class and working-class families in England (Cullinane & Montacute, 2020; Mowat, in press-b).

Marginalisation seen through the lens of social justice and as a form of oppression

Bell (2016) defines oppression as a durable, flexible and resilient concept that is used 'to embody the interlocking forces that create and sustain injustice' (p. 5) and which has a range of components or characteristic features, as summarised in Table 3.1.

The author attests that both those who oppress and those who are oppressed are dehumanised in the process. Further, oppression obscures the structural inequalities that create the conditions of people's lives which can lead to individualisation of the problem and a blame culture with people being held culpable for their own misfortunes (Brunila, 2011; Treanor, 2020a).

According to Adams and Zúñiga (2016, drawing from Hardiman, Jackson, & Griffin, 2013), structural inequality plays out at different levels – the individual, institutional and social/cultural, affecting attitudes and behaviour and occurring at both a conscious and unconscious level (see Figure 3.1).

At the individual level, bias and prejudice are negative attitudes towards marginalised or excluded groups rooted in unexamined stereotypes, reinforced through selective attention (paying greater heed to things that reinforce our prejudices and downplaying those that don't) and embedded within the dominant culture. They are often based on historical beliefs taken out of context; target characteristics of a group which may be shared by other groups who are

Marginalisation, Social Exclusion and the Impact of Poverty 47

Table 3.1 Components of oppression

Component	Characterised by
Restrictive	Structural and material constraints that significantly restrict opportunities and aspirations, leading to a lack of social mobility.
Pervasive	Seen as inevitable, unchangeable and institutionalised through pervasive practices that are grounded culturally and historically. Through a process of socialisation, they are gradually internalised and taken for granted.
Cumulative	Arising from past practices, the effects of oppression aggregate over time and can be seen in the micro-aggressions directed towards and experienced by oppressed people.
Socially constructed categories	The classification of distinct groups based on shared characteristics (e.g., race) presented as natural, inevitable and difficult to challenge.
Power hierarchies	The classification of social groups into hierarchies that confer advantage, status, resources, access and privilege to some groups that are denied to others, leading to a 'them' and 'us' culture by which subordinated or marginalised groups are seen as 'less than, inferior and/ or deviant' (p. 9).
Hegemonic and normalised	The effects of oppression become normalised to the extent that those who are oppressed don't recognise their oppression, which is seen as part of the natural order.
Internalised	The appropriation of stereotypes and biases encountered in everyday living into the belief system of the person through a process of socialisation.
Intersectional	How multiple forms of oppression coalesce, reinforce and re-constitute one another in the lives of individuals.
Durable and mutable	The resilience and ability of oppression to withstand attempts to challenge it.

Source: Derived from Bell (2016, pp. 5–15).

not discriminated against on that basis (e.g., the over-representation of ethnic minority, male youths subject to stop and search by the police in the UK); and/ or are over-generalisations which pay insufficient attention to diversity within a group (Adams & Zúñiga, 2016) (e.g., assuming that all children on the autistic spectrum are savants, as portrayed in the film, Rain Man).

Marginalisation as a subjective, situated and contextualised experience

My curiosity about marginalisation was first sparked by an encounter with a colleague who recalled her experience of attending a widening access to university event when a teenager. The lecturer leading the group informed everyone that the session was for youngsters from disadvantaged areas: my colleague looked

48 *Exploring and Understanding the Problem*

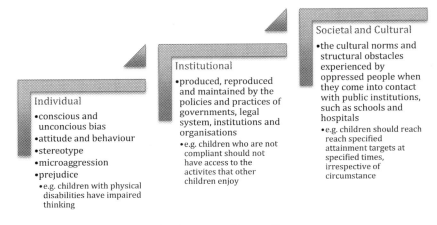

Figure 3.1 Illustration of levels of structural inequality.
Source: Derived from Adams and Zúñiga (2016, pp. 97–103).

around the room to see who they were, not aware that she was considered to be part of this 'marginalised' group.

Billy Connolly, the renowned Glasgow comedian, on reflecting on his childhood, observed that it was only when outside commentators drew attention to the grim living conditions that he became aware that he was considered to be poor and, therefore, disadvantaged.[1] Similar observations were made by elderly men who survived the blitz in Clydebank in the 1940s[2] who fondly reminisced about a childhood living in the tenements where every door was open and there was a genuine sense of community.

Patrick	There were no doors closed in the tenements at that time. And, as children, and when A'm gonna (I'm going to) meet you, I just walk into your house. I can walk inside any house in the street and walk into it and we'd all know each other.
Commentator	Cramped and crowded, tenement life was rough and ready but, for a child growing up there in the 1930s, it was like being part of one big family.
Patrick	That's what brought us all through that time. There was no, 'You're this or you're that.' You are all together.
Jack	Life was happy. We lived two up in the middle (in the middle house on the 2nd landing) wi' a room and kitchen wi' an outside toilet but it was fine. It's no' as if you knew anything else.

Despite living in cramped and basic living conditions, they did not experience their lives at that time as marginalised – to them it represented life, as they knew it. It could be argued that, in keeping with Bell's (2016) components of oppression,

Marginalisation, Social Exclusion and the Impact of Poverty 49

they had internalised the pervasive, hegemonic and normalised expressions of oppression in society, accepted as the natural order. However, an alternative perspective is to question the legitimacy by which groups of people can be categorised by others as marginalised, not recognising their individuality or lived experience.

Putnam (2015), returning 50 years later to the community in America (Port Clinton, Ohio) where he grew up in the 1950s, witnessed the loss of social cohesion and sense of community, irrespective of social class, of people looking out for each other. What he found was a divided community – prosperous families residing in second homes living side by side with families in poverty with virtually no communication or shared experiences between them: 'a community in which kids from the wrong side of the tracks that bisect the town can barely imagine the future that awaits the kids from the right side of the tracks' (p. 1).

Marginalisation – a complex concept manifested in multiple ways

Marginalisation is a highly complex concept that manifests itself in multiple ways across a range of disciplines but lacks a shared theoretical framework (Booth & Ainscow, 1998; Messiou, 2012a, 2012b; Petrou, Angelides, & Leigh, 2009; Pihl et al., 2018). It may or may not be discernable to the individual child or observer (Messiou, 2012a); may be expressed formally (e.g., through official policy) or informally (Petrou et al., 2009); and is situated in time and place (Munn & Lloyd, 2005; Razer, Friedman, & Warshofsky, 2013). If experienced over time, it may become internalised (Hjörne & Säljö, 2013; Skovlund, 2014) and become part of the lived experience of the individual child (Mowat, 2015b).

Marginalisation as a form of social construction

Adams and Zúñiga (2016) define social construction as 'the idea that norms, ideas and institutions that may now seem natural and inevitable actually grow out of historical and social processes' (p. 104). Messiou (2019) argues that, rather than marginalisation being an objective reality, it arises as a consequence of social constructions created through the social interactions within groups and the labelling which emanates from them. Whilst, on one hand, it cannot be assumed that children, so labelled, will experience their lives as marginalised, on the other hand, the needs of others (who do not fit readily into these 'marginalised' groups) may be ignored (Messiou, 2019). The author forwards four different ways of thinking about the 'fluid and complex nature of marginalisation' (2019, p. 308), encapsulated within Figure 3.2.

Marginalisation as a fluid and dynamic concept

The experience of marginalisation is not static. Children may move across boundaries (Messiou, 2012b): it is 'a dynamic concept that varies between contexts and times' (p. 17). This raises the possibility that *all* children may be subject to marginalisation at certain points and therefore opens the door to transformational practices

50 *Exploring and Understanding the Problem*

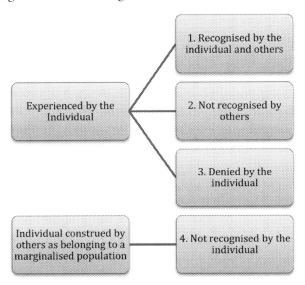

Figure 3.2 Representation of Messiou's (2019) conceptualisation of marginalisation.

in the creation of more inclusive schools (Messiou, 2019). Marginalisation may be experienced as transient and context related (Frisen, Hasselblad, & Holmqvist, 2012; Razer et al., 2013), but, for some children, it can become global and shapes their identity (Hjörne & Säljö, 2013; Macleod, 2013; Mowat, 2015b; Orsati & Causton-Theoharis, 2013; Skovlund, 2014).

Marginalisation – a normative concept

Social, cultural and historical norms and expectations shape our understanding of which individuals or groups (by dint of shared characteristics) we would consider to be marginalised, but, as highlighted in the previous cameos, it brings us back to the question about the legitimacy by which a child or young person who does not recognise their life as marginalised should be construed as such by others.

The relationship between marginalisation and social exclusion

Social exclusion – a state in which individuals or groups 'lack effective participation in key activities or benefits of the society in which they live' (Razer et al., 2013, cited in Mowat, 2015b, p. 457) – and marginalisation appear to be almost interchangeable in the literature, being two interrelated and interdependent processes (Hansen, 2012; Mowat, 2015b). Explanations for the marginalisation of individual children are often framed in terms of individual deficits in the child or young person and 'a lack of aspirations and capabilities,' disregarding the systemic influences on the life of the child (Vandekinderen, Roets, Van Keer, & Roose, 2018, p. 16).

Munn and Lloyd (2005) outline three processes associated with social exclusion: *relativity* (one is marginalised in relation to others within a similar context); *agency* (marginalisation arises from actions and/or circumstances and does not occur by chance); and *dynamics* (the interaction between sets of variables within the environment which together negatively impact on future prospects) (Mowat, 2008). Thus, a child living in poverty (*relative* to other children), arising from the direct actions of government with regard to fiscal and welfare policy (*agency*) may, through a combination of circumstances (*dynamics* – e.g., prejudice in society, lack of access to the same opportunities as other children), find themselves marginalised with their future prospects curtailed.

How marginalisation is understood

Within the literature, marginalisation as it pertains to children and young people is conceptualised in a range of ways, some of which relate to the discussion of inclusion and inclusive practice in Chapter 2. For example, pertaining to specific groups perceived to be specifically vulnerable to exclusion and stigmatisation (Ainscow, Booth, & Dyson, 2006a; Bottrell, 2007); social exclusion arising from a lack of equal opportunities, requiring the removal of structural and cultural barriers to learning and participation and associated with the 'inclusion for all' movement (Ainscow et al., 2006a; Messiou, 2012a; Petrou et al., 2009; Slee & Allan, 2001); and the conditionality in public policy which serves to marginalise and exclude to which Slee (2019) made reference. Others relate more to issues of social justice and equity, associated with an inequitable distribution of economic, social and cultural capital (Brann-Barrett, 2011); 'identity work' and resistance (Bottrell, 2007; Bright, 2011; Liu & Xie, 2017); and the social and relational aspects of poverty (Ridge, 2011). It is not implied that these are discrete categorisations, or, indeed, the only categorisations, but they highlight the inter-connectedness of the concepts under discussion (Mowat, 2015b).

Marginalisation as an affective state and as reflective of an 'ideal'

The feelings engendered by marginalisation cannot be separated from the state of marginalisation, highlighting the importance of marginalisation as a subjective state. To be marginalised is to have a sense that one does not belong and, in so doing, to feel that one is not a valued member of a community and able to make a valuable contribution within that community, nor to be able to access the range of services and/or opportunities open to others. In effect, to feel, and to be, socially excluded, looking in from outside (Mowat, 2015b).

Inherent within the notion of a 'marginalised group' are stereotypical assumptions that, firstly, there is a shared experience which can be associated with people who share certain characteristics – that of marginalisation; and, secondly, it can be equated with a global, stable state within a given population, failing to recognise the contextualised, subjective experience of the individual and conferring on them the status of 'other.' Such a position derives from dominant,

52 *Exploring and Understanding the Problem*

deficit (and often contradictory) discourses (Messiou, 2012b). Further, there is a shared conceptualisation of whatever it is they are being marginalised from – 'an ideal,' grounded in cultural and historical social norms, values, expectations and aspirations, with anyone seen as falling short perceived to be wanting in some way, deficient, disadvantaged and/or marginalised (Bottrell, 2007). There is a failure to recognise that not all will share these values and aspirations: some may offer resistance which can be construed as a form of resilience (though not often recognised as such) (Bottrell, 2007) and there can be legitimacy in such positioning (Mowat, 2015b).

An ecological perspective on marginalisation understood through the lens of resilience

The concept of resilience, deriving initially from the work of Garmezy, offers an explanatory framework for the variability in response of children facing similar adverse circumstances. It focusses on positive adaptation rather than explanations residing in psychopathology, poverty and post-traumatic stress (Condly, 2006; Kolar, 2011). Resilience can be understood as multi-faceted, mediated by context (Condly, 2006) and as an interactive process situated within time and place, operating across the lifespan (Kolar, 2011; Rutter, 2012). It is concerned with the wider social contexts and influences that impact on the individual child or young person within that context (Mowat, 2015b, 2019a; Rutter, 2012).

Within the multiple reciprocating systems with which the child interacts (e.g., home and school), the degree to which a child will demonstrate resilience in a given context is determined by the nature and quality of the interactions among the socio-ecological factors that facilitate the development of wellbeing under stress (Ungar, Mehdi, & Jörg, 2013). Rather than the locus for change being the child or young person (as exemplified in programmes such as 'Bounce Back!'[3]), it is seen as residing in adaptations at the different levels of the system: the greater the adversity to which the child is exposed, the more the child's capacity to adapt is dependent on the quality of the environment. Resilience understood as a process of adaptation (rather than a state of being [Kolar, 2011]) requires examination of both the risk mechanisms that make the child more vulnerable to adversity and the protective mechanisms that have the potential to promote resilience. If acting in synergy with each other, multiple risk factors (or conversely, multiple protective factors) may combine to have a more powerful effect than a single life-event (Mowat, 2015b, 2020a; Olsson, Bond, Burns, Vella-Brodrick, & Sawyer, 2003).

Towards a new conceptualisation of marginalisation

In addressing the two questions posed earlier in the chapter, 'What does it mean to be marginalised? and 'Marginalised from what?,' might it be the case that the degree to and ways in which a child will experience their life as marginalised and

Marginalisation, Social Exclusion and the Impact of Poverty 53

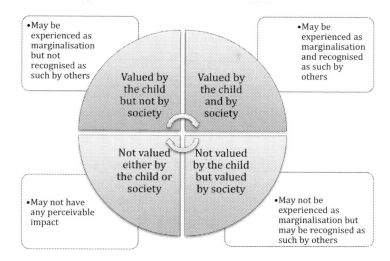

Figure 3.3 How marginalisation may manifest itself in relation to what is valued by the child and what is valued by society, if lacking.

Source: Modified from Mowat (2015b), Figure 3.4(a), with permission from SAGE.

be cognisant of it may depend upon the interaction between what is valued and held to be important by the child, what society values and the degree of congruence between the two (Mowat, 2015b) (cc. Figure 3.3)?

In turn, what the child values is shaped and filtered through their life experiences, which are a product of the interaction between the risk and protective factors in their lives, as outlined in Figure 3.4. Recognising that thoughts and feelings are inextricably linked (Gardner, 1999; Newton, 2014), these experiences are then interpreted by the child and filtered through their emotions.

Societal norms reflect collective values, aspirations and expectations of how people should behave towards each other, reflected within which are the ideals to which people within a culture aspire. Just as societal norms, values, aspirations and expectations are mediated by time, place and culture, so too are the risk and protective factors which together intertwine to determine the resilience of the child within a specific context and situation (Mowat, 2015b) (cc. Figure 3.4). All of the above are mediated by power relations (see Chapter 7), reflected within the political context, which create and act on on that context in a reciprocal relationship.

There is no doubt that the risk factors for some children (e.g., those living in poverty, within the care sector, ethnic and migrant populations, who identify other than heterosexual and who have *Special Educational Needs and Disabilities* [SEND]/*Additional Support Needs* [ASN]) are such that the likelihood of marginalisation is much greater. The discussion to follow focusses specifically on children living in poverty and the impact that this may potentially exert, recognising

54 *Exploring and Understanding the Problem*

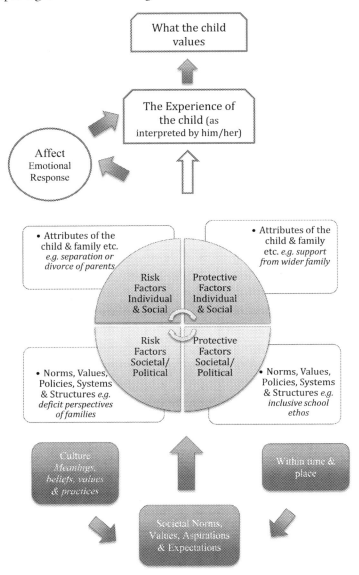

Figure 3.4 An ecological representation of resilience building upon Olsson et al. (2003) and other theorists.

Source: Modified from Mowat (2015b), figures 3.3 & 3.4b, with permission from SAGE.

the importance of *intersectionality* (how multiple factors [e.g., race, disability …] can intersect in the life of a child or young person to create discrimination or oppression). It is illustrated through the Scottish context and draws from Mowat (2018a, 2019a, 2020a).

> **Reflection Point**
>
> Think about a situation or context in which you have felt marginalised (but perhaps not something very traumatic). What was it about the situation that led you to feel this way? Use the models that have been presented within this chapter to help you to think through the factors that influenced the situation, both personal and external to you. From the insights gained from this, think of a child or young person whom you have been in contact with professionally and how the model might apply to their lives. How might this affect your responses towards them professionally?

Understanding the impact of poverty on the education and wellbeing of children and young people

In keeping with the previous discussion, the key argument forwarded is that children living in poverty cannot be regarded as a homogenous group to whom the same solutions can be applied. Nor can the problem be understood or addressed solely through education policy or the efforts of schools alone. It is highly complex and requires a sustainable, political solution focussed on social justice which integrates public policy across a range of spheres and which builds infrastructures of support around communities, schools, families and children (Mowat, 2018a, 2019a, 2020a).

The nature of the problem

Poverty impacts the lives of children in myriad ways, reflected in significant gaps in cognitive and emotional development and attainment from an early age (Sosu & Ellis, 2014) and poorer mental health and wellbeing outcomes manifest across the world, further exacerbated by the pandemic (World Health Organisation, 2020). Save the Children/UNICEF (2021) identified that around 60 million more children (than pre-pandemic) across the world could be living in poverty by the end of 2021. The effects of poverty are cumulative across the lifespan and impact not only on children's future outcomes but their present lives. It arises as a consequence of macro-economic, political, social and individual factors as they interact and impact on the lives of families and children, with income inequality being a key structural cause of child poverty (Treanor, 2020a). Levels of poverty are correlated with relative income gaps: the greater the inequality in societies, the greater the level of poverty (Wilkinson & Pickett, 2018; World Health Organisation, 2016).

Defining and measuring poverty

The definition and measurement of poverty is highly contested (McKinney, Hall, Lowden, McClung, & Cameron, 2012): the main classifications are *absolute,*

56 *Exploring and Understanding the Problem*

relative, persistent or *severe* (McKendrick, Mooney, Dickie, & Kelly, 2011). *Relative poverty* is defined as: 'living at a level of income that does not allow one to take part in the normal or encouraged activities for one's society' (Wolff, Lamb, & Zur-Szpiro, 2015). The measure adopted is of someone living in a household with less than 60% of the median income (Mowat, 2020a). Across countries affiliated with the Organisation for Economic Cooperation and Development (OECD), the measure takes account of both income and material deprivation (Treanor, 2020a). However, it fails to take account of other factors, such as disability in the family, which may exacerbate child poverty. Children living in *persistent poverty*, unsupported through the various transitions associated with childhood, are likely to experience cumulative disadvantage which extends into adulthood (Treanor, 2020a).

Poverty as dynamic

For many families poverty is not a persistent state but a state in which they are likely to enter and exit at different points, brought about by low-wage economies, unemployment and insufficient benefits. The failure to recognise the dynamic nature of poverty can lead to a 'them' and 'us' culture of blame where those living in poverty are held culpable for their circumstance, fuelled by government and media rhetoric in the UK (Treanor, 2020a).

During the pandemic, historically disadvantaged groups in the USA were disproportionately affected financially, widening inequalities (Perry, Aronsona, & Pescosolido, 2021). However, Treanor (2020a) argues that, even in periods of crisis and austerity, childhood poverty is not inevitable – government policy makes a difference.

Poverty as insidious

What is less easy to measure is the insidious nature of poverty and the cultures associated with it – how it eats into the psyche and impacts on the subjective wellbeing of families and children (Putnam, 2015). How poverty is understood politically drives public opinion (Treanor, 2020a). Within the media, portrayals and images of families living in poverty are invariably negative and the rhetoric is one of 'scroungers,' 'work shy,' 'teenage single mothers' and 'benefit cheats.' Yet, it has been established that, in 2018–2019, a quarter of children in the UK from working households were from low-income families (after account had been taken of housing costs) (C. Smith, 2020).

Poverty of aspiration

Aspirations are shaped by the interaction of a broad range of influences from the more immediate – family, neighbourhood, school – to wider macro-level systemic and social factors (J. White, 2018). Treanor (2017) debunks the myth of 'poverty of aspiration,' often forwarded as an explanation for under-achievement and a lack of social mobility. The author attests that it is not a lack of aspiration that

Marginalisation, Social Exclusion and the Impact of Poverty 57

stands in the way of progress for children living in poverty but a lack of cultural (know-how) and social (networks) capital in their communities compounded by multiple social and structural barriers related to inequalities in society.

Disproportionality in childhood poverty

There are some children who are at greater risk of experiencing childhood poverty than others through their family and social circumstance, such as living in a one-parent family, the number of children in the family, ethnicity and migrant status, disability in the family and specific work patterns (e.g., unemployment, zero-hour contracts). Those children living in poverty who themselves are more vulnerable (e.g., those in care, with a disability, a carer, refugees) are more likely to experience *severe poverty* (Treanor, 2020a).

Childhood poverty and adverse childhood experiences

There has been debate regarding whether or not poverty should be considered to be an *Adverse Childhood Experience (ACE)*. The concept arises from the work of Felitti, Anda, and Nordenberg (1998) in the USA and posits that the impact of childhood abuse, neglect or exposure to household adversity (e.g., alcohol abuse) in early childhood extends into adulthood, having major consequences for health and wellbeing and life chances.

D. Walsh, McCartney, Smith, and Armour (2019a, b), in a systematic review of the international literature, identify that the effect of ACEs can be cumulative – the greater the number experienced by a child, the greater the likelihood of adverse effects in adulthood. In Wales, those who had experienced 4+ ACEs were 20 times more likely to be incarcerated at any point in their lives. Further, children living in families where one or more of their parents have experienced ACEs are more likely to experience ACEs themselves, therefore breaking this cycle is imperative (Bellis et al., 2015).

In one of the few studies to gather data on children rather than adults, of children aged 7 years in Scotland in 2011–2012, around two thirds had experienced one or more ACEs and these were highly correlated with social disadvantage in the first year of life (Marryat & Frank, 2019). Treanor (2020b) observes that poverty, inequality and adversity in childhood often go hand in hand, with childhood abuse and neglect the most strongly correlated. However, she argues that the ACEs approach is flawed, as it does not take sufficient account of the social determinants of adversity, structural inequalities and discrimination in society:

> A fundamental flaw in the ACEs approach is that it focusses on the experiences of children as a result of their families rather than as a part of their families. It ignores the truism more readily understood in approaches to alleviate poverty: you cannot improve the circumstances of children without improving those of their family.
>
> (p. 481)

58 *Exploring and Understanding the Problem*

She cautions that the conflation of poverty and adversity can lead to unintended consequences for children and their families, with the potential to impede children's access to support and even legal entitlements.

Childhood poverty and education

Education is often seen as the route out of poverty, attenuating social and economic inequalities. However, not all children are equally placed to take advantage of what education has to offer, nor are all children equally valued. Education can present as 'yet another seat of inequality, an inhibitor rather than a facilitator of opportunity and outcomes' (Treanor, 2020a, p. 77, citing Reay, 2018).

The challenges faced by children living in poverty as they engage with schooling are often attributed to deficiencies in the child or the family (e.g., lack of innate ability, poor parenting) and attention devoted to remedying the perceived deficits rather than the structural and systemic causes of poverty. The congruence between the values and norms of middle-class homes and schooling creates a much easier transition for children from such backgrounds to 'fit in,' feel a sense of belonging and to achieve (Treanor, 2020a).

For some children living in poverty, schools can fulfil the function of a safe haven (Riley, 2017), building resilience in the child or young person (Henderson, 2013). A positive school ethos can play a key role in mediating the relationship between poverty and attainment (J. White, 2018). However, poverty-related factors can present as a barrier to participation in schooling and education, both directly (e.g., the costs associated with school subjects, such as home economics, and leisure activities), and indirectly (e.g., the financial vulnerability of the mother, impeding the capacity to create a loving home environment and to support learning) (Mowat, 2019a, 2020a; NHS Health Scotland, 2020; Treanor, 2016, 2020a; J. White, 2018).

The stigma of poverty

The stigma and shame attached to poverty leads some families and children to mask its impact on their lives, concealing from others its effects. This can lead to children withdrawing from the activities that other children enjoy (e.g., not informing their parents about school trips) and a reluctance of parents to engage with the school. The problem can be compounded by the dissonance between the culture of the school (which can be intimidating for some working-class parents) and the home, and the parents' own negative experience of school. Yet, the measures taken by governments to improve education systems, based on parental choice and competition between schools, make it much harder for parents who lack the 'know how' (or cultural capital) to navigate their way through the system to the advantage of their children, leading to greater socio-economic segregation (Treanor, 2020a).

Relationships are key

There is no doubt that the stresses on teachers working in disadvantaged areas are significant. When this is coupled with a lack of knowledge regarding the causes

Marginalisation, Social Exclusion and the Impact of Poverty 59

and consequences of poverty, it can lead to strained relationships between teachers and pupils and, for pupils, to low wellbeing, frustration, disengagement, truancy, and, ultimately, exclusion (Treanor, 2020a). Yet, the quality of relationships between teachers and pupils emerged as a key variable in fostering a sense of belonging and engagement in learning for youngsters with *Social, Emotional and Behavioural Difficulties* (*SEBD*), living in an area of multiple deprivation, who participated within a group-work intervention (Mowat, 2007, 2009, 2010a).

Changes in practice at the school level (such as provision of breakfast clubs); at the local authority level (such as sourcing cheaper suppliers of school uniforms); and the professional development of teachers, leading to heightened awareness, understanding and attitudes towards poverty, supported by 3rd Sector Organisations such as the *Child Poverty Action Group*,[4] can mitigate the impact of childhood poverty, reducing stigma and discrimination (NHS Health Scotland, 2020; Treanor, 2020a).

Childhood poverty in Scotland

The state of child poverty

In the period leading up to the pandemic (March 2021), 26% of children in Scotland were recorded as living in *relative poverty*, 23% in *absolute poverty* and 12% in *combined low income and material deprivation*. Whilst, over a 17-year period (1994/5–2011/2), rates of *relative* and *absolute poverty* fell (the latter by more than half from a starting point of 48%), recent trends indicate that *relative poverty* is slowly on the rise whilst *absolute poverty* has remained relatively stable (Scottish Government, 2021b). However, in comparison to the UK, reductions in childhood poverty have been greater and more sustained (Barnard, 2017; Mowat, 2020a). Children living with a mother under 25 are significantly more likely to be living in *relative* poverty (55% in the period 2015–2018), as are children living in a single parent or ethnic minority family (38% in the period 2017–2010) (Scottish Government, 2021b). Poverty rates vary significantly according to geographical location. Whereas one tenth of children in Shetland, an island community, live in poverty, this contrasts with a third in Glasgow (Mowat, 2020a; NHS Scotland, 2018).

How childhood poverty manifests itself

Poverty is generational and commences before birth, accumulating into the next generation (Treanor, 2012). Drawing from the *Growing up in Scotland* longitudinal survey (Bradshaw, 2011), it was established that children from low-income families are around 13 months behind in vocabulary and 10 months behind in problem-solving on entry to school in comparison to their more advantaged peers (Mowat, 2018a; Sosu & Ellis, 2014; J. White, 2018). Four-year old children living in the most deprived areas in the city of Glasgow were found to be three times more likely to experience mental health difficulties at age 7 than

60   *Exploring and Understanding the Problem*

those from the most affluent areas (Marryat, Thompson, Minnis, & Wilson, 2017; Mowat, 2019a).

The majority of children living in poverty remain in the same income quintile as their parents as adults, perpetuating inter-generational poverty, illustrative of the 'cycle of deprivation' (McKinney et al., 2012; Mowat, 2020a). The parents of children living in poverty are more likely to experience a range of adverse circumstances, such as mental health difficulties, relationship and financial problems and substance abuse (Treanor, 2012).

Eradicating child poverty in Scotland

Through devolution, Scotland has developed its own distinctive solutions to address the issue of child poverty. The Scottish Government has sought to eradicate child poverty through the *Tackling Child Poverty Fund* and through legislation, such as the *Child Poverty Strategy* (Scottish Government, 2014) and the *Child Poverty Act* (Scottish Government, 2017b), supported by an Action Plan (Scottish Government, 2016a) – *Fairer Scotland* – and subsequent Delivery Plan – *Every Child, Every Chance* (Scottish Government, 2018b). Articulating with UNICEF's goals for sustainability (UNICEF Office of Research - Innocenti, 2017), the aim is to have fewer than 10% of children living in *relative* poverty and fewer than 5% in *absolute* poverty by 2030 (Mowat, 2020a). Concerns are expressed, however, that efforts to eradicate child poverty will be counteracted by pressures on local authority budgets and UK welfare reform (Boyd, 2019; Freeman, 2017; McKendrick et al., 2016; Mowat, 2019a, 2020a). The third annual progress report (Scottish Government, 2021i) since the publication of *Every Child, Every Chance* acknowledges the challenges facing the Scottish Government in eradicating child poverty when in the midst of a pandemic but draws attention to achievements such as the launch of the *Scottish Child Payment* for eligible children under six years.

The poverty-related attainment gap

The poverty-related attainment gap is a global issue (Gomendio, 2017; OECD, 2016, 2017b, 2018; Parsons, 2016; Schleicher, 2014), residing within a culture of performativity (Ball, 2003; Solomon & Lewin, 2016), and deriving from social and economic drivers external to the school environment. It is sustained by neo-liberal economic forces and élitist structures (Parsons, 2016) which promote a culture of competitive individualism (B. S. Cooper & Mulvey, 2015; Mowat, 2020a; Slee, 2018a) and can be largely intractable, as observed in the USA (Dudley-Marling & Dudley-Marling, 2015).

The nature of the poverty-related attainment gap in Scotland

As previously intimated, the poverty-related attainment gap develops even prior to formal schooling (Bradshaw, 2011; Mowat, 2018a; L. Robertson & McHardy,

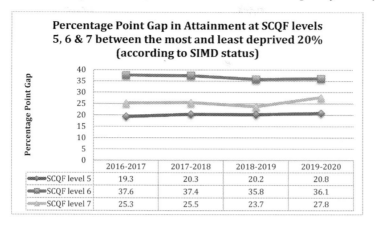

Chart 3.1 Illustration of trends in attainment between the most and least deprived quintiles of the Scottish Index of Multiple Deprivation.

Source: Scottish Government (2021h), derived from Table A1.1b.

2021; Sosu & Ellis, 2014). For example, in the early years, there is a 16% point gap between children living in the most disadvantaged quintile of the *Scottish Index of Multiple Deprivation* (SIMD),[5] in comparison to those in the least, regarding developmental concerns at 27–30 months (L. Robertson & McHardy, 2021). As children progress through their schooling, the gap widens, as represented in measures of progress in literacy and mathematics in the national curriculum – *Curriculum for Excellence* (Scottish Government, 2020b) – and in final destination statistics. Chart 3.1 illustrates the percentage point gap over a four-year period between students living in the most and least deprived quintiles of the SIMD at SCQF levels 5, 6 (Scottish Highers, which represent the entry point to Higher Education) and 7 (Advanced Highers). At level 6, this represents 82.7% of young people in the least deprived quintile achieving at least one Scottish Higher, in comparison to 46.6% in the most deprived quintile (Scottish Government, 2021h).

However, the SIMD is an imperfect proxy for poverty. Not all children living in Areas *of Multiple Deprivation* will be living in poverty (e.g., the children of professionals living in the community) and, as identified by McKendrick (2018), not all children living in poverty live in *Areas of Multiple Deprivation* (Mowat, 2020a). The latter may present a challenge to schools serving prosperous communities where there may be hidden pockets of poverty. Such schools may be less well geared up to support children and families in this circumstance and are unlikely to attract government funding to the same degree.

Intersectionality

Around one third of children living in poverty also have either additional support needs and/or are *Care Experienced*[6] children and young people (Mowat, 2020a;

62 *Exploring and Understanding the Problem*

Scottish Government, 2016b), compounding disadvantage. There are significant differentials in attainment for children recorded as having *Additional Support Needs* and *Care Experienced* in comparison to their peers. For example, only 16.1% and 30% of children recorded with *SEBD* and mental health problems respectively gained one of more passes at level 6 (Scottish Highers) (Scottish Government, 2021d). These statistics highlight the need for a nuanced and targeted approach in addressing the gap, recognising the multi-faceted aspects of children's lives. As argued by Dudley-Marling and Dudley-Marling (2015), 'No one is ever *just* poor. People living in poverty are also raced, classed and gendered, speak a particular language, and are members of particular ethnic and cultural groups' (p. 40).

Scottish attainment challenge

As discussed in Chapter 1, The *Scottish Attainment Challenge* (SAC) was launched in 2015, delivered through a range of policy initiatives and funding streams, including a *Pupil Equity Fund*.[7] The most recent evaluation of the programme at the time of writing (Scottish Government, 2021a), reviewing year 5, concludes that progress continues to be made regarding positive changes in practice and towards an inclusive education system. However, despite the positive perceptions of progress cited by headteachers through qualitative data and improvements in some measures, the gap in attainment seems largely intractable. The report acknowledges that it is difficult to ascertain the reasons behind any observed improvement and to ascertain causality.

Tensions within the system

An inherent tension lies in the fact that measures designed to improve the performance of children living in poverty (e.g., the introduction of new literacy strategies) may improve outcomes for all children with the potential for the gap to widen even further. A further tension lies in the imperative for governments to be able to demonstrate that public funds have been spent wisely, leading to a high accountability régime in which data is king and anything that moves is counted. This is illustrated in a word cloud drawn from the Executive Summary of the aforementioned progress report where the terms, measure, data, progress, report, improved and evidence are writ large (see Figure 3.5).

It could be argued that the emphasis on accountability is a distraction from where efforts need to be invested and could lead to a tendency towards the adoption of quick-fix initiatives which are easily measurable (e.g., focussing efforts on the children sitting on grade boundaries) rather than investing in long-term sustainable cultural change and more organic, bottom-up forms of school improvement which are not located in high accountability régimes. The locus of change as lying solely with schools is highly problematic, as schools, by their efforts alone, cannot close the gap. It is only when public policy coalesces, when social

Figure 3.5 Word Art illustration of the executive summary to the 4th interim report of the Scottish attainment fund.
Source: Scottish Government (2021a).[8]

justice lies at the heart of all public policy and leadership practices, and there is a will and resources to address the problem across public bodies that the potential to close the gap lies (Mowat, 2018a, 2018b, 2019a, 2020a).

Flipping the thinking

Treanor (2020a) asks us to 'flip the thinking:' to consider the value that children in poverty bring to a school, arguing that they should be valued and respected for who they are. For her, there needs to be a focus on both *distributive* (equal distribution of resources) and *relational* (relating to others as moral equals [Winter, 2018]) *equality*, developing strong school-family-child relationships as, by this means, children living in poverty can gain a sense of belonging to the school community. In seeking to meet the needs of all children who could potentially be marginalised, schools can truly become equitable, inclusive, and compassionate in their practice, creating empowering environments.

Reflection Point

What are the key messages to emerge for you regarding how schools can support and respond to families and children living in poverty in ways that are not stigmatising? What are the challenges for schools in responding at both a policy and professional level and how might they be overcome?

> **Additional Suggested Reading**
>
> *Confronting Marginalisation in Education: A Framework for Promoting Inclusion*
>
> *Routledge, 2012. Kyriakou Messiou*
>
> This is a really excellent book which provides not only great insight into how marginalisation manifests itself in education but also a framework through which teachers can come to a deeper understanding of how it presents within their own school, as seen through the eyes of children, through collaborative practitioner enquiry.
>
> *Our Kids, the American Dream in Crisis (Reprint Edition ed.)*
>
> *Simon and Schuster, 2015. Robert D. Putnam*
>
> This is a very engaging book which provides a social commentary on the loss of social cohesion and social and cultural capital over a 50-year period in a community in Ohio, USA, speaking to a growing chasm between rich and poor, impacting on the life chances of young people within the community and prospects for social mobility.
>
> *Child Poverty: Aspiring to Survive*
>
> *Policy Press, 2020. Morag, C. Treanor*
>
> This book focusses more broadly on poverty but devotes a chapter to poverty and education. It unearths many of the prejudices in society about poverty and identifies the structural roots of poverty. It would be of great value to school leaders and teachers who wish to develop a deeper understanding of the impact of childhood poverty.

Notes

1. BBC 2 documentary, 'Billy Connolly: Made in Scotland' (episode 2), broadcast on the 17th of August 2019.
2. BBC 2 documentary, 'Blitz: The Bombs That Changed Britain' (series 1, episode 3), broadcast on the 18th of August 2018. Series Producer Tim Kirby. Reproduced by kind permission of Wall-to-Wall Media, Warner Bros TV Production UK.
3. A social and emotional learning programme developed by Toni Noble and Helen McGrath to develop resilience skills in young people.
4. See the *Cost of the School Day Toolkit* https://cpag.org.uk/scotland/CoSD/toolkit
5. The SIMD draws on seven domains – income, employment, education, health, access to services, crime and housing – to determine areas of multiple deprivation. https://www.gov.scot/collections/scottish-index-of-multiple-deprivation-2020/
6. *Care Experienced* children (previously referred to as *Looked After and Accommodated*) are those who are under the auspices of the local authority, whether in residential care or not.
7. For information about the funding streams which support the Scottish Attainment Challenge, see the Scottish Government webpage https://www.gov.scot/policies/schools/pupil-attainment/
8. Excluding common words and words mentioned only once.

4 Schools as Places of Belonging or Exclusion
School Disaffection

Goals for Understanding

I. What barriers might schools present in terms of children's wellbeing and achievement and why is this the case?
II. How might school disaffection be understood differently?

This chapter focusses in greater depth on the school context and the importance of fostering socio-emotional wellbeing in children and young people. The basic premise is that the vast majority of teachers enter the teaching profession to make a positive difference in children's lives and the vast majority of school leaders are highly committed to their school communities. It has been established that schools can represent a place of safety and security that is otherwise absent in the lives of some children. However, as discussed in Chapters 2 and 3, for some children schools can represent places of exclusion and marginalisation, characterised by deficit discourses, leading to student disaffection and a blame culture, with communities, families, children and young people held culpable. It is important to recognise the complexity of schools as organisations and the difficulties they experience in responding flexibly to children's needs, particularly large secondary schools. This chapter therefore reframes the issue, exploring how schools can sometimes inadvertently disengage from children and young people. The chapter builds on the discussion of marginalisation and poverty in the previous chapter to explore the factors that can make schools either places of belonging or exclusion, commencing with an examination of the impact of the pandemic in this regard.

The socio-emotional and psychological impact of the pandemic on children and young people

Whilst much attention has been devoted within global reports, the literature, public policy and the media to losses in learning brought about by the pandemic and to learning recovery, increasingly attention is turning towards the

DOI: 10.4324/9780429467110-7

66 *Exploring and Understanding the Problem*

socio-emotional and psychological toll on children and young people (Lee, 2020; Mowat, in press-a; OECD, 2020; Wang, Zhang, Zhao, Zhang, & Jiang, 2020). The first global *State of the World Report* to focus on the mental health and wellbeing of children (UNICEF, 2021b) observes that the concerns that have arisen from the pandemic about the mental health of a generation of children 'represent only the tip of a mental health iceberg – an iceberg we have ignored for far too long' (p. 3). The report highlights the fragility of support systems for children and how the hardships experienced fall disproportionally on the most disadvantaged (p. 16).

The Chief Inspector for Schools in England noted that loneliness, boredom and misery became endemic during lockdown whilst the physical and mental health of children went into decline, felt most acutely by the youngest children whose development had been hampered, with some regressing in basic language and social skills (OFSTED, 2021). Parents, in a survey conducted by Save the Children, echoed these concerns as young children were missing out on activities essential for socialisation with limited opportunities for play and access to outdoor spaces (Mowat, in press-a; Save the Children, 2021). Public Health Scotland (2022) draws attention to similar concerns, advocating additional support to improve learning environments before the age of 2 and measures to encourage take-up of early learning and childcare opportunities.

However, adolescents are also at a key stage in development as relationships with peers take on a greater significance as they grow in independence and there is a heightened sensitivity to social relationships at this time. The disruption to networks of support and lack of physical contact brought about by lockdowns and school closures impacts their psychological wellbeing (Editor, 2020; Mowat, in press-a; Orben, Tomova, & Blakemore, 2020).

The Oxford Co-Space Longitudinal survey in the UK (Shum, Skripkauskaite, Pearcey, Waite, & Creswell, 2021) established a correlation between periods of restriction and behavioural, emotional and attentional difficulties in children, with those identified with *Special Educational Needs and Disabilities* (SEND) and those from low-income families continuing to show elevated health symptoms even when restrictions were eased (Mowat, in press-a). In England, the lack of face-to-face contact with children at risk of abuse and neglect led to a reduction in referrals to social services (a finding mirrored globally [UNICEF, 2020b]) and the anxiety brought about by disrupted relationships with staff and peers led to increasing incidences of self-harm in some children within the care system (OFSTED, 2021). Public Health Scotland (2022) draws attention to concerns about increased exposure to sexual exploitation and abuse with the potential to trigger lifelong mental health problems.

What the above highlights is the key role that schools play as places of learning but also places of belonging, a theme explored in this and subsequent chapters (see Chapter 13).

Schools as places of belonging or exclusion

Schools as agents of exclusion

Given that inclusion is amongst the avowed aims of education systems and schools across the world and is enshrined within the *Salamanca Agreement*, to which 92 countries are signatories, it seems contradictory, and perhaps even defamatory, to make the claim that schools can be agents of exclusion. However, systemic factors (e.g., the tendency for the clustering of pupils of low socio-economic status in 'lower performing' schools, with a concordantly greater risk of drop-out); inflexible, standardised curricula; exclusionary teaching approaches and inappropriate pedagogy; and/or unrealistic expectations of pupil behaviour which take little or no account of the individual circumstance of the child, cumulatively leading to a population of 'hidden drop-outs,' all conspire to create exclusionary contexts (Razer, Friedman, & Warshofsky, 2013).

It has been argued in previous chapters that the global neo-liberal drive has led to a focus on performativity at the expense of inclusive practice. This has led to the marginalisation of specific groups of children (Hedegaard-Soerensen & Grumloese, 2020) as teachers focus on the learning needs of the majority (Hedegaard-Soerensen & Grumloese, 2020): 'Concerns about diversity and inclusion fade into the background and marginalised children are overlooked and thus excluded' (pp. 641–2).

In Denmark, Larsen, Holloway, and Hamre (2019) observe a shift from a rights-based agenda to one of system optimisation and accountability and, at the level of the state, from welfare to competition, leading to a discrepancy between inclusion as a political project and in practice. This, in their view, has led to anomalies such as an expectation that grades will rise in a school despite an increasing number of children with additional needs and to restricted and normative understandings of what it is to be a 'successful student.'

Schools reflecting hierarchies of belonging and exclusion

Slee (2019) argues that, despite terms such as community, diversity and inclusion populating public policy documentation and a range of other media, schools, rather than being bastions of democracy and equality, 'reflect hierarchies of belonging and exclusion' (p. 910), rendering schools as places for *some* rather than *all* children, reflected in practices such as banding, streaming and special schools. In a study of the experiences of disabled children in Australian schools (Poed, Cologon, & Jackson, 2020), it was found that a significant minority (37%) of families were directed towards segregated provision with 70% of families having experienced some form of restrictive practice for their children (e.g., regularly being excluded from broader school activities such as choir, assemblies and excursions).

68 *Exploring and Understanding the Problem*

Exclusion as 'a stubborn foe'

According to Slee (2018b), exclusion, as a global phenomenon, is endemic and largely intractable in education: 'Inequality, and its fellow traveller, exclusion, are woven so tightly into the fabric of education, it often goes unacknowledged' (p. 11) – it is 'a stubborn foe' (p. 1). Fuelled by a resurgence of the far right, informed by neo-liberal ideology in which structural inequalities lead to academic underachievement, the language of inclusion has been misappropriated: 'the daily activity of exclusion is described as inclusion' (p. 28). Thus, he describes sets of circumstances in which children attend school only partially; in which they spend the bulk of their time in specially designated rooms (sometimes called 'inclusion rooms') apart from the regular classroom and in which access to other children at leisure times is restricted or mediated by adults; and, ultimately, children being withdrawn from mainstream provision to attend a special school.

Hedegaard-Soerensen and Grumloese (2020) reveal how even well-meaning teachers overlook the needs of some children in the classroom, seeing the inclusive agenda as something apart from everyday teaching to be directed towards specific groups of pupils who are the responsibility of specialised professionals and schools. They describe a child in the mainstream class, seated behind a screen with a Teaching Assistant, whom the classroom teacher makes no attempt to draw into the classroom activities or discussion. The authors draw attention to a 'collective indifference' to poverty, marginalisation and disadvantage, influenced by societal and cultural structures external to the school.

The above is captured in a vignette by Riley and Rustique-Forrester (2002) as a parent spoke despairingly about the experience of her son who had been put in an isolation room (code named 'ice' by the children) throughout the day because of difficulties in managing his behaviour:

> I went up to school and he was in a tiny room on his own. I said to them, 'You can't put him in here, it's like a prison. You have got to punish him but not like that.' They never had anything good to say about him no matter how small. Parents' evenings were terrible. Them and us!
>
> (Riley, 2017, p. 36, derived from Riley &
> Rustique-Forrester, 2002, p. 45)

In a study of disaffected young people in England, Riley (2017) observes:

> The young people were on the periphery of school life, their learning experience often fragmented, inconsistent and interrupted. Unable to conform in institutions which were alien to them, their behaviour could become inappropriate, challenging or even threatening. Relationships with their teachers were deeply important, yet frequently negative, and encounters with the school as a physical environment shaped their perceptions of how their school viewed them.
>
> (p. 35, cited in Mowat, 2019a, p. 214)

Schools as Places of Belonging or Exclusion   69

For these young people, school was characterised by a 'them and us' culture with a lack of trust between young people, school staff and families lying at the root of the problem: 'two alien tribes inhabited the divided world of the school, each speaking their own language' (p. 36, cited in Mowat, 2020, p. 359).

The concept of unconditional positive regard

Khon (2005), in a similar vein to the concerns raised by Hedegaard-Soerensen and Grumloese (2020), observes that, in a system where test scores in a restricted number of areas are valued more than more meaningful, holistic learning, *what we value* impacts on *whom we value*. Children who do not 'perform' or who, equally, do not 'conform' are seen as a liability. However, this does not just impact negatively on these children as it gives the message that *all children* are only accepted into the school community conditionally.

Drawing from Carl Rogers' concept of *unconditional positive regard* (Bozarth, 2007), Khon argues that, rather than valuing children for *what they do*, they should be valued for *who they are*. Treating all children with *unconditional positive regard* does not imply that teachers should condone under-achievement or behaviour that is not acceptable to the school community but, rather, the focus should be on the behaviour itself whilst letting the child know that he/she is a valued member of the school community.

Unconditional positive regard is a tenet of *person-centred psychotherapy* based on acceptance and respect, characterised by warmth and sympathy (Bozarth, 2007). Key aspects of the therapeutic or counselling process are *unconditional positive regard*, *empathy* and *congruence* (between the inner life of the person and their lived experience) (M. Cooper, O'Hara, Schmid, & Wyatt, 2007). Winter (2018) draws from these concepts, arguing that, as relationships are central to education, learning exists within systems of relationships (p. 347), providing scope for schools to become more egalitarian institutions as they focus on *relational equality* (see Chapter 3). However, within the constraints of a busy school and classroom environment with many competing demands, this is not easy to achieve, especially given that teachers respond more positively to children who conform to the culture and values of the school and less positively to those who do not (Hedegaard-Soerensen & Grumloese, 2020).

It calls into question approaches towards promoting positive behaviour premised on conditionality which use praise as a tool to promote 'desired' behaviours in contrast to genuine, heartfelt praise (I. Smith, 1998) delivered by a teacher with whom the child already enjoys a good relationship (Garwood & Van Loan, 2019). Likewise, token reward schemes, such as Jenny Mosley's 'Golden Time'[1] by which children who adhere to the 'Golden Rules' gain access to an activity denied to other children who do not. For children frequently excluded from what many would regard as normal school activities (e.g., painting, going to a disco, school trips) it is almost inevitable that, over time, this will impact on their sense of belongingness and connectedness to school and, ultimately, their disaffection from it and disengagement from learning.

70 *Exploring and Understanding the Problem*

However, as will be discussed further in Chapter 8, embracing *unconditional positive regard* across a whole school community is a significant paradigmatic shift for schools and their staff who have been at the receiving end of policy directives that advocate the use of praise and rewards in the name of promoting positive behaviour. For example, the UK Government's guidance to schools in England (DfE, 2022a) (at the time of writing, under consultation) states, 'Rewards and positive reinforcements should be applied clearly and fairly to reinforce the routines, expectations, and norms of the school's behaviour culture' (p. 12). *Unconditional positive regard* also challenges broader social norms whereby 'gold stars' and other incentives are often adopted within the family home, drawing on behaviourist approaches (see Chapter 6) and promoted by television programmes such as 'Super Nanny,' featuring Jo Frost.

Schools as places of belonging

A sense of belonging to school is associated with a range of positive indicators such as positive mental health and wellbeing and behavioural outcomes, social relatedness, academic achievement and successful school transitions (Korpershoek, Canrinus, Fokkens-Bruinsma, & de Boer, 2020; Mays et al., 2018; Prince & Hadwin, 2013; Riley, 2017; World Health Organisation, 2016). It is also associated with more positive perceptions of the value of schooling for long-term wellbeing, enhancing children's achievement motivation (Berryman & Eley, 2019), and with a mastery goal orientation (Korpershoek et al., 2020). Children with an enhanced sense of belonging have a more positive self-concept, a greater sense of self-efficacy and enjoyment of school and relatedness towards it and invest themselves in learning to a greater extent than children who do not (Korpershoek et al., 2020; Prince & Hadwin, 2013). It could be argued, however, that this is a cyclical relationship with these positive outcomes creating in the first instance or feeding back into enhancing a sense of belonging to school. Conversely, those who do not have a sense of belonging to school are more likely to have higher absence and drop-out rates (Korpershoek et al., 2020) along with other negative indicators such as mental health problems and substance abuse (Prince & Hadwin, 2013). The correlation between a sense of belonging and educational attitudes/aspirations is lower for children from lower socioeconomic backgrounds (Korpershoek et al., 2020).

Berryman and Eley (2019) draw on the definition of belonging forwarded by Watson (2005) as pertaining to 'the way in which students feel accepted, respected, included and supported by the educational communities and settings in which they are involved' (p. 989). Connectedness with the school community, characterised by warm relationships with peers and teachers and participation in school activities, is an essential element of a sense of belonging (p. 989).

For Slee (2019), belonging is key to inclusion, at the heart of which lies owning (taking responsibility for) and valuing *all* children. Indeed, Berryman and Eley (2019) attest that the two concepts are used almost interchangeably within the literature. They differentiate between belonging as being concerned with the internal state of the individual and inclusion as related more to formal policies, decisions and actions. Kovač and Vaala (2021) caution that the conflation of the two concepts can lead to confusion and impede the successful implementation of inclusion in practice.

For children identified with SEND, a sense of belonging may be integral to their motivational development and subsequent engagement and progress in learning, fostering positive self-perceptions and social inclusion (Prince & Hadwin, 2013). In exploring a series of vignettes of the experiences of a mother and her disabled son in a mainstream setting, Connor and Berman (2019) conclude, 'When individual children are accepted and appreciated for what they can do by those who surround them, they become part of a community and, in turn, can influence that community's thinking for the better' (p. 934).

In a plea for culturally responsive schools, Berryman and Eley (2019) caution that a relentless focus on excellence and equity (excellence for all) without an emphasis on belonging 'closes down discourses that open other ways of thinking and being' (p. 987), failing to give due consideration to aspects such as language, identity and culture. Without attention to *belonging, being* and *becoming,* children who are not part of the dominant culture become marginalised:

> ... if we also continue to champion visionary statements about all students 'reaching their potential', then impose a mono-cultural curriculum and evaluation regime in the name of equity and excellence, we will continue to see some students succeed but risk ongoing alienation of other groups within our student populations.
>
> (p. 998)

The authors argue for a focus on students' sense of belonging and wellbeing whilst reaching out to families and including them in the learning conversation, themes explored further in Chapters 11 and 12.

Student disaffection

It could be argued that a lack of connectedness or sense of belonging to the school community (perhaps created or exacerbated by some of the practices already under discussion) has led children to disengage from the school and what it stands for, making it more likely that they will exhibit the behaviours which will lead them to being excluded from school, either temporarily or permanently.

It could also be argued that the fundamental problem isn't so much that of children (and families) disengaging from schooling and what it represents, but that schooling itself has disengaged from the reality of children's lives, with a resultant mismatch between the needs of some children and what schooling has to offer, including aspects relating to pedagogy and the curriculum and inflexible approaches towards school discipline (see Chapter 8).

The lack of parity in esteem between Higher Education and vocational training (despite the introduction of University Technical Colleges in England)

72 *Exploring and Understanding the Problem*

(Atkins & Flint, 2015) has led to a skewing of the curriculum towards the academic, disenfranchising those who are not so academically inclined and providing fewer opportunities post-schooling for those so affected.

Addressing the above concerns isn't just a matter of 'tweeking' the curriculum and/or focussing on trying to make lessons more engaging but calls for a fundamental rethink of the relationship between schools and society; the purposes that schools serve (and for whom); and the relationship between schooling and education more broadly.

Reflection Point

To what degree would you consider schools to be places of belonging where children are valued for who they are? What barriers might need to be overcome to create such an inclusive environment?

Prejudice and bullying (see the discussion of oppression in Chapter 3)

> Only a ginger, can call another ginger 'Ginger,' yeah.
> When you are a ginger, life is pretty hard.
> The years of ritual bullying in the school yard.
> Lyrics to 'Prejudice' by Tim Minchin[2]
> (cited in Mowat, 2015b, p. 458)

A focus on prejudice

Children, even in infancy, have a grasp of issues around fairness, which, as they mature, develops into more complex understandings of morality, incorporating aspects such as rights and discrimination. When the implicit biases (related to social groups) which form during childhood are not challenged, this can lead to prejudice with some expressions of exclusionary behaviour representative of a manifestation of group identity. Children do not abandon social reasoning when making judgements about whether to include or exclude someone: they take account of both moral and group factors simultaneously (Killen & Rutland, 2013).

The authors attest that social exclusion is a fundamental aspect of social development which all children experience. The degree to which the exclusion is construed as fair or unfair will determine the consequences for the excluded child, which can be severe. Children often fall back on group norms, biases and stereotypes (ballet is for girls) when considering exclusion and inclusion for groups of children. As children become older, they become more aware of the role of social conventions in maintaining structure and order in society with previous, personally held, pro-social and inclusive attitudes subordinated into group norms. In all contexts examined (e.g., Muslim children in the Netherlands), children were able to make judgements relating to inclusion and exclusion, viewing some forms

Schools as Places of Belonging or Exclusion   73

of exclusion as unfair, yet, when group identity was threatened, they were able to justify these forms of exclusion (Killen & Rutland, 2013).

Bullying behaviours

It has been established that bullying (whether as perpetrator or victim) places children at greater risk of poorer subjective health and life satisfaction with those who have been bullied having less of a sense of belonging to school (Mowat, 2020a; OECD, 2017a; UNICEF Office of Research – Innocenti, 2016; World Health Organisation, 2016). Globally, a correlation has been established between bullying and age and gender and, in some countries, socio-economic status, with children living in more affluent countries less likely to be the victims of bullying (Mowat, 2020a; World Health Organisation, 2016).

Bullying, commonly defined as 'intentional, harmful behaviors carried out repeatedly by an individual or group against someone with less physical or psychological strength' (Chester, Spencer, Whiting, & Brooks, 2017, p. 2) takes a variety of forms – physical, verbal, relational and cyber. A critical element is an imbalance of power in the context of a relationship – it is 'a reciprocal and dynamic process of dominant relational behaviour' (Moore & Woodcock, 2017, p. 66), sustained through the interaction between the bully and the victim.

Children from an early age recognise bullying behaviours and are able to apply social-conventional and moral reasoning in their interpretation and thinking about incidences of bullying, aggression/conflict and play (Ey, Walker, & Spears, 2019). In England, boys are more likely to experience physical bullying and, girls, relational bullying (through the systematic destruction of peer relationships and social status). However, the negative impacts on health-related quality of life are significant for both boys and girls (Chester et al., 2017).

According to the Organisation for Economic Cooperation and Development (OECD), cyberbullying impacts more on girls than boys with around 15% of girls reporting being the victim of it in comparison to 8% of boys. Cyberbullying can be more corrosive than other more traditional forms of bullying, having highly detrimental consequences for the mental health and wellbeing of those targeted and, in extreme cases, leading to suicide (OECD, 2019).

Reflection Point

Do you consider bullying to be an issue within your school or organisation? What form does it take? Is there an anti-bullying policy in place and is cognisance taken of it? Are children and parents involved in discussions about the approach that the school should adopt?

74 *Exploring and Understanding the Problem*

The conundrum of school exclusions

The group of children who are most at risk of losing a sense of connectedness to school are those who have been excluded, either temporarily or permanently, some being taught in units attached to schools or discrete units. In England, Wales and Northern Ireland these take the form of Pupil Referral Units (PRUs) or Alternative Provision Academies; in Scotland, Secure Care Centres (formerly List D Special Schools, provided principally by the 3rd sector) or units (with various nomenclature) attached to schools.

The impact of exclusions on children and families

The impact of school exclusion on children and families is significant, affecting the child's mental health and wellbeing and social relationships, and interrupting learning, whilst creating stigma and shame and, in some cases, affecting the parent's employment (Parker, Paget, Ford, & Gwernan-Jones, 2016). School exclusions may serve to shift the burden of responsibility for the child from the school to the home. They are perceived as ineffective by parents and are considered to reinforce school avoidance (Parker et al., 2016). Associated with authoritarian discipline régimes, concerns are also expressed by pupils about the efficacy and the overuse (and sometimes inappropriate use) of school exclusions (McCluskey, 2006).

Exclusions and the criminal justice system

Both in Scotland and in Australia a strong correlation has been established between school exclusions and the criminal justice system, increasing significantly the likelihood of being imprisoned in late adolescence and early adulthood (McAra & McVie, 2010; Mowat, 2019a; K. Reimer & Pangrazio, 2020) and posing greater vulnerability to mental health difficulties and substance abuse (Dyer & Gregory, 2014). As such, it is advocated that a critical time for intervention is early-to-mid adolescence (McAra & McVie, 2010). An important mitigation and a consistent finding in the literature is the importance of a 'significant other' in the life of children and young people who is there for them and holds onto them in difficult times (Gough, 2016; Mowat, 2010a; K. Reimer & Pangrazio, 2020).

Exclusion and demographics

There are disproportionate rates of exclusion associated with certain demographics and these are highly persistent – boys; children with SEND; age (exclusions peak at ages 13–15); certain ethnic backgrounds (e.g., Black Caribbean); and those from low socio-economic backgrounds (McCluskey, Riddell, Weedon, & Fordyce, 2016). Unsurprisingly, these children are at much greater risk of disengaging from learning and dropping out from school (Stamou, Edwards, Daniels, & Ferguson, 2014).

Disproportionate rates of exclusion in the UK

However, there is a conundrum. If it is to be assumed that, fundamentally, children are the same across the UK, why should it be the case that there are vast differences in the rates of exclusion across the different nations which constitute the UK? 97.4% of permanent exclusions in 2016/17 were accounted for by pupils from England amidst increasing concerns about rising rates of permanent exclusion in both England and Wales. 7,720 permanent exclusions took place in England in comparison to only five in Scotland in this time period. With regard to temporary (or non-permanent) exclusions, Northern Ireland has the lowest % rate per population (2.14%) in comparison to England (4.67%) with a distinct downward trend in Scotland, in comparison to a rising trend in England and Wales (McCluskey, Cole, Daniels, Thompson, & Tawell, 2019).

In accounting for this discrepancy, the authors examine relevant education policy in England, Wales and Scotland and clear differences emerge. Scotland's policy – *Included, Engaged and Involved Part 2: A positive approach to preventing and managing school exclusions* (Scottish Government, 2017d) – places the emphasis on inclusion, the socio-emotional wellbeing of children and promoting positive relationships within the school community, stressing the importance of a positive school ethos and highlighting the long-term deleterious effects of exclusion on children's life chances. In contrast, the policy in England – *Behaviour and Discipline in Schools: Advice for headteachers* (DfE, 2016) – is more punitive in nature. Whilst the English document makes no reference to alternatives to exclusion (e.g., the use of restorative approaches), the Scottish and Welsh policies do so and they also stress the importance of early- and staged-intervention (McCluskey, Cole et al., 2019) (see Chapter 10). As explored in Chapter 8, the revised guidance on behaviour in schools (DfE, 2022a) (at the time of writing, under consultation), whilst emphasising to a greater extent the needs of specific groups, has a similar tone to the previous guidance.

Cole, McCluskey, Daniels, Thompson, and Tawell (2019), in examining the factors associated with the high exclusion rate in England, note the lack of an interdisciplinary approach towards reducing exclusions in schools with considerations of mental health, SEND and policies on promoting positive behaviour seen as separate entities rather than complementary aspects of inclusive practice. The authors cite a range of contributory factors for the rise in exclusions, such as a movement away from child-centred approaches to more rigid curricula and associated accountabilities and inspection régimes; financial constraints and concomitant reductions in Local Authority support for schools; and constant re-structuring of schools. This, coupled with practices such as 'off-rolling' children (putting pressure on families to remove their children from the school roll or face permanent exclusion) has led to the current crisis. The revised *Suspension and Permanent Exclusion* guidance (DfE, 2022d) (also under consultation at the time of writing), attempts to address the issue by highlighting that such informal exclusions are illegal.

76 *Exploring and Understanding the Problem*

However, both in Scotland (McCluskey, Cole et al., 2019) and Wales (McCluskey et al., 2016), not all is quite as it seems. There is evidence of the use of unlawful or 'hidden' exclusions which disguise the nature of the problem, such as a child being sent home without it being formally recorded; 'managed moves' through which a child is transferred to another school; abuse of part-time timetables; and increasing use of 'inclusion' or 'time-out' rooms to isolate the child. McCluskey et al. (2016) call for a renewed 'commitment to efforts to tackle inequality rather than focus on difference' (p. 537) (see Chapter 8).

Exclusionary mindsets

The medicalisation of normality

According to Slee (2019), the increasing emphasis on diagnosis (represented in the *Diagnostic and Statistical Manual of Mental Disorders* [APA]) has led to a reframing of what were once considered to be educational challenges or issues of classroom management – disengagement, disruption and underachievement – now being seen as 'problems of the mind,' requiring specialist intervention. He argues that much of the practice in schools is informed by *ableist* thinking and by the discourse of special needs (see Chapter 2), with considerations relating to children so affected – seen as 'a race apart' – being secondary to those without disabilities and with the existence of special schools and specialist provision serving to reinforce hierarchies.

Concerns around stigmatisation and labelling

A concern of many commentators is that the diagnosis which leads to a child being labelled and the provision of intervention to address need, particularly if it necessitates the removal of the child from the classroom or provision in specialist settings (either external to or within the school), carries with it the risks of stereotyping and stigmatisation (Riddick, 2012; Slee, 2013; Squires, 2012). This leads many to favour universal, rather than specific, interventions to support children and young people.

Labels fulfil a range of functions (e.g., creating a gateway to resources) (Bilton & Cooper, 2012; Hjörne & Säljö, 2013) and the degree to which they are regarded in a positive or negative light is contested (Mowat, 2015a). Some commentators have argued that it is the underlying negative attitudes within society that lead to stigmatisation rather than the label itself (Corrigan, 2006; Goffman, 1963; Mowat, 2015a; Riddick, 2012). It has been argued that the label ascribed to the child becomes all-consuming, impacting both on the child's sense of identity and perceptions of the child held by others: the label acts as a shortcut to shared understandings (negating the need to examine the specific circumstances of the child). Over time, the child internalises the label and is defined by it, limiting their aspirations (Hjörne & Säljö, 2013; Mowat, 2015a; Skovlund, 2014).

Labels as situated within a sociocultural and historical context

Labels are not objective realities devoid of context. They exist within a sociocultural and historical context and reflect societal norms and expectations. A range of commentators (Armstrong & Hallet, 2012; Hjörne & Säljö, 2013; Orsati & Causton-Theoharis, 2013) observe that expressions such as 'problem children,' 'serious misconduct' and 'aggressive behaviour' are used routinely within the classroom in an unexamined way, whilst behavioural norms, related to sociocultural constructs which reflect understandings of 'normal' or 'abnormal' repertoires of behaviour for children and young people, are taken for granted. The 'problem', arising from psycho-pathologising discourses, is seen as residing largely in inadequacies within the child (Macleod, 2006) or in parenting (Araújo, 2005; Macleod, Pirrie, McCluskey, & Cullen, 2013), leading to a discriminatory and stigmatising agenda, exclusionary practices and a 'them and us' culture (Araújo, 2005; Graham, 2008; Macleod, 2006a; Macleod et al., 2013; Mowat, 2015a; Slee, 2019).

Langager (2014) charts how, in Denmark, over as little as a seven-year period, psychological understanding of children's behaviour (e.g., related to abuse and neglect) shifted to psychiatric understandings. From being seen as 'young people who should "just pull themselves together and behave properly,"' (p. 284), they now have a clinical diagnosis of *Attention Deficit Hyperactivity Disorder* (ADHD). Likewise, Wienen, Sluiter, Thoutenhoofd, de Jonge, and Batstra (2019) in the Netherlands confirm the perspective that schools are 'a rich breeding ground for ADHD classification' (p. 659), with teachers themselves triggering the diagnosis (see further discussion of ADHD in Chapter 5).

The constraints upon schools as public institutions and the associated accountabilities lead to a focus on the structural, rather than relational, aspects of schooling, leading to an emphasis upon performativity, control and compliance (see Chapters 1, 7 and 8). Mowat (2015a), drawing from a range of commentators (Ainscow, Dyson, Goldrick, & West, 2012; Riddell & McCluskey, 2012; Slee, 2018b), argues that, if schools are to become truly inclusive learning environments, then there is a need for radical restructuring and an examination of social relationships within them. However, it is important to recognise that provision which may be construed by some as discriminatory and exclusionary may not be experienced in this way by the child concerned, the focus of the discussion to follow.

Exclusion as inclusion

In Chapter 3, a model of marginalisation was presented, building upon the work of Messiou (2012b) and other theorists, positing that whether a child experiences marginalisation is dependent upon a host of interrelated variables as they interact with each other in the life of the child, filtered through social norms, values and expectations and the subjective experience of the child, as interpreted by them (Mowat, 2015b). In a series of vignettes presented by Connor and

78 *Exploring and Understanding the Problem*

Berman (2019), the extraction from the mainstream classroom of the child for support for short periods of time was handled by the adults in a sensitive and responsive manner and was not experienced in an exclusionary way by the child.

A small case study of children on the autistic spectrum, some of whom were educated in alternative provision and had experienced multiple placements (C. Goodall, 2018), established that, for them, inclusion is a feeling, not a place, related to social justice, a sense of belonging and being valued and accepted. Mainstream provision had been experienced as exclusionary, with the children experiencing a sense of isolation, difficulties with inflexible pedagogy and a lack of teacher understanding:

> I was excluded and not included in a lot of ways such as making friends, socialising, in lessons etc. I was nearly always on my own and others would laugh at me if I didn't understand the work or got it wrong'.
>
> (p. 14)

In Scotland, Macleod (2013) found that, contrary to expectation, young people educated in specialist provision for children with *Social, Emotional and Behavioural Difficulties* (SEBD) (a List D school) had not experienced it as exclusionary. For her, the key determining factor is how they are treated: 'it is not the act of being labelled that in itself appears to be most significant, but the way in which it is applied, how it is used, by whom and the quality of the relationship between the labeller and the labelled' (pp. 72–3) (cited in Mowat, 2015a, p. 160).

Similarly, children, identified as having SEBN participating within a group work intervention in two local authorities in Scotland to support their socio-emotional development (Mowat, 2015a, 2019b, 2019c) responded differentially to being identified as being in need of support and to the intervention itself. Many demonstrated significant insight and sophistication in being able to balance the negatives with the positives and perceptions changed over time, allaying initial anxieties:

> Yes - definitely - glad I didn't just go to class and just skip it … because it really benefited me, and others because of the relationships - friends, family, classmates. Benefited all of the people around me. … It was helpful to have people to go to on the staff that I could talk to. … am really glad I was picked now even though I was singled out … I'm still focussed on my learning and doing well.
>
> Jennifer (pseudonym) (cited in Mowat, 2015a, p. 166)

Brief conclusion

This chapter has argued that much of what masquerades as inclusion/inclusive practice is, in itself, exclusionary. There is concern that what children may experience within what is construed as an inclusive environment (often equated with mainstreaming) may not facilitate their participation and learning and may lead to stigmatisation and marginalisation. In contrast, examples have been provided of what some might construe as exclusionary practices but which have not been experienced in this way. This accords with the argument forwarded in Chapter 2 about the fluid and dynamic nature of the relationship between inclusion and exclusion and the discussion of the subjective nature of marginalisation in Chapter 3.

Recognising that inclusive practice is not solely about policies, systems and structures but is fundamentally about the principles and values that guide how we lead our lives and the lives that we wish for our children, the imperative is to come to an understanding of the variables that interact in the lives of communities, families and children which create either a sense of belonging, exclusion (or otherness) in order to guide policy and practice with the goal of creating equitable, inclusive and compassionate schools. The themes of a sense of belonging to school and marginalisation are explored further in Chapter 11.

Reflection Point

Do you recognise some of the tensions and difficulties that have been identified within this chapter regarding the social exclusion of children? How does this manifest itself within your own context? Talk to children and young people, in a sensitive manner, about their own experiences of being included and excluded.

Additional Suggested Reading

Children and Social Exclusion: Morality, Prejudice and Group Identity

John Wiley & Sons Ltd. (2013). Melanie Killen and Adam Rutland

This book helps us to understand from a developmental perspective the basis of prejudice and how this leads to discrimination and social exclusion.

Working with Disaffected Students: Why Students Lose Interest in School and What We Can Do About It

Chapman Publications. (2002). Kathryn Riley and Elle Rustique-Forrester

This books offers insights into children's and young people's experiences of school and raises many important issues for educators regarding meeting the needs of children and young people for whom schooling lacks relevance.

Place, Belonging and School Leadership: Researching to Make the Difference

(Continued)

80 *Exploring and Understanding the Problem*

Bloomsbury Academic. (2017). Kathryn Riley

This book builds on Riley's earlier work but brings an international perspective to our understanding of schools as place of belongings or social exclusion. Offering guidance to both students and teachers who wish to investigate this topic within their own school setting, the book has many valuable insights for all.

See also recommendations in Chapters 2 and 3.

Notes

1. See https://www.circle-time.co.uk/were-starting-a-golden-time-revolution/
2. Reproduced by kind permission of Tim Minchin from the album 'Ready for This' recorded in the Queen Elizabeth Hall, London in 2008.

5 Understanding Social, Emotional and Behavioural Needs (SEBN)/Mental Health Needs (SEMHN)

> **Goals for Understanding**
> I. How might *Social, Emotional and Behavioural Needs (SEBN)/Mental Health Needs (SEMHN)* be understood?
> II. How might they present?
> III. What are some of the key challenges and tensions regarding SEBN/SEMHN?

The concept of *Emotional and Behavioural Difficulties* (EBD) is highly complex and has been described as challenging and controversial (Lopes, 2014). On the basis that the approaches adopted by schools to create discipline policies, manage behaviour and support children are shaped by understandings of the concept, the key aim of this chapter is to explore these understandings.

The concept cannot be separated or examined in isolation from considerations of school disaffection and exclusion, student motivation and school ethos and climate and the role of school leadership in this process. These are related, in turn, to children's more holistic experience of schooling and learning, including the curriculum and pedagogy. Nor can it be separated from the circumstances of children's lives in general and the influences on their development; how childhood is understood and theories of childhood development; how their sense of identity is formed; power dynamics; and recognition of the compulsory nature of schooling. These themes, building on discussions in earlier chapters, will be explored within this and subsequent chapters.

Thirty years ago, Furlong (1991) claimed that the entrenched positions of psychologists and sociologists with regard to this field of enquiry failed to grasp the complexity and inter-relatedness of the psyche and the social, leading to over-simplistic explanations for children's behaviour. Over the intervening time period, more sophisticated understandings have emerged, however, there is still a significant divide between how psychologists and sociologists frame children's behaviour and this has implications for policy and practice. Despite much scholarly work to try to achieve conceptual clarity, the concept of EBD has remained

DOI: 10.4324/9780429467110-8

82 *Exploring and Understanding the Problem*

elusive and is reflected in the wide range of nomenclature internationally and even across the UK. My preferred terms are as expressed in the title of this chapter but the default term, EBD, more widely used internationally, will be used predominantly within the chapter.

Understanding emotional and behavioural difficulties

Definitions and terminology

The term 'behaviour' (whilst often having negative connotations with regard to schooling) is a neutral concept: it is influenced by motivations, values, beliefs and attitudes, including biases and prejudices (Mowat, 2007). Behaviour is an expression of an emotional state, whether positive or negative. Being able to regulate one's emotions enables individuals to function effectively in society and to have good psychological wellbeing. Children who demonstrate good emotional regulation tend to have better social relationships and the converse is also true (Place & Elliott, 2014).

Globally, the concept is recognised in only a small but influential number of countries (largely Western) with the range of terminology adopted making international comparisons difficult (Lopes, 2014). It is a category applied uniquely to children (Thomas, 2014) and represents a shift from a medical to a psychological and/or sociological perspective (Bilton & Cooper, 2012; Cole, 2015). The *Organisation for Economic Cooperation and Development* (OECD) characterises EBD as 'students with behavioural or emotional disorders or specific difficulties in learning whose problems arise primarily from the interaction between the student and the learning context' (Lopes, 2014, p. 13). However, even across OECD countries there are very wide variations in what it is considered to constitute (Lopes, 2014).

According to Bilton and Cooper (2012), the term *Social, Emotional and Behavioural Difficulties* (SEBD) covers any manifestation (whether social, emotional or behavioural) which interferes with the educational engagement and capacity of the individual to engage with others and/or causes distress or harm to the individual. For them, the loose conceptualisation of the construct is advantageous in affording individual, socio-ecological or interactional explanations.

The nomenclature around the concept is not just a matter of semantics but represents different emphases and ways of thinking (mental models). For example, the 'D' in EBD within the American context represents 'disorders' (implying a medical model) whereas, within a European context, it represents 'difficulties.' Scotland and Wales have moved towards a paradigm of 'needs,' which is represented within SEBN, although the term SEBD is still used in Scottish Government publications. In some nomenclature, the social aspect is missing (as in the common use of EBD), yet, it must be highly evident that emotional and behavioural difficulties impact to a significant extent on the social sphere (Place & Elliott, 2014) and, conversely, social and environmental influences impact on emotional and behavioural states (Bilton & Cooper, 2012).

Understanding SEBN/SEMHN 83

The ordering of terms also implies a certain emphasis, as in BESD (*Behavioural, Emotional and Social Difficulties*) that was commonly used in England until the adoption of the *2014 Special Educational Needs and Disability (SEND) Code of Practice* (DfE & DoH, 2014). At this point, a new term, *Social, Emotional and Mental Health Difficulties* (SEMHD) was deployed in recognition that many children at risk of exclusion have risk factors and lack the protective resilience to promote good mental health (Cole, 2015; DfE, 2018b). The term was not intended to replace BESD and in subsequent documents the language of needs is employed (SEMHN), leading to a rather confusing picture.

Understanding the distinctions between the various terms (and related terms such as 'challenging behaviour' and 'disaffected behaviour') is highly complex with significant overlap with mental health disorders (Cole, 2015). EBD may co-present with other SEND (Landrum, Wiley, Tankersley, & Kauffman, 2014) or may arise as a secondary consequence of the difficulties which children experience in this respect (e.g., children on the autistic spectrum [Place & Elliott, 2014]).

Yet, there is a danger of seeing all children who fall under the umbrella of EBD (and its various manifestations) as being one homogenous group. Some argue that it is not wise to try to pin down the term definitively because of the complex and diverse range of ways in which children present (Munn, Lloyd, & Cullen, 2000) and there is resistance amongst educationalists towards the deficit language of disorders and disease (Cole, 2015).

A child presenting with *externalising* behaviours ('acting out behaviours,' such as aggression) may appear to be very different from a child with *internalising* behaviours ('inward acting behaviours,' which may present as school refusal, self-harming, etc.). However, such categorisations may, in themselves, represent an over-simplification as aggression and anger may mask other underlying emotions such as anxiety and fear, which are more normally associated with *internalising* behaviours.

Children exhibiting *externalising* behaviours, which impact directly upon the smooth operation of the classroom, are more likely to come to the attention of teachers and to be directed towards specialist services than children exhibiting *internalising* behaviours who may be overlooked in a busy classroom (Hayden, 2013; Place & Elliott, 2014). The distinction drawn between children who are diagnosed as having a disorder and other children who are not may be very tenuous (and context and/or culturally specific). Not all children who exhibit behaviours that would be regarded by some as problematic will receive a diagnosis.

The over-representation of specific groups

The over-representation of specific disadvantaged groups which can be seen regarding children diagnosed with SEND (Dorling & Tomlinson, 2016; Dyson & Kozleski, 2008; Slee, 2018b) is also evident regarding EBD (McCluskey, Cole, Daniels, Thompson, & Tawell, 2019). There is strong gender-patterning with boys much more likely to be categorised with *externalising disorders* than girls (Hayden, 2013; Place & Elliott, 2014), reflected globally in exclusion

84 *Exploring and Understanding the Problem*

statistics. This is particularly the case for boys from lower socio-economic backgrounds (Riddell & McCluskey, 2012) as illuminated in Scottish Government statistics where 80% of temporary exclusions are accounted for by boys (Scottish Government, 2018c).

In Scotland, high-incidence, non-normative categories in government statistics (such as SEBD) where professional judgement plays a significant role in the categorisation are more likely to demonstrate disproportionality and are strongly socially stigmatised (Riddell & Carmichael, 2019; Riddell & McCluskey, 2012). Children categorised as having SEBD, a rising trend, are the least likely to be in receipt of a *Co-ordinated Support Plan* (only 1.29%) which sets out their legal entitlement to support (Riddell & Carmichael, 2019). This, despite them representing the largest classified group of all children categorised as having *Additional Support Needs* (ASN) (Mowat, 2019a).

As discussed more broadly regarding SEND, there are also the well-documented dangers of the potential for stigmatisation and labelling and of ever-cascading numbers of children being categorised as having EBD globally. Slee (2013) highlights four key concerns as set out in Table 5.1.

Whilst there are some commentators who call for greater classification of disabilities including EBD (Mundschenk & Simpson, 2014) (exemplified in the *Individuals with Disabilities Education Act [IDEA]* and the *Diagnostic and Statistical Manual of Mental Disorders [DSM]* in the USA), Slee (2018b) attests that such classifications are pervasive and powerful reductive representations, marking individuals out in 'bolder, difficult-to-erase lines' – 'a caricature of their humanity' (p. 40). If we were to extend Bernstein's argument that classification in curricular areas serves to reinforce hierarchical power structures (Pluim, Nazir, & Wallace, 2021), then it could be argued that such classifications act in a similar way, framing perspectives on children in reductionist ways.

Mundschenk and Simpson (2014) maintain that an effective definition should be 'underpinned by reliable, rational and focussed observations and decisions about children and their behaviour' (p. 45). Yet, there is little recognition that

Table 5.1 Four key concerns associated with the categorisation of children and young people with EBD

Net-widening	The tendency for ever-increasing numbers of children to be diagnosed as having a range of disorders and directed towards alternative provision.
Accelerated disablement	In the quest for additional resources, the difficulties which children experience are 'enhanced.'
System segmentation	As children are directed towards the 'therapeutic margins,' resources are directed away from the centre and the opportunity for system reform, which could potentially benefit all children, lost.
School-to-prison pipeline	The tendency for those diagnosed with behavioural disorders to transition to the penal system.

Source: Derived from Slee (2013, p. 24).

Understanding SEBN/SEMHN 85

any such judgements cannot be separated from the world views, biases and prejudices that are brought to bear on the decision-making process and which form our understanding of the boundaries between what is considered 'normal' and 'abnormal' behaviour within a given context.

Implicit within any classification of EBD is a sense of cultural norms of behaviour that the student is perceived as deviating from, thus the student's emotional response, expressed through behaviours, cannot be separated from the sociocultural context in which it takes place. Rather than examining the root cause of the behaviours which may lie with the education system itself and its compulsory nature, Lopes (2014) attests that the prime response to perceived deviance from these cultural norms is towards managing the behaviour of the student. What is understood as *disordered behaviours*, perpetrated by *disordered people*, may be a logical response for those students for whom the school presents as an alien environment, as argued also by Graham (2008) (see Chapter 4).

Whose needs are being met?

Thomas (2014) claims that much of the discourse around the concept of EBD is 'psychobabble' drawn from a 'mélange of disparate metaphor and theory' (p. 21) based on tentative psychological theory, with the more recent emphasis on needs serving to accentuate rather than attenuate deficit and disadvantage (Mowat, 2019c). In the process 'the *school's* needs for order, calm, routine and predictability' transmute silently into the '*child's* needs for stability, nurture, security, one-to-one help or whatever' (p. 26). The author claims that this shifts the balance away from considerations of the environment of the school towards an understanding of behavioural difficulties as emotional disturbance, attributed to the disposition and individual circumstances of the child and seen through a child-centred, clinical lens, losing the opportunity for whole school reform and the creation of a more humane, congenial and inclusive school ethos.

EBD: 'an extreme, chronic condition'

On the basis that 'EBD is an extreme, chronic condition that does not respond to typical interventions,' Landrum et al. (2014) attest that 'special education can and should be an appropriate response in most cases' (p. 69). The use of the words 'should' and 'most' implies that they consider the special school to be the default position and the optimum environment. For them, it is the nature of the instruction that is of the essence. They claim that the intensity of response required is not determined by place, but there is an assumption that the 'typical interventions' offered are appropriate and sufficient in the first instance. There is little consideration given to the potential and actual detrimental effects of being educated in segregated provision or exploration of alternatives. However, the issue that they raise about the gap between the early signs of EBD developing in children and young people (which can manifest in pre-school

86 *Exploring and Understanding the Problem*

children), the formal recognition of a problem and the time before they are able to access appropriate services is a concern raised by many, during which time the difficulties experienced may augment and become intractable.

Round pegs in square holes

Despite the call for inclusive pedagogy for all learners, rather than specific pedagogies for specific groups (Florian, 2015; Florian, Black-Hawkins, & Rouse, 2017), there may be some legitimacy in the arguments forwarded by Landrum et al. (2014). The ways in which EBD present may make it more difficult for children to form trusting relationships with teachers within the normal classroom environment (Mowat, 2010a) and therefore approaches which afford opportunities for relationship building (such as counselling or group work) may be of value.

As previously argued, schools, particularly secondary schools, are, by their very nature, highly complex organisations which are not always able to respond flexibly to the needs of individual children even if well-intentioned. P. Cooper (2008) observes that the 'factory model of schooling' prevailing at the time (driven by externally imposed curricula and characterised by rigid authoritarian values) at best favours those children whose cognitive styles lend themselves to this form of instruction; at worst 'rewards conformity and passivity at the expense of intellectual curiosity, critical debate and creativity' (online). Whilst it has long been argued that inclusive schools should transform their practice (Slee, 2018b), rather than the school modifying to the needs of the child, the child is expected to fit into the norms of the school (Wheeler, 2010).

Cole, Daniels, and Visser (2013) make the case that, for a minority of children 'with' EBD, continued placement in mainstream schooling is not in their best interests if the key relationships between the child and school have broken down and the child does not feel valued and wanted. This, however, brings to the fore the need for schools to be places of belonging for *all* children and for *all* children to be valued unconditionally, as discussed in Chapter 4.

Reflection Point

How are children 'with' EBD described within your professional context and what are the underlying assumptions?

What are your views on the perspectives forwarded to this point and how do they accord with your professional experience?

The presentation of and explanations for EBD

It is not the intention in this part of the chapter to provide an in-depth clinical description of specific 'conditions' or criteria for diagnosis but it is important to provide some indication as to the broader categories and concerns whilst acknowledging the dangers of pathologising discourses.

Understanding SEBN/SEMHN 87

The nature and function of emotions

Oatley and Jenkins (1996) classify emotions and psychopathology in children under two categories – *externalising disorders* and *internalising disorders,* with the latter constituting both *anxiety* and *depressive disorders.* For the authors, emotions function principally to enable people to relate to their world: emotions that are deviant (that is, they are different from those of the majority of children) arise from atypical situations. The authors hypothesise that childhood psychopathology potentially arises through previous traumatic experiences which become part of the mental *schema* of the child and are triggered by future events which bear a resemblance to the initial event. Alternatively, children have deviant responses to emotional events (such as laughing at a sad occasion) or they lack emotional regulation, responding to events with heightened and sustained emotions.

Emotions, in themselves, are neutral: it is the purpose to which they are directed which will determine whether they are experienced negatively or positively (Faupel, 2013). Emotions operate at the moment, manifest physiologically (e.g., increased heart rate) and underlie motivation. Emotional responses are not just evoked in response to physical needs but also psychological needs, such as the need for social connection and belonging.

Emotions serve as a survival mechanism but, for some children who are in a perpetual state of fear, these heightened emotions over time can have long-lasting deleterious effects on their physical and mental health and on their capacity to learn. Particularly for abused and/or traumatised children, the anger that is generated may turn inwards. Self-harm and suicide or suicidal ideation are manifestations of displaced anger (Faupel, 2013).

Children who experience trauma over time, or who experience insecure attachment (see Chapter 6), and who therefore are in a high state of constant arousal, reacting more strongly to the normal stressors of life, may experience physiological changes in the body leading to raised levels of the stress hormone, cortisol. However, for those children exposed to severe and chronic stress, cortisol levels may be lower than expected due to cortisol receptors having shut down – a process known as 'down regulation' – a coping mechanism and possible defence mechanism (Gerhardt, 2004).

Externalising disorders

Externalising disorders, more prevalent in boys, manifest themselves through *Oppositional Defiance Disorder (ODD)* (most common in early childhood); *Conduct Disorder (CD)* (associated more with older children); and *Attention Deficit Hyperactivity Disorder (ADHD)*. Around 50–80% of children who have been diagnosed with *ADHD* have also been diagnosed with either *ODD* or *CD* (McGrath, 2014).[1] For those children for whom *externalising disorders* are stable over time, the ramifications include conflicts with parents and teachers, academic underachievement, peer rejection, depression and substance abuse (Heubeck & Lauth, 2014).

88 *Exploring and Understanding the Problem*

Externalising disorders manifest themselves in a wide range of ways detrimental to the forming and maintaining of children's positive social relationships, such as a lack of sensitivity to social cues (e.g., a child apologising to them) and a heightened threat response which leads them to misattribute hostile intentions to others, leading to an aggressive response. They can also present as highly manipulative, coercive behaviour, reflected in anti-social values and goals (McGrath, 2014).

However, Lopes (2014, citing Richters & Cicchetti, 2008), contests the assumption that the behaviours associated with *CD* are automatically indicative of a mental disorder, particularly when little account is taken of context. Such labelling is not innocuous because of the potential long-term deleterious effects: it is a self-perpetuating, enduring label with long-term negative consequences; it focusses attention on the individual rather than the environment; and, accordingly, it constrains the nature of the questions which potentially could have been posed relating to the environmental influences which shape the behaviour of the child.

Attention deficit hyperactivity disorder

ADHD is one of the most controversial and contested diagnoses, reflected in an extensive literature devoted to the topic over the past few decades. It is informed by biological, psychological and sociological paradigms and conceptualised differently within different disciplines, leading to a lack of definitive and unified explanations for its provenance and intervention strategies (Visser & Zenib, 2009). It is a clinical diagnosis of the *American Psychiatric Association (APA),* described in the *Diagnostic and Statistical Manual of Mental Disorders* to which reference has already been made. At the heart of the controversy lie questions as to the degree to which it can be considered to be a biomedical/neurological condition with a genetic basis or a social construct.

Initially diagnosed in the USA in the 1950s, it has become the most prevalent mental health disorder in children across the world (M. Smith, 2019) with an average prevalence rate of around 7% (Graham & Tancredi, 2019). It arose at a time when, not only did the behaviours associated with it – hyperactivity, impulsivity and inattentiveness – became more common, but when they were perceived as being more problematic than had formerly been the case (M. Smith, 2019).

ADHD is characterised by problems of attention, self-regulation and executive functioning which are in evidence prior to the age of seven in two different settings (Pavlidis & Giannouli, 2014). However, it may not become more noticeable until children enter primary school or even adolescence (Brown, 2015). According to the *Center for Disease Control and Prevention* in the USA, boys are three times more likely to be diagnosed with *ADHD* than girls.[2] Teachers are more likely to identify children who present with all aspects of the syndrome but are less likely to identify children who present only with the sub-type 'predominantly inattentive,' which is associated more with girls than boys (Moldavsky, Groenewald, Owen, & Sayal, 2013).

Variability in prevalence rates

Variability in the prevalence rates of *ADHD* globally has added to the controversy around the diagnosis (Bilton & Cooper, 2012). In Denmark, Madsen, Ersbøll, Olsen, Parner, and Obel (2015) establish that differential rates of diagnoses correlate with access to diagnostic resources, in contrast to the USA where contextual factors, such as socio-economic status (SES), spending on health care for children and/or differences in diagnostic practices, are all explanatory variables.

Within Scotland, there is a greater prevalence of *ADHD* in areas of deprivation (McCluskey & Lloyd, 2019). Machlin, McLaughlin, and Sheridan (2019) propose that changes in brain structure, arising from environmental factors such as lack of cognitive stimulation in the home, mediate the relationship between *ADHD* and socio-economic status.

Controversy around medication

Much of the controversy surrounding the construct arises from the use of medication, often as the first line of defence (McCluskey & Lloyd, 2019; Visser & Zenib, 2009; Wheeler, 2010). Concerns are raised about side-effects (such as loss of appetite, sleep disturbance); long-term impact (such as suppression of height and of weight gain); a lack of evidence for long-term efficacy and safety of medication; the addictive nature and potential abuse of the drugs administered; and questions around who really benefits, with questions posed about whether it is a form of social control (McCluskey & Lloyd, 2019; Wheeler, 2010). Moldavsky et al. (2013) found that teachers strongly endorsed non-pharmacological intervention for children with *ADHD* and expressed the view that medication should be seen as a 'last resort.'

ADHD: a complex, normative syndrome

ADHD is also a complex syndrome – it presents in different ways in different children (Brown, 2015) and, as previously discussed, co-presents with other *externalising disorders* and learning difficulties (Brown, 2015; P. Cooper, 2008; Pavlidis & Giannouli, 2014). All of us may experience characteristics of *ADHD* from time to time but it is its pervasiveness, chronic nature and the degree to which symptoms are experienced which marks it out (Brown, 2015). As such, it is a normative construct.

The impact of ADHD in childhood and adulthood

Children diagnosed with *ADHD* often experience a high degree of peer rejection, leading to conflict and confrontation, being seen by their peers as aggressive and immature. They experience many of the same difficulties (and therefore consequences) as children with *ODD* and *CD* in their social relationships

90 *Exploring and Understanding the Problem*

and communicate less effectively with other children (McGrath, 2014). For some children and young people, *ADHD* can extend into adulthood, impacting on employment and socio-economic status amongst other things (Bilton & Cooper, 2012), although hyperactivity tends to lessen with age (Brown, 2015).

Neurological explanations

ADHD has been associated with abnormalities in brain structure and functioning. It has also been associated with irregularities in the dopaminergic system which plays an important role in executive function, leading to difficulties in a wide range of areas such as inhibitory control that can have a significant impact on the capacity of the child to learn and regulate their behaviour (Pavlidis & Giannouli, 2014). It is well established that trauma, particularly in infancy and early childhood, can have a major impact on brain physiology (Gerhardt, 2004, 2013), extending into adulthood (Felitti, Anda, & Nordenberg, 1998), and reference has already been made to the mediating influence of modifications to brain structures on the relationship between *ADHD* and socio-economic status (Machlin et al., 2019).

Heritability of ADHD

ADHD is claimed to be highly heritable but no single gene is considered to be responsible – it is a complex mixture of genes interacting with each other (Brown, 2015; Graham & Tancredi, 2019). A quarter of children with *ADHD* also have a parent who has been diagnosed with the disorder and 30% have a sibling. However, it is recognised that heritability[3] is not indicative of the degree to which the environment plays a role (Brown, 2015).

Critiques of the biomedical perspective

M. Smith (2019) is amongst many authors who posit that the depiction of ADHD as a neurological disorder which is genetic in nature fails to take sufficient account of alternative environmental explanations and provides an over-simplistic account of the origins of the disorder. He characterises these explanations as being related, firstly, to changing expectations of how children should behave (e.g., the movement away from child-centred approaches in the USA) and, secondly, societal and environmental influences (e.g., fewer safe outdoor spaces for recreation and play).

Likewise, McCluskey and Lloyd (2019) draw attention to a wide range of social and environmental factors which can potentially underlie *ADHD*, raising concerns that the label diminishes children's individuality and humanity, lowers expectations and leads to determinist views on the part of the children themselves and those who seek to support them. They argue that, notwithstanding the diagnosis and label, there are creative means that teachers can use to support the learning of children so diagnosed which value them as learners.

Graham (2008) questions the degree to which children diagnosed with *ADHD* really do have a disorder, what defines the disorder and who decides, and whose interests are served by the diagnosis. She argues that parents are seen as being complicit in the diagnosis as it relieves them of any responsibility or blame for their child's behaviour. Largely missing in the explanations proffered for the disorder are the psychopathologising discourses implicit within schooling itself. The positioning of the child as 'deviant' and the encouragement of teachers to 'siphon off' such students to the margins, as argued by Slee (2013), results in *ADHD* acting as an 'escape clause' for schools.

Both Graham (2008) and Visser and Zenib (2009) observe the predominance of the biomedical paradigm, with the aetiology and intervention of *ADHD* often understood through a reductive lens which purports to represent objectified truth, driven by the media and medical expertise. The normalised medical discourse becomes the standard against which children are judged whilst other contradictory or competing discourses are marginalised. Despite the biomedical paradigm suggesting neurological dysfunction as being the key underlying cause for *ADHD*, Wheeler (2010) claims that there is no definitive test which can establish conclusively the existence of the disorder in an individual, with the criteria used to diagnose being highly subjective, dependent on the interpretation of words such as 'often,' 'unduly,' 'excessive,' 'markedly' and 'significant' (p. 259).

'THE SCIENCE' and controversies around classification

In contrast to these more nuanced understandings, Brown (2015) paints a picture of *ADHD* as representing incontrovertible fact, illustrated in the title of the article – *'ADHD: From Stereotype to Science.'* Pedagogical guidance is conspicuously lacking in the article. Instead, the author draws attention to the role that teachers can play in the diagnostic process.

This positioning is also borne out in an Australian study of pre-service teachers who make a clear distinction between the medical diagnosis (which they perceive positively) and the process of labelling (seen in a less positive light) which they attribute to the actions of teachers both pre- and post-diagnosis (McMahon, 2012). The predominance of bio-medical understandings within schools and Teacher Education Institutions had led the pre-service teachers to uncritically accept their role in the pathologising of children and towards the belief that pedagogical decision-making for this group of children depended on the medical diagnosis. Graham and Tancredi (2019) attest that the framing of *ADHD* as a medical, rather than an educational problem with implications for pedagogy, means that the modifications to instruction that could potentially be beneficial may never be considered or implemented.

In a similar vein, Wienen, Sluiter, Thoutenhoofd, de Jonge, and Batstra (2019) in the Netherlands draw on the perspectives of 30 primary school teachers regarding the classification process. For those who are critical of classification, amongst the key explanations forwarded are, 'it has no meaning for

92 *Exploring and Understanding the Problem*

teaching' – 'it neither explains nor clarifies anything worth knowing about the child' (p. 656). For some, any potential advantages of classification are outweighed by disadvantages, such as the long-term impact of labelling on the child (p. 656). The majority of respondents are largely positive about classification, seeing it as an explanation for the child's behaviour and citing potential benefits (such as promoting a more empathetic approach towards the child), but they also recognise some of the potential disadvantages. Many see it as a potential new starting point: an opportunity to create dialogue and mutual understanding between parents and teachers about the child's learning, with the classification bringing forth new intervention and support within the school setting.

The situated nature of the construct

Wienen et al. (2019) claim that insufficient account is taken of the situated nature of the classroom environment. For them, no child's behaviour can be understood in isolation from the broader social environment within the classroom in which judgements are based on situation-based comparisons. For P. Cooper (2008) and many other commentators, all judgements about appropriate or inappropriate behaviour are socially and culturally based, reflecting the values, attitudes and beliefs of the social group. This may be particularly of the essence with regard to more or less developed countries where children's life experiences may be very different (McCluskey & Lloyd, 2019).

According to Wienen et al. (2019), schools have become breeding grounds for *ADHD* diagnosis:

> In a broader social context in which educational performance is a major criterion for judging pupils' development, deviant behaviour and deviant performance have been turned into an attractive causal chain for a biomedical conception and explanation.
>
> (p. 657)

They draw from Hyman (2010) and Gambrill (2014) to claim that, through a process of reification, what is in essence a classification that lacks objective qualities – *ADHD* – becomes a direct explanation for the observed behaviour. In line with the arguments forwarded by Graham and Tancredi (2019), they attest that there is a failure to seek pedagogical explanations: to 'read, interpret and understand child behaviour and respond pedagogically to problems that teachers experience whilst teaching' (p. 659).

'Bobbing for alligators': a biopsychosocial perspective

P. Cooper (2008) identifies three major areas of theoretical exploration relating to *ADHD* and its provenance – cognitive research, neurobiological research and genetic research – all of which will have advanced considerably in the decade since the publication of his article. He draws on an analogy of 'alligators

Understanding SEBN/SEMHN 93

bobbing for poodles' to make the point that we all need to step outwith our frame of reference to look at issues and problems in new ways. He forwards a *biopsychosocial* perspective on *ADHD* that integrates across these three fields of enquiry. He makes the case that the polarised arguments which set biological explanations against social explanations for the learning and behavioural problems associated with *ADHD* are not helpful and, indeed, in his view, redundant. For him, *ADHD is* socially constructed with the school a major site for this construction but that does not negate biological and neurological explanations: some children are more pre-disposed towards the behaviours associated with *ADHD* through their biological and social circumstances. These children are disadvantaged in that they cannot meet the culturally based assumptions about what constitutes acceptable behaviour within a given context. His prime argument is that the better this *biopsychosocial* perspective is understood, the better placed schools will be to offer the educational experiences to promote engagement in learning – the school environment is key.

A synthesis

It can be seen that there is a broad, and largely irreconcilable, chasm between those who perceive and advocate for *ADHD* as incontrovertible 'science' and those who advocate for it as a social construct, not based on objective reality but situated in time and place and the associated cultural norms, dependent on subjective, comparative assessments which may not represent the holistic experience of children's lives. Such assessments may not take sufficient cognisance of the variables within the environment that interact with each other to create understandings of what constitutes norms of behaviour within a given context. This divide is representative of the philosophical positions that underpin the physical and social sciences – the nature of the social world and how social reality is understood (ontology) and the nature of knowledge (epistemology). P. Cooper (2008) draws attention to the dangers of adopting entrenched positions with regard to this debate but his advocacy of multi-modal approaches to intervention which combine medical, psychosocial and educational interventions may be anathema to those who argue against the pathologising of children's behaviour and/or who reject the use of medication as a potential solution.

In keeping with the title of Graham and Tancredi's article, 'In search of a middle ground …,' it is important to forward a perspective which moves beyond the groves of academia and offers insights to educators which can help them to steer a clear path through this tumultuous terrain and which recognises the genuine difficulties experienced by families and the challenges faced by schools in supporting children. So, what are the key messages that educators can take away from this and how can it inform their practice?

Firstly, acknowledgement of the complexities around the concept of *ADHD* and how it is understood. As advances in medicine cast light on the aetiology of *ADHD*, and will continue to do so in the future, it is likely that the biomedical paradigm will continue to prevail. It would be wrong for educators to cast aside

94 *Exploring and Understanding the Problem*

insights that can potentially be gained from this body of work to inform our understanding of the ways in which *ADHD* may present in children in order to inform pedagogy and practice, but it would be equally wrong for them to do so uncritically. They need to have the opportunity to engage in the controversies surrounding *ADHD* and to recognise that the way in which it presents is individual to each child – there is no such thing as the '*ADHD* child.' It is not the diagnosis in itself which is of the essence but how the wider school community and the classroom teacher can identify and remove potential barriers to learning to create the optimal learning environment for the child, including considerations of the classroom climate, curriculum and pedagogy, working collaboratively with the family and appropriate external agencies, irrespective of diagnosis.

Secondly, whilst avoiding the apportioning of blame (whether to parents, the child or the school), there needs to be an examination of policy at all levels of the system to explore the ways in which schooling itself may present as a barrier to the learning of children diagnosed with *ADHD*, recognising that what may be ascertained from this may be of benefit to all children. For example, consideration of the age at which children start formal schooling; the developmental stage of children (particularly for those children who are young for their cohort and for boys); the use of play-oriented, more active, pedagogies for younger children and learning which engages with nature and the environment; a responsive, flexible rather than rigid curriculum which takes account of the agency of children and has relevance to their lives; an emphasis on building trust, relationships and community rather than on behaviour management and inflexible discipline systems; and genuine, respectful partnerships with parents and external agencies.

Reflection Point

Where do you stand on the arguments presented regarding *ADHD* and why?

If appropriate, and with sensitivity, try to gain an understanding of how ADHD is viewed within your own professional context from the perspective of professionals, parents and children and young people themselves. What are the barriers they face and how might these barriers be addressed?

Additional Suggested Reading

The Routledge International Companion to Emotional and Behavioural Difficulties

Routledge 2013. Edited by Ted Cole, Harry Daniels and John Visser

This international companion brings together the expertise of a wide range of academics across the world to examine aspects of EBD. It is not a practical guide for teachers but is a very good starting point for someone wishing to immerse themselves in the field.

> **Critical New Perspectives on ADHD**
>
> *Routledge 2006. Edited by Gwynedd Lloyd, Joan Stead and David Cohen*
>
> Whilst this edited book was published some time ago, at the time of its publication it brought together a range of international expertise to bear on the subject of ADHD, forwarding alternative perspectives to the prevailing bio-medical model.

Notes

1. According to the *American Psychiatric Statistical Manual of Mental Disorders* (5th ed.) (The American Psychiatric Association (APA), 2013), *ODD* is characterised by symptoms/behaviours associated with angry/irritable mood; argumentative/defiant behaviours; and vindictiveness, presenting as either mild, moderate or severe. *Conduct disorder* shares many of the same characteristics but is more severe in form, encompassing behaviours such as aggression to people and animals; destruction of property; deceitfulness or theft; and serious violation of rules which, for some children, is also accompanied by impaired emotional functioning/limited pro-social emotions (e.g., lack of remorse), leading to significant impairment in functioning in social and academic spheres for children.
2. https://www.healthline.com/health/adhd/adhd-symptoms-in-girls-and-boys
3. See https://ghr.nlm.nih.gov/primer/inheritance/heritability

6 Looking through the Lens of Developmental Theory to Understand Social, Emotional and Behavioural Needs (SEBN)/ Mental Health Needs (SEMHN)

Goals for Understanding

I. How do developmental theories shape our understanding of children's behaviour?

II. Why does this matter?

As intimated in Chapter 5, how the behaviour of children and young people (C&YP) is understood cannot be separated from the range of contextual factors (whether related to the individual child and family circumstance, schooling, or broader issues of public policy) which impact on the life of the child. These explanations are also rooted in understandings of the nature of childhood and childhood development (see Chapter 2). A range of commentators has sought to classify the theories that underpin explanations of children's behaviour, in the process exploring issues relating to the formation of a child's sense of identity (Head, 2014) and power and agency (Porter, 2006).

Schools are complex, busy environments. It is unlikely that any senior leader or teacher in a school would stop to pause and think about which theory (or more likely, theories) informs their response to indiscipline and/or shapes their school discipline policy. They are even less likely to consider whether some of the theories which underpin policy and practice within the school are incompatible with each other (or are internally inconsistent) and may be giving out mixed, and sometimes, conflicting messages to the school community (see Chapter 7). Yet, these theories (often understood in common sense terms and reinforced through the media – for example, 'Super Nanny' and the 'naughty step') – do, indeed, shape policy and practice in schools and in homes.

Newman and Newman (2016) classify developmental theories as biological (e.g., *attachment theory*); environmental (e.g., learning theories such as *behaviourism* and *social learning theory*); and an interaction between the person and environment (e.g., *cognitive social-historical theory* [Vygotsky] and *bioecological theory* [Bronfennbrenner]). This chapter examines the most apposite theories for schools and the philosophies underpinning them, using the classification system of Newman and Newman.

DOI: 10.4324/9780429467110-9

Biological theory

Attachment theory

Attachment theory is one of the most influential explanatory theories for children's behaviour, stemming from the work of John Bowlby in the 1930s, deriving from an eclectic mix of disciplines (Music, 2017). He observed that the infant's strong urge to be with their mother has evolutionary roots and is common to other species (Robinson, 2014).

Philosophical basis

Early patterns of attachment and the bonds of affection formed between an infant and caregiver create the crucial building blocks for future fulfilling relationships and shape the child's ability to form close relationships at all stages of their life (Music, 2017; Newman & Newman, 2016). By meeting the child's physiological and psychological needs, the child gains the confidence to explore their environment, knowing that there is a *safe haven* for comfort and a *secure base* to which to return (Gillibrand, Lam, & O'Donnell, 2011; Robinson, 2014). Such feelings become *internalised* (incorporated into the *internal working model* of the child), leading to effective emotional self-regulation in adult life (Robinson, 2014).

Nature of the theory

Attachment theory is characterised by different stages as the infant begins to form an *internal working model* (or *mental model*) of the caregiver – a representational and emotional map which incorporates expectations of how the caregiver will respond to their needs (Music, 2017; Newman & Newman, 2016; Robinson, 2014). As the child grows in independence (2–3 years upwards), more abstract representations of attachment emerge, such as trust, affection and approval. At this stage, a *securely attached* child recognises that the mother may not always be present but will return and respond to their needs (Gillibrand et al., 2011).

Given the complexity of modern family relationships and changes in child-rearing patterns, it may not always be the case that the principal caregiver is the mother and nor can it be assumed that *affectional bonds* will form with only one person. The infant will form a hierarchy of relationships with the 'significant others' in their life (Main, Kaplan, & Cassidy, 1985), whether members of the immediate or wider family (Music, 2017), early childcare specialists or carers (Wilson-Ali, Barratt-Pugh, & Knaus, 2019), depending on factors such as the constancy, quality and responsiveness of care (Newman & Newman, 2016).

Bowlby's work on the impact of *maternal deprivation* (whether through neglect, illness, bereavement or other circumstance) in disrupting the attachment process is crucial in highlighting the importance of a 'continuous, warm and intimate relationship' (p. 246) for the healthy development of any child (Gillibrand et al., 2011). Early disruption to this pattern can lead to emotional

98 *Exploring and Understanding the Problem*

insecurity and disturbances in meaningful relationships in later life (Lyons-Ruth, 2007).

Further development of the theory: Ainsworth's 'strange situation'

Ainsworth (Wall, Ainsworth, Blehar, & Waters, 2014) explored the nature of the attachment between the caregiver and child through a laboratory experiment – the *Strange Situation* – a seven-stage procedure used to observe the child's response to the return of the caregiver after a period of absence. It is characterised by episodes of increasing stress – initially, the infant is exposed to a stranger with the caregiver present; latterly, the infant is exposed to a stranger when the caregiver is not present (Newman & Newman, 2016).

Initially, three *attachment types* were identified – *securely attached*, *insecure-avoidant* and *insecure-resistant/ambivalent*. However, at a later point, researchers interested in atypical development (Main & Solomon, 1990) identified a fourth *attachment type – insecure – disorganised*. This type of attachment is more commonly observed in families with parental dysfunction or pathology, such as associated with bereavement, separation or divorce (Gillibrand et al., 2011).

Studies carried out in the home environment by Ainsworth and colleagues established that *attachment types* are associated with different parenting styles, leading to different types of observable behaviours in infants. For example, *securely attached* babies cry less, are more cooperative and greet their mothers more positively on reunion whereas babies characterised as *anxious-avoidant* cry a lot, are difficult to soothe but yet are distressed by separation (Newman & Newman, 2016). In general, *securely attached* infants have parents who are more sensitive to their needs and who are consistently available in contrast to parents of *insecurely attached* infants who are less responsive. *Insecure ambivalently attached* infants, who greet the return of the mother with a mixture of proximity seeking, resistance or anger, tend to have parents with inconsistent parenting styles and, the group of greatest concern to psychologists – *insecurely disorganised*, have been subjected to unpredictable and traumatising parenting (Music, 2017). Hesse and Main (2016) hypothesise that it is the conflicting and simultaneous needs of the child to approach and yet to flee from the parents that create disruption to the child's patterns of behaviour.

Correlation between parental states of mind and child attachment styles

Main et al. (1985), in seeking to compare *attachment styles* in early childhood to adult functioning, introduced the *Adult Attachment Interview*, focussing not so much on the events experienced in people's lives, but how they make sense of and represent them. The authors establish four key patterns of adult response set out in Table 6.1 which correlate to the *attachment styles* or patterns of their children (Main et al., 1985; Music, 2017).

Looking through the Lens of Developmental Theory 99

Table 6.1 The characteristics of adult responses to the adult attachment interview

Classification of caregiver responses	Representation of childhood experiences	Attachment pattern of offspring
Secure autonomous	Coherent narrative taking cognisance of emotional experience and others' life experiences	**Securely attached**
Pre-occupied	Angry, inconsistent and confused responses which lack self-reflection	**Insecure-ambivalent**
Dismissing	Positive, brief descriptions of childhood which give a restricted, non-emotive response	**Insecure-avoidant**
Unresolved-disorganised	Incoherent, poor reasoning and bizarre thinking, with discontinuities and abrupt changes	**Insecure-disorganised**

Source: Derived from Main et al. (1985) and Music (2017).

A key aspect of this body of work is that it serves as an explanation for how *attachment styles* can be perpetuated across generations but it also demonstrates that early childhood experiences need not be determining (Music, 2017).

Main et al. (1985) hypothesise that the capacity of the adult to create coherence in their lives through *reflective self-functioning* may play a determining role in the creation of emotional security in adulthood. Adults with positive memories of their childhood are more likely to be open in their relationships with their offspring (leading to *secure attachment* in their children). In contrast, those who block out memories (dismissive) or are emotionally burdened by them (pre-occupied) are more likely to lead to *insecure attachment*, arising from *internal working models* laid down through early experiences which act to restrict and, in some cases, distort the information available to the child. In observing 6-year-old children in the home environment in unstructured incidents, the ways in which children interacted with their caregiver, both verbally and non-verbally, were consistent with the *attachment styles* identified at one-year-old, indicating stability in attachment style.

Emotional regulation and maternal sensitivity and attunement

A key function of the caregiver is to help the infant to regulate their emotions. Caregivers who are unable to enter into the emotional states of their baby (e.g., unable to soothe them) tend to perpetuate this regulatory problem in their infants, leading to *insecure* patterns of attachment (Gerhardt, 2004). Children who do not experience sensitivity in the caregiver are exposed to higher levels of the stress hormone, cortisol (Gerhardt, 2013; Lyons-Ruth, 2007), but *securely attached* children of an anxious disposition can over-ride this hormonal response (Lyons-Ruth, 2007). These impacts can extend beyond early childhood. Bender, Sømhovd, Pons, Reinholdt-Dunne, and Esbjørn (2015) found

100   *Exploring and Understanding the Problem*

a relationship between early attachment patterns, emotional regulation and anxiety in early adolescents.

A study of four month-old infants established that the degree of co-ordination between caregiver and infant (through, for example, the emotions expressed in facial expressions and tone of voice) was predictive of *attachment style* at age one. However, it was the mutuality of this process that was key – how the mother and infant responded to each other rather than solely how the mother responded to the infant (Beebe et al., 2010; Music, 2017). The *internal working models* that the infants had *internalised* through interactions with the mother were carried into the interactions they had with strangers, indicating that they were taking their expectations of interactive styles into other relationships (Music, 2017).

The degree to which the caregiver is able to respond promptly, appropriately and consistently to the needs and is able to attune to the emotions of the infant is essential in determining the emotional safety of the infant and the nature of attachment bond whilst also creating the optimal conditions for learning and for emotional wellbeing (Gerhardt, 2013; Gillibrand et al., 2011).

The intentionality of the infant

Arising from processes that commence even prior to birth and from the development of a trusting bond between caregiver and infant (Trevarthen, 2011), the infant signals intentions, feelings and experiences about a shared world, initially to closer family members and then, with the assistance of companions and teachers, more widely (Trevarthen, 2011; Trevarthen & Delafield-Butt, 2015). Such a process occurs by means of the reciprocal 'mirroring' of actions and utterances between the caregiver and infant, through, for example, playful games and songs, building a shared expressive repertoire (Trevarthen, 2011; Trevarthen & Delafield-Butt, 2015). When a trusting bond is lacking, perhaps because of depression in the mother, it leads to stress within the baby, impeding the capacity of the brain to generate open and trusting communication (Trevarthen, 2011).

Intersubjectivity

An infant's trajectory for emotional growth is facilitated or inhibited by the context of his/her family and culture which either supports or threatens it. Such processes are dependent on the development of the right hemisphere of the brain which shapes the capacity for self-awareness, empathy, identification with others, *intersubjectivity* and forming a stable and coherent sense of self (Schore & Schore, 2008). *Intersubjectivity* is described by Lyons-Ruth (2007) as 'a capacity to attribute to others a mental state similar to one's own' (p. 598). It is a form of social referencing through which the infant or child learns to regulate and modify their emotional responses and actions through the affective responses of the adult (Music, 2017). It is a process of shared meaning-making – a conscious interaction with the world (Trevarthen & Delafield-Butt, 2015, 2016).

Looking through the Lens of Developmental Theory 101

Freedom from overwhelming anxiety is essential for the infant's capacity to explore and learn about the social world, and for their capacity for *intersubjectivity* (Lyons-Ruth, 2007). The author argues that, rather than *intersubjectivity* being seen as a part of the goal-orientated behaviour of the infant or as part of a hierarchy of needs, it should be seen as being 'a condition of our humanity and as an essential function of mind' (p. 602) which cannot be switched off at will.

Attachment styles/patterns as adaptive: Crittenden's Dynamic Maturational Theory of Attachment and Adaptation (DMM)

Later theorists have contested the stability of *attachment styles or patterns,* arguing that, throughout the lifespan of the child, attachment patterns will vary in response to changing contexts and are almost always adaptive to the prevailing environment at the time (Crittenden, 2008; Music, 2017). As children mature, they develop more complex information processes that enable them to develop more sophisticated strategies in response to danger. They may develop different strategies in their responses to different adults, which become *internalised representations* of themselves in relation to others (Crittenden, 2008).

This may bring into question the notion of a unique, enduring *attachment style* for each child and the emphasis, inherent within Bowlby's theory, on *critical* stages of development, indicating that the child may be more adaptable to circumstance than initially considered to be the case. More recent advances have highlighted the importance of a *sensitive* period in the child's development when affectionate bonds are more readily forged (Gillibrand et al., 2011).

Cultural considerations

Schore and Schore (2008) draw attention to the embedded nature of attachment within a cultural context. There is a danger that a theory that derives from the cultural values, norms and expectations of Western societies may not be applicable across different cultures. Indeed, there are significant variations in how children are classified across nations with some categories not represented at all in some cultures (Gillibrand et al., 2011; Music, 2017). Gillibrand et al. (2011) hypothesise that such differences may arise from how certain attachment behaviours are interpreted and valued in different cultural contexts (e.g., the degree to which a culture values independence and social responsibility in children), associated with differing child-rearing practices and cultural expectations of both children and adults.

Contemporary conceptualisations

In drawing from the work of theorists who embrace a broader conceptualisation of *attachment theory,* such as Schore and Schore (2008), Lyons-Ruth (2007) and Trevarthen and Delafield-Butt (2016), it could be argued that explanations which do not take sufficient account of the *intentionality* and rich inner life of

102 *Exploring and Understanding the Problem*

the infant or child and the *intersubjective* expressions between the caregiver and child are not adequate in providing a full account of the attachment between caregiver and infant. Trevarthen (2006) argues that *attachment theory*, in its classical form, does not pay sufficient attention to the inventiveness and curiosity of the child and the needs of the child for companionship and confirmation from a mentor or companion in play and learning. Lyons-Ruth (2007) claims that current understandings should embrace positive components of the infant-caregiver relationship, such as maintaining the baby's positive relationships with others. Such insights and the observation from Lyons-Ruth (2007) that there is now a convergence of developmental, behavioural, biological and evolutionary theory would indicate that contemporary understandings of *attachment theory* extend beyond biological theory, as classified by Newman and Newman (2016).

Reflections on attachment theory

Attachment theory has been highly advantageous to educators in offering explanations for children's behaviour that are not rooted in deficit understandings of the child and deviance and providing a shared vocabulary with other professionals. However, the explanatory framework takes little or no account of the sociological factors (e.g., poverty, poor-quality housing) that may impact on the capacity of the caregiver to be able to create a loving home environment and to demonstrate the maternal sensitivity and *attunement* which are more likely to lead to *stable* attachment. This can lead to a deficit positioning of parents (mothers, in particular); an automatic assumption that any child presenting with *Social, Emotional and Behavioural Needs (SEBN)/Mental Health Needs* (SEMHN) can be attributed to *insecure attachment* and related parenting practices, perhaps leading to an inappropriate and inadequate response; and a failure to examine or recognise that there might be aspects of the school environment which may be a contributory factor in the child's presentation or to locate the problem in wider public policy. Despite the more recent findings that attachment styles over the lifespan may not be as stable as postulated initially by Bowly, there is still a danger of determinism, not only with regard to the child in the present, but to the future projections of the child as a parent which could impact on how adults interact with the child, leading to a self-fulfilling prophesy.

Environmental theory

Behaviourism

Behaviourism is credited to the work of pioneering psychologists at the end of the 19th and beginning of the 20th centuries. The key underlying philosophy of *behaviourism* is that learning does not occur at a conscious level but is a *conditioned response* to stimuli (Phillips & Soltis, 2004). Any educator who uses praise and rewards to incentivise the behaviours they wish to foster in children and/ or who observes the mantra to notice good behaviour and ignore less desired behaviours is drawing on insights from *behaviourist theory*. There are two key forms of *behaviourism* – *classical* and *operant conditioning*.

Classical conditioning (Pavlov)

Drawing on the renowned experiment with dogs, Pavlov established that, if they were exposed simultaneously, consistently and repeatedly to two *stimuli* (*the neutral stimulus* – the sound of a bell; and the *unconditioned stimulus* – food), the dogs, over time, associated the sound of the bell with food, eliciting a *conditioned response* (salivation), even if the food were not present. The dog has made a *conditioned response* (salivation) to the now *conditioned stimulus* (the bell) (c.c. Figure 6.1).

However, if the pattern is broken (the dog is no longer fed when the bell is rung), the *conditioned response* will no longer be elicited, although recurrence of the pattern will re-establish the relationship, if more weakly. What this implies is that the *conditioned response* is responsive to changes in the environment (Newman & Newman, 2016).

Events not identical but similar to those that have been *reinforced* through *classical conditioning* also elicit a similar response, thus learning can be *generalised* beyond a specific context but it can also lead to biases and stereotypes. Through the same mechanisms, individuals can be taught to discriminate between different stimuli but, if there is a simultaneous tendency towards making a response and inhibiting a response, this can lead to anxiety and stress in the individual. *Conditioned* responses formed in early life can endure into adulthood (Gillibrand et al., 2011; Newman & Newman, 2016). For example, if a child has come to associate a certain stimulus with pain, this can lead to anxiety in later life even when the stimulus presents as no threat (Newman & Newman, 2016).

Operant conditioning: trial-and-error learning

Thorndike, in studying the behaviour of cats, observed a process of trial-and-error – the gradual association between a *stimulus* and *response*. Unlike Pavlov's theory, the *stimulus*, when applied to people, could be both an external or internal

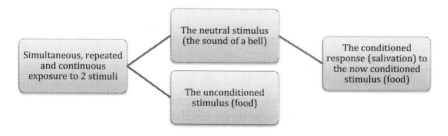

Figure 6.1 Representation of *classical conditioning* as described by Newman and Newman (2016).

104   *Exploring and Understanding the Problem*

(thought or emotion) phenomenon and the *response,* any behaviour that occurs in reaction to the stimulus (Newman & Newman, 2016). Responses to a *stimulus* that elicit positive emotions (*the law of effect*) and which are reinforced through repetition (*the law of exercise*) are more likely to recur, becoming an automated habit, forming sets of learned behaviours. Conversely, a *stimulus* that elicits negative emotions and/or which occurs infrequently is less likely to recur (Newman & Newman, 2016; Phillips & Soltis, 2004). Whereas *classical conditioning* requires a pre-existing *reflex* linking some natural *stimulus* and *response,* Thorndike's theory of learning is not dependent on a pre-existing *reflex* as any *response* to any *stimulant* can be *conditioned* by immediate *reinforcement* (Phillips & Soltis, 2004).

Operant conditioning: the role of reinforcement

Skinner built on the work of Thorndike, focussing on the modification of behaviours arising from the consequences of those behaviours (Newman & Newman, 2016). The premise is that behaviours can be encouraged or inhibited through *reinforcers* which take the form of reward or punishment (Gillibrand et al., 2011). The key mechanisms are illustrated in Table 6.2. It was found that *intermittent,* rather than *continuous, reinforcement* is more likely to sustain the desired behaviours over time and leads to more durable learning (Newman & Newman, 2016).

A challenge of *operant conditioning* is that the desired behaviour needs to be there in the first place to be *reinforced.* Newman and Newman (2016) and Gillibrand et al. (2011) describe a process of *shaping* whereby the desired behaviour is broken down into steps that are *reinforced* at each stage until, eventually,

Table 6.2 The key mechanisms of operant conditioning

Encouragement of desired responses		*Inhibition of undesired responses*	
Positive reinforcers	When a desired behaviour is in evidence it is reinforced (e.g., through praise and rewards) to make it more likely to occur, for example, 'Look how nicely Jenny is sitting up in her seat.'	**Extinction**	Inhibiting the undesired behaviour through not responding to it in the expected way (e.g., ignoring a child having a tantrum) or through distraction.
Negative reinforcers	Designed to increase the rate of desired response when discomfort or displeasure is removed, often conditional in nature, for example, 'You'll be able to join in with the other children if you play nicely.'	**Punishment**	A negative consequence of an undesired behaviour which can take the form of withdrawal of positive reinforcement or privileges or other more overt forms of punishment.

Source: Newman and Newman (2016).

the desired behaviour is in place. However, failed attempts to shape a child's behaviour, such as eventually giving in to a child's demands, can lead to *reinforcement* of the non-desired behaviour.

Thus, *operant conditioning* is a means of establishing desired behaviours where there are *contingencies* (whether *positive* or *negative reinforcers, extinction* or *punishment*) that exert influence on the individual. In contrast to *classical conditioning* where the responses of the individual are considered to be *reflexes* occurring at a subconscious level, the individual is considered to be able to make voluntary choices about whether or not to respond depending on the anticipated consequences of their behaviour (Newman & Newman, 2016).

The influence of this theory can be seen in approaches such as *Assertive Discipline* and *Applied Behaviour Analysis* whereby children's behaviour is framed in terms of 'choices' and 'consequences' (see Chapter 8). Critics of *operant conditioning* question the degree to which experiments (carried out in a laboratory often with animals) are replicable or generalisable to the real-world, complex scenarios in which people interact with each other in multiple environments (Gillibrand et al., 2011).

Critics of *behaviourism*, in general, argue that there are limitations to the theory, that it is based on a limited understanding of science and that it cannot account for all human learning. Social movements, such as 'Me Too,' 'Black Lives Matter' and 'Reclaim the Streets,' cannot be explained adequately (if at all) through *reflex responses* or *operant conditioning*. The implications of *behaviourism* in framing understandings and approaches to school discipline will be examined in Chapter 8.

Social learning theory

Bandura

In contrast to *behaviourism, social learning* theory recognises the social dimension of learning and the important role that cognition, culture and context play within it (Pritchard & Woolard, 2010). Bandura, the key exponent of the theory, proposed that individuals across the lifespan learn to modify their behaviour through paying attention and adhering to *social norms* and observing the behaviour of others who *model* behaviour which acts as a template for future action (Gillibrand et al., 2011; Newman & Newman, 2016).

What distinguishes this theory from *behaviourism* (and *classical conditioning*, in particular) is that these are not automatic, *reflex* responses – there is an element of judgement involved (Newman & Newman, 2016). Whether a child will imitate the behaviour of the *model* is influenced by aspects such as the child's expectations, understanding of *social norms* and beliefs relating to the appropriateness of the behaviour (Gillibrand et al., 2011). The capacity of the child to exercise judgement is indicative of the development of *self-efficacy* – 'a person's belief about how effectively he or she can control herself, her thoughts or behaviours, particularly when intended to fulfil a personal goal' (p. 34). In the process, the child is

106 *Exploring and Understanding the Problem*

exercising *agency* (intentional acts based on people's beliefs about their ability to control events) (Bandura, 1997; Moses, Rylak, Reader, Hertz, & Ogden, 2020).

This theory emphasises the role that significant adults and other influences (including social media) can potentially exert on the developing child's behaviour (whether for good or bad) through the *modelling* of behaviour or through the absence of positive *role models* (a concern that is often raised with regard to the absence of positive male *models* in children's lives [Parkes, Riddell, Wight, & Buston, 2017]). Children themselves act as *role models* for each other, which is particularly apt within the context of concerns about bullying behaviours.

Situated learning

A more contemporary social learning theory emanating from the 1990s arises from the work of Lave and Wenger. It is a complex theory that is beyond the scope of this discussion to examine in depth. Lave and Wenger were concerned with three key aspects – learning, meaning and identity – through what is described as *legitimate participation in communities of practice* (Lave & Wenger, 1991; Wenger, 1998; Wenger, McDermott, & Snyder, 2002). Lave and Wenger (2006) observed that people, often regarded as unskilled or lacking in knowledge, were able to learn complex sets of skills when participating within *communities of practice*. Initially, on the periphery of activity, people acquire not only the skills-set required but gradually take on the identity of a member of that community along with the norms, expectations, practices, beliefs and values associated with it. The *community of practice* creates the conditions for meaning-making, and its social structures – its power relations, and its conditions for legitimacy (e.g., formal qualifications) – define the possibilities for learning (p. 24).

According to Wenger (1998), a *social theory of learning* integrates four elements related to: the *social structure* of the *community of practice* and how it is constituted; the *situated experience* of the individual within the *community of practice*, arising from the social interactions of the group; the *social practices* of the group – its everyday activity; and how *identity* is constituted through the interaction between the individual and the group. *Communities of practice* are an integral aspect of people's lives and take many shapes and forms – families, workplaces, church communities, clubs .... According to this theory, learning is concerned with engaging with, and contributing creatively to, the practices of the community and is not a separate activity apart from our lives (Wenger, 1998).

Thus a child, through an introduction to and participation within the school community, gradually learns what it *is* to be a student within that school; what the norms, expectations, practices, beliefs and values of the school community are (and how these relate to the other *communities of practice* in which the child participates – the family, the Brownies etc.); the hierarchies amongst peers (the 'popular girls') associated with age-groups, gender/sexual orientation, socio-economic status and disability; and the differentials in power between children and adults (and between different adults in and associated with the school) and how this manifests itself. Over time, they take on the identity of what it is to *be* a student within that specific school, in whichever form of identity this takes, given that there can be communities within communities, some of which may be more conforming than others. Thus, this theory extends far beyond Bandura's theory of the *modelling* of behaviour through observation and highlights that the *culture* of the school is crucial in shaping the *social norms* of the school and the values and beliefs of all who participate within that community, including children.

Interaction between person and environment

Cognitive social-historical theory (sociocultural theory)

Theorists of the 20th century who have stressed the social and cultural dimension of learning are Dewey, Bruner and Vygotsky. These theorists are the pillars of *social constructivism*, the key principles of which are that learning is a social process rooted in prior experience and learners construct their own sense of reality through their engagement with the world, interpreting and making sense of their experiences (Pritchard & Woolard, 2010).

Dewey (1915) conceives of the child as an active learner within a social and cultural context engaging in authentic tasks in a process of meaning-making, drawing upon the symbolic system of language, with the role of the teacher being to give direction to the child's learning. Bruner (1973) conceives of the child, not as an assimilator of facts, but as an active problem-solver, interacting with his world in a reflective and analytical way. This is facilitated through the construction of *mental models* or *formal schemata* by which new knowledge is classified and from which inferences can be drawn (Mowat, 2008).

Vygotsky's sociocultural theory

Vygotsky's *sociocultural theory* builds on *social constructivist* principles. According to Vygotsky, learning – a conscious, deliberative, metacognitive act (A. Moore, 2007) – takes place within a cultural and historical context that shapes thinking processes, represented through *cultural tools*, such as language, that are created and shared, shaped and changed over time (Learoyd-Smith & Daniels, 2014; Newman & Newman, 2016).

Learning gradually becomes *internalised* through observation, listening and imitation as the child becomes more competent. The adult *mediates* the learning of the child through *scaffolding* (a concept similar to *shaping*), providing a secure framework for learning and acting on the *Zone of Proximal Development* (the differential between what a child can achieve on his or her own and what can be achieved when supported by a knowledgeable adult) (Pritchard & Woolard, 2010).

Looking at children's behaviour through this lens negates the premise of *behaviourism* that behaviour arises from subconscious processes. Children are sense makers and it is through social interaction and the *scaffolding* of their learning by knowledgeable adults *mediating* the learning process that children can come to an understanding of their behaviour and are able to make informed

108 *Exploring and Understanding the Problem*

judgements about it. They create a *mental model* or *action schema* of their world that encompasses expectations of how others will behave towards them and guides their actions. This does not come about through the manipulation of *reinforcers* – children are seen as social beings who have *agency* and who are moral agents in their own right.

Instrumental Enrichment (Feuerstein, Rand, Hoffman, & Miller, 1980), an approach which seeks to develop students' social adaptability through developing real-life problem-solving skills, and *Support Groups* (Mowat, 2007) (see Box 6.1) are both informed by *social constructivism/sociocultural theory* as are *humanistic* approaches to school discipline (see Chapters 9 and 10).

Box 6.1

Support groups: philosophical underpinnings

Support Groups (Mowat, 2007) are a group-work intervention to support pupils who have been identified as having SEBN. The key premise of the approach is that, through teaching for understanding,[1] pupils can come to an understanding of the values, beliefs and motivations that underlie their behaviour, in the process developing self-regulation and empathy towards others. Through participating in a range of mediated activities, led by a Support Group Leader,[2] pupils have the opportunity to explore their behaviour in a safe environment. Pupils set individual targets for improvement with the support of their Support Group Leader but there is no reliance on rewards or sanctions inherent within the approach. The key focus is on building relationships and trust.

Source: Mowat, J. (2007).
Using support groups to improve behaviour.
SAGE Publications, London.

Bioecological theory

Bronfenbrenner's *ecological theory* (Bronfenbrenner, 1979, 1986), later modified to include a biological perspective (Bronfenbrenner & Morris, 2006), is one of the most influential and comprehensive theories of human development located in the everyday experiences of people, such as issues around parenting, early childcare and education. It illuminates a process by which people through the course of their lives try to make meaning of the varied settings in which they function, impacted by community, societal and cultural forces. It is recognised that, just as the wider environment exerts a force on the individual, so does the individual shape the external environment in a reciprocal process (Newman & Newman, 2016), no better exemplified than in the efforts of the Manchester United footballer, Marcus Rashford, to procure free school meals for children living in poverty in England, bringing about a U-turn in government policy.

Looking through the Lens of Developmental Theory 109

The Eco-system

Bioecological theory places the individual child at the centre of a series of concentric circles, each representing a different layer of the system (Gillibrand et al., 2011). The dynamic interactions at all levels of the eco-system create the conditions for children's development (Bronfenbrenner, 1986; Gillibrand et al., 2011).

- *The microsystem*: The features of the immediate environment of the child and how this is experienced and perceived by the child. The child plays an active part in the activities and interactions associated with the multiple settings in which they participate – the family and siblings, classroom, clubs and societies ... (Gillibrand et al., 2011; Newman & Newman, 2016).
- *The mesosystem*: The interactions between two or more settings within which the child interacts and the pressures exerted by these settings (Newman & Newman, 2016). For example, a teacher might notice that a child is subdued and ask the family if there are any circumstances that might have brought this about. Through participation in these related settings, children come to an understanding of *social norms* and expectations of behaviour and a child's sense of identity is formed (Newman & Newman, 2016).
- *The exosystem*: These are the contexts in which the child is not directly involved but still exert influence on his/her life, including the wider family (Gillibrand et al., 2011). For example, the working pattern of the caregiver, and changes related to it, are likely to have a direct influence on how much time can be spent with the child in supporting learning at home.
- The *macrosystem*: The broader cultural and societal context that frames the relationships at all other levels of the system, incorporating cultural values, norms, laws, customs and other social influences on the child's development (Gillibrand et al., 2011; Newman & Newman, 2016).

When an individual faces recurrent difficulties in maintaining control and integration of behaviour across a range of contexts, this can lead to *dysfunction*. Some environments – described as *chaotic systems* – such as associated with systemic poverty, undermine development (Newman & Newman, 2016). Bronfenbrenner's later work also recognises the *chronosystem*, changing contexts over time affecting all levels of the system (Bronfenbrenner, 1994), particularly relevant to the 'shifting sands' of the pandemic (see Chapter 12).

The key strength of Bronfenbrenner and Morris's *bioecological* model is recognition of individual difference (the biological aspect) whilst also recognising the forces at all levels of the *ecosystem*, from the most immediate circumstances of the child's life to the broader societal and cultural context, which impact the child's life and the child's growing sense of identity (the ecological aspect).

From this perspective, in understanding children's behaviour, consideration needs to be given to the genetic, biological and social determinants of behaviour. Further, cognitive development, learning and academic achievement cannot be considered as apart from the sociocultural factors that exert such a significant influence on the

110 *Exploring and Understanding the Problem*

lives of children and young people (Gillibrand et al., 2011). As such, this theory sits alongside and complements other theories of children's learning and behaviour such as *attachment theory, social constructivism* and *social learning theory.*

What bioecolgical theory affords

Bioecological theory helps us to understand systemic issues, such as how public policy affects the lives of families (issues of poverty, housing, access to a living wage and benefits, etc.) within an ever-changing landscape. However, public policy does not exist in a vacuum: it, in turn, is shaped by societal and cultural norms (which arise from a historical context) and what is valued by society at any particular time. Having that broader perspective can help to prevent the negative discourses around inadequate parenting, single mothers, the 'feckless' unemployed and 'disturbed, deviant children' – the 'bad, mad or sad' (Armstrong & Hallet, 2012; Macleod, 2006b; Mowat, 2010b) – and focusses attention towards potential solutions which impact at all levels of the system, rather than focussing solely on the level of the child. For Learoyd-Smith and Daniels (2014), the imperative is to transform the cultures of schooling in which culture is seen as something that is created rather than 'out there' (p. 147). Thus, in trying to come to an understanding of a child or young person's behaviour, a range of issues could be examined, such as the nature of the social interactions within the environment and external forces which could potentiate the child's behaviour, for example, separation of the parents (Newman & Newman, 2016).

Such an approach is demanding – it requires an in-depth understanding of the child and the circumstances surrounding the child: schools need to know their families. It recognises the need for strong inter-disciplinary and multi-partnership working and partnerships with parents, as might be exemplified in some staged-intervention approaches, all of which can prove to be challenging. However, *by intervening at the level of the problem and the root causes underlying it,* rather than simply addressing the manifestations of the problem (the child's behaviour), it is hoped that such an approach will lead to more meaningful and sustained change over time (see Chapters 9–12).

A synthesis

There is an extensive range of developmental theories which underpin our understanding of children's behaviour and which create their sense of identity. Whilst some of these theories complement each other, others, such as *behaviourism* and *social constructivism,* are entirely incompatible. These differences are explained by understandings of the nature of children and childhood; how reality is understood; how knowledge is constructed; the nature of power relations, particularly between children and adults (see Chapter 7); the purposes that education, and schooling, in particular, is intended to serve; and the relationship between education and society. Depending on the stance adopted, individuals will take a position with regard to the theories examined and this will underpin their attitudes towards school discipline. The implications of the above will be examined in the next two chapters.

Reflection Point

This chapter has outlined a range of developmental theories that offer explanations of how learning occurs and children's behaviour. Which of these theories do you consider to be the most powerful in explaining children's behaviour and why? In examining your own professional context, how do you see the various theories playing out? Do you see a problem with practices associated with *behaviourism* sitting side by side with those that are influenced by other developmental theories, such as *attachment theory* (which is reflected in nurture [see Chapter 9])?

Additional Suggested Reading

Theories of Human Development (2nd ed.)

Psychology Press 2016. Barbara and Philip Newman

This text examines an extensive range of theories of human development, not just related to children.

Nurturing Natures: Attachment and Children's Emotional, Sociocultural and Brain Development

Routledge 2017. Graham Music

This insightful text provides a comprehensive account of the influences on children's early development, encompassing areas such as attachment theory, play, trauma, resilience and moral development.

Why Love Matters: How Affection Shapes a Baby's Brain

Routledge 2004. Sue Gerhardt

A very powerful book which explores the importance of loving relationships to healthy brain development in infants and the impact of this on future emotional and physical wellbeing.

Notes

1. Drawing on the *Teaching for Understanding Framework* (Wiske, 1998) developed by Emeritus Professor David Perkins and colleagues at Project Zero, the Harvard Graduate School of Education.
2. Normally a Pastoral Care or Support for Learning Teacher who has received training and support in the delivery of the approach.

Part III

Towards New Understandings

Challenging Orthodoxies and Building Community through Relational Approaches

The initial two chapters in this part of the book critique the concept of behaviour management and school discipline policies in the UK (England and Scotland), tracing influences back to the USA. The final two chapters offer an alternative perspective, focussing on building community through relational approaches to promoting positive behaviour.

DOI: 10.4324/9780429467110-10

7 Challenging the Orthodoxies of Behaviour Management through an Examination of Power, Influence and Authority

---

Goals for Understanding

I. How can current and often implicit understandings of behaviour management and school discipline be problematised to develop alternative understandings and approaches?

II. How are power, influence and authority understood as they pertain to school discipline and behaviour management?

III. What is the relationship between power and school disaffection as portrayed within the literature?

The previous chapter explored theories of human development and how they shape our understanding of children, how adults interact with children and where agency lies within the relationship between children and adults. This chapter will examine these relationships in greater depth, focussing on how concepts such as power, influence and authority are understood from the perspective of various theorists as a preliminary to critiquing policy and practice in Chapter 8.

Porter (2006) provides a very valuable critique of theories which underpin approaches to behaviour management, categorising the various theories and approaches on a continuous scale from 'laissez-faire' through 'egalitarian,' 'mixed-authoritarian' to 'autocratic,' depending on the degree to which power is perceived as lying with the teacher or pupil. According to this scale, more egalitarian theories/approaches (such as *humanism* and *solution-focused* approaches) are characterised by more equal power relations between teacher and pupil whereas more authoritarian theories/approaches (such as *assertive discipline*) position the teacher as having a great deal of power with the pupil having relatively little.

Porter's conceptualisation sees power as being finite – as the power of the pupil increases, so does the power of the adult diminish and vice-versa. However, this understanding of the relative power between adults and children may be over-simplistic and could underlie some of the concerns that teachers may hold with regard to relinquishing 'control' in the classroom. Might it not be the case that, through fostering pupil agency and participation (see Chapter 11),

DOI: 10.4324/9780429467110-11

116 *Towards New Understandings*

the agency of both teacher and pupil increase? And, might it also not be the case that by diminishing opportunities for pupil agency and participation, teachers may diminish their own agency if power is not understood as control but relative? It should also be recognised that, even in more egalitarian approaches, power differentials between teachers and pupils will still be significant because of the authority invested in the teacher (see the discussion of authority to follow).

As will be explored further in this and subsequent chapters, pupil (or student) agency, as it pertains to behaviour and school discipline, tends to be portrayed in limited and reductionist ways (in terms of the 'choices' that pupils make about their behaviour, the same 'choices' often determined by adults). The term within this context is rarely defined. Yet, pupil agency has been identified as one of a set of variables that promotes belonging and engagement within a caring school climate (Pope & Miles, 2022). Understood more broadly, Moses, Rylak, Reader, Hertz, and Ogden (2020) define pupil agency in terms of students' capacity to act in ways that are congruent with their beliefs, capacity for self-regulation and self-reflection and ability to take control and take ownership of their own learning (p. 124). Drawing from J. Robertson (2017), the authors describe it as a practice-embedded construct that informs the work of teachers, involving 'reflection and restructuring of traditional roles between teachers and students to share power and control over learning' (pp. 219–20) (see Chapters 11 and 12 for further discussion).

The vignette below (see Box 7.1), derived from a popular column in the *Times Educational Supplement Scotland*, whilst clearly 'tongue-in-cheek,' illuminates and brings to the fore issues of power and is illustrative of a deficit perspective of, and uncaring (some might say, callous) approach towards children. It was not untypical of many of the articles and opinion pieces that I read at that time in the same publication and in the wider media (reflecting commonly held views),

---

Box 7.1

Extract from TESS

... the more my classroom looks like a prison, the happier I will be. Ideally, I'd like it to resemble a still from the Nuremberg Rallies, with row upon row of attentive students, facing the front and saluting the air with the "quiet signal", while their desks march across the room with unwavering military precision. While other teachers promote "tangible buzz," I prefer abject fear. I believe that if you can instil enough terror at the start of the lesson, you're less likely to have to squander the rest of your life scouring the yard for the kids who default on handing in homework.

Anne Thrope (pseudonym)

Source: Extract from TESS,
9 November 2012, p. 31, kindly provided by Henry Hepburn,
News Editor of the *Times Educational Supplement Scotland*.

including the weekly pronouncements of the self-professed, 'Behaviour Guru,' Tom Bennett, who, at a later point, played a key role in shaping UK government policy on school discipline (see Chapter 8). Such a stance is reflective of a sense of 'kids being out of control' (Wright, 2009) with zero-tolerance approaches to school discipline being seen, by some, as being the solution (see Chapter 8).

How issues of power, agency and autonomy are reflected in developmental theory and the implications for school discipline policy

The discussion in the previous chapter highlighted the wide variation in how children and childhood are understood through the lens of human developmental theory. Just as such theories set out a portrayal of the child, likewise, they also portray how adults act towards and respond to the child. Inherent within such understandings are power relations between children and adults with varying degrees of agency attached to both child and adult. These range from more authoritarian to more egalitarian positions. For example, *behaviourism* provides little scope for the agency of the child (other than 'choosing' [or not] to respond to the stimuli [operant conditioning]) whilst placing significant power and authority in the hands of the adult. Likewise, the infant is seen as largely dependent on the nurturing of the caregiver (*attachment theory*), although later theorists stress the *intentionality* and *intersubjectivity* of the child. *Social learning theory* stresses the self-efficacy of the child (Bandura) as an observer and active participant within their environment (Lave and Wenger); *sociocultural theory* sees the child as an active sense-maker interacting with his/her environment with learning mediated by the adult; and *bioecological theory* positions both the child and the adult as being 'acted on' by the various systems that make up the *ecosystem* whilst also 'acting on' the ecosystem and therefore having agency to a degree. Regarding each of these theories, the degree to which the child is able to exercise *autonomy* (being able to determine what to do and how to do it [Brophy, 2010; Deci, Vallerand, Pelletier, & Ryan, 2011]) will be constrained by the degree of *agency* afforded the child.

As explored in the previous chapter, all of the above will have implications for school discipline policies and for how adults and children interact with each other within the school setting. It can be argued that holding multiple, often incompatible, understandings of children and childhood; of how adults behave towards and respond to children; and of power relations between adults and children is clearly not tenable when considered rationally, yet many school discipline policies and practices are founded on a mishmash of such understandings with *nurture, restorative practice* and *solution-orientated* approaches sitting alongside 'positive behaviour' policies that are founded on rewards and sanctions, on actions and consequences. Given the importance that schools and school leaders attach to vision and values, what mixed messages are being given out to the school community at large? The counter argument offered is that schools and teachers need a 'mixed bag' of strategies and solutions and what matters is

118   *Towards New Understandings*

what works (in itself a problematic concept [Biesta, 2007]). This sits alongside the reification of *evidence-based practice* with John Hattie's work in the ascendancy.

The previous chapters have argued that behaviour is a neutral concept, influenced by motivations, values, beliefs and attitudes, and is an expression of our emotional states. The concept of behaviour management implies that something – 'behaviour' – has to be managed but the implicit understanding is that it has to be *managed by others*. There is little or no recognition of the child as a moral agent with internal drives where the role of adults who come into contact with that child is to 'give direction to the child's learning' (a reference to the work of John Dewey). Early pioneers in understanding moral development, such as Judy Dunn (Dunn, 1987; Dunn, Maguire, & Brown, 1995) and the later work of Colwyn Trevarthen (2011) establish that infants develop a moral sense, demonstrating affection, joy, pride and shame in their shared experiences with the caregiver and interactions with others. Even when a case is made for self-discipline or self-regulation, it is often in pursuit of conformity to the norms of behaviour within the school and is not directed towards the flourishing or *self-actualisation* of the child (a reference to Carl Rogers' *person-centred therapy* [see Chapter 4] but also Maslow's *hierarchy of needs* [see Chapter 9]), recognising that *self-actualisation* is understood in different ways within the respective bodies of work.

What is clearly evident from the above is that understandings of children and childhood underpin and are reflected in theories of human development and learning and strongly influence the approaches that are adopted with regard to behaviour management and school discipline. However, it could also be argued that much of this occurs at a subliminal level. I would suspect that, other than those who have had explicit training in approaches such as *nurture* or *restorative practice*, the vast majority of teachers would struggle to articulate the theories and philosophical positioning behind the discipline policies and practices within the school and few would consider that it matters. Practices are adopted because 'they are a good thing': they worked at the school down the road or the classroom next door, or sometimes because they are the 'flavour of the month' and appear to make sense at a common sense level. Who could see praise, rewards and Golden Time (even the name has an aura about it) other than as a good thing? After all, we all like recognition for our efforts, don't we? This, and subsequent chapters, will argue that behaviour management is no longer a construct of value and that other alternative approaches to nurturing the development of children and constructs are more relevant to meeting the needs of today's children within schools.

Understanding school discipline and issues of power, authority, agency and autonomy

Exploring concepts

Behaviour management and school discipline, whilst distinct, are inextricably linked and can be distinguished from classroom management (which is concerned with the smooth running of the classroom), although the boundaries are fluid.

Challenging Orthodoxies: Power, Influence and Authority 119

Discipline is often seen as being synonymous with punishment. The aphorism, 'Spare the rod, spoil the child,' whilst no longer so prevalent, undoubtedly reflected historical attitudes towards child rearing and schooling. It is not so long ago that Scottish schoolchildren endured 'the tawse' (or Lochgelly – a leather strap) and it is a measure of how far we have come that spanking of children is now illegal in Scotland[1] (one of the first countries in the world to do so).

Clark (1998) observes that the terms 'discipline' and 'control' are often used interchangeably, in his view, erroneously: 'Just as 'discipline' is used as a euphemism for 'control,' and 'self-discipline' for 'self-control,' so 'disciplining' is used as a euphemism for 'controlling' and 'punishing' (p. 295). He draws a distinction between 'disciplined children' who comply because they subscribe to the value of the activities in which they are engaged (see the discussion of *self-determination theory* in Chapter 11) and 'controlled children' who comply because they recognise the authority of the teacher (see the discussion of authority to follow). Rather than a focus on control, he argues for discipline understood as children's capacity to learn and be supported in becoming moral agents with the key element being consideration of the principles that ought to govern the conduct of establishments concerned with the welfare of children.

Within a school context, MacAllister (2017) attests that discipline can be understood both in terms of policies and practices which 'locate pupil obedience to rules, norms and teacher authority' (p. 69) and in relation to disciplines of knowledge. Rather than a focus on self-discipline and the self-absorption that can arise from it, MacAllister advocates for personal discipline, arguing that 'pupils should be supported to develop a sense of responsibility and care for others' (p. 11).

The concepts of self-regulation (of emotions) and self-control (often used synonymously), the latter associated with more deliberative and conscious altering of responses (Schmeichel & Baumeister, 2004), are much more commonly used than the concept of self-discipline but should be seen as distinctive from it. Khon (2001) cautions that the term self-discipline can be understood in different ways: to describe a child who is truly autonomous in their behaviour (not contingent on the actions of adults or the presence of the adult) or the child who is compliant and conforming but who lacks autonomy. It follows therefore that agency and autonomy (see Chapter 13) are key concepts in understanding the concept of self-discipline.

A crisis in school discipline

MacAllister (2017) argues that, despite the generally acknowledged crisis of discipline in many schools in the UK, the real crisis lies in the confusion about the purposes that school discipline serves and those it *ought* to (p. 2). Over-simplistic explanations, which locate the problem as residing solely in the individual child, fail to take account of the complexity of the school as a social institution and the school in relation to its wider community and see the behaviour as the *cause* rather than a *symptom* of the problem. For him, school discipline has been

120 Towards New Understandings

hijacked in the service of 'a narrow agenda of training, control, punishment and examination' (p. 2) from which many children have become disengaged, rather than thinking deeply about what discipline and education *actually* and *should* mean – its nature and purpose. An over-reliance on narrow accountability agendas and on zero-tolerance discipline policies do little to avert or mitigate the perceived crisis.

Theoretical perspectives on school discipline

MacAllister (2017) explores the philosophical positioning of a range of theorists on the purposes that discipline should serve within schools and more broadly. Whilst there is a degree of consensus with regard to school discipline acting as a process of socialisation, transmitting culture and ways of knowing and being (thinking, feeling, acting) from one generation to the next, and being essential for the moral development of the child, it is the means by which this is to be accomplished that distinguishes the different philosophical positions. These understandings are rooted in the cultural and historical contexts of the time (see Table 7.1).

How concepts such as power, authority, autonomy and agency are understood more generally and in relation to school discipline varies significantly from the perspectives of various theorists. Despite holding quite distinctive views as to what discipline means and entails, Kant (1724–1804), Durkheim (1858–1917) and Foucault (1926–1984) are in agreement that discipline is imposed on pupils and that both discipline and punishment constrain pupils and mould them into what society expects of them (MacAllister, 2017). For Kant and Durkheim, this process of socialisation would lead, in their view, to individual growth, autonomy and social cohesion. Foucault, in contrast, believed that the process of socialisation into laws, traditions and bodies of knowledge is not necessarily beneficial, carrying with it a damaging *normalising* power and leading to docile, conforming workers of the future. For him, teaching becomes coercive when it seeks to develop in pupils norms of acceptable behaviour (MacAllister, 2017).

Discipline as surveillance

Whilst, over time, more punitive régimes have gradually been replaced with what are generally portrayed as more humane responses to indiscipline (such as removal of privileges, detention and exclusion), for Foucault, these approaches are largely coercive, located within a context of increasing surveillance, serving to act as a deterrent for future transgressions, preserving the social order (Andrejevic & Selwyn, 2019).

Whilst the dystopian state, reflected in the development of facial recognition technologies to determine people's moods, emotions and affective states (Andrejevic & Selwyn, 2019), may seem far from a reality in today's classrooms, the use of digital technologies to track attendance and behaviour in schools is

Challenging Orthodoxies: Power, Influence and Authority 121

Table 7.1 A summary of the key philosophical positions of Kant, Durkheim, Dewey, MacMurray, Wilson, Peters and Hirst on (school) discipline

Philosopher	Philosophical position	Ultimate goal
Immanuel Kant (1724–1804)	Discipline is inherently negative. It seeks to curb undesired behaviours. Being able to think autonomously first requires the child to acquire discipline and follow the rules of others.	The betterment of humanity and moral development of the child, the latter achieved through socialisation into school rules.
David Émile Durkheim (1858–1917)	Durkheim shared a similar philosophy to Kant but did not believe that all children were capable of rationally forming universal moral laws.	Serving society.
John Dewey (1859–1952)	'Discipline is a disposition of persistence and endurance in the face of challenge and difficulty'. Schools serve to transmit valued ways of thinking, acting and feeling to children. Order is established through communication rather than rules. Discipline in education should foster student agency.	In the pursuit of significant learning, directed towards individual growth and social democratic renewal and concerned with promoting community and better social order.
John MacMurray (1891–1986)	Human feelings are the foundation upon which education and discipline should be built. Discipline should primarily be about the fostering of personal relationships and overcoming egocentricity.	In the pursuit of the betterment of self and others.
John Wilson (1928–2003)	School discipline and the socialisation of children are vital for moral education and development and should initiate students into rules that are impersonal and apply to all.	Moral education and development.
Richard S. Peters (1919–2011) & Paul Hirst (1946–2003)	Advocates of self-discipline, students need to work hard and be disciplined by knowledge if they are to come to an understanding of it – discipline is not something apart but integral to learning.	In the pursuit of learning.

Source: Derived from MacAllister (2017).

122 *Towards New Understandings*

becoming increasingly prevalent across the world and video cameras in school grounds are commonplace. Whilst the public recording of the names of children who misbehave on the board (as initially advocated in *Assertive Discipline*) may seem trivial in comparison (apparently critics had 'misinterpreted the use of names and checks on the board as a way of humiliating students' [Canter & Canter, 2001, p. 72]), it is all part of the surveillance culture that Foucault draws to attention, drawing a parallel with Bentham's Panopticon (a central tower located in the centre of a prison for surveillance purposes).

Discipline as objectification

Foucault does not restrict his critique to the disciplinary processes associated with behaviour management. He considers a range of mechanisms as serving the purposes of discipline – heightened surveillance, exclusions, examinations and league tables (MacAllister, 2017) – represented nowadays within the increased accountability measures associated with the global market economy and in the commodification of education. Reflected also in the ascendancy of the Organisation for Economic Cooperation and Development (OECD) (see Chapter 1) with teachers becoming increasingly objectified ('manipulated, shaped, trained' [Foucault, 1991, in Schwan & Shapiro, 2011, p. 98]) as they are held accountable for the results of their pupils. This occurs not only at a local level but nationally, at the macro (the school)- and micro- (the individual pupil) level as complex systems of national comparators and the tracking of individual pupil progress have become firmly entrenched. It could be argued that such practices could also be construed as part of the surveillance culture to which Foucault refers – a form of discipline, although they are rarely seen in this light. Foucault argues that the exercise of discipline is not confined to the political élites but is diffused across society, working through decentralised networks, reproduced in multiple small, discrete acts, concerned with the docility and utility of the individual (Schwan & Shapiro, 2011).

The above is reflected in the multiplicity of small, discrete acts taking place on a daily basis in countless schools across many lands, enforcing dress codes, movement across the school and classroom routines and regulations that serve to reinforce the authority of the school as an institution and that of the individual teacher. Whether one believes that this is a good thing or not, it is important to recognise that it is a representation of power in action, designed to foster compliance in children and even staff who may feel an obligation to comply in enforcing the rules, whether or not they fundamentally agree with the practices and underlying values.

Fundamentally, school discipline, seen through this lens, is concerned with the maintenance of the system and in preserving the social order rather than being primarily concerned with meeting the needs of children, although it will often be couched in the language of dignity, respect and other *humanistic* concepts (see Chapter 9).

Influence, power and authority

Macleod, MacAllister, and Pirrie (2012) examine the relationship between authority and teacher/pupil relationships. They draw from the earlier theoretical framework of Wrong (1979) who conceptualises authority as one of four forms of power which, in turn, is conceptualised as a form of influence that is intentional in nature. Whilst Wrong's theory is not specific to education, it has applicability to it and value in setting out a model that helps to explain the rationale for why pupils would obey (or not) although it does not address whether they ought to (Macleod, Fyfe, Nicol, Sangster, & Obeng, 2018). Wrong (1979) builds on Bertrand Russell's definition of power as being, 'the production of intended effects,' by defining it in terms of the actors involved and as a disposition to act: 'power is the capacity of some persons to produce intended and foreseen effects on others' (Wrong, 1979, Chapter 1- e-reader). Intentionality is a key aspect of power that distinguishes it from normal social interactions, although there may be unanticipated and unplanned for outcomes that may arise as a consequence (Wrong, 1979).

Hearn (2012) distinguishes between social power as 'power to' and 'power over,' the former concerned with the capacity to realise ends either individually or collectively, the latter with the control of one individual over another, raising questions about who should exercise power, how much and over whom (p. 6). However, in contrast to the generally held view as to the undesirability of 'power over,' the author argues that the two are inextricably linked: it is the exercise of 'power over' that leads to 'power to.'

Macleod et al. (2012) observe that teacher authority is rarely considered in discussions of the classroom dynamic. The concept is often conflated with that of power and is under-theorised, yet, it is central to understanding the nature of classroom interactions and of discipline. In the authors' view, this has led to a narrow conceptualisation of authority as control or force (the dominant discourse being that of 'strategies to control unruly behaviour' [p. 494]) and a focus on pupil behaviours and discipline, neglecting other possible understandings of the nature of the authority between teacher and pupils, including personal authority. Key features of the four forms of power as identified by Wrong are set out in Table 7.2 which I have extrapolated to the school context.

Authority differs from the other three forms of power in that it is dependent on the nature of the source of the power as perceived by the recipients of it. Thus, it is a form of power that is relational in that it lies in the interactions between pupils and teachers (Macleod et al., 2018). The different bases of authority – *coercive, by inducement, legitimate, competent* and *personal* – can be differentiated by the degree to which the individual is motivated to obey (Macleod et al., 2012). According to the theory, a child, for example, who recognises the *legitimacy* of the teacher to exercise discipline, will seek to obey, as would a child who has a sense of affinity with the teacher and wishes to please (*personal authority*). In contrast, a child who does not believe that the teacher has the capability of or desire to impose discipline (*coercive authority*), or who does not value the *competency* and expertise of the teacher, would be more inclined to disobey.

124 *Towards New Understandings*

Table 7.2 A brief synopsis of forms of power

Power as:			*Child's response*
Force	Physical or biological force (deprivation of basic needs) which may be actual or threatened (symbolic and a form of coercion) and/or psychological violence (e.g., bullying, emotional abuse).		The child obeys to avoid punishment in whichever form it takes.
Manipulation	When the individual who is seeking to influence another through their actions does not make their intent explicit. Inducement by rewards is a form of manipulation if the aim is to maintain the power balance. It may be achieved through direct or indirect actions (e.g., through making changes in the environment which act as a catalyst for changes in behaviour).		The child's obedience is contingent on receiving a desired outcome (reward, praise, status …).
Persuasion	Whilst seemingly more benign, it is classified as a form of power as it represents a means by which one individual may achieve an intended effect on another's behaviour. There is potentially, however, a greater prospect of reciprocity and agency on the part of the recipient who, depending on the circumstances, can make their own case and choose or not whether to acquiesce.		The child may choose to obey, believing that it is in his/her best interests to do so.
Authority	Compliance is induced as a consequence of the perceived status of the source of the authority and the affordances associated with it (e.g., access to resources). It takes four forms:		
	Coercive	A form of authority achieved through the threat of force but is dependent on the perception of the authority (whether the state, institution or an individual) as having the capability and intention of using it.	The child's belief in the authority of the teacher is contingent on the expectation that the teacher has the capability and intention of using whichever force is required to impose discipline. The child obeys to avoid reprisals.
	By inducement	The offering of rewards to bring about obedience. However, the threat of withdrawal of the reward can be experienced as coercion.	The child obeys to either receive the inducement or avoid it being withdrawn.

(Continued)

Challenging Orthodoxies: Power, Influence and Authority 125

Table 7.2 A brief synopsis of forms of power *(Continued)*

Power as:			Child's response
	Legitimate	Where the state/institution/ individual exercising authority is acknowledged as having the right to do so (based on shared group norms and values) and there is an expectation of compliance on the part of those who are subject to it. The powers exercised are seen as mandatory rather than something over which the individual can exercise judgement. However, this is dependent on the individual recognising the legitimacy of the power.	The child obeys because he/she believes that the teacher, through their position and the things that go with it, has a right to exercise authority over him/her.
	Competent	Where authority arises out of the competence (knowledge and skill) of the individual exercising it. The subject of the authority obeys on the basis of the authority's perceived superior competence, which is seen as serving the best interests of the subject's interests and goals.	The child obeys because they recognise the expertise, knowledge and skill that the teacher possesses and this is something that the child values in achieving their goals.
	Personal	Personal authority rests on the attributes of the individual exercising power – it is not coercive or contingent on inducements.	The child obeys out of a sense of personal affinity with the teacher, seeking to please.

Source: Derived from Wrong (1979), Chapters 2 and 3.

Wrong (1979) makes the case that the forms of authority are permeable and can overlap. For example, a classroom teacher could be seen to exercise *legitimate* authority by dint of their status and position (and what it affords), qualifications and formal apprenticeship into the profession; to exercise *competent* authority through their subject and pedagogical expertise; and to exercise *personal* author-ity through the creation of a positive climate for learning founded on trusting relationships. He/she may also exercise *authority by inducement*, through the use of praise cards, stickers, Golden Time ..., and through *coercion* – 'If you don't finish this task, you will be kept in over break.'

126 *Towards New Understandings*

It is likely that many teachers may morph through the different forms of authority in the course of their working day but it is also highly likely to be the case that some teachers are more pre-disposed towards some forms of authority than others and this may depend on their worldview (formed, over time, through their interpretation of their life experiences) as well as aspects of their personality and underlying motivations. In a small-scale empirical study across a range of educational settings, Macleod et al. (2018) found it to be the case that authority relationships are multi-faceted with different forms of authority relationships inextricably bound. The authors identify a further form of authority – that of *care and commitment*, drawing on both *competent* and *personal authority* but sufficiently distinctive to deserve a separate categorisation. Understandings of teacher authority are framed by visions of what the *school* should be and by the hidden structures of schooling (Macleod et al., 2012). For example, whether the vision is egalitarian, child-centred or driven by a narrow accountability and neo-liberal agenda.

Any experienced teacher will know that the classroom environment is highly complex. How power relations operate in a classroom (or, more broadly within the school) is not contingent solely on the relationship and/or interactions between any one individual and another and how they are interpreted, both cognitively and emotionally (as might be understood through the lens of *symbolic interactionism*[2]). Pirrie and Rafanell (2020) make the case that authority should be seen as 'continuously negotiated, challenged, accepted, defined and ultimately constituted in and through the dynamics of interactions' between all members of the classroom community (p. 112). They attest that teacher authority may be a quality that arises as a consequence of relationships between pupils and teachers and between pupils themselves (as argued by Wrong).

Authority as situated

How individuals frame concepts such as authority is also situated in time and place and cultural norms. Over my lifetime, living in Scotland, I have seen a significant cultural shift with regard to how authority figures (those whom Wrong would describe as having *legitimate authority*) are perceived – whether in relation to people in high office, politicians or the professions. In my childhood, people were generally much more deferential towards authority figures and rarely brought into question their judgements. A child getting into trouble at school would have been more likely to be given a 'skelp o'er the lug' (Scottish vernacular for 'slap across the ear') when they reached home than the parent arriving at the school gate to make a complaint (please note that I am not, under any circumstances, advocating the former approach!). There may be a wide range of potential reasons for this, including greater access to information through digital technologies and freedom of information acts; the influence of social media; the rise of celebrity culture; and a greater awareness of rights which have been ratified through legislation.

Politicians in the UK and the USA have undermined faith in public expertise and institutions. In June 2016, The Financial Times declared, 'Britain has had enough of experts,' commenting on the pronouncements of Michael Gove, Justice Secretary of State at the time. This now seems ironic in the light of the pandemic and the constant references to 'THE SCIENCE.' In the USA, shocking scenes unfolded as an unruly mob descended upon and desecrated the Capitol building, leading to death and injury, fuelled by Trump's unfounded claims that 'THE ELECTION WAS STOLEN' – described by the Daily Telegraph as 'Anarchy in the US' (07 January 21) – a day of infamy that will go down in history. Such actions threaten the legitimacy of the electoral system that underpins both democracy and the constitution of the USA.

There is no value judgement implied here: just an observation that the *legitimacy* and *competency* of authority figures (and the bodies they represent) is increasingly being brought into question and this is also the case for the classroom teacher. It is represented within the commonly expressed viewpoint, 'Respect has to be earned,' and is not an entitlement that goes with the role of classroom teacher.

The relationship between school disaffection and the 'deviant' student

Slee (2015), in his frustration at the relentless quest for quick solutions, tips and strategies to address the problems presented by pupil behaviour (represented in the ubiquity of texts such as 'Getting the buggers to behave' by Sue Cowley with its advice on 'how to deal with the class from hell') and the attribution of the problem to either pathological dysfunction in the child or inadequacies in parenting, turns to the work of theorists such as Furlong, Cooper and Rose who offer alternative perspectives.

The key thrust of sociological research in the late 20th century focussing on school disaffection, building on the work of Durkheim, shifted the focus away from pathological explanations of deviance to explanations rooted in the environment, understood as an adaptive, 'rational' and 'normal' response to adverse circumstances. However, Furlong (1991) observes that concerns around *social structures* (constraints on agency) and power, including issues of social class which lie at the heart of sociological understandings of school disaffection, in themselves, are not sufficient to account for it: 'Children do not reject school simply because they are working class ... What is more, pupils do not reject abstract social structures, they reject real teachers going about their day to day business of schooling' (p. 297). In an attempt to reconstruct a sociological theory of school deviance, he argues that the starting point has to be a psychological perspective.

The hidden injuries of schooling

The key issues for Furlong were failure to acknowledge the emotional response of children to what he describes as the *hidden injuries of schooling* and the assumption that children are 'rational and knowing individuals' (p. 295) who are able

128   *Towards New Understandings*

to logically appraise the situations in which they find themselves and exercise appropriate judgement. Indeed, this is a key tenet of many of the approaches towards behaviour management in which children are deemed to have made, or make, 'choices' about their behaviour. It could be argued that the extent to which a child is able to make rational choices based on an informed appraisal of a situation may be a matter of degree and dependent on a range of variables, such as their capacity for self-reflection and developmental stage. As highlighted by Killen and Rutland (2013), and as discussed in Chapter 4, even young children develop a moral sense and are able to rationalise the decisions that they make.

From his perspective, whether or not pupils are able to offer an explanation for their behaviour, it is only part of the story as rejection of school is almost always an emotional response on the part of the pupil to the contexts and situations in which they find themselves. In order to understand the roots of disaffection and why school evokes such strong emotions in pupils, there is a need to understand how, through schooling, 'power is used to change young people and insist that they change themselves' (p. 298). Drawing from the literature, he acknowledges that the school itself may be the source of the negative emotions or, alternatively, it may be a 'site' where children give vent to their emotions, having roots outwith the school, recognising that these may be interconnected (p. 296). Furlong's analysis resonates with the work of theorists such as Riley (see Chapters 5, 6 and 13) and with earlier bodies of work such as 'Tell Them from Me' (Gow & McPherson, 1980), which is a harrowing account of the experiences of school of young people in the late 1970s.

Furlong (1991) argues that the starting point for understanding pupils' response to schooling is to recognise that schools not only seek to impose certain ways of behaving on pupils but to construct pupils in particular ways: 'we insist that they *come to see themselves* and organise their lives in these ways' (p. 298). Whilst not drawing from Foucault, the parallels between this account and Foucault's arguments about the construction of identities are clear. It is this fundamental drive to change people, and to draw on the power that the school affords to achieve this end, that makes it such an emotionally strong experience for children and young people (C&YP). The 'injuries of schooling' may lead to repression of emotions (arising from feelings of being excluded and devalued), which, for some, may lead ultimately to disruption and truancy, seeking encouragement and solace from their peers. Whilst many pupils will find means of dealing with their repressed feelings of rejection, Furlong (1991) identifies two groups for whom this will not be the case: those who are so injured that it leads them to vent their aggression and challenge the authority of the school, forming a sub-culture within the school (as identified in the works of Hargreaves and Ball[3]); and those who are already emotionally vulnerable and for whom even the most basic demands of schooling will lead to conflict and rejection (p. 305), though it can be surmised that some pupils will transcend both groups. He explores three routes through which 'hidden injuries' are created – the production of ability, values and occupational identity, as set out in Table 7.3.

Challenging Orthodoxies: Power, Influence and Authority 129

Table 7.3 The production of the 'hidden injuries of schooling'

The production of	Characterised by
Ability	Differences in ability between pupils are accentuated, legitimated and lived, created through the organisational structures of schooling and through curricula, pedagogy and assessment.
Values about knowledge, behaviour and aspirations for the future	Historically and culturally situated and aligned with the values of the educated, white, aspiring middle class. Certain forms of knowledge, codes of behaviour and aspirations for the future are valued over others with pupils from middle-class homes sharing a 'class cultural affinity' with teachers, which, along with other desired attributes (e.g., being good at sport), serves to exclude others.
Occupational identity	Schooling being one of a range of factors, such as the employment market, networks (related to social capital – see Chapter 12), which, through formal qualifications, either opens the door to opportunities, or excludes.

Source: Derived from Furlong (1991, pp. 299–304).

Furlong (1991) argues that schooling is a highly demanding and, often, ambivalent experience for pupils, with teachers acting as the gatekeeper for both affirmation and rejection. To imply, therefore, that pupils' response to schooling is solely rational does not take account of the emotional distress they experience or the vulnerability of such pupils. For him, school deviance, whilst generally understood through a sociological lens, has both a psychological and an emotional dimension but this does not mean that the problem should be individualised.

Whilst Furlong's work stems from 30 years ago, as a former Depute Head in a Secondary school serving an area of deprivation, dealing on a day-to-day basis with matters of indiscipline and with children regarded as deviant and their families, I recognise the truths in Furlong's work and the humanity it represents. Schools, in themselves, represent the expectations of society – for an educated, productive and, dare one say, compliant workforce – and, whilst there have been significant changes in the values and norms of society (the 'Me Too,' 'Black Matters' and 'Reclaim the Streets' movements representative of these changes), many of the elements of the structures identified by Furlong are still heavily represented and, indeed, in some cases, amplified, with the emphasis on international comparators and testing in today's schools. Therefore, the issue is still, as highlighted by Furlong, to identify those aspects of the educational structures within schools which are most likely to lead to 'hidden injuries'; to seek to address them in innovative ways; and to challenge orthodoxies within society which lead to them being present in the first place. For Slee (2014), there is a need for more nuanced and sophisticated means of understanding the phenomena of pupil

130 *Towards New Understandings*

disengagement and disaffection from a multidimensional perspective which then becomes incorporated into educational reform.

Brief conclusion

The discussion in this and previous chapters has highlighted the complexity of and inherent tensions within what is often taken for granted and unquestioned ways of thinking about the nature of children and childhood (and therefore our responses as adults towards them); about power, influence and authority and how it is exercised; about agency and where it lies; about school discipline and the classroom dynamic; and how we understand pupils who disengage from learning and from school and whose behaviour is considered deviant. In the process, it has highlighted the inadequacies in our understandings of school discipline and the redundancy of reductive concepts such as behaviour management that will not serve us well as we embrace the challenges of creating equitable, inclusive and compassionate schools in the future. The concluding chapters will offer an alternative paradigm to behaviour management and means of building community in schools.

Reflection Point

With regard to your own professional context, how do the arguments forwarded within this chapter resonate with your own experience? What forms of power and authority are represented within your organisation and what ends do they serve? What forms of authority do you call upon in exercising your role as an educator and/or leader of learning?

Additional Suggested Reading

Behaviour in Schools. Theory and Practice for Teachers (3rd ed.)

Open University Press 2014. Louise Porter

This is the 3rd edition of a really excellent text that moves beyond the critique of various approaches towards school discipline in the 2nd edition to a broader exploration that encompasses aspects such as parental engagement and resolving issues around bullying and aggression.

Reclaiming Discipline for Education

Routledge 2017. James MacAllister

This text draws from a range of theorists and philosophers (past and present) to examine the nature of discipline in schools, leading to an exploration of more contemporary understandings which stress the importance of relationships and community.

Notes

1. The Children (Equal Protection from Assault) (**Scotland**) **Act** 2019.
2. A sociological theory, attributed initially to Mead (1863–1981) but further developed by Goffman (1922–82) and other sociologists (principally in the Chicago School), which focusses on the interactions between individuals and the symbols by which they are transmitted, for example, language, body language, gestures, which collectively create meaning. For *symbolic interactionists* there is no objective social reality – the *social self* develops through the interactions between individuals (Giddens and Sutton, 2017, pp. 84–5).
3. Hargreaves' study of Lumley Secondary Modern School and Ball's study of Beachside Comprehensive.

8 Challenging the Orthodoxies of Behaviour Management through a Focus on Policy and Practice

---

Goals for Understanding

I. How are power, influence and authority expressed in policies relating to school discipline in the UK and where does agency lie?

II. What are the influences upon this?

Having examined how power, influence and authority are understood within an educational context from the perspective of a range of theorists, this chapter explores how this manifests itself in policies relating to school discipline in the UK, in particular England and Scotland, tracing this back to influences from policies emanating from the USA and *zero-tolerance* approaches. As the distinction between school discipline and behaviour management is so blurred within the literature, the concepts are used interchangeably within the chapter and the term 'exclusion,' rather than 'suspension', is adopted. The term children will denote both children and young people within the chapter. The terms student and pupil reflect the use of the terms within the source documents.

The wider policy context

Both in the USA and the UK, discourses of behaviour management have dominated policy and practice. MacAllister (2017) attests that the view that discipline should first and foremost initiate students into impersonal rules that apply to all (as advocated by Kant, Durkheim and Wilson) is pervasive. It is exemplified in *zero-tolerance* approaches which may lead to long-term negative consequences for students and do not foster responsibility in students for their learning and behaviour. He is not arguing that rules, in themselves, are not of value – they set expectations both within the school and within wider society – but, in too many cases, they do not serve the interests of students well.

DOI: 10.4324/9780429467110-12

Policy in the USA

Chapter 1 outlined some of the key policies, such as *No Child Left Behind* and *Race to the Top* in the USA. Whilst such policies were well-intentioned, aiming to reduce educational inequalities, they reside within a neo-liberal agenda which fosters competition and emphasises accountability, leading, almost inevitably, to *zero-tolerance* behaviour policies as schools seek to 'raise the bar' (L. Darling-Hammond, Cook-Harvey, Flook, Gardner, & Melnick, 2018). Yet, the *American Psychological Association* in 2008 came to the conclusion that *zero-tolerance* policies are largely ineffective in improving behaviour in schools and making schools a safer place to be for students (Skiba & Losen, 2015).[1] Indeed, they may be likely to trigger further exclusions from school in the future and create schools which have a less, rather than more, conducive climate for learning (MacAllister, 2017).

Skiba and Losen (2015) and MacAllister (2017) chart how *zero-tolerance* policies emerged in the USA in the 1980s in response to mounting concerns about school safety, later mandated by the Clinton administration (1993–2001) through legislation, reflected in much of the literature on this subject emanating from the USA. The increasing prevalence of law enforcement officers on school premises together with the diminishing role of teachers being 'in loco parentis' had led to the escalation of even minor infractions of indiscipline being dealt with by the criminal justice system. It also led to an increase in school exclusions which fell disproportionally on historically disadvantaged groups, such as ethnic minority students and students with disabilities. Even when controlling for poverty, race remained as a significant predictor of school exclusions, and exclusions, in themselves, are a risk factor for longer-term negative outcomes, such as contact with the juvenile justice system, school drop-out and incarceration as an adult, described as the school-to-prison pipeline. A study conducted in Charlotte-Mecklenburg Schools in the USA established a correlation between rates of school exclusion and stricter school discipline régimes in adolescence, and a substantially higher rate of arrests and incarcerations as adults, applying across all of the schools' population, but affecting disproportionally males and minority groups (Bacher-Hicks, Billings, & Deming, 2021).

By means of a federal discipline directive, the Obama administration (2009–2017) sought to address the higher proportion of students of colour in USA schools who were disciplined in comparison to their peers (Skiba & Losen, 2015). The basis of the directive was that school discipline policies could violate human rights if they led to 'disparate impact,' even if there had been no discriminatory intent (Blad, 2018). However, critics of the directive raised concerns that it was too 'heavy-handed' in approach and did not allow school officials to exercise discretion. The Trump administration (2017–2021) rescinded the guidance and, in response to the Parkland (and other school campuses) shootings, advocated that school staff should be armed instead (Blad, 2018).

Examination of a 2018 edition of *Educational Leadership* (a USA journal) focussing on behaviour management reveals a wide range of perspectives on

134 *Towards New Understandings*

school discipline and behaviour management, from those which clearly stem from more authoritarian approaches such as *Assertive Discipline (AD)* and *Positive Behaviour Support (PBS)* to more *humanistic* approaches (see Chapters 9 and 10)[2]. For example, whereas M. Anderson (2018) focusses on consistency in the application of behavioural consequences and what they afford (or not), Scanfeld, Davis, Weintraub, and Dotoli (2018) argue that a focus on rules and consequences wastes the time that should be devoted to learning goals, advocating instead a common creed with which the school community can align. Jung and Smith (2018) proclaim, 'Tear down your Behaviour Chart,' asking for teachers to pose the question, 'Stop asking "what's wrong with that student?" and start figuring out what has happened to that student' (p. 16) – a very clear steer towards *trauma-informed practice* (see Chapter 9). Milner, Cunningham, Delale-O'Connor, and Kestenberg (2018) are also aligned with a more *humanistic* approach, focussing on caring and belonging, effective instruction and a commitment to social justice, observing that those children most frequently targeted for punishment in school mirror the same demographic (race, gender, socio-economic status) as those who populate USA prisons. They caution:

> … too many teachers see classroom management as a way to *control* students. They attempt to control how students think, when they speak, how (or whether) they move, and where they complete their work. But far from being a constructive part of education, attempts to control students can have a damaging effect over time, and they tend to be met with increasing resistance as students grow older – which can lead to intensified problems.
>
> (p. 86)

What the above indicates is that, whilst there is a growing movement towards more *humanistic* approaches to school discipline in the USA, the fact that the arguments need to be made in the first place indicates the entrenchment of more authoritarian and *zero-tolerance* approaches, which have been highly significant in shaping district- and school-level policy and continue to be influential not just in the USA but beyond, as the discussion to follow will evidence.

Authoritarian approaches to school discipline

Armstrong (2018) describes a 'manage-and-discipline' approach to school control (deriving from Foucault's treatise on power [see Chapter 7]), based upon a set of assumptions about children's behaviour which are conceptually muddled and are not grounded in understandings of developmental psychology about child and adolescent behaviour. Key underlying core assumptions are:

1 Behaviour can be quantified and controlled;
2 Students' behaviour can be reduced to variables which can be manipulated and managed;
3 Given the right skills and training, teachers can control the classroom;

Challenging Orthodoxies: Policy and Practice   135

4   Technical, professional skills to induce student compliance are required by teachers;

5   Students who do not respond are a threat to the orderly classroom.

(Armstrong, 2018, p. 1000)

The work of Bill Rogers, a worldwide expert on behaviour management, has been highly influential in promoting less punitive and skills-based approaches to behaviour management. His advocacy of 'positive discipline' is associated not only with the language adopted by teachers but with a range of non-verbal behaviours (such as tone of voice and eye contact) which he claims, if adopted globally, can 'convey a positive managerial tone' (MacAllister, 2017, p. 18, citing Rogers, 2011, p. 8). Rogers (2002) acknowledges the unequal power forces within the classroom and advises teachers to see their power '*for*, and power *with* our students rather than merely power over others' (parallels with Clark's distinction between power *to* and power *over* [see Chapter 7]) but, when one examines the range of strategies advocated, they are largely based on *behaviourism* and the same 'bag of tricks' we find in other approaches which come from the same stable – 'directed choices,' consequences.' MacAllister (2017) raises concerns about Rogers' failure to acknowledge that the strategies he advocates are manipulative (one of Wrong's [1979] categorisations of power [see Chapter 7]).

Head (2007) argues that the basic premise of authoritarian approaches resides in student deficit, leading to reductionist and pessimistic views of children (Head, 2007). Slee (2015), likewise, claims that behaviour management approaches are myopic in their positioning of the problem as attributable to individual student pathology or to a failure of child-rearing practices within the family, leading to the development of more authoritarian, rather than *authoritative*, teachers (p. 5) and failing to give consideration to wider considerations as to why children may present with behavioural issues.

Head (2007) maintains that, whilst such approaches may be popular in schools (asserting the teacher's right to establish order on students and providing clarity with regard to the nature of behaviours to be targeted), ultimately, they do little to address the roots of the behaviour and the strategies adopted lose impact over time. It can be observed that, whilst much of the discussion is couched within the language of caring, the means adopted to achieve the desired ends do not align with (and, indeed, contradict) this philosophy and, ultimately, such approaches are about the control of students by adults (Head, 2007; Khon, 2001; Porter, 2006).

Porter (2006) identifies two behaviour management approaches as lying towards the autocratic end of the continuum, described as authoritarian – *Assertive Discipline* and *Applied Behaviour Analysis*[3], of which *Positive Behaviour Support* in its various guises is a manifestation of the latter. A common feature of these approaches (and others of a similar vein, such as *Discipline with Dignity* [Curwin, Mendler, & Mendler, 2008]), is that they largely derive from the USA but have since had global reach and have exerted considerable influence in thinking about behaviour management and school discipline. The following

136 Towards New Understandings

discussion critiques *Assertive Discipline* and *Schoolwide Positive Behaviour Support (SWPBS)*, the latter as described by Young, Caldarella, Richardson, and Young (2012) and applied within the context of secondary schooling.

A comparison between assertive discipline and schoolwide positive behaviour support

Assertive Discipline is an approach developed in the USA in the 1970s by Lee and Marlene Canter (Canter & Canter, 2001) the basis of which is that teachers need to be more assertive in their approach to classroom discipline, setting 'consistent, positive behavioural limits' (p. 7). *SWPBS* is an evidence-based, data-driven, problem–solving, schoolwide approach to promoting positive behaviour, seeking to counter *zero-tolerance* approaches in the USA (Armstrong, 2018).

Despite the ubiquity of the former approach, the evidence base for it is very limited and anecdotal with little consideration of potentially deleterious effects or children's rights (Porter, 2006; Render, Padilla, & Krank, 1989). In contrast, there is extensive literature on both *Positive Behaviour Support* and *Schoolwide Positive Behaviour Support* but Armstrong (2018) observes that, despite Federal Funding in the USA to support implementation, the approaches have not been successful in reducing exclusion rates in US schools overall, although the author cites a range of studies where *SWPBS* had been successful in this respect when carefully implemented.

Philosophical underpinnings of the approaches

Whilst both approaches are distinctive in their own right, they are firmly rooted in *behaviourism* with its emphasis on the reinforcement of desirable behaviours and the elimination of less desirable behaviours (see Chapter 6). This is represented in the emphasis on praise, token reward systems, corrective actions *(AD)* and the creation of behavioural expectations (for which naturalistic consequences are to be given if 'expectations' are not met) in *SWPBS* (Young et al., 2012) (Wrong's *power by manipulation*). Both approaches stress the importance of adults modelling pro-social behaviours, drawing from Bandura's *sociocultural* theory (see Chapter 6). Whilst *SWPBS* recognises that environments shape behaviour, the key principle underlying *Assertive Discipline* is that, in order to ensure fairness and equality, other than in exceptional circumstances, the same due process needs to be applied consistently to all children: 'Students must know that misbehaviour carries with it a corrective action – every time' (p. 153).

The nature of the approaches

For Canter and Canter (2001) *(AD)*, the solution to 'problem behaviour' rests in the implementation of a discipline plan – a hierarchy of actions through which, it is believed, students will move to a higher form of self-management (in keeping

Challenging Orthodoxies: Policy and Practice   137

with theorists, such as Kant, Durkheim and Wilson who maintain that it is only through the induction into rules and routines that pupils will be able to self-discipline [see Chapter 7]). In contrast, *SWPBS* relies on a much more complex three-staged-intervention approach and embraces a wide range of interventions, such as *social and emotional learning*, but the role of interprofessional and multi-agency working is not recognised.

Critique of the approaches (see the discussion of power, influence and authority in Chapter 7)

The almost exclusive focus on the child as the unit and agent of change

Despite the emphasis on relationships, school culture and understanding the developmental needs of children in *SWPBS*, the almost exclusive focus on the child (and the observable behaviours of the child) as the unit and agent of change negates and deflects attention away from other variables within the immediate and wider environment (including public policy) that impact on the life of the child and have the potential to make a difference. Whilst Canter and Canter (2001) draw attention to the importance of high-quality teaching and learning, thereafter, scant attention is paid to it.

Discipline as a form of coercive control: if it looks like a duck, walks like a duck ...

The premise of both approaches is that students will only behave when adults control their behaviour, predicated on the indelible right of teachers to exercise *legitimate authority* (as described by Wrong, 1979) in their classrooms. An irony of both approaches, but particularly *Assertive Discipline*, is the degree to which students are able to exercise so little autonomy and agency in the classroom but are still held to be fully responsible for the 'choices' that they make about their behaviour (often determined by the same adults – 'You chose to push Samantha and therefore you have chosen to sit by yourself' [Canter & Canter, 2001, p. 148]). 'Choices' when imposed (an oxymoron in itself) in this manner by adults represent coercion to achieve compliance to unexamined norms (see the discussion in Chapter 7 of Wrong's *coercive authority* and Furlong's *hidden injuries* of schooling).

The positioning of all behaviour as deliberative (especially when one considers children as being in a stage of development) is highly questionable and would not stand up to scrutiny. There is an overwhelming sense of adults, no matter how well-intentioned, doing things *to* rather than *with* students, rather than helping them come to an understanding of their behaviour at a deeper level and to develop self-responsibility (beyond the reductionist 'making choices') and genuine autonomy (being able to determine what to do and how to do it).

The advocacy of positive reinforcers, both overt and covert – what Wrong (1979) would describe as exemplifying *power as manipulation* and *authority*

138 *Towards New Understandings*

by inducement – is regarded as entirely unproblematic (see the discussion of token-reward systems and *self-determination* theory in Chapter 11). When praise, encouragement and token reward systems become a means to an end, rather than an expression of authentic relationships (even if, I would argue, they may appear to be welcomed by those students in receipt of them), a clear message is given to *all* students that they are only accepted conditionally within this classroom (Khon, 1999, 2005) (see Chapter 4). There is a failure to recognise that the withholding or withdrawal of positive reinforcers (or the conditionality associated with them) is a manifestation of *coercive authority,* as described by Wrong (1979). The message that is conveyed to children is that it is acceptable to manipulate the behaviour of others to get your own way and to exclude others who do not 'conform' from their activities.

Despite the 'soft language' and the avoidance of words such as 'punishment,' the following, derived from *AD*, is indistinguishable from, 'Do as you are told, or else!' – 'Sarah, you have a choice. Either come outside with me or you will have to go to Mr Boyer's office' (Canter & Canter, 2001, p. 152). The authors maintain that 'corrective actions' should never embarrass or humiliate a student and should not be regarded as punishment, yet keeping a student back from class is considered to be highly effective because, 'That one minute delay really gets to them, believe me. Everybody's moved on and they're left behind' (p. 65).

SWPBS, with its advocacy of milder forms of punishment, such as time out (regarded by the authors as having minimal negative effects), is portrayed as an alternative to more punitive approaches towards school discipline. However, there is no evidence provided in support of these claims and it cannot be assumed that what is intended by adults to be experienced with minimal negative effect is experienced in the same way by children. Khon (2001) sums it up, 'Someone who wants to know whether a given intervention is punitive can find the answer not in a book on discipline but in the child's face' (p. 41).

The over-reliance on hierarchical forms of discipline, particularly as exemplified through the discipline plan in *Assertive Discipline,* almost inevitably leads to an acceleration in exclusionary practices whereby fairly minor infractions of indiscipline (which potentially could have been diffused if a less rigid approach had been adopted) may lead to consequences that are severe for the student, far out of proportion to the initial offence. This is of particular concern when little consideration is given to individual circumstances.

Brief conclusion

There is no doubt that, of the two approaches, *SWPBS* offers a much more sophisticated and comprehensive understanding of the classroom dynamic but its reliance on behaviourist principles and practices is, in my view, its Achilles Heel. Whilst the approach recognises the primacy of relationships in underpinning a climate for learning, somehow or other, in the very detailed processes underpinning the approach and the unquestioning advocacy of tokenistic reward systems (and their alter-ego, naturalistic consequences), the focus on relationships gets lost.

Challenging Orthodoxies: Policy and Practice   139

> **Reflection Point**
>
> Where do you stand on these issues? What influence do you think these two approaches have had in shaping school discipline policies in your country and context?

The discussion to follow explores issues of power and authority as expressed through English and Scottish policy on school discipline. The term student will be used in the English context and pupil in the Scottish context to reflect more normal usage.

School discipline: the policy context in England and Scotland

The policy context in England

As I am writing this chapter, the Guardian proclaims, '"Written off – at five": children in England dumped in unfit "schools"' (Seale, 2021). The journalist reports on the concerns raised by two OFSTED (Office for Standards in Education, Children's Services and Skills) inspectors that children, as young as five, on being permanently excluded from school are being re-allocated to unregistered 'schools,' often 'in unsuitable accommodation, with unqualified staff, and may be receiving little in the way of education.' Whilst the focus of this discussion will not be on *Pupil Referral Units* or other alternative provision, what the discussion seeks to highlight is how we got to this shocking and appalling position in the first place.

Educational policy in England is beset with contradictions. Whilst some claim that the educational policy of the Conservative government (2010-) is 'made up on the hoof,' Percival (2017) argues that it is strongly ideologically bound. A key challenge has been the lack of systematic gathering of data on student behaviour, other than surveys conducted by teaching unions (NUT 2012, Association of Teachers and Lecturers, 2014 and NASUWT 2019), which may be subject to bias. This gap has led to conflicting messages in the media, from OFSTED and the teaching unions, all of which will have their own agenda, with school discipline constantly in the spotlight (MacAllister, 2017).

Social and Emotional Aspects of Learning (SEAL)

A key plank of New Labour (1997–2010) policy was the introduction of the *Social and Emotional Aspects of Learning* (SEAL) *Programme*, a staged-intervention approach to develop key socio-emotional skills in children. Initially introduced in primary schools but thereafter developed in the secondary sector, it offered a flexible package of materials and support to be tailored

140 *Towards New Understandings*

to the needs of individual schools. However, the national evaluation of the programme was equivocal: it had not demonstrated the desired impacts across a range of areas such as social and emotional skills and pro-social behaviour (Humphrey, Lendrum, & Wigelsworth, 2010). The authors identify a range of factors which may have impacted on the implementation, such as a lack of fidelity to the approach, difficulties in sustaining the momentum of the programme, competing imperatives and unrealistic expectations of what could be achieved within the time frame.

A new trajectory

It came as no surprise that the incoming Conservative/Liberal Democrat coalition in 2010 and later Conservative government took policy in a new direction. Given the disdain shown towards 'experts' by the then Secretary of State for Education, Michael Gove, and towards educationalists in general (Tickle & Ratcliffe, 2014) (together with the strong vein of anti-intellectualism within and towards the teaching profession itself [Humes, 2020; Percival, 2017]), it was hardly surprising that the government turned towards the populist commentator and self-professed 'Behaviour Guru' – Tom Bennett, a former columnist in the *Times Educational Supplement* and author – to advise on policy in this area.

Typical of Bennett's response to a problem posed by a teacher struggling to maintain discipline is the following:

> You are doing the right thing: laying down the law, setting the boundaries, then enforcing them. ... If you give up, they will renew their disobedience; if you persist, the clamour will dissipate and you will be gifted with another classroom entirely, one governed by law and structure. It seems far away now, but keep setting detentions, make them severe, make them boring and full of hard work. Make them places no sane pupil would want to be, make the class learn that you will not be crossed, because you care about them and you know that the rules need to be there in order for them to learn. You'll get there. Good luck.
>
> Tom Bennett [Behaviour Guru], TESS, 9th Nov 2012, p. 27

If one digs beneath the bonhomie, and what might be assumed to be a genuine concern for the situation of the teacher, what is revealed is a perspective on students which is at best disrespectful and, at worst, callous. The underlying assumption is that it is only through submission to the will of the teacher that children will behave. His response aligns with Wrong's conceptualisation of power as *force* in which the *authority* of the teacher is an unquestioned right by dint of their role and is exercised through *coercion* (Wrong, 1979). The juxtaposition of care with force and the assumption that effective learning arises through unquestioning adherence to rules is resonant of *authoritarian* approaches to school discipline, as discussed. It is an over-simplistic analysis of the complexity of the situation which takes little or no account of the micro-interactions within the classroom (Pirrie & Rafanell, 2020) and/or of the importance of building relationships within the classroom setting.

Such positioning is not uncharacteristic of the policy landscape at the time in England. Government guidance offered to schools (DfE, 2011b) makes explicit and increases the powers available to schools to 'unequivocally restore[s] adult authority to the classroom' (e-report). However, commentators critique the notion that authority can be built through the use of force (MacLeod, MacAllister, & Pirrie, 2012; Pirrie & Rafanell, 2020). Further policy documents (DfE, 2011a, 2012) reinforce this authoritarian stance on school discipline, the former document portraying authority as 'strategies for controlling unruly behaviour' (Macleod et al., 2012, p. 494), and the latter morphing almost immediately into a discussion of 'poor behaviour,' negating the notion that adults within the setting exhibit behaviour of any consequence (Pirrie & Rafanell, 2020).

MacAllister (2017) is strongly critical of the *Department for Education* (DfE) 2014 report, *Behaviour and Discipline in Schools*, strongly influenced by Tom Bennet's managerial stance. He draws from Bennett's book (T. Bennett, 2010), citing the six key behaviours for teachers, all of which are aimed towards dominating the classroom (justified on the basis that teachers care about their pupils and want them to achieve):

1 It's what you do, not what you say;
2 Act tough;
3 Talk like you expect to be heard;
4 Think about how you move;
5 It's your room;
6 Don't blow your top (p. 17).

It could be argued that all teachers should care about their pupils and want them to achieve and no-one should be arguing for a classroom where anarchy reigns, but is this the learning environment that you would want to create for your classroom? Or, if you are a parent, for your child to experience? There is no sense whatsoever of a classroom as a community with a common purpose or of pupils playing any role in creating such a community.

The DfE report on *Behaviour and Discipline in Schools* (DfE, 2016), the purpose of which is to set out the powers and duties for school staff, has a similar managerial tone, as illustrated in Figure 8.1.

Indeed, relationships, learning, pupil participation and voice, school ethos and climate, *Special Educational Needs and Disabilities* (SEND) and inclusion (other than adherence to legislation and punishment being proportionate), pastoral care and staff development seem to be largely absent from the main body of the document. Parents are referred to only with regard to the clear communication of the policy and expected standards of behaviour and whether or not notice of detention should be offered to them.

Figure 8.1 Word Art representation of *Behaviour and Discipline in Schools*.
Source: DfE (2016).

'Creating a culture: How school leaders can optimise behaviour'

This DfE commissioned report (T. Bennett, 2017) focusses on identifying strategies and themes that can be shared across schools whilst purporting to recognise the saliency of contextual factors. Bennett's research-light report (drawing principally from OFSTED reports and the *Education Endowment Foundation*) identifies themes which are considered to be associated with the most 'successful schools' to be achieved through key strategies, such as 'designing routines that students and staff should follow … which corridor side to walk down, how to queue for lunch' (p. 8). Impediments to 'improvement' are identified but neither 'success,' 'improvement' nor 'management skills' are defined or articulated. Recommendations are forwarded for the DfE to consider, such as the creation of internal 'inclusion' units; making it mandatory for new headteachers to demonstrate their command of 'cultural levers;' and providing training opportunities for senior leaders focussing on 'strategies' and 'best practice' (p. 11).

Bennett advocates that not only should schools seek to influence outward manifestations of pupil behaviour, but they should also seek to influence student character and attitudes (p. 12). The report propagates the notion that it is through the pursuit of better behaviour that better learning can be achieved. There is neither recognition that the learning in which pupils are asked to engage may be deficient in the first instance nor recognition that, indeed, it may be the converse that is the case (in keeping with Head's arguments, see the discussion to follow).

In keeping with *Assertive Discipline*, Bennett claims that the route to autonomy and independence can only be achieved through initial compliance: 'Compliance is only one of several rungs on a behavioural ladder we hope all

Challenging Orthodoxies: Policy and Practice   143

our students will climb, but it is a necessary one to achieve first' (p. 23). There is no evidence whatsoever offered in support of this assertion. Other than a brief reference to a former *Initial Teacher Training* report authored by Bennett, any real consideration that relationships should underpin the culture of the school is distinctly absent. The strategies forwarded in support of building and maintaining the school culture are entirely unproblematised, and there is little acknowledgement of the literature which emphasises more *humanistic* approaches to achieving a positive climate for learning.

Whilst recognising the very hard work that many school leaders and teachers invest in promoting positive behaviour within their schools, the case studies exemplify this authoritarian stance, in some instances propagating a *zero-tolerance* approach to school discipline. Students are exposed to impersonal rules applied to all, regardless of circumstance. For example, in Ebbsfleet Academy, situated in a deprived area of England, it is advocated that there should be 'attention to detail – strict rules, weekly equipment checks, detentions for such things as rubber or pen missing, uniform infractions, colour of hair' (p. 26). For a child living in a dysfunctional home or a home where a parent may have mental health difficulties or may struggle to put food on the table, coming to school without a rubber or pen would be highly unlikely to be a priority for that child or family. Such practices, in my view, are likely to lead to the stigmatisation and marginalisation of the most disadvantaged students.

Even in the examples offered which are indicative of a more humane approach, throughout, there is a sense of the unquestioned authority of the teacher to impose discipline on children. Given the appointment of the 'UK's strictest headteacher,' who believes that children are born with 'original sin,' to head up the UK Government's Social Mobility Unit (D. White, 2021), the resurgence of *zero-tolerance* approaches is hardly surprising. What comes across is a joyless environment where little individuality is afforded to either staff or pupils. The overt use of power to enforce routines, uniformity, 'the ideal school student' (p. 40), even social norms, chimes with Furlong's concerns about the fundamental drive to change people, leading, ultimately, to children rejecting what school has to offer.

The vision of the school is that of an authoritarian institution where things are done *to* students rather than *with* them; where students have little agency or voice; where staff are seen as legal custodians of discipline and where there is no room for dissent (any senior leader who does not buy into the vision [described as 'unsuitable members'] is 'curated' – moved into a different position [p. 32]); where school governors and senior leaders act as the long-arm of the government, rather than primarily serving the interests of their students; and where parents only serve as the recipients of information about the expected standards of behaviour of their children to which they are expected to conform. Within such a context, the *hidden injuries* of schooling will be many and many children will fall by the wayside to be discarded by society as being of little value, as illuminated by the Guardian article, alluded to earlier in the chapter.

144 *Towards New Understandings*

Subsequent developments

In April 2021, as part of a drive for a 'strong behaviour and discipline policy,' Gavin Williamson, the former Secretary of State for Education, announced that termly behaviour surveys would take place in schools (Belger, 2021), supplementing the DfE's behaviour hubs project (partnering up schools with a 'strong record' with those considered to be struggling). The subsequent White Paper, published on the 28th of March, 2022 (DfE, 2022c), proposed that national behaviour surveys should take place annually. In June 2021, the DfE launched a consultation (DfE, 2021) on its approach to behaviour management strategies, in-school units and managed moves. In response to the Timpson review of school exclusion (DfE, 2019b), the focus of which is to ensure that practice is lawful, reasonable, fair and a last resort, and taking cognisance of the *Children in Need Review* (DfE, 2019a), focussing on 1:10 children (over a six-year period) in receipt of statutory social care support, the UK government launched a further consultation on revised *Behaviour in Schools* guidance and *Suspension and Permanent Exclusion* guidance in February 2022 (DfE, 2022b).

The revised guidance on suspensions and permanent exclusions in England (DfE, 2022d) (at the point of writing, still under consultation [DfE, 2022b]) sets out the legal duties of local authorities, governing bodies and schools. As described in Chapter 4, for the first time, the guidance addresses the issue of *off-rolling*, the practice of removing a pupil from the school roll without using a permanent exclusion when the removal is primarily in the best interests of the school rather than the best interests of the pupil (Owen, 2019), highlighting that it is both unacceptable and illegal, and *managed moves* (a pupil being removed from the school register to be registered in another school or off-site provision).

Its companion document – *Behaviour in schools: Advice for headteachers and school staff* (DfE, 2022a) updates the previous guidance (T. Bennett, 2017). However, rather than setting a new direction, if anything the authoritarian tone and top-down approach which characterised *Creating a Culture …* is even more in evidence. The role of members of the school community is understood in restricted and reductionist ways: headteachers formulate, lead, communicate and reinforce the behaviour policy; staff should be trained to ensure that they embody the school's culture; parents support the policy; and pupils obey it. There is no sense of a collaborative approach, based on relationships, trust and building community (see Chapters 11 and 12 to follow). There is an unquestioning stance that the only way to ensure a climate for learning is through the imposition of sanctions and rewards (spelt out in great detail), routines and even the advocacy of teacher scripts (reminiscent of *Assertive Discipline*). In keeping with *zero-tolerance* approaches, we are informed that 'disruption is not tolerated' and schools should have rules with consequences for breaking them.

On a more positive note, there is much greater recognition of meeting the needs of pupils with specific circumstances, such as those with SEND (see sections 33-7), and putting interventions in place, particularly with regard to the safeguarding of the child (see sections 96-100), but the thinking is made clear when an exemplification is offered of 'a pupil with ... dyslexia who may seek to distract from the fact that they find it difficult to access written material' (section 34). This, to me, lies at the heart of the issue. The 'problem' is the child seeking to distract – not the failure of the school to accommodate the learning needs of the child.

There is a failure also to distinguish between consistency ('inconsistency teaches pupils that boundaries are flexible which can encourage further misbehaviour' [section 40]) and fairness and to recognise the need for a responsive approach not only for children with specific circumstances but for *all* pupils that allows teachers to exercise their professional judgement and discretion (as should be the case for a professional workforce), treating each child or young person as an individual. Such a deficit perspective on children is concerning (reminiscent of 'give them an inch and they'll take a mile') and sets up a 'them' and 'us' barrier to the forming of trusting relationships between pupils and teachers. The approach currently advocated is not compatible with the stated aim that the school behaviour policy should be inclusive: the authoritarian stance of this report not only dehumanises, but teaches children (and adults) that they are inconsequential – cogs in a wheel.

As discussed in Chapter 4, despite the heightened attention to SEND, the tendency to see behaviour as a separate entity (Cole, McCluskey, Daniels, Thompson, & Tawell, 2019) is still in evidence and there is a lack of an integrated approach to meeting the needs of children. The report refers to the updated guidance on mental health and behaviour in schools (DfE, 2018a) but, other than the emphasis on creating an orderly and safe environment and the need to give consideration to the specific circumstances of children with mental health issues (e.g., ensuring that a detention does not clash with a medical appointment), there is little emphasis on the wellbeing of children.

This takes place within the context of a sharp increase in the number of children presenting with mental health needs and a decrease in the number of referrals to specialist services during the pandemic (The Children's Commissioner, 2022), despite an increase of 4.4% in NHS spending since 2019/20 in real terms. In contrast to the other jurisdictions in the UK that offer access to counselling services for schools, England does not have statutory counselling services in schools.

The policy context in Scotland

A data-informed system

In contrast to England, the Scottish Government has been gathering data on perceptions of behaviour in schools since the inception of the *Behaviour in Scottish Schools Surveys* in 2006 which was built on the earlier commissioned surveys conducted by the University of Edinburgh in 1990 and 1996 and a broad range of work focussing on alternatives to inclusion (Munn, Lloyd, & Cullen, 2000).

146 *Towards New Understandings*

A key finding of the most recent survey (Black, Eunson, Murray, Zubairi, & Bowen, 2016) is that the strongest predictor of behaviour in Scottish schools is school ethos. The research team found that student behaviour is inextricably bound with school ethos, relationships and engagement in learning, with a positive school ethos being associated with a sense of 'community' or 'family' 'where all pupils, their parents and staff feel known, included, valued, safe, supported and cared for' (p.86). Shared values, strong leadership, communication and openness amongst staff, and account being taken of the views of others, particularly pupils, were also identified as important aspects of school ethos.

In keeping with previous surveys, the majority of staff considered that they encountered good behaviour around the school and in classrooms *all* or *most of the time* and were confident in their ability to create a positive climate for learning. However, concerns were expressed about a perceived increase in low-level indiscipline in primary schools since the previous survey in 2012, attributed principally to the increasing use of digital technologies amongst pupils and changing parent-child relationships. Whilst differences emerged between practices to promote positive behaviour in the primary and secondary sectors, the principal approach adopted in both sectors is the promotion of a positive school ethos and values, supported by *nurture* and *restorative practice.*

Many of the approaches adopted within Scottish schools have much in common with the recommendations of the 2017 DfE report in England (e.g., the use of reward schemes and detention), but the tone of the two reports could not be more different. It is clear that, in Scotland, *the bottom line is respectful and trusting relationships,* very clearly demonstrated in the following aspects of teacher behaviour which were important to pupils: 'being happy/smiling, being enthusiastic, using humour, being calm and not shouting' (p.43).

However, whilst a survey can provide a very valuable overview, it does not cast light on the everyday experiences of staff working in schools at the far end of the spectrum, particularly those schools situated in areas of deprivation, as implied by the factor analysis carried out by the research team. For these schools, the main findings of the report may not hold true. The failure to recognise this issue may lead to a sense of complacency and a failure to direct resources, guidance and support towards these schools.

Scottish policy: from a focus on behaviour to a focus on relationships

In response to concerns about indiscipline and rising exclusion rates in Scottish education at the turn of the millennium, the Scottish Executive set up a *Discipline Task Force* which led to the publication of 'Better Behaviour- Better Learning' (Scottish Executive Education Department, 2001), the premise of which is that, through improving behaviour, better learning will ensue. The report offered 36 recommendations to be implemented nationally, by the local authority and the school, amongst which were the formulation of policies relating to pupil care, welfare and discipline.

The report represented a seismic shift, articulating explicitly that pupils identified as having *Social, Emotional and Behavioural Difficulties* (SEBD) were to be considered as having *Special Educational Needs* (SEN) (a group who to this point had been regarded largely as undeserving of support [Hamill, Boyd, & Grieve, 2002]). Head (2007) argued that, if SEBD is to be regarded as a learning difficulty, then addressing the problem should be treated in the same way as addressing any other learning difficulty – through a focus on learning. Therefore, better learning should foreground better behaviour, rather than the converse.

He critiques the emphasis within the report on 'positive behaviour' and 'positive discipline' (used interchangeably) – expressed through the use of rules, rewards and sanctions, drawing from *behaviourism* and redolent of the work of Canter and Canter, arguing that such approaches are counter to a rights and empowerment agenda which the policy sets out to promote.

In contrast to England, the Scottish Government did not focus on a single approach to promoting positive behaviour (as represented in SEAL in England) but developed a range of approaches that local authorities and schools could take forward, supported by a team of national advisors – latterly, the *Rights, Support and Wellbeing Team*. Thereafter, a series of policy documents promoting positive behaviour and health and wellbeing emanated from the Scottish Government and the associated public body, *Education Scotland*, as set out below.

Positive Behaviour in the Early Years (Dunlop et al., 2008)

This study, conducted in two local authorities in Scotland with 0–6-year olds, established that the vast majority of children were considered to display positive behaviour in early years settings. However, around a fifth of pupils were considered to be presenting with varying degrees of concern, particularly boys. A key recommendation was the incorporation of more challenging and engaging learning activities for children in early years settings, building on the work to promote positive behaviour (Dunlop et al., 2008).

Better Relationships, Better Learning, Better Behaviour (Scottish Government, 2013)

This report emphasises pupil wellbeing to a greater extent than previous reports. However, there is no clear rationale for the foregrounding of relationships and learning as pre-requisites for better behaviour, other than an observation that those learning communities that focussed on social and emotional learning and creating a positive school ethos seemed to fare better. The emphasis is placed on creating a climate for learning rather than on the quality of the learning *per se* as being the pre-requisite for improving behaviour and this has continued to be a feature of subsequent policy documents:

> Developing good relationships and positive behaviour in the classroom, playground and wider community is essential for creating the right environment

148 *Towards New Understandings*

for effective learning and teaching. Where children and young people feel included, respected, safe and secure and when their achievements and contributions are valued and celebrated, they are more likely to develop self-confidence, resilience and positive views about themselves.

(p. 5)

Included, Engaged and Involved (parts 1 and 2)

These two policy documents update and set out the legal obligations of local authorities and schools regarding school attendance and school exclusions, respectively. The latter (Scottish Government, 2017d) has an entirely different tone and emphasis from the equivalent guidance in England (DfE, 2022a), highlighting relationships as being the most critically important aspect of schooling and emphasising the importance of pupil wellbeing. The joined-up thinking that underpins the report is clearly evident in the word-art image that appears at the beginning of the report, reproduced in Figure 8.2. The report explores the negative impact of school exclusion on children, on their attainment and involvement with the criminal justice system, and advocates a preventative approach, focussing on early and staged intervention (linking to *Getting it Right for Every Child*

Figure 8.2 Illustration from *Included, Engaged and Involved* (Part 2).

Source: Scottish Government (2017d), reproduced with permission from the Scottish Government.

[GIRFEC] [see Chapter 9]) and a responsive approach which takes account of individual circumstance, emphasising that exclusion should be a last resort.

Developing a Positive Whole-School Ethos and Culture – Relationships, Learning and Behaviour (Scottish Government, 2018a)

This policy document (Scottish Government, 2018a), drawing from the 2016 survey and from a children's rights perspective, foregrounds the promotion of positive relationships and behaviour in order to improve schools' ethos and culture. It could be argued, however, that this is a reciprocal, rather than a uni-directional, relationship. Drawing on 'research' (unspecified), the report advocates for an 'authoritative school climate' in which high expectations and structure are balanced with warmth and support, on the basis that such a climate is correlated with higher attainment and better pupil wellbeing.

A comparison between policy documents

A simple content analysis of the various policy documents reveals some interesting findings, as illustrated in Charts 8.1–8.5.

Whilst recognising that this is an over-simplistic way to examine these policy documents, the dominance of 'behaviour' in contrast to 'learning' and 'relationships' is marked in both the *Early Years* (Dunlop et al., 2008) and 2013 policy documents (Scottish Government, 2013), despite the foregrounding of 'relationships' and 'learning' in the title of the latter. However, relationships feature to a much greater extent than in the initial policy document (Scottish

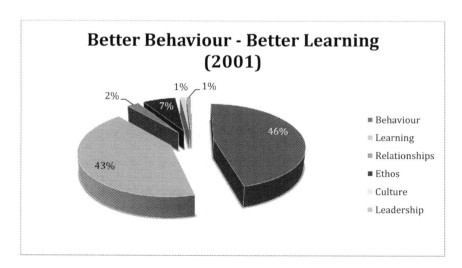

Chart 8.1 Content analysis of *Better Behaviour – Better Learning* (Scottish Executive Education Department, 2001).

150 *Towards New Understandings*

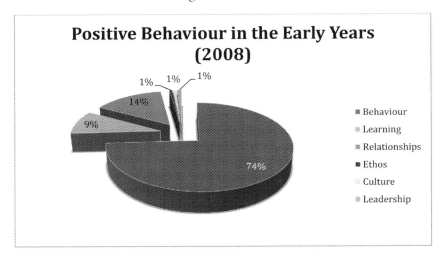

Chart 8.2 Content analysis of *Positive Behaviour in the Early Years* (Dunlop et al., 2008).

Executive Education Department, 2001) in subsequent policy guidance. Given the importance that is attached to school ethos and the role of leadership in creating a shared vision and culture for learning in the school, as exemplified in the *National Improvement Framework* (Scottish Government, 2020c), it is surprising how little these feature, even in later policy documents.

The more recent emphasis on *trauma-informed practice* in Scottish schools (Education Scotland, 2017a; Public Health Scotland, 2017), supported by the funding of a national development officer (Scottish Government, 2018a) to develop an understanding of the impact of trauma, stress, bereavement and loss on children, is intended to lead to a more caring and compassionate approach in working with children.

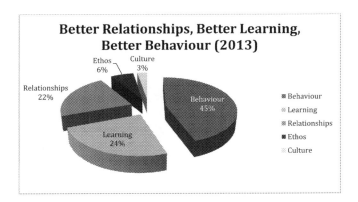

Chart 8.3 Content analysis of *Better Relationships, Better Learning, Better Behaviour* (Scottish Government, 2013).

Challenging Orthodoxies: Policy and Practice 151

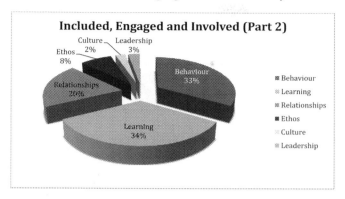

Chart 8.4 Content analysis of *Included, Engaged and Involved* (Scottish Government, 2017d).

These developments should not be seen in isolation from the policy framework and legislation relating to *Additional Support Needs* (as outlined in Chapter 2); *Curriculum for Excellence; Getting it Right for Every Child* (GIRFEC); the *Rights Respecting Schools* agenda and non-statutory guidance offered to schools on the incorporation of the UNCRC (*United Nations Convention on the Rights of the Child*) in Scotland (Scottish Government, 2021c); and interventions to support positive mental health, such as the Scottish Government's commitment to placing a counsellor in each secondary school (Scottish Government, 2020a). Nor should they be considered in isolation from the *Professional Standards for Scottish Teachers* (2021) (GTCS, 2021) which place a clear responsibility upon all teachers, student teachers and school leaders to promote positive relationships and behaviour and contribute towards the creation of a positive school ethos.

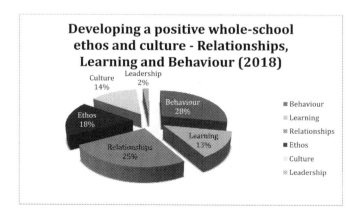

Chart 8.5 Content analysis of *Developing a Positive Whole-School Ethos and Culture: Relationships, Learning and Behaviour* (Scottish Government, 2018a).

152 *Towards New Understandings*

A synthesis

It will be evident in the discussion to this point that there clearly is a different narrative at play in the policy rhetoric of each nation and this may go some way to explaining the different outcomes in terms of school exclusions (Cole et al., 2019; McCluskey, Cole, Daniels, Thompson, & Tawell, 2019). It is evident that, in Scotland, there is a greater emphasis on a holistic and integrated approach across different aspects of education and public policy. There is a danger, however, in seeing the approaches adopted towards school discipline and behaviour management in the two nations as polarities – the commonalities may be greater than the differences. It would be wrong to imply that 'everything in the garden is rosy' in Scottish schools regarding school discipline but what is more in evidence is a greater consensus between policymakers and practitioners, a much clearer roadmap for the way forward and a focus on relational approaches. Key issues to emerge relate to how the teaching profession is regarded in each nation, teacher professionalism, agency and autonomy. These will be picked up in the final chapter.

Conclusion

It is very tempting when faced with concerns in the media and wider society regarding 'youth in crisis' and mounting concerns about school indiscipline to call for 'more of the same' – tougher sanctions, rigid discipline policies and to see the solution as resting in a 'carrot and stick' approach. I hope that this chapter will have encouraged deeper reflection on these matters. I would draw readers' attention to the words of Detective Chief Superintendent John Carnahan (CALA Childhood Practice, 2013), former head of the *Violence Reduction Unit* in Glasgow which focussed on reducing knife crime, who cautioned that 'you can't police your way out of this problem; locking people up is not the answer to this,' advocating that the way to achieve a reduction in violence is to invest in the early years.

Similarly, the way to improve behaviour in schools is to invest in children and in the workforce, ensuring that they have the highest quality, professionally-trained teachers in front of them who teach with a sense of social justice, care and compassion and with children's rights to the forefront, able to exercise their professional judgement, a theme that will be developed further in the final chapter. The chapters to follow explore *relational* approaches to building community in schools.

Reflection Point

What influence do you consider public policy has in terms of framing understanding of this complex issue and responses to it? Do you agree with the arguments forwarded in the second half of the chapter? If not, why not? What arguments (and evidence) would you bring to bear on the problem?

> **Additional Suggested Reading**
>
> *Positive Behavior Support in Secondary Schools: A Practical Guide*
>
> *The Guilford Press, 2012. Ellie Young, Paul Caldarella, Michael Richardson and Richard Young*
>
> This book provides a comprehensive and detailed account of Positive Behaviour in Schools on a schoolwide basis as applied within the Secondary school.
>
> *Beyond Discipline: From Compliance to Community*
>
> *Merrill Education/Prentice-Hall, 2001, Alfie Khon*
>
> Whilst this book was published some time ago, it is one of the most influential texts critiquing *authoritarian* approaches to school discipline, arguing that the focus should be, instead, on fostering community.
>
> *Using Support Groups to Improve Behaviour*
>
> *Sage Publications, 2008. Joan G Mowat*
>
> This is my own book that describes a targeted approach to supporting the socio-emotional learning of pupils in a secondary school through a social constructivist approach. The book provides practical guidance for implementation and a CD of materials. The evaluation of the work formed the basis of my PhD – 'Teaching for Understanding within the Affective Field,' strongly influenced by the work of Emeritus Professor David Perkins, Harvard University and Howard Gardner's work on Multiple Intelligence Theory. The approach was developed further and implemented in primary schools with a grant from the Esmée Fairbairn Foundation.
>
> *Please see suggested additional reading for Chapter 7.*

Notes

1. The *Education Endowment Foundation* in the UK, similarly, found little evidence in support of the efficacy of *zero-tolerance* approaches, yet they seem to be in the ascendancy in England.
2. *Educational Leadership*, published by the Association for Supervision and Curriculum Development (ASCD).
3. For a discussion of *Applied Behaviour Analysis*, see Porter (2006), chapter 3.

9 Building Community through Nurture and Trauma-Informed Practice

---

Goals for Understanding

  I. How can a climate for learning be created that is not based upon behaviourist approaches and/or rigid systems of discipline but upon building relationships and community?
 II. How might nurture and trauma-informed practice inform our understanding of how to build community in schools and meet individual needs?
III. What role can multi-agency/interdisciplinary working play in the process and what are the facilitators and barriers to success?

This chapter is the first of two chapters focussing on *relational* approaches to building community within the school, exploring how we can create a climate for learning that is not based upon *behaviourist* approaches or rigid systems of discipline. A *relational* school 'puts creating and strengthening the ties of human connection as its number one goal, something that is written through its policies and actions' (Finnis, 2021, p. 2). *Relational* approaches are founded on *humanism*. The chapter examines and critiques two key approaches – nurture and trauma-informed practice. It concludes with an exploration of multi-agency/interdisciplinary working in meeting individual needs.

Humanism

Humanism has its roots in the progressive education movement, associated with theorists such as John Dewey (Porter, 2006), and is reflected in contemporary pedagogical approaches such as cooperative learning. It was developed further in the person-centred therapy of Carl Rogers (M. Cooper, O'Hara, Schmid, & Wyatt, 2007), founded on *relational* approaches to working with people. According to the tenets of *person-centred therapy*, if the right conditions prevail and people are treated in a 'fundamentally positive, respectful and empathetic way,' they will 'grow in a positive, pro-social direction' (p. 57) in a process of

DOI: 10.4324/9780429467110-13

Building Community through Nurture and Trauma-Informed Practice   155

self-actualisation (Bohart, 2007). It is a model based on growth and development (not on deficit perspectives), which, in turn, is based on the characteristics of:

a   Congruence (the individual is at one with himself/herself);
b   Care – unconditional positive regard (non-judgemental and not conditional on behaviour – 'If, then') (see Chapter 4);
c   Empathy.

Compassion

Care and compassion lie at the heart of the two approaches under consideration in this chapter – nurture and trauma-informed practice. Yet, compassion features little in the educational literature (Oplatka & Gamerman, 2021). Compassion constitutes an awareness of the suffering of others, an empathetic concern but also a desire to alleviate such suffering (Bartholomay, 2022; Oplatka & Gamerman, 2021). Carla Shalaby (McKibben, 2021) and Causton, MacLeod, and Pretti-Frontczak (2021) make a case for *compassionate discipline*, the latter presenting a three-part framework founded on love, kindness and compassion.

School ethos and climate

There is an extensive literature which points to the importance of school ethos and climate in creating the conditions for promoting equitable and inclusive learning communities based on authentic and trusting relationships (Botha & Kourkoutas, 2016; L. Darling-Hammond & DePaoli, 2020; Lopez, 2017; Mowat, 2010a; Munn et al., 2009; O'Donovan, Berman, & Wierenga, 2015). Such an approach calls for collaboration (Mulholland & O'Connor, 2016) and a focus upon building community (Botha & Kourkoutas, 2016; Kohn, 2001; Sergiovanni, 1994).

Tew and Park (2013) claim that the behaviour of individual pupils arises from an interaction between their personal histories and their experience of school life, the latter shaped by the ethos of the school, expressed through the formal and hidden curriculum. School climate, as defined by the *Organisation for Economic Cooperation and Development* (OECD), relates to:

> ... the quality of social relations between students and teachers (including the quality of support teachers give to students), which is known to have a direct influence on motivational factors, such as student commitment to school, learning motivation and student satisfaction, and perhaps a more indirect influence on student achievement.
>
> (OECD, 2009, p. 91)

The discussion to follow focusses on the two aforementioned *relational* approaches to promoting a positive climate for learning. Please refer to the discussion of developmental theories in Chapter 6.

156 *Towards New Understandings*

Nurture

Nurture groups first emerged in the 1970s in London, developed through the pioneering work of Marjorie Boxall in response to concerns about large numbers of vulnerable children entering the school system with emotional and behavioural needs (Nolan, Hannah, Lakin, & Topping, 2021). P. Cooper (2004), citing Bennathan and Boxall (2000), defines the nurture group as '... a school-based learning environment specifically designed for pupils whose difficulties in accessing school-learning are underpinned by an apparent need for social and individual experiences that can be construed in terms of unmet early learning needs' (p. 176).

This discussion initially focusses on the traditional manifestation of nurture – nurture groups – before exploring the phenomenon of nurture as a whole school approach.

Nurture: the six principles

The six nurture principles are informed by attachment theory but other theories, such as *sociocultural theory*, have also informed practice in schools (P. Cooper, 2004; Garner & Thomas, 2011; Lyons, 2017).

Children's learning is understood developmentally

On the basis that children's socio-emotional development, even from infancy (Dunn, 2000), is inextricably linked with their cognitive development (Colley, 2012; Wilson & Wilson, 2015) and, in keeping with *sociocultural theory* (Vygotsky and Bruner) and Piaget's *cognitive developmental stage theory*,[1] this principle recognises that there may be a disparity between the stage of development which would normally be associated with the child's chronological age and their socio-emotional development (P. Cooper, 2004; Wilson & Wilson, 2015). The nurture group serves to facilitate the stages of development that may have been missed due to *insecure attachment* by providing enriching, nurturing learning experiences within a child-centred environment (P. Cooper, 2004; Greenwood, 2020).

The classroom offers a safe base

Central tenets of attachment theory are the role that the caregiver provides in creating a safe base from which the child can securely explore their world (Gillibrand, Lam, & O'Donnell, 2011; Newman & Newman, 2016; Robinson, 2014) and the *attunement* of the caregiver to the needs of the child (Cubeddu & MacKay, 2017; Gerhardt, 2004, 2013; Lyons-Ruth, 2007).

Maslow's theory of motivation (Maslow, 1970) sets out a hierarchical structure of dependency that needs to be overtaken cumulatively if a child is to reach their full potential (Wilson & Wilson, 2015). For an infant for whom physiological,

Building Community through Nurture and Trauma-Informed Practice   157

safety, security and connectedness needs have not been met, or have been met inconsistently (*insecure resistant attachment*), their *mental* (or *internal working*) *model* of the world, expectations of how people will behave towards them and their neurological responses to perceived threat are very different from a *securely* attached child (Couture, 2013; Gerhardt, 2004, 2013; Hughes & Schlösser, 2014; Wilson & Wilson, 2015). Such children may exhibit patterns of *avoidant* (avoiding closeness and relationships) or *resistant/ambivalent* (both clinging and resisting) behaviours associated with *insecure* attachment (Greenwood, 2020).

The regular routines of the nurture group setting and the positive relationships that arise between teacher and pupil through sensibility to the needs of the child and emotional proximity create a sense of safety and security, facilitating positive outcomes for children (Couture, 2013; Greenwood, 2020).

Nurture is important for the development of wellbeing

Early attachment patterns and the degree of *attunement* between caregiver and child (see Chapter 6) determine the degree to which the infant is able to regulate their emotions effectively (Gerhardt, 2004, 2013; Lyons-Ruth, 2007), impacting also on the stress and anxiety levels of the child (Bender, Sømhovd, Pons, Reinholdt-Dunne, & Esbjørn, 2015; Gerhardt, 2004, 2013). The nurture setting affords the building of trusting relationships with an attachment-figure who can model pro-social behaviours (Bandura, 1997) and *scaffold* the learning of the child (Doyle, 2004) (a reference to *sociocultural theory*) within an emotionally secure environment.

Language is understood as a vital means of communication

Sociocultural theory stresses the important role of social contexts in learning and the role that *cultural tools* play in the process, key among which is language (Learoyd-Smith & Daniels, 2014; Newman & Newman, 2016; Pritchard & Woolard, 2010). As language develops in the infant, the child's sense of self is greatly enhanced and it becomes an important mental tool, enabling children as they grow to think more clearly about their own emotions and those of others (Wilson & Wilson, 2015).

Language is important in helping children to come to an understanding of their world, both emotionally and socially, and to *internalise* the natural order of things. It also facilitates emotional communication, a central aspect of good relationships. It is through language and dialogue within the family unit that infants develop a moral sense, become *attuned* to the feelings of others and develop social understanding (Bennathan, 2013; Dunn, 2000, 2004). Dialogue plays an important role in supporting children and young people (C&YP) with *Social, Emotional and Behavioural Needs* (SEBN)/*Social, Emotional and Mental Health Needs* (SEMHN) through *relational* approaches such as nurture (Hibbin & Warin, 2020), setting appropriate boundaries for behaviour (Greenwood, 2020).

158 *Towards New Understandings*

All behaviour is communication

This is perhaps one of the most important principles as it reframes how children's behaviour is understood (and therefore how adults should respond to them). Rather than behaviour being framed in terms of 'mad, bad or sad' (Macleod, 2006b; Sinclair, 2005), all behaviour is understood as a needs-based form of communication (Hibbin & Warin, 2020). Behaviour is an outward expression of inner states and is a form of unconscious communication (Greenwood, 2020). This is portrayed very effectively on the cover of Greenwood's book – a child with his head in his hands over his desk with the subtitle, 'Why can't you hear me?' An important implication is that the non-verbal cues of C&YP are just as important as any verbal communication.

Greenwood has created a framework of observed behaviours, their possible meanings and possible causes. For example, a child who is always finding fault or criticising others could be understood as easing their own feelings of not being good enough, a response to hurtful criticism of the child in the past (Greenwood, 2020, App 3). However, it would be important to exert caution, as there could be a potential danger of reading too much into or misinterpreting children's behaviour.

Transitions are significant in the lives of children

Transitions are an inevitable part of life and a natural process (J. M. Davis, Ravenscroft, & Bizas, 2015; Greenwood, 2020). The degree to which children are able to cope with the transitions in their lives (whether big or small) and grow from them is dependent on the degree of support they have experienced with regard to previous transitions and the opportunity presented to process the transition through supportive dialogue (Greenwood, 2020). For children with a *chaotic/disorganised* pattern of attachment, any change in routine, such as the absence of a teacher, can provoke a panic reaction and disruptive behaviour (Greenwood, 2020). The established routines of the nurture setting and the *scaffolding* of change by adults help the child to anticipate and cope with the transitions they face and provide an opportunity for children to process the associated changes through dialogue (Greenwood, 2020).

Nurture in action

Since the inception of nurture groups in the 1970s, different models of nurture have emerged. There are deviations from the classic model, which are described as variants.

The 'Classic' nurture group

The 'classic' nurture group generally consists of a special unit of up to 12 children, aged four-to-eight years, in a mainstream school, staffed by two adults (a teacher and a teaching assistant) who create a nurturing environment

Building Community through Nurture and Trauma-Informed Practice 159

and act as role models for the children in the nurture group. Children attend the unit for a short-term, fixed duration after which they will be integrated back into the mainstream classroom. The groups generally run for four-and-a-half-days a week and provide a structured intervention that offers opportunities for *social and emotional learning*, curriculum-based tasks and play (Nolan et al., 2021). The setting is usually equipped with soft furnishings, a book corner, toy storage and role-play materials (Kourmoulaki, 2013). The provision of food serves both a physiological and symbolic function (Boxall, 2013). Children in the nurture group maintain contact with children within their class throughout the intervention, with contact increasing as they re-integrate into the mainstream classroom (P. Cooper, 2004; Hughes & Schlösser, 2014).

The Boxall profile

A key aspect of nurture is the use of the Boxall profile – a normative diagnostic instrument (Bennathan & Boxall, 2013) which assesses the social, emotional and behavioural functioning of the child, including academic engagement (Colley, 2009), in order to plan for focussed intervention (Allison & Craig, 2014). The Boxall profile provides a framework for structured observation of children in the classroom that is completed by professionals who know the child best. It consists of two sections: the *Developmental Strands* and the *Diagnostic Profile*, each constituting 34 items from which an individual pupil profile is created, showing areas of strength and developmental needs (Allison & Craig, 2014).

Variant models of nurture

Over time, variants of the 'classic' nurture approach have developed, such as part-time provision (Cooke, Yeomans, & Parkes, 2008) and adaptations to the approach for secondary settings (Colley, 2009, 2012; Colley & Seymour, 2021; Garner & Thomas, 2011; Kourmoulaki, 2013). The latter draws on insights from psychological developmental theory, neuroscience and attachment theory to focus on the developmental needs of adolescents (Choudhury, Charman, & Blakemore, 2008; Cooke et al., 2008; Garner & Thomas, 2011). Colley (2009) and Garner and Thomas (2011) identify features of secondary nurture provision which distinguish it from the 'classic' nurture model, set out in Table 9.1.

Some of these variants may raise issues about fidelity to the principles and practice of the 'classic' nurture group (Garner & Thomas, 2011; Grantham & Primrose, 2017), but it could also be argued that it is important for initiatives and interventions to be responsive to differing and changing contexts and needs and, as argued by Cefai and Cooper (2011), culture. Increasingly, there is a focus on nurture as a whole-school initiative, informed by nurture principles (M. Coleman, 2020; Nolan et al., 2021; Warin, 2017).

160 *Towards New Understandings*

Table 9.1 Features of secondary nurture which make it distinctive

Colley (2009)	Garner and Thomas (2011)
Nurture serving as part of a broader framework of support	Relationships between nurture staff and pupils are on a more equitable footing, based on mutual respect rather than a nurturing role
Reflecting the needs and concerns of adolescents	A greater focus on *social and emotional learning*
Part-time attendance	The secure base had a broader function of support
Credibility derived from success	A need for extended support beyond intervention to combat a lack of support from the wider school and home
The safe base may represent multiple locations	

Source: Colley (2009) and Garner and Thomas (2011).

Nurture as a whole-school approach

In keeping with a more general trend towards universal rather than targeted approaches towards supporting the mental health and wellbeing of C&YP, there has been a movement towards whole-school nurturing approaches, often in parallel with the operation of nurture groups within the school. Hybrid models emerge, such as an approach described by Webber (2017) which integrates attachment theory with the PACE (playfulness, acceptance, curiosity and empathy) framework.

The attention on nurturing schools has manifested itself not only at the level of the individual school but also in national and local authority initiatives. For example, the Scottish Government has produced a set of national guidelines and a framework for evaluation (Education Scotland, 2018) to inform the implementation of whole-school approaches to nurture in Scottish schools that integrate policies such as *Getting it Right for Every Child* (see the discussion to follow) with nurture principles and practice. Local authorities, such as Glasgow City Council (Education Scotland, 2018; Grantham & Primrose, 2017) and Renfrewshire (Carleton, Nolan, Murray, & Menary, 2021) have been highly proactive in developing nurturing approaches within their schools.

P. Cooper and Whitebread (2007) found that the positive impact of the nurture group extends beyond the group itself. In schools that had nurture provision, pupils with SEBN who did not attend the nurture group fared better than in schools without. The authors attribute this to the dialogue between nurture and mainstream staff but H. Bennett (2015) cautions that the effects may not be attributable solely to the nurture group.

Whilst acknowledging the disparity between the affordances of a small-group setting and a mainstream classroom, Cubeddu and MacKay (2017) found that nurture teachers more frequently and consistently *attuned* to the learning and emotional needs of their pupils than did classroom teachers. Drawing from MacKay (2015), they forward a research agenda for nurture in education, which, I suggest, could also operate as a model for nurture provision, taking account of differing levels of need. A simplified version, focussing on the latter, is set out in Figure 9.1.

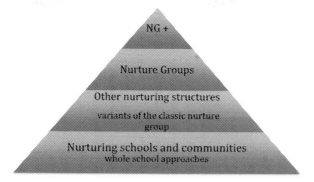

Figure 9.1 Modification of MacKay's (2015) research agenda for nurture in education.
Source: MacKay (2015), cited in Cubeddu and MacKay (2017).

The importance of school leadership in creating a culture of shared nurturing values (Warin, 2017), committed and attuned to nurture principles (M. Coleman, 2020), is identified as a key variable for success.

A focus on impact

The 'classic' nurture group and its variants

Two of the more recent literature reviews of nurture groups in both primary and secondary settings establish that provision had had a positive impact in addressing SEBN/SEMHN, at least in the short term. However, the authors observe that there are few longitudinal studies that follow the progress of C&YP beyond intervention (H. Bennett, 2015; Hughes & Schlösser, 2014) and issues emerged around the research design, rigour and transparency of some studies (Hughes & Schlösser, 2014).

Hughes and Schlösser (2014) found significant improvement in at least some of the strands of the Boxall profile, though this varied from study to study and according to age and stage. Some of the findings between studies were contradictory. The authors took account of the rigour of the studies in balancing various perspectives.

H. Bennett (2015) found that nurture groups had impacted on all levels of the system, from the individual to the societal level as set out in Table 9.2. However, the author argues that effects at the school level should be treated with caution as schools investing in nurture groups may already have a more positive ethos in the first instance, being more disposed towards *relational* approaches.

The greatest improvements relate to the *developmental* rather than the *diagnostic* strand of the Boxall profile, suggesting that children with challenges within this strand are likely to derive the greatest benefit from nurture provision (H. Bennett, 2015).

162 *Towards New Understandings*

Table 9.2 Impact of nurture groups classified according to level

Level of impact	Nature of impact
Individual level	Reduction in acting out behaviours
	Increased self-regulation
	Less likely to be excluded
School level	Benefits extended to children with SEBN beyond the nurture setting
	Increased capacity to support children with SEBN
	Increased commitment from staff in their work and professional learning opportunities
	More flexible and responsive pedagogy
	A respite from children participating in nurture groups creating a calmer classroom for all
Home–school interface	Positive impact extended into home
	Teachers able to exert a positive influence on children's behaviour despite continuing negative influences at home
Societal level	A cost-effective intervention in comparison to residential placement for children with SEBN.

Source: H. Bennett (2015).

The conditions that were identified as influencing outcomes related to the characteristics of the children themselves; the composition of the nurture group, teacher characteristics, its size; the provenance of the nurture group, nature ('classic' or part-time) and duration; and the degree of integration with the wider school – commitment to pupils' needs, quality of relationships, collaboration, leadership (the creation of a vision for change) and communication (H. Bennett, 2015).

Nurture as a whole-school approach

Nolan et al. (2021), in a systematic review of the literature, found that the research which focussed specifically on whole-school approaches was sparse and 'generally poor in quality, lacking clear evidence and tending to the anecdotal' (p. 22), with no evidence of follow-up beyond intervention. The authors identify characteristics of a whole-school nurturing approach, among which are 'a positive role model from teachers' and 'incorporation of attunement, warmth and connection' (p. 12).

Critique of nurture

Whilst it is evident that nurture has much to offer children, families and schools, the robustness of the evidence base, particularly as it applies to variants of nurture, secondary nurture and whole-school nurturing approaches, needs to be considerably strengthened, with some papers having almost an evangelical tone.

Building Community through Nurture and Trauma-Informed Practice   163

There is insufficient attention directed towards the issue of transferability and sustainability of learning beyond the nurture setting,[2] compounded by a lack of longitudinal studies.

However, the key concern of commentators is the deficit perspective on parents/caregivers and the failure to adopt a more ecological perspective which may potentially offer alternative explanations for children's behaviour, including the environment of the school itself. There is a danger that any manifestation of behaviour, which is perceived as being outwith the norm, will be rationalised in terms of attachment theory, whether or not this is appropriate. The over-reliance on teacher judgement, and the accordant lack of triangulation, not recognising the subjectivity inherent within this, is problematic.

There is insufficient heed paid to the literature relating to inclusive education that draws attention to the potential drawbacks of identifying children as being in need of additional support and excluding them from mainstream activities and class. Although it could be argued that this should be balanced with the potential benefits which may not be potentiated within the setting of a mainstream class (Mowat, 2015a) and the dangers of not intervening (Kauffman, 2005), at the very least, these concerns should be acknowledged and addressed within the nurture literature to a much greater extent (see Chapters 2 and 4).

The more recent focus on nurturing schools is to be welcomed and may act as a counter to the above, however, there is a danger that the term becomes all-embracing and fidelity to the nurture principles then becomes an issue, serving to undermine, rather than further, nurture in schools. There perhaps needs to be an additional category added to MacKay's model (Cubeddu & MacKay, 2017) which reflects this concern – that of nurture-informed practice.

Trauma-informed practice

In parallel with the growth of nurture in schools, there has been a focus on trauma-informed practice. This was fuelled initially by the work of Felitti, Anda, and Nordenberg (1998) in the USA on _Adverse Childhood Experiences_ (ACEs) which established a correlation between childhood trauma and a range of adverse experiences in later life, expressed in health and social inequalities. The study identified ten ACEs, classified under _abuse, neglect_ and _household adversities._ The total number of adversities reported by an individual determines their ACEs score. Trauma-informed practice has also been informed by insights into the physiological changes that take place in the body in response to early experiences of trauma or stress and how these shape brain development and the activity of related stress hormones (Gerhardt, 2004, 2013; Greenwood, 2020).

The lines between trauma-informed practice and nurture are blurred. For example, much of the rationale provided for a focus on whole-school nurturing approaches by Nolan et al. (2021) is located within concerns relating to trauma, yet _insecure_ attachment is not one of the ten ACEs identified by Felitti and colleagues. It could be argued that _insecure_ attachment can potentially be a pre-cursor for neglect and abuse or arise from household adversity (such as

164 *Towards New Understandings*

mental illness), but it could not be argued that this is always the case. This is not to deny that *insecure attachment* is likely to be experienced traumatically by the individual child and Greenwood (2020) and Gerhardt (2004, 2013) make a very strong case for this. The Scottish Government has provided guidance for schools, drawing out the relationships between nurture, ACEs and trauma-informed practice in schools (Education Scotland, 2017a).

The relationship between ACEs and deprivation

ACEs have been shown to be more prevalent in areas of deprivation (Couper & Mackie, 2016; Lacey, Howe, Kelly-Irving, Bartley, & Kelly, 2020; Marryat & Frank, 2019; Public Health Scotland, 2017; D. Walsh, McCartney, Smith, & Armour, 2019a). As discussed in Chapter 3, Marryat and Frank (2019), in one of the few studies examining ACEs in children, found that they were highly correlated with socio-economic disadvantage in the first year of life. Children coming from the most deprived homes were 10 times more likely to have 4+ ACEs than children from the least deprived homes. Other variables which made it more likely that a child had 4+ ACEs were gender (male), born of younger mothers and living in an urban environment.

A clear relationship between the risk of experiencing ACEs or maltreatment and socio-economic position (SEP) has been established. This holds true across different countries, different measures of ACEs and SEP, and the age at which ACEs are measured. It is an area that has been significantly under-researched (D. Walsh et al., 2019a). One exception is the more recent study conducted by Lacey et al. (2020), drawing on data from the *Avon Longitudinal Study of Parents and Children* (ALSPAC) from cohort 1991–1992. The research team examined the data to identify clusters of ACEs and the associations between the clusters and poverty and gender. Poverty was associated with the likelihood of all of the individual ACEs, with the exception of the death of a close family member. Children in poverty were more likely to experience multiple adversities. The strongest relationships were with sexual abuse, mother's mental health problems and parental separation.

The effects of unsupported trauma

Greenwood (2020) examines, in depth, the effects of unsupported trauma, whether relating to abuse, neglect, looked after children or those exposed to domestic abuse. She identifies unconscious processes that arise when trauma is experienced, such as *repression,* when ideas, experiences and impulses, in response to trauma, are automatically pushed into the unconscious and therefore 'not known' or remembered, but which may be expressed in other ways, such as acting out (p. 48).

She highlights the importance of *emotional containment* – 'the experience of being and feeling held and understood, or thoughtfully "wondered about" in someone's (initially the mother's) mind' (p. 58) – in young children as they

Building Community through Nurture and Trauma-Informed Practice 165

develop, and the role of the caregiver in this process. Such a process fosters emotional capacity and security, mediating brain function related to the child's experiences. It is dependent on the caregiver's capacity to offer such experiences, taking on board the anxiety or pain of the child. Children who experience *emotional containment* develop the capacity to contain emotional experience, and to think and talk about it, essential for the processing of such experiences. This provides them with the resilience to withstand trauma.

Practice and impact

As trauma-informed practice takes many forms, it is not possible to provide a definitive account of how it is operationalised. The boundaries between trauma-informed practice and *social and emotional learning* can be loose. Much of the earlier literature (which tends to emanate from the USA) focusses not so much on practice with children but on the professional development of staff (Cohen & Barron, 2021; Douglass, Chickerella, & Maroney, 2021; Koslouski & Stark, 2021). The work on developing a systems or schoolwide approach to developing trauma-informed practice is in its infancy and little researched (Chafouleas, Pickens, & Gherardi, 2021; Cohen & Barron, 2021; Koslouski & Stark, 2021). A literature review of trauma-informed high schools in the USA (Cohen & Barron, 2021) found a lack of rigour in study design and little commonality between the studies, approaches adopted within schools and outcomes. However, Chafouleas et al. (2021) consider that the groundwork has been laid in creating a trauma-informed framework which 'integrates a whole child, culturally responsive, and healing-centred system approach' (p. 221) in K12[3] settings in the USA.

Critique of trauma-informed practice

One of the key criticisms of trauma-informed practice is its decontextualised nature (Chafouleas et al., 2021; D. Walsh et al., 2019a; G. M. Walsh, 2020), leading to a failure to consider the socially situated nature of trauma likely to impact C&YP (e.g., racism, homophobia) (Chafouleas et al., 2021). As such, the opportunity to probe the social structures that contribute to these experiences and how they may be perpetuated within the school environment is often missed. The individualisation of the problem depicts families and pupils as being in deficit – as damaged or deficient (Chafouleas et al., 2021), whilst paying 'limited attention to features of system implementation within schools or influences from outside of schools (socio-ecological, cultural context)' (p.5).

D. Walsh et al. (2019a), drawing from Bywaters, Bunting, and Davidson (2015), cite the 'lack of joined up thinking about poverty and child abuse and neglect in the UK' (p. 1091). On the basis that poverty and socio-economic inequality are underlying causes of ACEs (Lacey et al., 2020), they allude to the current debate as to whether poverty should be regarded as an ACE,

166 *Towards New Understandings*

an argument that has been dismissed by others as 'conceptually muddled,' relating to issues around causality (Treanor, 2019) (see Chapter 3).

Further, a range of commentators make the case that the ACEs score approach is flawed – it treats all adversities as being of equal weighting, irrespective of their nature, severity or context, and pays scant attention to the patterning of adversities and the importance of this for student outcomes (Lacey et al., 2020). Nor is there recognition of the potential danger of pathologising what might be regarded as normal behaviours in response to trauma (Mowat, 2019a).

Teachers are neither clinicians nor psychotherapists, nor should they be. Whilst many are well-intentioned, an unthinking application of ACEs theory could reinforce deterministic thinking about children and families, leading to labels such as 'ACEs kids' and 'He's got 4,' and a lowering of teacher expectations. As argued above, the individualisation of the problem and the failure to examine the life of the child in the round, recognising the complex interactions of the ecosystem of which he or she is a part, leads almost inevitably to a focus on 'fixing the child,' rather than focussing on building resilient communities.

No matter the debates surrounding ACEs theory and practice and the argument that the ACEs movement is 'a simplistic solution to complex social problems' (G. M. Walsh, 2000, p. 456), a *relational* and compassionate approach to supporting children who, for any reason, have experienced adversity in their lives can only be welcomed. This, however, needs to be accompanied by an equal focus on social and economic policy to lift families out of poverty and address inequalities in society, as argued by D. Walsh et al. (2019a), and the adoption of a bio-ecological perspective and response (c.c. Box 9.1).

Box 9.1

Case study

Addison, Casimir, Mims, Kaler-Jones, and Simmons (2021) explore how a trauma-informed, equitable and culturally responsive approach to mindfulness can impact positively on student wellbeing. Drawing on their experience, they describe the start of the school day for Rachel (a fictional character), a 7th former who is excited to be going to school. After experiencing a school culture characterised by over-surveillance – 'Bell rings in one minute' … '25 SECONDS!'. 'Late. Your weren't in your seat at the bell' – 'The teacher then instructs the class to close their eyes, imagine their favourite place to be, and take three deep breaths' – Rachel is no longer excited by school. The authors draw on this cameo to illustrate how this scenario could have been very different, drawing on cultural knowledge, prior experience and frames of reference to connect to students' lives.

Source: Case Study deriving from Addison et al. (2021).

Building Community through Nurture and Trauma-Informed Practice 167

Reflection Point

Reflecting on the case study and the discussion of nurture and trauma-informed practice, what issues does the case study raise for you about the policies and practices to promote positive discipline in schools? Can nurture and trauma-informed practice sit side-by-side with rigid discipline systems and behaviourist approaches (see Chapters 7 and 8) to school discipline?

In bringing all of the discussion together, what are the key lessons that can be learned to inform *relational* approaches to building community within schools?

Meeting individual need through integrated children's services, staged intervention and multi-agency/interdisciplinary working

Whilst there has been an increasing emphasis on universal, as apart from targeted, approaches to intervention, it is generally recognised at the level of government/ state that there is a need for a hierarchy of provision that extends from universal approaches to those more targeted towards individual need, with the publication of the *United Nations Convention on the Rights of the Child* (UNCRC) acting as a catalyst for global policies which focus on the holistic development of the child (L. Darling-Hammond & Cook-Harvey, 2018; L. Darling-Hammond, Cook-Harvey, Flook, Gardner, & Melnick, 2018). This has led to a movement towards integrated children's services and a reconfiguration of the workforce (Forbes, 2018). Within Scotland and England, this is supported by *Codes of Practice* (DfE & DoH, 2015; Scottish Government, 2017a, 2017e) that set out the statutory guidance under which the different professions who have responsibility for the care and welfare of C&YP must comply.

Evidence from studies of interagency[4] collaboration in children's services indicates that integrated intervention in pre- and school-based initiatives can lead to improvements in the functioning and behaviour of C&YP and can lead to better coordination of services and earlier identification of need (M. Cooper, Evans, & Pybis, 2016, citing C. Oliver, Mooney, & Stratham, 2010).

A Scottish case study

Within Scotland, the *Children and Young People (Scotland) Act 2020* enshrines children's rights in law, constituting the statutory basis for the national practice model, *Getting it Right for Every Child (GIRFEC)*. GIRFEC is a multi-agency approach that requires professionals from a range of agencies to collaborate together in a coordinated way to improve outcomes for C&YP. A modified version of the staged intervention framework that underpins GIRFEC and which guides decision-making is set out in Table 9.3.

168 *Towards New Understandings*

Table 9.3 The Scottish government's staged intervention model

Level	Identifying	Supporting
Level 1 Universal	Professionals identify a child or young person in need of support or planning which can be met within the existing setting.	A support plan is put in place to support the child or young person from within resources to be monitored and reviewed by school and parents. An Individualised Educational Programme (IEP) may be required.
Level 2 Single agency plan	Situation not resolved. Advice and support sought from outside specialists within educational services (e.g., educational psychologist).	Support put in place drawing on services outwith the school but within educational services, monitored and reviewed by a multi-disciplinary team. IEP in place.
Level 3 Multi-agency plan	Situation not resolved. Advice and support sought from specialists from agencies outwith educational services (e.g., clinician).	Support put in place drawing on a range of services outwith the school, as required, monitored and reviewed by a range of professionals and parents. Coordinated support plan considered.

Source: Scottish Government (2017a), adapted from Chapter 3, Section 31, with permission of the Scottish government.

GIRFEC is guided by eight principles to guide practice: C&YP should be safe, healthy, achieving, nurtured, active, respected, responsible and included (SHANARRI). Two further frameworks – the *My World Triangle* and the *Resilience Matrix* – support the process (Scottish Government, 2017a).[5] The *Individualised Educational Programme* and *Coordinated Support Plan* are documents, arrived at through consultation with relevant stakeholders, which set out the educational objectives to be achieved by the child and the additional support required in order to achieve them. The latter is a statutory document prepared by the education authority when at least one agency, beyond education services, is involved in supporting the child. Whilst not a statutory requirement, it is recommended that a *lead professional* should act to coordinate the support offered to a child or young person with complex needs (level 3 of the staged intervention model) and a *named person* (e.g., health visitor, Pastoral Care Teacher) should act as a single point of contact with the family (all levels) (c.c. Box 9.2).

Additional support for learning: statutory guidance 2017

It is important to recognise the important role that support staff within a school (e.g., learning support assistants, school nurses) can play in supporting the

Box 9.2

Exemplification of level 3

Louise, aged 6, is the oldest of three children. The school is concerned about her short concentration span, poor communication and aggressive behaviour towards other children. The family receive support from the local family centre and there have been regular multi-agency meetings to coordinate support. For the previous six months, all three children have been on the child protection register because of concerns of neglect and each now has a Child's Plan. At the most recent review of Louise's Child's Plan it was highlighted that her communication skills remained poor despite an individualised educational programme being in place. A speech and language therapist assessed Louise and advised the school about more appropriate learning and teaching approaches and objectives and helped to develop new appropriate education targets within the Child's Plan. There is one overall action plan which incorporates child protection measures and the steps being taken to address her additional support needs.

(Scottish Government, 2017a)

Source: Case study derived from the Statutory Guidance to the *Education (Additional Support for Learning) (Scotland) Act 2004 as amended*, Chapter 3, point 91, reproduced with permission from the Scottish Government (Scottish Government, 2017a).

wellbeing of C&YP and in breaking down barriers between staff and students (Littlecott, Moore, & Murphy, 2018). Likewise, students themselves can act to support the positive mental health of their peers through peer support schemes as in the Mental Health Foundation Peer Education Programme.[6]

Multi-agency/interdisciplinary working

It has long been established that multi-agency working is highly complex and that there are many barriers to successful partnership (Forbes & Watson, 2012). There is a range of terminology to describe the practice of agencies and professionals working together to support C&YP, reflecting different nuances and emphases (M. Cooper et al., 2016; Forbes, 2018). I have used *multi-agency* to signify more than one agency working with a family or young person and *interdisciplinary* to signify the collaboration between professionals from different disciplines in providing *solution-focussed* support across the wider network of professional relationships and structures (as exemplified in the case study above). In a study conducted in two schools in the UK catering for C&YP with SEMHN, it was established that support (offered through an on-call service and regular interventions) provides opportunities for reflection and for coping strategies to develop in C&YP (Dillon & Pratt, 2019).

170 *Towards New Understandings*

The facilitators and barriers to multi-agency/interdisciplinary working

M. Cooper et al. (2016) carried out a systematic review of interagency collaboration relating to children and young people's mental health, examining the facilitating and inhibiting factors that impacted on outcomes. For them, a limiting factor in much of the research in the field is that it emanates from the perspectives of the professionals themselves and focusses to a significant extent on processes rather than outcomes, with interagency collaboration seen, in an unquestioning manner, as generally 'a good thing' with 'a feel good rhetoric' (p. 326). The findings are largely consistent with an earlier study conducted by Atkinson and Herrick (2006) (although there are differences in emphasis) which classified facilitators into four categories: *facilitative working relationships*, *multi-agency processes*, *resources for multi-agency work* and *management and governance*. The key findings to emerge from the systematic review are set out in Table 9.4, classified according to this categorisation.

Other facilitators (e.g., joint meetings, positive personal relationships, co-location of services, joint case conferences) and inhibitors (e.g., a lack of senior

Table 9.4 Facilitators and barriers to interagency collaboration

Facilitators	*Manifested in*	*Inhibitors*	*Manifested in*
Facilitative working relationships			
Mutual valuing, respect and trust	Reciprocity, appreciation and supportive attitude	Lack of valuing, respect and trust	Feeling patronised and being treated in an arrogant way
Good understanding across professionals/ services	Practical knowledge of policies, referral criteria, roles and responsibilities and empathy towards alternative perspectives	Poor understanding across professionals/ services	Misunderstandings, misconceptions and/ or stereotypical views about what other professions provided and how they worked, leading to inappropriate referrals and difficulties in accessing services
		Differing perspectives/ cultures across professionals/ services	Different understandings of children's problems, priorities, goals and cultures
Joint training	Staff development or training activities in which professionals from different disciplines are trained together		

(Continued)

Building Community through Nurture and Trauma-Informed Practice 171

Table 9.4 Facilitators and barriers to interagency collaboration *(Continued)*

Facilitators	Manifested in	Inhibitors	Manifested in
Multi-agency processes			
Good communication across professionals/ services	Quantity (frequency and regularity) and quality (clarity, transparency and streamlined) of communications	Poor communication across professionals/ services	Poor quality (ineffective and unclear) and difficulties in contacting professionals from other disciplines
Clear protocols on interagency collaboration	For example, agreed referral criteria and clear role demarcation	Confidentiality issues	Unwillingness to share information and differing policies and cultures regarding confidentiality
Resources for multi-agency work			
Named link person	Facilitating interagency collaboration		
Management and governance			
Senior management support	Commitment to interagency working and roles being aligned with it		

Source: Derived from M. Cooper et al. (2016, pp. 337–9).

management support, lack of accountability, unrealistic expectations of other services) were identified less frequently in the studies examined within the review. In general, collaborative initiatives were evaluated positively and interagency collaboration seen as helpful and important by professionals, parents and carers.

Effective multi-agency and interdisciplinary working requires great commitment and investment in systems, structures and resources, yet, a failure in policy and practice can have devastating consequences for C&YP and their families, as high-profile cases in the UK and beyond have demonstrated. It would seem that a key imperative in breaking down the barriers that present would be interdisciplinary training/education both pre- and in-service, identified in 10 of the studies as a means of facilitating interagency collaboration.

Brief summary

This chapter has focussed on two specific *relational* approaches – nurture and trauma-informed practice – in creating a climate for learning in which all C&YP can flourish and thrive and on the importance of an integrated multi-disciplinary approach to identifying and addressing need. The following chapter focusses on Restorative Justice/practice as a whole-school *relational* approach.

172 *Towards New Understandings*

Additional Suggested Reading

Understanding, Nurturing and Working Effectively with Vulnerable Children in Schools

Routledge, 2020. Angela Greenwood

This book provides both theoretical and practical insights into supporting C&YP who have experienced trauma in their lives, integrating theory from nurture with that of trauma-informed practice in an engaging manner. It provides an in-depth account of how trauma manifests itself through unconscious processes and explores each of the nurture principles. It is an invaluable resource for educators who wish to develop *nurture* and *trauma-informed* practice in a thoughtful way.

Notes

1. For a discussion of Piaget's *developmental stage theory*, see Gillibrand et al. (2011), Developmental Psychology, chapter 2.
2. Please see 'An Explorative Case Study of a Scottish Secondary School Nurture Group Focusing Upon the Transfer of Learning from the Nurture Group to the Wider School Setting,' an EdD thesis by Leanne, Reid Black, submitted to the University of Strathclyde, March 2022, for whom I was 1st supervisor.
3. School settings from kindergarten through to age 18 in the USA.
4. Whilst I would normally refer to inter-agency, I have adopted the form, inter-agency, as this is the form used by the author.
5. See Chapter 3. https://www.gov.scot/publications/supporting-childrens-learning-statutory-guidance-education-additional-support-learning-scotland/pages/4/
6. https://www.mentalhealth.org.uk/projects/peer-education-project-pep

10 Building Community through Restorative Justice/Practice

> **Goals for Understanding**
> I. What are some of the tensions between universal and targeted approaches to intervention and how can the transfer of socio-emotional learning be facilitated best?
> II. Building on the previous chapter, how might restorative justice/practice inform our understanding of how to build community in schools and meet the needs of individual pupils?

This chapter builds upon the previous chapter to examine and critique a whole-school, *relational* approach to creating a climate for learning and building community within the school – *restorative justice/practice*. A key challenge for any intervention is the transfer of learning from the discrete context of the intervention (e.g., the nurture group setting or a *restorative conversation* [see the discussion to follow]) to the wider context of the school. Therefore, the discussion of *restorative justice/practice* is prefaced by an exploration of some of the challenges and tensions in facilitating the *transfer* of learning whether from targeted interventions or whole-school, universal approaches (in keeping with the discussion of staged-intervention in Chapter 9) to wider contexts.

Universal vs. targeted approaches to intervention: the 'sticky-problem' of transfer

As previously intimated, there has been a momentum towards universal, as opposed to targeted, approaches to intervention that is evident in all three approaches under discussion in this and the previous chapter – *nurture, trauma-informed practice* and *restorative justice/practice*. There is a range of reasons why this is the case, some of which were explored in depth in Chapter 2, such as a movement away from practices which are perceived to be exclusionary (Slee, 2018b, 2019) and which may lead to the potential for stigmatisation and labelling (Mowat, 2015a; Riddick, 2012; Slee, 2013); an advocacy of inclusive pedagogy (Florian, Black-Hawkins, & Rouse, 2017); and a recognition that inclusive approaches which

DOI: 10.4324/9780429467110-14

174 Towards New Understandings

support some children may be beneficial to all and therefore should be extended to all, as illustrated in the nurturing schools movement (see Chapter 9).

A strong case was made in Chapters 6-8 for the need for a coherent vision and cohesive approach to promoting positive relationships and a climate for learning within schools, underpinned by compatible, rather than conflicting, theoretical and philosophical positions. A key consideration relates to the degree of congruence between the philosophical underpinnings, principles and practices of the intervention and the ethos and climate of the school, and the degree to which this may impact on the transferability of what is learned within the discrete setting of the intervention to real-life situations, the broader environs of the school and to the home and community.

Transfer is a 'sticky problem' that is largely under-researched (particularly with regard to the *affective* domain) yet has applications across a range of fields (e.g., thinking skills, policy borrowing). It would not be going too far to suggest that the problem may arise largely through what Brookfield (1995) would describe as an unquestioning, causal (if ... then) assumption that what is taught and assumed to be learned (and perhaps even measured) will automatically transfer to wider contexts. Perkins (1992) identifies this as the *Bo Peep theory* of transfer – *leave them alone and they'll come home.*

Perkins (1992) describes much school-related learning as 'fragile' – it fails to embed, manifests itself in gaps in students' knowledge and cannot be called upon in real-life situations (Mowat, 2008). For example, students may go through the motions of responding when prompted (as might be the case in a *restorative conversation* – see the discussion to follow) but revert back to what Perkins describes as *naive knowledge* – their intuitive beliefs, prejudices and assumptions – when in a real-life situation. However, the degree to which a failure of transfer can be attributed to a failure of initial learning or a failure to apply the learning in new contexts, problems or situations – a problem of *transfer* – is a matter of judgement (Perkins & Salomon, 2012).

Perkins and Salomon (2012) argue that it is not just *whether* the transfer of learning can occur that is the issue *but under what conditions for learning*[1] (p. 248). When the transfer concerned relates to *socio-emotional* learning, this is not just an issue about cognition and pedagogy but about the climate for learning within the classroom, ethos within the school and the modelling of pro-social behaviours by adults within the setting of the school.

Perkins and Salomon (1989) identify two processes – *low* and *high transfer* – that make it more or less likely that transfer will occur. They focus on the nature of the knowledge/skills to be assimilated and the degree of congruence between the initial context for learning and the context for transfer. In a later paper (Perkins & Salomon, 2012), they create a three-stage model of transfer, illustrated in Figure 10.1.

Whilst it is presented as a three-stage model, the authors argue that it is not necessarily the case that the model will be experienced at a conscious level and nor may it be experienced sequentially. They highlight the role of *motivation* and *dispositions* towards action, evident in all three stages of the model. For example, a child or young person who has been exposed to ideas about anger management

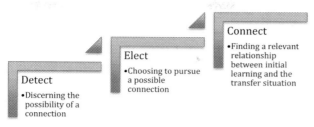

Figure 10.1 Model of transfer.
Source: Perkins and Salomon (2012).

and a range of strategies to be deployed needs to be open to recognising a situation where it might be applied (*detect*); be disposed towards and have the motivation to look for possible connections between the insights gained and the context in which they find themselves (*elect*); and to make the connection with the prior learning *in situ* (*connect*).

Failure to *detect*, *elect* or *connect* may lead to a failure of transfer – described by Perkins and Salomon (2012) as '*sometimes a bridge too far*' (p. 253). The authors draw attention to the difficulties of transfer 'in the wild' – in real-life situations where ingrained responses impede the transfer of learning, compounded by an *entity mindset* (Dweck, 2000, 2002, 2006; Dweck & Elliot, 1983; Yeager, Scott, & Dweck, 2012) where learners lack belief in their capacity to learn through adversity and too readily give up. Many teachers will be only too familiar with this phenomenon.

Perkins and Salomon (2012) synthesise the two aforementioned models, as illustrated in Table 10.1.

Table 10.1 A synthesis of two models of transfer

	Assimilation of knowledge/skills	*Congruence between contexts*	*Detect-elect-connect*
Low transfer	The knowledge and skills are routine in nature	The contexts for learning are similar	As transfer arises more automatically from habit, requiring less cognitive effort, a degree of motivation or a disposition to act may still feature but is less crucial
High transfer	In order to assimilate the new knowledge/skills, greater reflection is required and explicit connections made	The differential between the two contexts is wider	Demands extensive cognitive effort and significant motivation or dispositional drivers

Source: Derived from Perkins and Salomon (2012).

176 *Towards New Understandings*

The learning and skills to be developed in children and young people (C&YP) through approaches such as nurture, restorative-and trauma-informed practice are not routine in nature, nor is it necessarily the case that there is congruence between the context of intervention, the wider school environs and the home environment, as previously argued. For example, in a study of nurture groups in secondary settings, Kourmoulaki (2013) found a considerable discrepancy between the ethos of the nurture group and the ethos of the school, to the extent that the nurture groups appeared to be detached from the day-to-day business of the school. Similarly, in a primary school setting, Warin (2017) established that the staff in the nurture setting and other teaching staff were 'singing from different song sheets.' In these circumstances, the learning within the nurture setting is likely to be undermined and transfer of learning to the wider school and home environment, impeded. This implication can be extrapolated beyond nurture to the other *relational* approaches under discussion.

Engle, Lam, Meyer, and Nix (2012) contrast two means of framing learning contexts – *bounded* and *expansive*, the latter of which leads to more meaningful transfer. The former is characterised by a restricted context – the broader applicability of the learning is not examined or explored. In contrast, *expansive* learning contexts emphasise the meaningfulness and applicability of the learning beyond the immediate context, creating an expectation that what is being learned will have relevance to other settings and encouraging students to have greater agency in their learning.

Through investing in developing the knowledge, understanding, empathy and expertise of the whole school community, not only will the conditions for reinforcement, transferability and sustainability of learning be created but also a sense of community within the school, hence the focus on whole-school approaches.

Restorative justice/practice or approaches

Restorative justice (RJ) is interdisciplinary in nature, rooted in the criminal justice system and developed through a range of disciplines. How it is understood and operationalised reflects disciplinary norms and philosophical assumptions (Cremin, Sellman, & McCluskey, 2012; Hollweck, Reimer, & Bouchard, 2019). A generally held view, however, is that it is a mediated process to address harm (Bevington, 2015) in which a third party acts to facilitate a discussion by which an offender is held accountable for their actions and offers reparation to the victim. It is concerned with peace-making, dispute resolution and rebuilding relationships (MacAllister, 2017).

Schiff (2018), however, cautions that the language of 'victim' and 'offender,' developed within the criminal justice system, is insufficiently nuanced to capture the fluid nature of relationships within schools – 'Wednesday's offender is often Tuesday's victim' (p. 122). She cautions that the use of labels of this nature can be potentially damaging, leaving students feeling increasingly distanced from each other and stuck with labels that can be intractable. For her, *restorative justice* should have a different focus in schools: 'creating and maintaining a values-based climate where strong relationships form the foundation of restorative culture' (p. 122), lending itself to the terminology of *restorative practice* or *approaches*.

Finnis (2021) makes a distinction between *restorative justice* and *restorative practice*, the former concerned with repairing harm (as described above); the latter, a much more expansive concept – a 'way of being' (p. 10) which extends beyond to a systemic and relational shift for enabling and building healthy relationships and providing a whole-school framework to promote a positive school ethos and climate (see the discussion of *restorative justice* as *transformative*, to follow). *Restorative practice* seeks to proactively build community and *social capital* (see Chapters 11 and 12) within and beyond the school community, working with families to create a safe and secure environment for C&YP.

However, this distinction is not in evidence in much of the literature where the terminology of *restorative justice/practice/approaches/measures* is used interchangeably, depending on the preference and context of the author. In the discussion to follow, I shall use the terminology adopted by the author, defaulting to *restorative practice*, which is my preferred term.

Restorative practice in schools

Restorative practice (*RP*) is generally understood as an empathy-based philosophy, falling under the umbrella of peace education (K. Reimer, 2019), which is regarded as an alternative to more punitive and zero-tolerance approaches to school discipline (Mullet, 2014; Schiff, 2018; Teasley, 2014; Vaandering, 2014; Velez, Hahn, Recchia, & Wainryb, 2020). It requires a significant shift away from traditional approaches to school discipline that are sanction-led and determined by an authority figure (K. Reimer, 2019) towards beliefs that community building and strong relationships can potentiate behaving well for its own sake (Gregory, Ward-Seidel, & Carter, 2021). It shifts the attention and emphasis away from rules to the repairing of relationships (Riestenberg, 2012). It aims to build community and civic engagement (Riestenberg, 2012), building bridges between teachers and children and between schools and communities (Finnis, 2021). It emphasises the inherent worth and wellbeing of individuals and relies on a 'relationship-based, dialogic framework that contrasts with the more common hierarchical, power-based structure' found in schools (Vaandeering, 2014, p. 64).

Colombi, Mayo, Tanyu, Osher, and Mart (2018) acknowledge the difficulties facing schools in implementing *relational approaches* and building community when educators feel inadequate in coping with C&YP who present with challenging behaviour. Yet, they observe that exclusionary practices not only do not work but also serve to exacerbate the problem, ultimately making all children feel less safe and secure within the school. Their perspective on RP is *transformative*, seeing it as a vehicle to enhance learning and encourage self-responsibility and empathetic relationships, building classroom communities that are 'based on collective agreements, authentic communication, and reflective dialogue' (p. 156).

178 *Towards New Understandings*

Velez et al. (2020) claim that *RP* contributes to student wellbeing through promoting student agency and voice, increasing perceptions of fairness and justice in schools. However, they note a disjunction between theory and practice, observing that careful attention needs to be paid to the environment, people, culture and history of the specific community. They draw attention to the potential for *RP* to impact positively on school climate, students' sense of self and student behaviour and forward insights into successful implementation, noting that educators' beliefs and attitudes matter (see K. Reimer [2019, 2020] to follow). They recommend that *RP* should be integrated fully into the school on a long-term and continuous process and not regarded as simply a toolkit of strategies.

Restorative practice as understood by C&YP

In an endeavour to understand how RP is understood by C&YP, the Scottish Government commissioned research on the topic (Vaswani & Brown, 2022).[2] However, rather than a study of *restorative practice in situ*, the research paradigm adopted was based on a short-term intervention that introduced the concept to C&YP and explored their responses to a series of scenarios. This, in my view, limits the value of the findings, as they are not derived from the direct experience of RP. It was found that C&YP demonstrated a nuanced understanding of RP, recognising the harm not only to the person affected but also to the perpetrator(s), extending to family, friends and bystanders. RP was seen as potentially beneficial to both parties who had been affected, particularly in the case when serious harm had occurred. The report highlights the importance of child-friendly approaches to RP and the need for preparation and support for the process.

Restorative practice in action

RP is developed through facilitated *restorative conversations* (Cremin et al., 2012) which can be informal in nature, taking place in the classroom and wider environs of the school, or can be formalised through *restorative conferencing, restorative circles* (K. Reimer, 2019) or *peer mediation* (Bevington, 2015) with a focus on dialogue and understanding the perspective of others (K. Reimer, 2019). Through the use of *restorative questions* involving both parties, the aim is to seek to understand what happened, the effects on others, what restitution is required and what can be learned to reduce the risk of further harm (Bevington, 2015; Cremin et al., 2012). According to Finnis (2021), *restorative practice* is about 'making the implicit explicit, making the invisible visible,' (p. 31), providing a framework for practice and concerned with shifting the culture within the school.

Restorative practice and school discipline

Vaandering (2014) argues that the situating of RP within the discourses of behaviour and classroom management and largely authoritarian school structures is problematic as it inadvertently reinforces the power structures already in place

Building Community through Restorative Justice/Practice 179

within the school, conflicting with the underlying philosophy of the approach. In a study of implementation in Ontario, insufficient attention had been devoted to structural and institutional influences and the inherent power relations within the school (see Chapter 7), leading to decontextualised practices.

In contrast, Schiff (2018), in reflecting on the 'school to prison pipeline' and the disproportionate representation of 'minority youth' in the American justice system, maintains that *RP* can serve to redefine school discipline policies, minimise exclusionary practices and promote inclusive values but only if initiatives are placed within a broader framework of political, cultural and policy contexts, giving consideration as to how institutional bias and structural racism act as an impediment to implementation.

Flexible consistency in approach

In a small-scale study conducted in a primary school in England, the degree of congruence between *RP* and the values and practice of a school was found to be an important variable in successful implementation (Bevington, 2015), leading to more thoughtful and reflective responses from both staff and pupils. Whether this emerges from the school's existing practice or from its engagement with *RP* is uncertain. The findings mirror those of Vaandering (2014) in that the tension between the philosophy and practice of *RP* and the rigidity of school discipline structures emerged as an issue. Teachers drew on their professional judgement to resolve this tension, adopting a more nuanced, responsive approach of 'flexible consistency.' They identified a range of reasons why *RJ* may not always be appropriate within a specific context (e.g., low self-esteem of the child) but it is interesting to observe that power relations did not emerge as a concern, perhaps indicating a lack of awareness of the issue amongst teaching staff.

Restorative practice and imbalances of power

When one considers relationships within schools that are characterised by an imbalance of power, such as bullying, much of the literature relating to *RP* largely regards this as unproblematic. A review of the literature in the USA (S. Darling-Hammond et al., 2020) focusses only on the impact of *RP* on the incidence of bullying behaviours. McCluskey (2011) questions the assumption that involvement of the victim in *restorative practices* is necessarily 'a good thing.' She shares the concerns of other commentators about over-simplistic and dichotomous understandings of who is right and who is wrong in a given situation, failing to recognise 'the dynamic flows of power in schools' (p. 2). Riestenberg (2012) observes that, due to unequal power relations, peer mediation is not effective in resolving issues relating to bullying, however, she does advocate for skilled adult mediators to fulfil this role.

Cremin et al. (2012) question the degree to which adults, who are ultimately responsible for the wellbeing of C&YP, can ultimately be neutral and objective when facilitating *restorative conversations*. It could also be argued that the

180 *Towards New Understandings*

unequal power relations between teachers and pupils could place undue pressures on C&YP within a *restorative conversation* (or to agree to it in the first instance).

Separating the child from the behaviour

Riestenberg (2012) makes a distinction between the offending behaviour of the child and the person of the child, arguing that, although the behaviour itself is harmful, the child should be treated as a valuable member of the community, with the capacity to behave differently with the support that *RP* affords. This is in keeping with the arguments forwarded in Chapter 4 regarding Carl Rogers' concept of *unconditional positive regard*, one of the defining principles of *person-centred therapeutic practice*.

She draws on a case study of an adolescent boy (Kyle) who made sexually explicit drawings of another boy (Pete) and his family and left them in a common area of the school. During the *restorative conference* set up by his social worker, at which, Pete, his parents, Kyle and his Dad and a social worker were present, Kyle apologised for his actions and agreed to create posters about bullying prevention, which he took along with him when he went along to elementary classes to share his story.

Whilst the author presents this as an example of separating the child from the behaviour, recognising the worth of the child, to come back to my previous point, although the reparation may have been experienced positively by Kyle (we can only surmise this), given the unequal power relations within the *restorative conference*, what pressure did Kyle feel during it to comply with the suggestions forwarded and did he feel able to express any disquiet about what was expected of him?

This is not to condone Kyle's behaviour in any way, nor his responsibility towards others, but what rights and agency did he have during the *restorative conference*? To say that he had forfeited his rights (as many would do) would be counter to the notion of *unconditional positive regard* and the separation of the harmful action from the child. This is not to negate the value of *restorative conferencing* but to draw attention to some of the hidden complexities.

Restorative practice as coherence

K. Reimer (2020) draws on Antonovsky's concept of *coherence* (Antonovsky, 1979) as a lens through which to understand *RP* in a Canadian primary school. Antonovsky examined the lives of people who had experienced chronic and severe stress in their lives. He proposed that it is the ability of an individual to make sense of their inner and outer environments in the midst of daily stress that leads to healthier lives, that is, *coherence*. For him, a sense of *coherence* stems from a view of life that is *comprehensible, manageable* and *meaningful* (see Table 10.2), therefore the degree to which societies in general, and schools in particular, facilitate or impede the development and maintenance of a strong sense of *coherence* is the issue.

Building Community through Restorative Justice/Practice 181

Table 10.2 Synthesis of discussion of the concept of coherence, deriving from a range of literature as cited by K. Reimer (2020)

	Form and nature	*Implications for schools*
Comprehensibility	Having form and structure – predictable	Students, consistently, over time, feel safe and accepted in the school environment
Manageability	Confidence that most things will turn out well in the future – challenges can be overcome either individually or with assistance	Building self-efficacy in students, teaching strategies for conflict resolution and having resources available in times of crisis and distress
Meaningful	Experiences are rewarding and engaging	Students are able to participate in decision making

Source: K. Reimer (2020, pp. 408–9).

K. Reimer (2020) observes that schools are rarely seen as the site in which students can actively contribute to developing a sense of *coherence*. Nor is there clarity about what they are trying to achieve through *RJ*. However, she establishes that the use of *restorative justice*, and *restorative circles*, in particular, within the school created a strong sense of *coherence* in students within her study. She attributes this to the understanding of educators in the school that *RJ* is fundamentally about relationships, engagement and transformation of the culture of the school, concerned with building community and respectful relationships – both the individual and the collective thrive. This is in contrast to narrower understandings of *RJ* as being a reactive, specific response to harm or student behaviour issues.

The above is reflected in the distinction to be made between *RJ* as *transformative* or *affirmative* (K. Reimer, 2019). Drawing from Nancy Fraser's theory of justice, K. Reimer (2019) characterises the former as 'a radical paradigm shift with the potential to address social injustices and power imbalances' (p. 6) whereas the latter is concerned more with addressing the individual behaviour of the student without addressing the underlying injustice. The former relates to building community whereas the latter can potentially manifest itself as a behaviour management tool to reinforce existing hierarchies and to engender obedience and student compliance (see Chapters 7 and 8).

In contrasting how *RJ* was practised in this Canadian elementary/primary school and a secondary, comprehensive school in Scotland (the former ethnically diverse, the latter ethnically homogenous but both with a much higher proportion of students from low-income backgrounds than average), K. Reimer (2019) found distinct differences in philosophy and approach to the implementation of *RJ* not only at the level of the school itself but at the national level. In Canada, what appeared at the state level to be systemic fragmentation, at the local level manifested itself in autonomy and agency. Whereas, in Scotland,

182 Towards New Understandings

while a range of policies nationally pursuing a transformative agenda gave the impression of internal coherence, at the local level this coherence broke down:

> I encountered a continuum of beliefs as staff members questioned how restorative and inclusive practical schooling could actually be. By the time RJ reached the classroom, pupils experienced an incoherent mixture of transformative, mutually respectful relationships alongside authoritarian, punitive ones that depended on the particular individuals involved and the particular context.
>
> (p. 69)

The key differences between implementation of *RJ* in the two contexts are set out in Table 10.3.

The contrast can be seen in two exemplifications provided by the author, both describing incidences of conflict between pupils.

Canadian	... And a girl, too, she got, she was being, she felt like she didn't belong to the school because someone was being racist to her. ... And the other boy that was, like, yelling at her and stuff started laughing and calling her names in Arabic and swearing at her, making fun of her parents, making fun of her. But then we helped her with the problem. We walked her away, we calmed her down, we made her laugh, we played with her, we gave her cookies, and some of us gave her gum. We talked to her and we talked to the boy, too. (p.66)
Scottish	Like, maybe four, like, three weeks ago. One of my pals was standing on a railing, and I was under him. And he jump off and land. . . grabbed onto me and smacked my head on the ground. But that was like.. . I was.. . so I just got up and whacked him. That stopped him. Ha. (p. 62)

In the former (Canadian context), the students drew on what they had learned about *RJ* to put it into practice. In the latter (Scottish context), it was found that pupils who felt that they could handle conflict themselves did so through force, seen in this case as self-defence. My own recollections as a Depute Head chime with this as parents often defended the rights of their child – 'You stick up for yourself, son,' indicating that this is a wider cultural issue. Indeed, this is commented upon by one of Reimer's respondents:

> I think the whole Scottish education system is one that's been based in the past on punishment. And people work because the consequence of not working is that you're punished. You know, and so people will do things because, or behave because of the consequence of not behaving.
>
> (p. 61)

Whilst much has been achieved in Scotland in turning around what were exceptionally high exclusion rates, this indicates that we still have a long way to go

Building Community through Restorative Justice/Practice 183

Table 10.3 Comparison between *RJ* as enacted in a Canadian elementary/primary school and in a Scottish comprehensive secondary school

	Canada	Scotland
The national context	Systemic fragmentation	Outwardly coherent but with mixed and contradictory messages
Goals	For students to take responsibility for their actions Engaging in collaborative problem-solving Empowerment – giving students a voice Restitution – making things right	Social engagement (building empathy, relationships and connections) intermingled with social control Inherent belief in the teacher as the final authority – the emphasis was on *making* the pupil understand the *teacher's* perspective Focus on pupil behaviour and how to improve it Lack of coherence in the values and beliefs underpinning *RJ* in schools
The student experience	A complex web of relationships A respectful, supportive and welcoming ethos Support was not universal but students had confidence and faith in both their teachers and their peers (often without adult help) to resolve conflict Teachers were trusted to resolve issues through *restorative circles* Students felt that they were part of a community and had a voice – they were part of the solution School rules seen as being concerned with safety and 'getting along' Students saw the actions of teachers – whether in terms of creating rules, enforcing rules or supporting needs – as making sense	Complex and varied pupil interrelationships Strongly reliant on adults to mediate conflict Vast majority of students felt respected by adults Teacher response to behaviour deemed as disruptive was dealt with inconsistently, sometimes aggressively (shouting) and perceived as unfair by some students Students did not feel that their opinions affected decisions A lack of reciprocal trust – students perceived that their teachers did not trust them

Source: K. Reimer (2019).

(see the discussion of power, influence and authority in Chapter 7 and approaches to school discipline in Chapter 8).

It could be argued that the author is not comparing like with like. The challenges faced and the scale of the endeavour in embracing *RJ* and transforming the culture in secondary schools in comparison to elementary/primary schools is potentially much greater due to the complexity and size of the institution and

184   *Towards New Understandings*

the entrenched nature of pupil behaviour and attitudes (influenced and formed over their elementary/primary schooling).

However, the author draws attention to the mixed and contradictory messages emanating from the guidance offered to schools on the *Education Scotland* website which calls for transformation on the one hand whilst also depicting *RJ* affirmatively as 'one of the best behaviour management tools available to teachers,' with the advocacy of sanctions if the approach appeared not to work on the other (p. 55). In this context, it is hardly surprising that there is a lack of coherence in the approach adopted on the ground within the Scottish case study school.

A key finding of the study is that it is not the implementation of *RJ* in itself that is the crucial element, but the predominant relational objectives in the school and the understandings of *RJ* (whether *affirmative* or *transformative*) held by individual educators: 'How educators view and use *RJ* fits into their broader understandings of school purposes, practices and relationships' (K. Reimer, 2019, p. 50). The author maintains that national policy or leadership does not primarily sway the perspectives of educators, which indicates a significant challenge for school leadership teams in implementing *RJ*. It raises questions for the author about the role of relationships in schools – whether in the quest of fostering social control or facilitating social engagement? (K. Reimer, 2019). This, to me, would be a key point and chimes with arguments made in previous chapters. She cautions that it is the *affirmative* approach to *RJ* that predominates, losing its potential for transformation.

Restorative approaches (RA) – a conundrum

MacAllister (2017) argues that *restorative approaches* cannot in themselves account for how schools might become less punitive and more educational other than in response to conflict events. For him, *restoration* and *transformation* are very different and competing processes that cannot co-exist and therefore cannot be used to describe the same goal: the former entailing a return to the status quo; the latter entailing something becoming *different and new* (p. 112). He argues that there is an onus on schools to not only restore relationships when they have broken down but to foster more open, respectful, caring and communicative relationships in the first instance. Whilst *RA* seeks to create less punitive and conservative cultures, they are unlikely to be able to do so if used in isolation.

He draws on an example of a primary school in England that had replaced its previous reliance on reward schemes, Golden Time and sanctions by a relationships policy founded on *RA*. The headteacher took the view that the root of much inappropriate behaviour is a failure to meet the needs of children: 'schools fail children and potentially cause further discipline problems when they punish "bad" behaviour rather than seek to understand it' (p. 115).

Finnis (2021) makes a similar point – 'all behaviour is nothing more than a display of unmet needs' (p. 16), attuning with to the discussion of nurture and

Building Community through Restorative Justice/Practice   185

trauma-informed practice discussed in Chapter 9. For him, meaningful learning only takes place in the context of meaningful and authentic relationships. Like the headteacher above, he asks, 'Can we stop talking about behaviour and start talking about relationships instead? And belonging? If we do have to have a behaviour policy, can it actually be all about learning and achievement?' (p. 49) (attuning with the arguments of George Head as discussed in Chapter 8). For him, working restoratively is about working *with* students and creating a sense of belonging – it isn't about having less authority but more to do with *how* authority is exercised (see the discussion of power relations in Chapter 7), recognising that building community is only ultimately achievable when all are invested in it.

Whilst recognising the veracity of McAllister's argument regarding the incompatibility of restoration and transformation, it could be argued that the *socio-emotional learning* that takes place in the context of *RA* (the *restorative* element) may, over time have a *transformative* element and impact positively on the individual and, ultimately, on the ethos and climate of the school, creating a feedback loop and facilitating the more open, respectful, caring and communicative relationships he desires.

A framework for restorative practice

The lack of coherence in philosophy and implementation that K. Reimer (2019, 2020) drew attention to is also apparent in a study conducted by Gregory et al. (2021) in the USA, illustrated through the confusion of a leader responsible for implementing *RP*: 'I'd like to better understand … when do we call the behavior specialists versus when do we call the guidance counselors versus when do we send someone to [the Restorative Justice Co-ordinator] … versus when it's the principal' (p. 163).

A key challenge amongst *RP* leaders was the shift from hierarchical discipline structures to encouraging educators to take responsibility for preventing and de-escalating conflict within their classrooms, whilst balancing this with teachers feeling supported in their role. This is within a context in which media reports and surveys indicate that some teachers feel insufficiently supported and with insufficient training to handle student misconduct.

The authors forward a framework for *RP* implementation to guide school leaders, framed around three pillars – *laying the foundations, capacity building in staff, students and families* and *tiers of support* (see Figure 10.2). Much of the discussion in the next two chapters focusses on these elements.

The role of teacher educators

Hollweck et al. (2019) turn their attention to the role that Teacher Educators can play in embedding *RJ* and *relational* pedagogy and argue that the way to bring about the paradigmatic shift needed is to create such a culture amongst those tasked

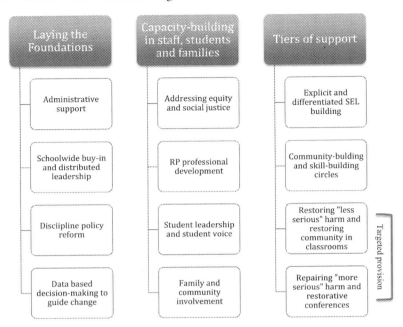

Figure 10.2 Framework to guide implementation of *restorative practice* for school leaders.

Source: Gregory et al. (2021).

with implementing *RJ* in the classroom. Thus, providing opportunities for trainee-teachers to experience *RJ* pedagogies, 'the building, maintaining and repairing of relationships in their own teacher education classrooms' (p. 263), is a key imperative for the authors, whilst recognising the complexities in achieving this.

Recent developments within the field

More recent work within the field focusses on how RP can be integrated with other *humanistic* and *relational* approaches within schools and integrated with broader theory (McCluskey, Riestenberg, & Thorsborne, 2019). Colombi et al. (2018) describe how schools in the Oakland Unified School District in Alabama, USA, took forward a multi-tiered approach to *RJ*, integrating it with *trauma-informed practice* and other interventions considered to be compatible with *RP*, disrupting the social norms that lead to exclusionary practices.

A brief reflection

What is evident from the above is that it is not just schools that lack a clear sense of what *RJ* seeks to achieve within educational settings but the literature itself.

Building Community through Restorative Justice/Practice 187

K. Reimer (2019, 2020) brings this to light in her discussion of *transformative* v *affirmative* understandings of *RJ*.

Given that *restorative practice* in schools has its roots in the criminal justice system, it is hardly surprising that much of the writing reflects the *affirmative* perspective or, as in the case of the guidance emanating from *Education Scotland*, an uneasy mix of the two. This then raises issues about fidelity to the principles and values of *RP* and the need to clarify what these are, as without this, the Scottish experience, as highlighted by Reimer in the case study (recognising that this may not be representative nationally), will be replicated far and wide. Without being clear about the principles and values underpinning *RP*, it may not bring about the transformational change that is desired and may, indeed, be deemed to have failed by many practitioners who have only understood it at the instrumental level.

Gregory et al. (2021) draw from a range of theorists who highlight the dangers of programmes that are not implemented with high fidelity (e.g., under-resourced and/or short-term initiatives). There is a world of a difference between an unthinking completion of a 'restorative template' with minimal discussion in an individual booth, separated from peers (euphemistically called the 'inclusion' room), immediately after an altercation in a classroom, and a carefully facilitated *restorative conversation* carried out at an appropriate time and place by a respected and respectful adult. Whilst schools may appear to be adopting similar strategies, what this indicates is the importance of the underlying purposes, values and beliefs and understanding of the principles of *RP*.

This is not to imply that the Scottish experience was entirely a negative one – the author acknowledges that it brought about a kinder form of discipline, but it still was firmly embedded within the paradigm of behaviour management: 'simply another tool for solidifying compliance and meting out punishment,' rather than creating 'an environment of and for student engagement that challenges traditional systems of discipline, facilitates learning, and embodies peaceful and just societies' (p. 50). It is this focus on building community through the creation of just societies that informs the final chapters of the book.

Reflection Point

On a continuum from *affirmative* to *transformative* approaches, where would you see your school or organisation lying? What would need to happen for it to shift towards a more *transformative* approach? What are the challenges?

What is your perspective on the issue of power relations with regard to *RP* (not just between children but between children and adults)? If it is an approach that is adopted within your organisation, how aware are people about this issue and how much consideration is given to it in implementation?

188 *Towards New Understandings*

Additional Suggested Reading

Getting More Out of Restorative Practice in Schools: Practical Approaches to Improve School Wellbeing and Strengthen Community Engagement

Jessica Kingsley Publishers, 2019. Edited by Gillean McCluskey, Margaret Thorsborne and Nancy Riestenberg

This edited book draws from the perspective of a range of authors to explore how *RP* can work in partnership with other initiatives such as trauma-informed practice and mindfulness and work in partnership with parents.

Circle in the Square: Building Community and Repairing Harm in School

Living Justice Press, 2012, Nancy Riestenberg

I have recommended this text not just because it provides an in-depth understanding of the principles and practice of *restorative measures*, and *restorative circles* in particular, but also because it provides multiple examples of it in action. The moral conviction of the author comes across strongly – it is a book with soul and is a very accessible, enjoyable read.

Independent Thinking on Restorative Practice: Building Relationships, Improving Behaviour and Creating Stronger Communities

Independent Thinking Press, 2021, Mark Finnis

This is not an academic text nor is it a 'how to' guide. In the initial chapters it sets out an impassioned case for *RP* in schools, placing it within the context of school culture, community and relationships, thereafter exploring the nature of the various practices associated with it. It would be an excellent text for anyone unfamiliar with the approach wishing to find out more about it.

Notes

1. The authors' emphasis.
2. It should be noted that the report uses the term *restorative justice*, representative of its provenance – the Children and Young People's Centre for Justice at the University of Strathclyde.

Part IV

Empowering the School Community

The final part of the book draws together the threads of the previous chapters to bring forward new insights into how to create equitable, inclusive and compassionate schools that are not based on reductionist neo-liberal ideology (and the policies emanating from it) nor restricted understandings of behaviour management but on creating an empowering environment within which all children can flourish. The initial chapter builds on the theme of community through the creation of participative and collaborative school cultures. The final chapter examines how to build capacity for change in the system and at the level of the school, highlighting the role of school leaders as change agents for social justice.

DOI: 10.4324/9780429467110-15

11 Working Collaboratively Together to Empower the School Community through Pupil Participation and Parental Engagement

> **Goals for Understanding**
> I. What does community mean within the context of a school?
> II. How can theories of motivation inform our understanding of classroom climate?
> III. How might community be built through the mechanisms of enquiry, pupil voice and parental engagement and what are some of the tensions and challenges in this respect?

This chapter builds on the discussion of *relational approaches* to building community in schools to examine in greater depth how we understand community, classroom climate and the role of pupil participation and parental engagement in creating empowering school communities, building capacity for change within the system (a theme to be developed further in the final chapter).

What community means within the context of a school

Community lies at the heart of *humanist* behavioural philosophy (Porter, 2006) but is a community any organisation or collection of people in one place? How we understand community is informed by a range of theoretical insights, from the work of Lave and Wenger (1991, 2006) on *situated learning* and *communities of practice* (see Chapter 6) and the German concept of *gemeinschaft* (Sergiovanni, 1994) to the body of work focussing on a sense of belonging and connectedness to school (Riley, 2017) (see Chapters 3 and 4), as illustrated in Figure 11.1.

What is clearly evident is that community cannot be restricted to proximity and location. Indeed, MacAllister (2017) argues that, in today's digital world, and with the increased movement of populations, community transcends 'geographic boundaries, nationality, ethnicity, historic, legal and cultural ties, or shared religious or cultural values' (p. 125). For him, community is concerned with networks of relationships where pursuit of the common good is valued above individual gain and where people work collectively together with this common purpose in mind. Synthesising the above, it can be seen that community

DOI: 10.4324/9780429467110-16

192 *Empowering the School Community*

Figure 11.1 Illustration of community.

Source: Drawing from Lave and Wenger (1991, 2006), Sergiovanni (1994) and Riley (2017).

is about the shared experiences, histories and values, sense of connectedness, affinity and relatedness of people to each other as they collaborate together through shared repertoires with communal purpose and in a joint enterprise to achieve a common goal.

Schools, as educational establishments, have learning at their heart, but, as has been argued throughout this book, they are fundamentally *relational* in character and it is only through understanding and fostering the relationship between learning, relationships and wellbeing that they can achieve their purpose. Fullan (2021) identifies four key drivers for change in education, one of which is 'wellbeing and learning' (the human paradigm) which he contrasts with 'academics obsession' (the bloodless paradigm). Wellbeing extends beyond *social and emotional learning* (SEL) to encompass 'equity, and a greater focus on purpose, meaning and connection to the world' (p. 17): for Fullan, 'wellbeing is learning' (p. 14).

Sergiovanni (1994) describes the defining characteristics of schools as communities as being 'the bonding together of people in special ways and the binding of them to shared values and ideas' (p. 4). V. Coleman and Osher (2018), drawing from Chavis and Lee (2015), describe communities, characterised by trust, belonging, safety and caring, as transformational where people within the community have individual and collective agency. For Riley (2017) (drawing from the perspective of school leaders), security, belonging and mutual trust

Working Collaboratively Together to Empower the School Community 193

are essential to counter the negativity which many children and young people (C&YP) face in their lives through racism and other forms of prejudice. Khon (1999) describes the community of the school or classroom as:

> A place in which students feel cared about and are encouraged to care about each other. They experience a sense of being valued and respected; the children matter to one another and to the teacher. They have come to think in the plural: they feel connected to each other: they are part of an "us." And, as a result of this they feel safe in their classes, not only physically but emotionally.
>
> (pp. 101–2)

He argues that such a community is dependent on authentic and respectful relationships between adults and children where the former do not hide behind a professional persona but take a genuine interest in the children under their care, setting a powerful example in so doing. It fosters cooperation and collaboration amongst children, rather than competition, within the context of an engaging curriculum.

Whilst all of these conceptualisations differ in emphasis, an ethos of care and compassion lies at the heart of creating inclusive school communities. The discussion to follow focusses on the climate for learning within the school understood through the lens of motivational theory, and, in particular, Deci and Ryan's *self-determination* theory (Deci, Vallerand, Pelletier, & Ryan, 2011).

The climate for learning within the school: insights from motivation theory

The key tenet of *self-determination theory* is that environments promote *intrinsic motivation* when they fulfil three innate psychological needs: *autonomy* (being able to determine what to do and how to do it), *competence* and *relatedness* (affiliation with others through pro-social relationships) (Brophy, 2010; Deci et al., 2011). Deci et al. (2011) describe *intrinsically* motivated behaviours as being 'engaged in for their own sake' whereas *extrinsically* motivated behaviours are 'instrumental in nature' (p. 328).

Deci et al. (2011) identify four types of *extrinsic motivation*, determined by the degree to which behaviour has become *internalised* (a process through which behaviours, which are externally driven, when reinforced over time become part of the normal, unconscious repertoires of the individual). The model is illustrated in Table 11.1.

It might be considered that *integrated regulation* is fundamentally the same as *intrinsic motivation* as both are forms of autonomous self-regulation, however, the authors argue that the latter is characterised by the intrinsic worth of the activity itself (e.g., a love of reading) whereas the former is characterised by the activity being important to the individual because of the desired outcome (e.g., winning a medal at the Olympics).

194   *Empowering the School Community*

Table 11.1 The four types of extrinsic motivation

	Forms of extrinsic motivation	Manifestation
Process of internalisation	**External regulation**	The behaviour arises out of external contingency (praise/reward/punishment)
	Introjected regulation	A form of internal coercion which arises out of external contingency (e.g., arriving on class at time to avoid a sense of guilt)
	Identified regulation	Whilst the motivation is extrinsic, the individual has come to value the activity (e.g., devoting additional time to studying to pass an examination)
	Integrated regulation	The extrinsic motivator has become fully integrated with the individual's coherent sense of self – values, needs and identities (e.g., identification with being a good athlete)

Source: Derived from Deci et al. (2011).

In terms of pupil behaviour, *intrinsic motivation* would be characterised by a child 'doing the right thing' out of a genuine care and consideration for others whereas *integrated regulation* would be characterised by a child 'doing the right thing' because they have come to regard good behaviour as a pre-requisite for succeeding at school, which is something that they value. If the goal of the school is *compliance* of the child (see Chapter 8), rather than *flourishing* (a concept which has come to the fore also in the field of character education [Narvaez, 2015]) and *self-actualisation*[1] (Bohart, 2007; Maslow, 1943), then either forms of motivation would be regarded as being of equal value.

The relationship between agency, autonomy and control

The concepts of *agency* (see the discussion of *sociocultural theory* in Chapter 6) and *autonomy* are closely related but not the same. It could be argued that, to be *autonomous*, one requires *agency*. Both concepts, however, can be understood as being relational to the degree of *control* exercised within an environment (cc. Figure 11.2), whilst recognising the mediating role that *internalisation* plays.

Building upon the discussion of power relations in Chapter 7, and examining the relationship between the degree to which student behaviour is *controlled externally* and the degree to which students are *intrinsically motivated* to learn and to behave in ways that are congruent with their values and internal drives, pupil behaviour can be considered to arise from an interaction of these two continuums and can be classified accordingly as *constrained, contingent, dependent*

Working Collaboratively Together to Empower the School Community   195

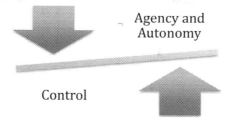

Figure 11.2 A visualisation of the relationship between control and agency/autonomy.

or *self-actualising* (see Table 11.2). *Self-actualisation* is not a process of looking inwards in a narcissistic way – it is the means by which individuals have a sense of self, of worth and are able to maintain and enhance this state (Bohart, 2007; Sanders, 2007) – to fulfil their potential.

Table 11.2 The relationship between the continuums of control/agency and autonomy and self-determination

		Dependent	*Self-Actualising*
Agency and autonomy	↑	Seeking direction Seeking approval Avoiding negative outcomes	Flourishing if the right conditions to promote learning and positive relationships are in place
		Contingent	*Constrained*
Control		Compliance (the reinforcers are salient) Disobedience (the reinforcers are not salient or have lost their power)	Rebellion Rejection Frustration Withdrawal (seeks to follow own path) Reluctant compliance Compliance (reinforcers of no consequence – the child would have behaved well and applied themselves to their learning irrespective of rewards or sanctions, assuming that the values of the child are congruent with those of the school) May not fulfil potential
		Extrinsically Motivated	**Intrinsically Motivated**

196 *Empowering the School Community*

Some may argue that it is not possible for a child or young person to be afforded *agency* and *autonomy* within an overly controlling régime, therefore the top left quadrant should be blank. However this model, whilst presented in the form of a framework, represents a continuum, therefore it could be argued that the *agency* and *autonomy* of the child or young person are compromised within an *extrinsically motivated* environment, leading to varying degrees of *dependency*.

This model attests that the imposition of controls through the use of external reinforcers on children who are otherwise *intrinsically motivated* to learn and behave with consideration towards others could have a range of unanticipated negative consequences, leading potentially to a failure to realise their potential. This contrasts with the commonly held view that the imposition of controls on otherwise well-behaved children has a neutral effect.

What, also, if the *intrinsic motivation* of the child is not directed towards the values of the school? Within an overly controlling régime, it is likely that many of the identified responses would still hold true, other than *compliance (reinforcers of no consequence)*. Within a classroom where *agency* and *autonomy* are afforded and, as described, the right conditions to promote learning and positive relationships are in place (an important caveat), there is a greater likelihood of the child or young person fulfilling their potential within a more *affirming* environment, in keeping with the three conditions – *autonomy, competence* and *relatedness* – which create *intrinsically motivating* environments (Deci et al., 2011).

Reactive vs. proactive approaches to school discipline

The continuum of *control* and the degree to which *agency and autonomy* are afforded to the child can also be related to the degree to which approaches to school discipline can be regarded as *reactive* or *proactive*, classified as *fostering compliance, punishment/exclusionary, responsive to need* and *relational/participative* (see Table 11.3). It should be noted, however, that approaches that are classified as *responsive to need* and which may initially be implemented in response to circumstance (e.g., bereavement counselling) may also be *proactive* and/or preventive in nature, depending on the orientation within a specific context and whether it is regarded as a discrete, targeted intervention or a whole-school approach (see Chapter 10).

As argued in previous chapters, approaches towards school discipline are not neutral: they are informed by understandings of childhood development and childhood, other relevant bodies of theory and an extensive range of historical and cultural influences. School discipline policies that constitute a hotchpotch of approaches from all four quadrants give out very mixed messages to the school community, lack coherence and may not be congruent with the espoused values of the school. So, how do we move towards more *relational* and participative school cultures?

Working Collaboratively Together to Empower the School Community   197

Table 11.3 The relationship between the continuums of control/agency and autonomy and the degree to which approaches to school discipline and promoting positive behaviour are pro-active

		Responsive to need	*Relational/participative*
Agency and autonomy afforded	↑	Solution-orientated approaches Restorative practice/ approaches (if affirmative – see Chapter 10) Counselling Therapy Nurture groups Support groups Feuerstein's instrumental enrichment	Pupil voice Restorative practice/ approaches (if transformative – see Chapter 10) Pupil enquiry Peer support & mentoring Nurturing schools Anti-bullying policies (if directed towards prevention) Programmes focussing on building resilience Social and emotional learning Trauma-informed approaches Pupils involved in devising the mission statement for the school and school rules/regulations Volunteering Participation in schemes such as the Duke of Edinburgh Award Focus on community and relationships
		Punishment/exclusionary	***Fostering compliance***
Control		Punishment exercises Removal of privileges (or what should be entitlements) Detention Naming & shaming régimes Removal from classroom Sin bins (or however they are euphemistically called) Referrals to senior staff Contact with parents/ guardian (after the event) Suspension/Temporary exclusion Removal from the school roll Pupil Referral Units (PRUs)	School discipline policies & regulations around uniform/dress code etc. Praise & rewards (when used as a means of manipulation) /Golden Time etc. Award schemes Assertive discipline (and other similar approaches)
		Reactive approaches	**Pro-active approaches**

198　*Empowering the School Community*

Reflection Point

With regard to your own context:

Table 11.2
Which of the cultures represented within the model would characterise your school or organisation most - *constrained, contingent, dependent* or *self-actualising?* What makes you think this? How might you move towards a *self-actualising/flourishing* (not in the sense of being focussed on self) *culture?*

Table 11.3
In examining your own context (or looking in from outside), in which quadrant would you consider your school to lie? What makes you think this? How coherent is the policy towards school discipline (see Chapters 6-8)? How might you move towards more *relational* and *participative* approaches to building community within the school?

Towards more relational, inclusive and participative school cultures

Chapter 7 argued that the construct of behaviour management, with its undertones of *external control*, is no longer apposite as we move forward in the 21st century. But how do we move schools from a *reactive* culture of *control* to one that foregrounds relationships and participative cultures and which also meets the needs of individual pupils, particularly those who are most disadvantaged?

A focus on school culture – cultivating the garden

Stoll (2007) argues that school improvement is not just about systems, structures, curricula ... but, 'requires an understanding of and respect for the different meanings and interpretations that people bring to educational initiatives, and the nurturing of the garden within which new ideas can bloom' (p. 106). The garden to which she refers is the culture of the school. The culture of a school is unique, is influenced by external forces (see Chapter 1), and is situated in its past histories, its taken for granted 'ways of doing things around here' and the underlying assumptions, values and beliefs held by the school community: it is 'the glue that holds everyone together' (p. 96). Finnis (2021) describes school culture as 'the complex and broad set of relationships, values, attitudes and behaviours that bind a specific community, consciously and unconsciously' (p. 29). He observes that a new culture does not come about by conscious planning on the part of the individual, nor does it come about overnight or by a rebranding: 'it is created by sharing a vision, beliefs, values and behaviours that breathe life into the organisation' and is a collaborative venture (pp. 31–2).

Insights from the literature on change management indicate that the starting point for any change process is to understand the context and culture of the school as interventions that do not impact at the cultural level may fail to embed or be sustainable (Stoll, 2007) and may be seen and experienced

Working Collaboratively Together to Empower the School Community 199

as peripheral to the life of the school (Kourmoulaki, 2013). Three authors who have sought to offer insights into how schools can become more inclusive in their practice through an enquiry approach are Kathryn Riley (sense of belonging – see Chapters 3 and 4); Lani Florian and colleagues (inclusive pedagogy – see Chapter 2); and Kyriaki Messiou (confronting marginalisation in education – see Chapters 3 and 4). The discussion to follow compares and contrasts the rationale for and approaches adopted within the three texts as a means of discerning key messages to inform the journey towards more inclusive, equitable, *relational* and participative cultures in schools.[2]

The rationale for action and focus for enquiry

For Riley (2017), the key imperative is that schools should be places of opportunity where all C&YP can flourish, helping them to develop their sense of identity and engagement with the world (p. 6). The identities of C&YP are shaped by how schools reach out to and connect to their communities – their cultures, practices and beliefs (pp. 12–3). For schools to become places of opportunity for all, they need to be friendlier institutions with relationships at their heart, developing an understanding of the lives of C&YP beyond the school gates and connecting with their communities and the outside world (p. 45). An enquiry approach offers insights that can inform the approach of school leaders in creating schools where C&YP can thrive and fulfil their potential and where staff can become highly reflective in their practice (p. 7).

Messiou (2012b) believes that exploring how marginalisation is experienced by C&YP through enquiry enables teachers to 'reach out to all children, irrespective of the labels assigned to them, with the aim of creating inclusive classrooms' which respect the diversity of all learners, in the process removing barriers to participation and learning (p. 4).

On the basis of the argument that high levels of *inclusion* can be compatible with high levels of achievement, Florian et al. (2017) advocate for inclusive pedagogy as an approach to teaching and learning which supports teachers in responding to individual difference but in ways that do not marginalise students who are treated differently from others (Florian et al., 2017).

Whilst it can be seen that the focus of each text is different, with Riley having a much broader perspective of the school in relation to its community, all are focussed on the creation of more inclusive school environments which respect diversity and individual difference through a process of enquiry. The work of Riley and Messiou is more *relational* in focus, with the latter exploring the degree to which C&YP, irrespective of categorisation, are truly included in the full life of the school community. Table 11.4 summarises the foci of enquiry.

The enquiry approach and its rationale

All three approaches are based on frameworks designed to facilitate and guide the process of collaborative enquiry, acting as a scaffold for reflection,

200 Empowering the School Community

Table 11.4 The foci of enquiry for Riley (2017), Messiou (2012b) and Florian et al. (2017)

Riley	Messiou	Florian et al.
Is this school a place where all children, young people and adults feel they belong? If not, what are we going to do about it?	How can schools engage with students' voices in order to confront marginalisation and promote inclusion?	What is the nature of the relationship between the inclusion of some children and the achievement of all? Are there strategies which can raise the achievement of all children, whilst safeguarding the inclusion of others who are more vulnerable? What changes can a school make to ensure high levels of inclusion as well as high levels of achievement for all its children?

learning, policy and practice. The frameworks of Messiou and Riley are highly participative. Both conceive of researchers working in collaboration with teachers and students to investigate an issue, using a wide range of data-collection methods, including visual methodologies (such as drawing) and other age-friendly approaches – 'Message in a bottle' and role-play being examples of such.

For Riley (2017), engaging in enquiry is a means of building capacity in the school, investing in the professional development of teachers and involving C&YP in meaningful decisions about their education and welfare, fostering agency. Both frameworks commence with an in-depth examination of the school context, allowing voices to be heard and building trust. Thereafter, a process of sense-making and sharing of the data leads to a series of identified actions to create inclusive school communities (see Table 11.5). Messiou's framework is cyclical in that step 4 – *dealing with marginalisation* – leads back into the cycle.

Both approaches are located within considerations of children's rights, citizenship and democracy; the empowerment of C&YP; and recognition of the valuable contribution they can make and insights they can bring as valued members of the school community (Messiou, 2012b; Riley, 2017). However, Messiou (2012b) cautions that the views of C&YP can sometimes reflect the dominant perspectives within the school and raises concerns that the voices of those who are disadvantaged are rarely heard.

The framework of Florian and colleagues is of a different nature – *a Framework For Participation* (Florian et al., 2017) that enables understanding of the educational experience of a child or group of children within the classroom and

Working Collaboratively Together to Empower the School Community 201

Table 11.5 A comparison between Riley's *Framework for Belonging* and Meesiou's *Framework for Promoting Inclusion*

Framework for belonging (Riley, 2017)		Framework for promoting inclusion Messiou (2012b)	
Step 1	Making sense of the context	**Step 1**	Opening doors: enabling voices to emerge
		Step 2	Looking closely: bringing concerns to the surface
Step 2	Looking through the prism of place and belonging to understand the importance of place and belonging	**Step 3**	Making sense of the evidence: sharing data with learners
Step 3	Being and becoming a place maker, building trust, developing the knowledge and capacities of staff; and harnessing the creative potential of young people to create schools which are places of belonging and inclusion (p. 138).	**Step 4**	Dealing with marginalisation: encouraging inclusive thinking and practice

Source: Derived from Fig 1.2, Messiou (2012b) and Box 9.2, Riley (2017), and modified from Mowat (in press-b), Table 11.1.

beyond. The four sections of the Framework and underlying principles are set out in Table 11.6.

Through the framework, teachers, working in collaboration with a critical friend, can explore understandings of achievement, *inclusion* and the relationship between achievement and *inclusion* through sets of searching questions such as, 'Do you think that it is more acceptable to include some children and young people, rather than others, in this school/class/group etc.? If so, who would you include? And, who not? Why?' (Box 10.2, p. 150).

The role of school leaders as 'place makers'

The role of school leadership in achieving the desired outcomes is only fully considered in Riley's text. The key aspect for Messiou (2012b) is the role of school leadership in facilitating the process towards the authentic engagement with students' voices and gaining the support and commitment from staff in this regard. Florian et al. (2017) draw attention to the importance of school ethos and culture.

For Riley (2017), the key imperative for school leaders is to gain greater insight into how schooling is experienced by C&YP in order to make schools 'great places to be' where C&YP can thrive; where staff can become 'outstanding and reflective professionals' (p. 7); and where people can be comfortable in

202   *Empowering the School Community*

Table 11.6 The *framework for participation*

	Participation and	Underpinned by five principles
Access	Being there	Participation concerns all members of a school's
Collaboration	Learning and working together	community and all aspects of school and classroom life;
Achievement	Supporting everyone's learning	Participation and barriers to participation are
Diversity	Recognition and acceptance	interconnected and continual processes; Participation is concerned with responses to diversity; Participation requires learning to be active and collaborative; Participation is based on relationships of mutual recognition and acceptance (p. 49).

Source: Florian et al. (2017), derived from Chapter 4.

their identities and have a sense of belonging (p. 136). School leaders shape the spaces (physical and emotional) where C&YP can flourish and their voices heard, shaping the norms, values, beliefs and expectations of the school community, creating places of *inclusion* or *exclusion* (pp. 29–30).

> School leaders set the framework for belonging or exclusion, influencing how young people view society and their place within it. How leaders think, decide, act and reflect – and draw on their roadmap to create a roadmap of possibilities – is critical to the wellbeing of children and adults. Leaders' aspirations and practices shape young people's beliefs about themselves and send messages to communities about how they are viewed. Their expectations set the professional agenda.
>
> (p. 7)

They strike a balance between responding to external demands and meeting the needs of the school community for safety, belonging and agency (p. 136).

Reflecting on the approaches: what can be learned?

Whilst each approach is distinctive, there are commonalities that direct us towards building inclusive school communities. Key amongst these are an enquiring mind, open to new possibilities; a focus on school improvement; the primacy of relationships and trust and an inclusive school culture and ethos; respect for diversity and difference; care and concern for all pupils, but particularly those who are more likely to be marginalised; a collaborative, participative approach which is rooted within children's rights; an empowering agenda which

Working Collaboratively Together to Empower the School Community 203

creates space for the voices of C&YP and develops the capabilities of staff and students; a recognition of the importance of the interface between the school and its community and respect for the cultures, practices and beliefs of that community, even if they do not fully align with those of the school; and the important role of school leaders as 'Place Makers' (Riley, 2017) and facilitators (Messiou, 2012b). It is about creating a school community where all members feel valued and affirmed, have a sense of belonging and are included in the day-to-day activities of the school and in learning.

The discussion to follow will build on the work of the aforementioned authors to examine and critique two approaches to building community through participative and collaborative school cultures – pupil voice and participation and parental engagement.

Building community through participative and collaborative school cultures: pupil voice and participation and parental engagement

Pupil voice and participation

The work of Riley and Messiou is grounded in creating the conditions under which the voices of students are not only heard but are acted upon. Students are seen not as the objects of research but as active participants within and shapers of it. The work of all three sets of authors is very firmly based within a human rights paradigm and the *United Nations Convention of the Rights of the Child* (UNCRC) (as explored in Chapter 2), building on the early pioneers in the field (such as Jean Ruddock) and more contemporary understandings of research with children (such as the work of Mary Kellett, 2011).

Fielding (2007), in his tribute to the work of Jean Ruddock, identifies key contributions in furthering the field of enquiry. Amongst these are insights that the promotion of *student voice* is essentially about inclusive school communities and human flourishing; engaging deeply with the purposes that schooling serves, and the underlying principles and values; and transformation of the deep structures of schooling (see Rudduck & Flutter, 2000).

Rudduck and Fielding (2006) caution that the ascendency of student voice can lead to surface compliance – to a quick response that focusses on "how to do it" rather than a reflective review of 'why we might want to do it' (p. 219). They identify three aspects that need to be attended to: recognising the constraints of *unequal power relations* between teachers and students (see Chapter 7); the *authenticity* of consultation and participation as perceived by students; and *inclusion* (see Chapters 2 and 4) – ensuring that the voices of 'the silent – or silenced – students' are heard, not just the voices of the more articulate, well-performing and compliant (p. 228). A key argument is that C&YP are afforded greater agency and autonomy in their everyday lives than within school and their capabilities are underestimated within the latter environment.

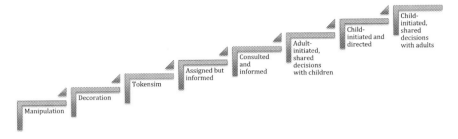

Figure 11.3 A representation of Hart's ladder of participation.
Source: R. A. Hart (1992).

Hart's *Ladder of Participation* (R. A. Hart, 1992), which sets out a continuum from the tokenistic participation (in projects) of C&YP to active citizenship, has also been highly influential in informing approaches to *student participation*, as set out in Figure 11.3., but it also provides a valuable framework for considering *student voice* (Messiou, 2012b).

However, contemporary scholars caution that *student voice* can be subverted to serve purposes other than those initially envisioned by Rudduck and other early pioneers. Influenced by Foucault's critique of the coercive use of power as a mechanism for creating the *objectified being* in the name of preserving the social order (Andrejevic & Selwyn, 2019) (see Chapter 7), they raise concerns that *student voice* may become a mechanism of control. Mayes (2020) draws from an ethnographic study in Australia in which *student voice* became enmeshed within an initiative to develop *Positive Behaviour Interventions and Supports (PBIS)* (see Chapter 8). Student researchers investigated how the student body was feeling at school and was then involved in devising the recognition system through which students received behaviour tokens for demonstrating desired behaviours. Whilst some students who had been involved in the process appreciated that their voice had been heard and acted upon, other students voiced concerns that their aims had been hijacked and subverted. What comes across is the wisdom of these young voices.

Rebecca	We wanted it to be about student voice and us making a change in the school that would benefit the students. …
Faisal	Our focus was on more, so education and students actually wanting to come to school and learn rather than being rewarded for behaviour. It was more about learning than just simple behaviour. I mean, I could sit there quietly and not learn anything. It's more about – I actually sat there one day just daydreaming and I got a RESP award, just being quiet.
Rebecca	That's what we kind of aimed for. As [Faisal] said, we were aiming for improved education. We wanted people in the school to learn. (p. 461)

Working Collaboratively Together to Empower the School Community 205

An earlier study (Leach & Lewis, 2013) demonstrates the dangers of unquestioningly seeing student voice as a 'good thing,' not recognising the unintended consequences that can arise. In a small-scale study of circle time,[3] conducted with an upper primary class in a UK school, the researchers found that, rather than the approach providing an emotionally safe place for children to be able to express themselves and for *social and emotional learning*, it became an occasion when 'children can all too easily be left feeling isolated, vulnerable, threatened and stigmatized' (p. 50).

The authors draw on the concepts of *space, boundaries* and *power* to deconstruct the experiences of the children. Particularly in the circumstance when circle time is used as a mechanism for *restorative practice* (see Chapter 10), they found that, rather than children having an 'authentic voice,' they were being controlled and manipulated in ways that could leave them open to bullying and being discriminated against. An example is provided of a boy from another class who was repeatedly naughty being brought to the circle to be told by older children how 'sad and cross' they were with him, leading to the child becoming distraught.

What both of these case studies demonstrate is that, when due consideration is not given to unequal power relations (between adults and C&YP and between C&YP themselves), to the 'authentic' voice (rather than the 'manipulated' voice) of the child or young person and where there is not an inclusive, caring and compassionate culture, *student voice* may inadvertently cause harm. This means that *student voice* and *participation* (along with any other approach or intervention) need to be approached from a critically informed, reflective, moral and ethical perspective.

Within the UK, initiatives to promote *student voice and participation* have taken place, not only at a local level but also at an international level through the *Rights Respecting Schools* movement and at a national level through government and the work of the third sector. For example, the representation of C&YP in children's parliaments (e.g., Children's Parliament, Scotland; Welsh Youth Parliament) and in cross-party parliamentary working groups (the *Cross-Party Group for Children and Young People*[4], Scotland); the appointment of Children's Commissioners in the constituent parts of the UK to ensure children's rights and to give them a voice; the advocacy of charities such as the *Mental Health Foundation*; and consultations with C&YP, such as the recent consultation conducted by the Scottish Government in partnership with the Children's and Youth Parliaments (Scottish Government, 2021f) (part of the *Muir review* of the education system).

Reflection Point

What are the key messages that you would take away from this discussion to inform your approach to promoting student participation and voice within your organisation (irrespective of sector)?

206 *Empowering the School Community*

Parental engagement

Education does not just take place at school. If children are to realise their potential, it is important that schools engage fully with parents as partners in the process of learning. As discussed in Chapter 3, the pandemic brought into sharp relief, at a global level, inequality of access to resources (UNESCO et al., 2020) and the infrastructure required to support home learning (UNICEF, 2021a; UNICEF & International Telecommunication Union, 2020) and highlighted the key role of parents in this regard.

However, what do we mean by parental engagement? Is it the parents who attend parent consultation evenings and/or the school concert? Sit on the Parent Council/Board? Engage in fundraising? Chat informally to school staff at the school gate? Respond to consultations? Help children with their homework? Take their children to a museum? Is it the efforts of schools to get 'buy-in' for their policies, as advocated by proponents of *Assertive Discipline* (Canter & Canter, 2001)? Some might say that it is all of these things, but that would be to misunderstand the fundamental distinction to be made between *parental involvement* and *parental engagement*.

The conflation of parental involvement and parental engagement

One of the key difficulties with regard to this field of study is the conflation of *parental involvement* with *parental engagement*. Within the literature, the terms are frequently used synonymously with both terms often understood as engagement with the school (parental presence) rather than engagement with the learning of the child within the home (J. Goodall, 2013). Yet, it is claimed that it is the latter which impacts on the attainment and achievement of C&YP more than any other non-school variable, such as the educational attainment of the mother (Harris & Goodall, 2008). In a study conducted in England, whilst all of the school community considered parental engagement to 'be a good thing,' teachers, parents and students understood it in different ways (Harris & Goodall, 2008).

A continuum of practice

J. Goodall and Montgomery (2014) make a distinction between *parental involvement* and *parental engagement* but do not perceive them as being binaries: rather they reside along a continuum, from *parental involvement with school* to *parental engagement with children's learning*, the latter requiring greater commitment and ownership from the parent than the former. The model is a three-stage process as illustrated in Figure 11.4.

The continuum represents a goal to be achieved but does not diminish the importance of *parental involvement*: whilst it represents a continuous process, it does not necessarily imply a simple, clear progression from one point to the next.

Working Collaboratively Together to Empower the School Community   207

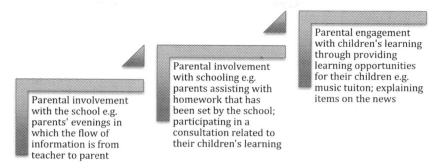

Figure 11.4 Continuum of parental engagement in children's learning.
Source: J. Goodall and Montgomery (2014).

As one moves along the continuum, *agency* for children's learning gradually shifts from the school to the parent, as illustrated in Figure 11.5.

The continuum does not represent a transfer of all *agency* from the school to the parent, but a more equitable distribution: at the final stage, the learning of the child is a shared responsibility between school and home, moving away from a conceptualisation of 'parents-supporting-schools.'

Economic, social and cultural capital and parental engagement

It could be argued that the degree to which the goal of *parental engagement with children's learning* can be achieved may be dependent on the *economic, cultural and social capital* of the parent. Harris and Goodall (2008) note that the *social capital* of middle-class families (e.g., culturally supportive social networks) enables them to form more trusting relationships with the school. Not all families can afford to send their children to music lessons (*economic* and *cultural capital*); have the necessary knowledge and understanding to be able to know how to support learning in the home or sufficient in-depth understanding of subject matter or skill to be able to do so (*cultural capital*); or have the family connections so that, 'Uncle John can help you out with your Science project' (*social capital*).

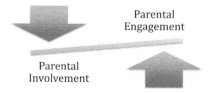

Figure 11.5 The shifting of the locus of *agency* from school to parent along the continuum towards *parental engagement*.
Source: J. Goodall and Montgomery (2014).

208 Empowering the School Community

Insufficient account is accorded within the literature to the unequal power relations (see Chapter 7) between school staff and parents (related to *agency* and where it lies) and this can be exacerbated when the *cultural* and *social capital* of the school is at odds with that of the community or with groups of parents within the community (see the discussion to follow). There can also be a danger of perceiving *parental engagement* through the rosy glow of cultural and middle-class values of a 'golden era' – measuring out the ingredients as Mum and child spend time baking together.

Deficit perspectives on parents and families and the narrative of 'hard to reach parents'

There is a tendency to perceive parents living in disadvantaged circumstances as being less concerned with the learning of their children and having lower aspirations for their future (J. Goodall, 2021; Treanor, 2017). These deficit perspectives are pervasive and are expressed in a myriad of ways within schools ('What can you expect? Look at his parents!'). They are also, unfortunately, perpetuated through the literature in expressions such as 'hard to reach parents,' implying that parents are somehow 'difficult,' 'obstructive,' or 'indifferent' (Crozier & Davies, 2007, p. 295). It is also argued that teachers conflate 'hard to reach parents' with under-performing students, whether or not this is the case (Harris & Goodall, 2008).

The conflation of *parental involvement* with *parental engagement* also leads to a tendency towards equating a lack of presence, or involvement with the school, with a lack of learning within the home, which may not necessarily be true (particularly when cultural influences are considered [Crozier & Davies, 2007; Fenton, Ocasio-Stoutenburg, & Harry, 2017]). It may also lead to narrow conceptualisations of what home learning constitutes and entails (equating it with the formal learning that takes place in school) and who is involved with it, failing to recognise the learning that takes place through the daily interactions within the home and beyond.

In a small-scale study in a Scottish primary school investigating *parental engagement* through the eyes of young children, Cameron (2021) found that home learning manifests itself in an extensive range of ways, including those that further social responsibility and the socio-emotional development and life skills of the child, and was engaged in by all family members and the extended family. This included the children themselves who supported the learning of their siblings, leading the author to the perspective that the emphasis should be placed on *family engagement* rather than more narrowly on *parental engagement*, recognising the reciprocity in learning (both cognitive and affective) between family members.

The Scottish government recognises the importance of family learning in its policy *Learning Together* (Scottish Government and the Convention of Local Authorities in Scotland [COSLA], 2018) which informs practice in Scottish schools. However, even valuable programmes to support *parental engagement* in the UK, such as the *Family Connects* programme (Lord et al., 2020), run by *Save the Children,* make no reference to the role of the extended family in fostering engagement in learning. Tett and Macleod (2020), in a small-scale Scottish study of primary schools located in socio-economically deprived areas (Tett & Macleod, 2020), establish that deficit perspectives held by headteachers of parents had a detrimental effect, but this could be mitigated by family learning programmes as they increased the knowledge and agency of families in supporting their children's learning. Drawing on the work of Auerbach (2010) and Green (2017), they examined the issue through a tripartite framework (c.c. Figure 11.6).

Kalil and Ryan (2020) observe that parents in disadvantaged circumstances have the same desires as other parents to engage in activities with their children that promote learning but they are less likely to do so. The authors postulate that financial strain and family stress, described by Treanor (2016) as *financial vulnerability*, impede the emotional and cognitive capacities of the mother in ways that make it more difficult for her to interact with her children in ways that are intellectually stimulating and emotionally nurturing.

In a more recent paper, J. Goodall (2021) addresses the deficit discourses which can arise in the literature on *parental engagement*, concerned that theorists are in danger of perpetuating the very problems of social injustice that they are seeking to address. She highlights how discourses around a 'culture of poverty' (Gorski, 2008) (pervasive and seen as inter-generational) play out in the relationships between staff and parents/families. As discussed in Chapter 3, it positions individuals as being architects of their own fate, arising from personal choices to do with attitudes and beliefs which are passed from one generation to the next. Such a culture 'absolves the system, by ignoring the institutional and structural elements that create and perpetuate poverty' (p. 100), leading to an 'othering' ('us' from 'them') which acts as a barrier between the school and parents in these circumstances.

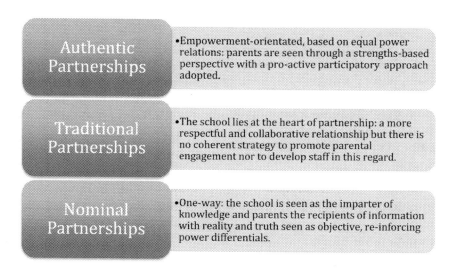

Figure 11.6 An interpretation of Tett and Macleod (2020, pp. 457–8).

210 *Empowering the School Community*

This can give rise to considerations about the degree to which those who represent the parent community (e.g., on the parent council) are truly representative of it, with the voices of more assertive, middle-class parents (Crozier & Davies, 2007) (whose *social* and *cultural capital* may more clearly align with the school [Scanlan & Johnson, 2015]) being more likely to be heard. Crozier and Davies (2007) observe that 'there are differences between getting parents through the school door and ensuring they have an equitable role in democratic participation in the school' (p. 306). Scanlan and Johnson (2015) argue that efforts to engage parents who have traditionally been marginalised (e.g., through poverty, race, ethnicity), even when well-intentioned, can reinforce power differentials and the power of the more privileged (as argued above), the implication of which is that school leaders need to examine more critically how power relations shape partnerships with the school.

The difficulties of reaching out to families who, for any reason, may not appear to be engaging with any level of the continuum outlined by J. Goodall and Montgomery (2014) are very real. My own experience in supporting the professional development of prospective headteachers clearly demonstrates the commitment and dedication directed towards the issue. However, the problem is often understood in terms of the influences and constraints on parents (e.g., poor experiences of schooling themselves) rather than on the barriers that the school itself may present to *parental engagement* (Crozier & Davies, 2007). Therefore, the starting point in establishing effective partnerships with parents is to examine how the school may have inadvertently distanced itself from its community and from parents and families, creating barriers to effective communication through its systems and structures but also through the *internalisation* of negative discourses, leading to misunderstandings and a lack of trust on both sides of the divide. L. Darling-Hammond, Cook-Harvey, Flook, Gardner, and Melnick (2018) stress the importance of *relational trust,* grounded in partnerships with families, as 'the "connective tissue" that holds improving schools together' (p. 43).

Rothstein-Fisch and Trumbull (2008) explore a range of cultural barriers to effective home-school relationships. For example, the all-too-human tendency to deem approaches to child development and education that differ from the orthodoxies of the school as being unenlightened or wrong, leading to a failure to draw on the *cultural capital* of families (the knowledge that they have of their children) in seeking solutions to problems. Within a context of the unequal power relations between professionals (from the dominant culture) and family members (from the non-dominant culture), the former perspective holds sway. Lacking cultural understanding of the family's child-rearing and educational goals, there is a danger that home-school relationships will be undermined. Recognising the different expectations that parents from different cultures have of schools and of their role in supporting their children's learning, the authors explore a wide range of approaches adopted within a 'Bridging Cultures' project to address cultural barriers.

Scanlan and Johnson (2015) argue that parental interactions with the school occur on multiple sites (e.g., church-based groups; community organisations).

Working Collaboratively Together to Empower the School Community 211

Schools that are successful in reaching out to more marginalised groups do so through multiple spaces and sites, developing mutually respectful relationships and demonstrating a willingness to engage with families in community spaces which 'provide a more level playing field for relationships,' reducing power differentials (pp. 167–8).

Harper (2015) poses the questions, 'Do educators truly value parents involvement and the knowledge that they bring about their children to the educational table?' … 'Do they truly have a voice?' (p. 78). She observes that some educators regard parents as a nuisance and place restrictions and barriers around their involvement, seeing it as an intrusion on their professionalism. In her view, rather than C&YP rejecting schooling, it is schools that reject children and hold their parents at arm's length, noting that the natural enthusiasm that young children have for learning is 'snuffed out' as educational policies and practices stifle curiosity and crush enthusiasm. Whilst some might reject this criticism as overly harsh, when one considers the disaffection of many teenagers with learning, it cannot be denied that there is something at the heart of schooling that is not resonating with some C&YP, nor is it meeting their needs (see Chapter 4).

Fenton et al. (2017) advocate examining one's own culture and how it interacts with the communities that the school serves. Through valuing and learning about the community and the knowledge that families have about their children, and through the exchange of knowledge between home and school, the *social capital* that parents need to be able to navigate the school can be grown. If schools are to move forward in building policies premised on *relational* approaches to promoting positive behaviour (as described in the previous two chapters), then building partnerships with parents, not focussed on gaining 'buy in' for pre-ordained policies, but on genuine collaboration and respect, is a crucial element of this. To return to the work of Kathryn Riley and Roger Slee, 'Is this school a place of belonging and inclusion for all parents and families or just for some?'

The final chapter explores issues around *culturally responsive leadership* in the quest for truly equitable, inclusive and compassionate schools.

Reflection Point

If you were to pose the above question of your organisation (irrespective of the sector), what would your answer be and how would you go about ascertaining this? If you come to the conclusion that, perhaps not, or not as much as you would like, how would you go about remedying the situation in a participative and collaborative manner? (perhaps drawing from some of the enquiry approaches adopted within the three texts under discussion earlier in the chapter).

How do you understand the distinction to be made between *parental involvement* and *parental engagement* and how is it generally understood within your school(s)? What implications are there for policy and practice in moving forward?

Additional Suggested Reading

Improving Learning through Consulting Pupils

Routledge, 2007. Jean Ruddock and Donald McIntyre

This book draws on research carried out for the *Teaching and Learning Research Programme* in England, examining the potential to engage with student voices on learning and teaching, pupils' perspectives on what facilitates or acts as a barrier to learning and perspectives on the consultation process itself.

Narrowing the Achievement Gap: Parental Engagement with Children's Learning

Routledge, 2017. Janet Goodall

This book attunes both with the discussion of the poverty-related attainment gap and how to address it (see Chapter 3) and the discussion in this chapter about the value of parental engagement. Chapter five – *Parental Engagement for all Parents* – is particularly relevant to the discussion in this chapter.

See also the following books that have been recommended in previous chapters:

Place, Belonging And School Leadership: Researching To Make The Difference

Bloomsbury, 2017, Kathryn Riley

Confronting Marginalisation in Education: A Framework for Promoting Inclusion.

Routledge, 2012. Kyriaki Messiou

Achievement and Inclusion in Schools

Routledge, 2017. Lani Florian, Kristine Black-Hawkins and Martyn Rouse

Notes

1. The concept of self-actualisation is not understood in the same way in Maslow's *Theory of Motivation* as it is in the field of psychotherapy and counselling, which with regard to the latter, is not regarded as individualistic.
2. A condensed discussion of, and comparison between, Riley (2017) and Messiou (2012b) can be found in Mowat (in press-b)
3. A *Social and Emotional Learning* (SEL) approach advocated by Jenny Mosley which is widely adopted in primary schools in Britain in which children are invited to share their most personal experiences with the teacher and other students as they sit around a circle in what is considered to be an emotionally-safe environment in which they are portrayed as having an 'authentic voice.'
4. Of which I, at the point of writing, am a member.

12 Empowering the School Community through Socially Just and Culturally Responsive Leadership

> **Goals for Understanding**
> I. How can we build capacity for change at all levels of the system and work collaboratively together in the creation of equitable, inclusive and compassionate school communities through creating empowering environments?
> II. What are the tensions and challenges that need to be overcome, particularly when leading in times of crisis?

This chapter integrates the themes of the earlier chapters to focus on what needs to happen if the vision of equitable, inclusive and compassionate school communities is to be realised. The role of school leadership is crucial in achieving this end, as is investment in the professional development of staff. The chapter explores what it means to be a *socially just leader*, reaching out to and working collaboratively with the school community, and how capacity can be built within the system to enable this to happen. The starting point for the discussion to follow is to look at how schools can create the conditions for change through *capacity building*.

Building capacity for change

The expectations upon schools have grown exponentially over the past few decades, reflecting societal changes and norms, and, accordingly, the role of school leaders has become increasingly complex. Whilst it is crucially important, individually and collectively, to be committed to the principles of *inclusion*, *equity* and *social justice*, in itself it is not enough to bring about the transformational change that is required. In order to be able to embrace change, a school community needs to be in a state of readiness for it and this will only come about through the efforts of the school leadership team in building capacity within the school. Scanlan and Theoharis (2015) describe the role of effective school leaders in eliminating educational inequalities as setting the direction for improvement and ensuring that organisational structures support improvement by building the capabilities of staff and including a range of stakeholders in decision making.

DOI: 10.4324/9780429467110-17

214 *Empowering the School Community*

Likewise, Apple et al. (2022) describe the role of school leaders, concerned with social justice, power and emancipation, as playing 'an important role in shaping vision, strategy, and the path into the future, in ways that must be responsive to local needs and contexts, whilst recognising the particular challenges facing education settings within their broader communities' (p. 3).

What this implies is that the school as an institution needs to be understood as part of a wider ecosystem. The policies and actions of school leaders are framed and constrained by societal expectations, norms and values and by the broader political spectrum (global, national and local) that determines the resources afforded to schools that facilitate *capacity building* or not. In turn, schools, and their communities impact collectively (and sometimes individually) on policy formation in a two-way process. This calls for both operational and strategic leadership and a focus also on leadership at the systems level: what Fullan describes as *systemness* – a commitment to contributing to, and benefitting from, the larger system (Fullan, 2021).

Capacity building, as it pertains to *social justice*, needs to be understood in relation to a broader range of concepts pertaining to the role of school leaders, as set out in Figure 12.1. The four key dimensions – *building capacity, creating the culture, strategic leadership* and *leadership for social justice* – are all strongly interrelated. Indeed, it could be argued that *creating the culture* is an aspect of *building capacity* and that *capacity building*, in turn, impacts on the culture of the school – they mutually modify each other.

Osher (2018) defines capacity as being a product of technical and socio-emotional competence and supporting conditions. A state of readiness for change arises from a combination of capacity and motivation towards a desired goal (weighing up the potential benefits and risks) at both the individual and organisational levels of the school.

For Fullan (2008), *capacity building* is concerned with 'competencies, resources and motivation.' Those who are high in capacity possess knowledge and skills, attract and use resources wisely and are committed to getting things done *collectively* and *continuously* (the author's emphasis) (p. 57).

Hooper and Bernhardt (2016) describe *capacity building* as being related to deliberative actions to build the knowledge, skills and dispositions of the leader whilst simultaneously attending to organisational learning, focussed on a shared vision for improving student learning. This is to be achieved through attending to three forms of leadership:

- *Instructional leadership*: ensuring a rigorous and coherent instructional programme aligned to a shared vision;
- *Adaptive leadership*: ensuring learning and equity by defining approaches for leading data-informed continuous improvement and establishing a shared vision;
- *Transformational leadership*: cultivating conditions that create respectful and culturally responsive engagement and collaboration in the service of enabling a vision for learning and equity (p. 4).

Socially Just and Culturally Responsive Leadership 215

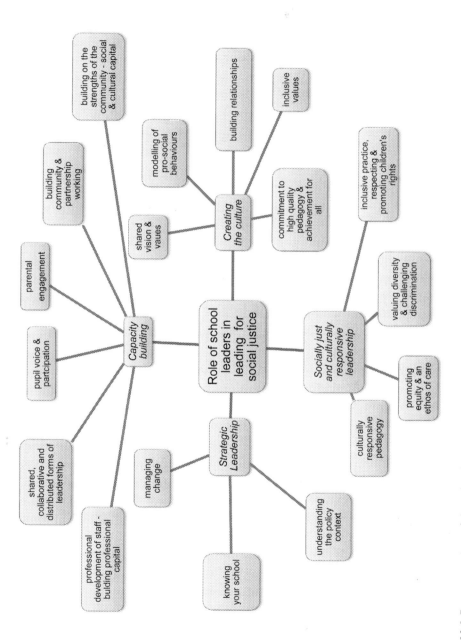

Figure 12.1 Representation of the role of school leaders in leading for social justice.

216 *Empowering the School Community*

The emphasis on building a 'purpose-driven shared vision,' arrived at through consultation and collaboration and based on values, beliefs, purpose and a clear understanding of the school as a system, is in keeping with the broader literature on *capacity building*. However, the emphasis on leadership residing within the individual (as expressed through *instructional, adaptive* and *transformational* leadership) is out of keeping with more contemporary understandings of leadership as a *collaborative* (Hallinger & Heck, 2012) and a *shared* (Goksoy, 2016) endeavour, not just restricted to those in formal positions of power (*positional leadership*) but exercised informally by members of the school community (MacBeath, 2020; Mowat & McMahon, 2018; Waterhouse & Møller, 2009).

MacBeath (2020) argues that the relationship between leaders and followers is more fluid than often portrayed: it is not the actions of individuals that are critical for leadership practice but the interactions amongst them. This is in keeping with Spillane's perspective. For him, leadership is distributed amongst a community and resides within the interdependent interactions between people, within formal and informal networks (Spillane, 2006). Thus, leadership becomes a property of the organisation itself, a *sociocultural* process (see Chapter 6) that emerges from the use of cultural tools (such as language), expressed through them and the artefacts arising from them (e.g., the school mission statement), rather than being regarded as solely invested in the individual.

The implication of the above is that, whilst those who hold *positional leadership* will ultimately be held accountable for the policies and practices of the school, *all* within the school community have a collective and individual responsibility towards achieving the shared vision of the school.

However, whether each individual within a school perceives themselves as 'a leader' or wishes to take up the mantle of leadership more formally is a matter for debate (Torrance, 2013a, 2013b). The degree to which leadership is *distributed* – 'in the gift of the headteacher' (Torrance, 2013b), perceived often as a form of delegation or relinquishing some authority or power (MacBeath, 2020) – or *distributive* (MacBeath, 2006, 2020), arising from the *agency* and *autonomy* of those within the school community, may be determined by the degree to which those in formal positions of authority have created the conditions that promote inclusive, participative school cultures. What is evident is that *capacity building* is dependent on a collaborative effort to build a shared vision for improvement based on an intimate knowledge of the school in relation to its wider environs, and the courage, commitment, human and professional capital (Hargreaves & Fullan, 2012) and resources to see it through.

Capacity building to promote social justice at district level (USA)

R. G. Smith and Brazer (2016), in their study of the practices of district superintendents in the USA, found that ensuring stability was an important consideration for the superintendents but there were threats to this in various shapes or forms, such as competing interests (e.g., the relative power and voice of more affluent families), intensified by cuts in budgets. Within the districts, there were numerous 'undiscussables' deeply embedded within the areas of race, resources

Socially Just and Culturally Responsive Leadership 217

and teacher practice, and recognition that they needed to be addressed if more equitable outcomes were to be achieved.

> The board of education has fundamental ideological differences around the issue of race, to the point where it has created a real dysfunction on the board. There are some board members that believe it is racist to even look at scores by race. ... The issue of race is still there, you know. And they're not willing to talk about it ... I would say a large percentage of teachers in their heart of hearts don't believe that the kids can do it, even though we're demonstrating, you know, increased performance (Superintendent Feset).
>
> (p. 71)

They conclude that the key issue is for superintendents to see their districts as requiring 'continual nurturing of capacity, stability and learning' (p. 77).

Leadership for social justice

Conceptualisation of leadership for social justice

How *leadership for social justice* is understood and enacted is dependent upon how the concept of *social justice* itself is understood, related also to the concept of marginalisation (see Chapter 3). For Bell (2016), *social justice* is both a process and an end-goal. The former relates to democratic, participatory and inclusive practices which are respectful of human diversity and group differences; the latter concerned with the 'full and equitable participation of people from all social identity groups in a society that is mutually shaped to meet their needs' (p. 3). It is concerned with 'reconstructing society in accordance with principles of equity, recognition and inclusion' (p. 4).

Socially just leaders

Whilst there is a literature focussing on high-level strategies to promote *equity*, there is a limited literature which examines the day-to-day practices of *socially just leaders* in fostering inclusive cultures (Forde, Torrance, & Angelle, 2021). Yet, these leadership practices are essential in challenging the low-level forms of discrimination – the *micro-aggressions* – that create hostile environments for children and young people (C&YP) and which can have a profound impact on their learning and wellbeing. The authors, drawing on case studies of school principals conducted in the USA and Scotland, found that *relational leadership* and the building of *relational trust,* based on an *ethic of caring* (Noddings, 1988, 2010), lay at the heart of *socially just leadership.* Edwards-Groves and Grootenboer (2021) describe *relational trust* within a school setting as 'entangled in the social exchanges, mutually understood responsibilities and designations, and interactions and relationships formed among key stakeholders' (p. 264).

218 *Empowering the School Community*

Table 12.1 Modification of Table 1.2

Joint enterprise	Mutual engagement	Shared repertoire
What are we learning to pursue? For example, creating an inclusive school community	Who is engaged in this learning? For example, all within the school community	How are we pursuing this? For example, the promotion of student voice …

Source: Scanlan and Theoharis (2015).

Socially just schooling

For Scanlan and Theoharis (2015), *socially just schooling* is characterised by:

1 Ambitious academic goals which are held and met by all students;
2 A welcoming school community in which students are proportionally distributed across all groupings within the school;
3 Where one's identity is affirmed and not discriminated against (p. 3).

It is not an isolated activity but can be achieved through *communities of practice* (see the discussion of *sociocultural theory* in Chapter 6) and the associated key principles of *joint enterprise, mutual engagement* and *shared repertoire* (see Chapter 11, Figure 11.1). These three principles translate into a simple framework that can be used to interrogate practices in schools as set out in Table 12.1.

Principles of courageous leadership

Blankstein and Noguera (2015) argue that the binaries that are drawn between the achievement of *excellence* and *equity* are not helpful: 'social progress is contingent upon expanding opportunities for all' (p. 6). They draw on five principles of courageous leadership if their vision of 'excellence through equity' is to be achieved (see Table 12.2).

Table 12.2 The five principles of courageous leadership

Five principles of courageous leadership	
Getting to your core	The moral purpose of leadership – understanding the value of the endeavour and how it connects to personal and collective mission and values
Making organisational meaning	Bringing coherence to the system and a strong rationale for action
Ensuring constancy and consistency of purpose	Being steadfast in the face of setbacks
Facing the facts and your fears	Drawing on data to inform improvement
Building sustainable relationships	Fostering respect, trust and mutual responsibility

Source: Blankstein and Noguera (2015).

Socially Just and Culturally Responsive Leadership   219

Building inclusive school communities

Ainscow and Sandill (2010) stress the important role of school culture in building inclusive school communities, arguing that *inclusion* cannot be divorced from either the context in which practices develop or the social relations that create and sustain the culture. For them, the starting point for change is a detailed audit of current practice and addressing, and sometimes challenging, entrenched ways of thinking.

Socially just schools – tensions and dilemmas

B. Francis, Mills, and Lupton (2012) identify a range of dilemmas in the achievement of *socially just schools*, such as the tension between teacher professionalism and *autonomy*, versus *accountability*; and diversity of provision, versus comprehensive equality. They argue that many of these dilemmas may require a re-imagining of what constitutes a school, going beyond 'affirmative' approaches to addressing social injustice to a transformation of the system.

A focus on the system

Fullan (2016) reflects on the changes that need to happen at the systems level to achieve equitable school systems. He identifies three necessary components: commitment to improvement from all schools within the system; a set of core strategic elements that need to be in place (e.g., build leadership at all levels); and the need to monitor outcomes and use them as a lever for improvement across the system.

Drawing from Hargreaves and Shirley (2009) who argue for a 'Fourth Way' of systems change focussed on democratic process, restoring greater *autonomy* to the teaching profession and greater engagement between schools and parents and communities, Chapman and Ainscow (2021) pose the questions:

- What can be done to promote equity within education systems?
- What are the barriers to progress?
- How might these barriers be overcome? (Ch 1, electronic source).

One of the conundrums of leadership for *social justice* and, in particular, the pursuit of *equity* is the emphasis on data to inform improvement (as advocated by Blankstein and Noguera [2015], Smith and Brazer [2016], Hooper and Bernhardt [2016] and Fullan [2016]) which has the potential to become an end in itself, feeding into a *neo-liberal* agenda (see Chapter 1). This can lead to a culture of accountability and to practices which may, inadvertently, create further discrimination and disenfranchisement (e.g., setting and streaming). The focus becomes one of measurement rather than learning and the learning becomes directed towards what can be readily measured. This, if combined with rigid instructional programmes (rather than responsive, *inclusive pedagogy* [see

220 *Empowering the School Community*

Chapter 11]) and *zero-tolerance* approaches to school discipline (see Chapter 8), is highly likely to marginalise C&YP further and may not lead to the 'respectful and culturally responsive engagement and collaboration' desired by Hooper and Bernhardt.

Social justice leadership as politically loaded

Gümüş, Arar, and Oplatka (2021) draw attention to the 'deep-rooted social and organisational practices' (pp. 94–5) that present as a challenge to school leaders in creating *socially just school* communities. They observe that understandings of *social justice* and *social justice leadership* in every culture and society are politically loaded and deeply rooted in power dynamics that define and demarcate the boundaries of what is possible. Reay (2012), commenting on public policy in the UK, observes that political parties, for their own ends, have misappropriated *social justice*, placing the burden for remediation on the individual rather than on society (the infamous 'Get on your bike' reference to the unemployed by the former Conservative MP in the UK, Norman Tebbit, comes to mind) and ignoring structural aspects (such as social class) that create inequality in the first instance.

What the above indicates is that *social justice leadership* is highly complex and reflects the multitude of different ways in which the concept of *social justice* itself is understood, the inherent tensions and dilemmas (B. Francis et al., 2012) and the different fields of enquiry which have informed these understandings (Gümüş et al., 2021). It cannot be separated from the wider political context, nor the *neo-liberal* forces that shape education systems across the world (see Chapter 1).

Reflection Point

To what degree do you recognise *socially just leadership* within your school or organisation? What insights can be gained from the discussion above to inform your understanding of it and how it can be achieved?

Leadership for social justice in unprecedented times

As described in previous chapters, there is an emerging literature which talks to the significant impact that COVID-19 has had on the lives of families and children at a global level (OECD, 2020; UNICEF, 2021a; World Health Organisation, 2020). The UNICEF global report focussing on the mental health and wellbeing of C&YP during the pandemic (UNICEF, 2021b) calls for a strengthening of leadership to create a strong vision for change and a solution-focussed approach, working with a range of stakeholder partners across a range of sectors.

A systems perspective

Fullan (2020) argues that COVID-19 has exposed the fault-lines that were already present in education systems across the world prior to the pandemic (e.g., the stagnation in improvements to learning outcomes) but also provides an opportunity to re-imagine what might be possible. Within a swiftly changing landscape, characterised by chaos and ambiguity, school leaders became 'de-skilled' as they were faced with challenges that they had never encountered before. From this chaos, he believes that education should become a transformational agent of society to 'build equitable public school systems that become the lifeblood of thriving societies that benefit individuals and collectives' (p. 27).

However, Sahlberg (2020) cautions that, unless we stand back and re-imagine a 'new normal,' and, more importantly, focus on the 'how' and 'why' of change rather than just the 'what,' it is likely that schools, post-pandemic, will revert back towards the status-quo, particularly within the context of tightening budgets. He cautions against an over-emphasis on policy in transforming schools:

> If we really want to transform our schools, we should expect less from policy-driven reforms and more from the visionary leadership of principals, professional wisdom of the teachers, and passionate engagement of students as change-makers (blog).

This message is very much in keeping with arguments forwarded within this and the previous chapter about empowering the school community.

A school leadership perspective

Within a context in which there were no precedents or blueprints to steer school leaders through the pandemic, Harris and Jones (2020) argue that school leadership practices are unlikely to be ever the same and that most existing leadership preparation programmes will need a radical re-think in order to remain relevant. They highlight that the pandemic has brought to the fore the importance of *relational trust* and *context responsive leadership*, dependent on *distributive* forms of leadership and recognising 'the wealth of additional expertise, knowledge and local capacity' (p. 246) of the community.

How senior leaders in schools see their role is shaped by many different forces that interact with each other in a complex web, both personal (e.g., values, beliefs, motivations) and external to the individual (e.g., the political context for leadership [see Chapter 1]). When one variable shifts, it is likely to have a knock-on effect on other variables, creating a new or altered normality.

McKinney and Head (2021) observe that such an altered normality typically arises from sustained engagement with others in which 'we come to assimilate the nuanced experiences and perspectives of others in a new way' (blog). Within the swiftly shifting sands of the pandemic, characterised by constantly changing

222 Empowering the School Community

government directives often conveyed through the media, and the unprecedented demands on school leaders in seeking to reach out to and support their school communities, it is almost inevitable that they (and other staff members) would come to see their role in new ways.

Supporting the school community during lockdown

As Course Leader for *Into Headship*[1] (a one-year Masters-level preparation programme of study) in a Scottish university, working with colleagues, I wanted to understand how former and current students on the programme had sought to support their school communities during lockdown (in particular, the most disadvantaged families) and the challenges that they anticipated as schools emerged from lockdown. I also wanted to ascertain the ways in which the programme had prepared them for the challenges they faced and what suggestions there were for modifications to it. Forty-four students, drawn from the primary and secondary sectors and special schools, completed an electronic survey, comprising mainly qualitative open-ended questions. Two-thirds of respondents were from the primary sector, fairly representative of the group as a whole.[2]

The challenge of equity

One of the key challenges faced by these aspiring headteachers was the necessity to ensure equitable access to high quality learning for all pupils. Whilst not restricted to issues pertaining to *digital inclusion* (a key concern across the world [UNICEF, 2021a]), the findings indicate that these senior leaders had gone to extraordinary lengths to ensure that pupils had access to learning materials (digital and non-digital) and digital technologies, and that staff, parents and pupils were up-skilled in the use of digital platforms and technologies, all accomplished under extreme pressure of time.

> Our school had set up Glow[3] blogs at the beginning of the session as a means of communication between school and parents. We made the decision at the start of lockdown to use these in order to post suggested learning activities. We also posted a weekly check-in within each class blog page where we encouraged our pupils to post a comment. We reviewed these weekly and where we noticed a pattern of a pupil not commenting I made a check-in phone call to make sure everything was okay.
>
> (Primary sector)

The challenge of inclusion

In response to the crisis, local authorities had set up school hubs to support more vulnerable pupils, serving a cluster of secondary and primary schools within an area, and many of the respondents were responsible for managing the hubs, including staffing. There were significant challenges in ensuring the welfare of more vulnerable pupils, as there was considerable disruption to many of the services that work with schools to support children:

> Child protection routines, procedures etc. from other agencies were often held up which became quite frustrating as no children's panels were meeting, some really serious child protection issues being dealt with via online environments with poor connections - those were particularly hard.
>
> (Primary sector)

There was evidence of a pro-active approach towards reaching out to families who normally did not engage well with the school and of a compassionate and caring approach, extending far beyond just the welfare of the child:

> We had certain families that didn't engage and as a staff we identified these families and decided on appropriate communication to 'check in' e.g. email, call or visit from teacher or senior leader. The focus here was on pastoral care rather than the learning.
>
> (Primary sector)

> One particular family had a real sore time and I was able to organise sofas for them and even small things like Easter eggs for the children.
>
> (Primary sector)

> At one point I was delivering a bike to a young person to help them travel through their local community more safely as they were too scared to walk and delivering Easter eggs to get young people and parent to answer the door.
>
> (Secondary sector)

Changing conceptualisation of the role of senior leaders

It is evident from the above that these senior leaders saw their role as not just being concerned with the safety, wellbeing and learning of students and staff within the school but they were equally concerned for the welfare of families, and particularly those living in disadvantaged circumstances. This extended to concern and support for the mental health and wellbeing of parents and caregivers, providing practical support to families: 'Parents were offered and could access support from our pastoral care staff/DHTs (Depute Head Teachers) as well as financial support from our Family Opportunities Team at the school. This included, ... food vouchers, advice with housing, debt and utilities' (Secondary sector).

Many emphasised the importance of relationships, of building *relational trust*, 'knowing your families,' and adopting a flexible, responsive approach.

> It has been so hard not 'seeing' our children and this highlighted the importance and value of the relationships we build with families ... we felt

224 *Empowering the School Community*

an overwhelming sense of responsibility for our whole school community and at times struggled to accept that there were limitations in what we could actually do. We had to support staff and families without overwhelming them and at times this was really difficult to do as everyone was reacting and coping in different ways. Due to this a uniform approach for all wouldn't work so we had to make professional judgements with the knowledge and information we had on individuals before and during lockdown.

(Primary sector) (Mowat, in press-b)

Those who had invested in *capacity building* and building relationships prior to the pandemic were more able to rise to the challenge and be less overwhelmed by it. One respondent reflected honestly:

I personally think that we had not established a strong enough relationship with these families before lockdown. I believe that they would have engaged more with us during lockdown if the relationship had been there initially. This has highlighted the need to focus on engaging and working with these identified families to build a strong relationship with the school when moving forward after lockdown.

(Primary sector)

The depth of care and compassion was extraordinary when one considers the extensive pressures and expectations upon senior leaders in schools, including balancing the pressures of home-life with the job:

As a leader, I have had to deal with many challenges throughout my career, however, I cannot think of anything that comes close to leading during a pandemic, and in the most unprecedented times we have ever seen. I felt that as a leader, the need to be able to demonstrate optimism and resilience whilst juggling the many other demands that were placed upon me, such as working from home, home schooling, continuing with my studies, whilst ensuring that my family and friends were safe and well both physically and mentally. With many feeling scared, isolated, stressed and overwhelmed, I felt my role as a leader was to be there and get on with the role, working with senior colleagues in leading and serving our school community, demonstrating the leadership that is expected and required of a senior leader.

(Secondary sector)

The vast majority of respondents considered that the programme had prepared them well to face the challenges posed by the pandemic, particularly the professional reading, focus on critical incidents and on building community, and the networks they had built during it had sustained them through the pandemic.

I believe that Into Headship has had a profound impact on my confidence and maturity as a school leader. Although I may not always know the answer,

Socially Just and Culturally Responsive Leadership 225

I have a real self-belief in building and working with my colleagues and the wider school community towards a shared vision.

(Primary sector)

Brief reflection

I was immensely proud of these former and current *Into Headship* students in their efforts to support their school communities during lockdown. Students on the programme had been participating within a *Community of Practice* (see Chapter 6), on a joint enterprise of professional learning (Mowat, 2020b), in the process building both *cultural* and *social capital* (see the discussion to follow), the latter manifested in strong bonds and networks of support. During the programme they had not only engaged with theories of leadership but with theories of *social justice* and *inclusion* (represented also in the *Professional Standards* for headteachers in Scotland [GTCS, 2021]), embracing many of the themes within this book.

It is very likely that they, like many of their contemporaries across the world, experienced the 'de-skilling' to which Fullan referred. However, the programme had provided them with the networks of support and resilience to rise to the challenge to the best of their ability, in the process coming to a deeper understanding of the school in relation to its community and the important role that they, as senior leaders, play in the process. The key issue is whether the insights gained in the pandemic will act as a catalyst for positive change in the future, as envisaged by Fullan (2020) and Harris and Jones (2020), or, as cautioned by Sahlberg (2020), in the absence of a clear vision for change, revert back to prior ways of thinking and knowing.

Building social and cultural capital through creating an empowering school culture

The concepts of *social* and *cultural capital* are means of understanding at a deeper level the circumstances of people's lives and, in particular, the relationship between culture, status and material resources (Adams, Hopkins, & Shlasko, 2016). Chapter three drew on the work of Robert Putnam to illustrate how, in the town where he grew up, over time, a sense of community, networks of support and levels of trust and reciprocity had diminished as *social capital* reduced. Those who were prosperous and those who were poor became as two separate tribes, diminishing in the process *cultural capital*.

In crude terms, *social capital* refers to '*who* one knows' – the social networks that an individual is a part of – whereas, *cultural capital* refers to '*what* one knows about' (Adams et al., 2016). Both forms of capital are not unique to those in the upper echelons of society, albeit that they may take different forms and exercise different degrees of influence and power. The cumulative advantages of *social, cultural* and *economic capital* determine the degree to which individuals and groups can leverage power and maintain their status across generations (Adams et al., 2016).

226 *Empowering the School Community*

According to Spillane and Sun (2020), *social capital* is 'embedded in the relationships among people' (p. 2). Access to resources that can enable an individual's capability is influenced by the structure of these relationships (e.g., whether weak or dense) (p. 2). However, this is not dependent solely on the strategic efforts of individuals to build networks, but the nature of the networks to which they belong (the 'old boys' club' comes to mind). This is determined, in turn, by the institutional practices, norms, and regulations which set the parameters for how individuals interact with each other within the organisation (Spillane & Sun, 2020).

Spillane and Sun (2020) maintain that school principals can build *social capital* through attending to the norms, expectations and quality of interactions amongst the school community (including between the school and families); through influencing school climate and establishing high expectations of student performance; and through building facilitative school structures, creating opportunities for collaboration and the establishment of *relational trust.*

In a study of the leadership practices of newly appointed principals, the authors establish that principals adopted three main strategies to build *social capital – being present* by being visible and approachable; *channelling relationships* to transform the nature of interactions within and amongst stakeholder groups; *and building infrastructure* to support the process.

Empowering the school community

The concept of empowerment has recently come to the fore in education, championed by the Organisation for Economic Cooperation and Development (OECD) (Gomendio, 2017), although it is often framed through a *neo-liberal* lens and related to systems and structures. Within the context of leadership being exercised at all levels of the system, Forde and Torrance (2021) discuss the tension between *autonomy* and collaboration and centralised and directive government approaches focussed on achieving a narrow set of attainment outcomes.

However, drawing on *self-determination theory* (see Chapter 11), the notion that one can 'empower' or 'motivate' an individual, group or organisation is questionable: I would argue that both empowerment and motivation come from within. What we can do, however, is to create motivating, affirming and empowering environments that afford *agency* and *autonomy*. Three mechanisms by which schools can build *social* and *cultural capital* are student voice and participation, parental engagement (see Chapter 11) and building and strengthening links with the wider community. The last of these will be the focus of the next discussion.

The school and its wider community

A key issue to have emerged in the discussion of *relational* approaches to promoting positive behaviour in Chapters 9 and 10 is the importance of congruence both internal (e.g., the philosophical underpinnings of approaches adopted within the school) and external (e.g., between the values of the community, home and school). There is a growing literature, particularly in the USA, about the importance of *cultural responsiveness*, not only with regard to the curriculum (e.g., children of colour recognising themselves in the portrayal of everyday life, culture, art and history) and pedagogy, but also in terms of building *relational trust* both internally and between the school and its wider community. Such an approach values the community and what it has to offer and is based on a capabilities perspective (M. Smith, 2018; Ward, Bynner, & Bianchi, 2021) rather than a deficit perspective. It is an inclusive, collaborative approach that recognises and values diversity, seeks to create a bridge between the school and its community and is concerned with creating *culturally responsive learning environments* and empowering the school community.

The centrality of cultural competence and responsiveness

K. Francis and Osher (2018) claim that the inbuilt biases and prejudices which are held individually and collectively within the school community can be challenged through developing *cultural competence* (e.g., self-awareness), developing mindsets that value and address diversity. *Cultural competence* recognises the real barriers that children and families face in engaging with schooling. It seeks to address these barriers through addressing issues relating to *availability, accessibility, affordability, appropriateness* (effectiveness and quality) and *acceptability* (congruence with belief systems) of services; *identity safety* (sense of belonging and of being valued); and through examining issues of privilege and power (pp. 83–4). The key issue then becomes one of creating *culturally responsive* learning environments and the role of school leadership in this quest.

Culturally responsive school leadership

Culturally responsive school leadership focusses on improving outcomes for all children, but particularly those who are more prone to marginalisation (Scanlan & Johnson, 2015). It requires an approach that moves beyond a 'food and festival approach' to one that raises critical consciousness of the ways in which schools themselves may inadvertently reinforce inequalities and blame students and families for situations outwith their control (pp. 166–7). It constitutes several elements:

- High expectations of student achievement;
- Incorporating the history, values and cultural knowledge of the communities served by the school into the curriculum;
- Developing a critical consciousness more generally of inequities in society;
- Creating inclusive organisational structures that empower students and families from diverse racial and ethnic backgrounds (p. 166).

Hooper and Bernhardt (2016) consider the modelling of *cultural responsiveness* by school leaders as being the hallmark of *equity*, the key focus of which is the leader's engagement and interaction with the local community served by the school. *Culturally responsive* school leaders are concerned with building the systems, structures and relationships that enable the cultural identity of each individual to be affirmed and in creating a sense of community with which all can identify. At the heart of *cultural responsiveness* is knowledge and understanding of the circumstances of families, recognising diversity and the variability in family situations and providing opportunities for participation.

However, the individual identities of members of the school community may impact on their ability to identify with the community created within the school. As such, *being culturally* responsive places an onus on school leaders to consciously recognise their own biases, assumptions and prejudices towards others who identify with cultural groups other than their own and for intentional engagement and interaction (Hooper & Bernhardt, 2016).

The authors perceive interaction as lying on a continuum, as set out in Figure 12.2.

They regard engagement with diverse cultural groups as 'a journey rather than a destination' that has the potential for conflict arising from 'cultural dilemmas' rooted in differing perspectives, conflicting cultural values, historical bias and power differentials (p. 113), requiring an adaptive and responsive approach to resolving difficulties.

V. Coleman and Osher (2018) identify a set of principles that should inform *community engagement* amongst which is the need to value all perspectives and to recognise that culture matters. For them, engagement should go beyond tokenism and be community driven towards a model of *shared leadership*, characterised by a strong bidirectional relationship and final decision making at the community level. This could be characterised as a *working with* rather than a *doing to* relationship between the school and its community.

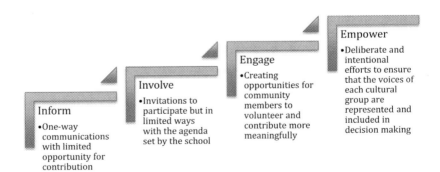

Figure 12.2 A model of cultural responsiveness of school leaders.

Source: Derived from *Creating Capacity for Learning and Equity*, figure 7.3, edn. 1 by Mary A. Hooper and Victoria L. Bernhardt, Copyright © 2016 by Routledge. Reproduced by permission of Taylor and Francis Group.

Price (2008) argues that the *social capital* that resides within communities is often untapped by schools, particularly that of voluntary and community groups. The issue then becomes one of how to engage with and release the positive energy of the community in ways that are constructive and productive and has value for a young person's development. Scanlan and Johnson (2015) identify a common element across approaches as being the importance of investing in building *social capital*. Through bringing together parents and school personnel across racial and economic groups, *bridging social capital*[4] (Putnam, 2001) can develop which has the potential to strengthen the relations between school and families.

In the USA, Rothstein-Fisch and Trumbull (2008) describe a range of approaches adopted within the 'Bridging Cultures' project that are designed to promote a sense of community and harmony, offering choice to students in the types of activity and the way in which activities are organised, and tapping into students' sense of shared responsibility. Whilst many of the strategies adopted could be applied readily to other classroom contexts, the key aspect is that they are based on a cultural understanding of children and families, recognising that the *collectivist* values that may be espoused in the home, representative of many cultures across the world, may be at odds with the *individualistic* culture of the school, particularly in Western societies.

Reflection Point

To what degree would you consider that your school or organisation has built strong ties and networks of support with its community? What are some of the barriers and opportunities that may present?

Whilst much of the discussion around *culturally responsive* schools emanates from the USA, is there a danger that this discussion may seem less relevant to schools in less culturally diverse communities? Yet, we need to prepare our C&YP to live in culturally diverse societies. How might this barrier be overcome and what can be learned from the discussion above?

A new paradigm

As previously intimated, a new paradigm is required as schools traverse and move beyond the pandemic. One not based on the limited, reductionist and potentially harmful paradigm of behaviour management and oft associated practices (such as *zero-tolerance* approaches); or narrow and confused understandings of discipline and the purposes that it serves, as argued by MacAllister (2017) (see Chapter 8), but based on building community and relationships, underpinned by the values and practices of equity, inclusion, care and compassion and concern for the well-being of the child or young person, within an empowering school ethos.

As argued in Chapter 8, behaviour management approaches frequently do not extend beyond the fostering of compliance and socialisation into unquestioned norms and values; do not recognise the moral agency that C&YP bring to the table nor their capacity to take responsibility for their own behaviour and learning; and understand student *agency* in very limited and reductionist ways. They do little to promote students' understanding of their behaviour and their relationships with others and are focussed on the achievement of short-term objectives (compliance) at the expense of the holistic development of the child or young person, often to the detriment of long-term objectives towards a well-rounded individual with a sense of social responsibility (Khon, 2005, 2008; MacAllister, 2017). They focus on the *symptoms* rather than the *causes* of what is perceived to be deviant behaviour (MacAllister, 2017), failing to challenge the systemic roots of such behaviour. They often fail to recognise or acknowledge alternative ways of creating a positive environment for learning through *relational* approaches, creating a false dichotomy between strict régimes and chaos (Khon, 1999, 2005) or, alternatively, bring together approaches which have entirely different philosophical and theoretical bases (such as nurture and token-reward schemes). Such policies do not recognise the professionalism of teachers, nor their capacity to exercise judgement in a responsive, caring and compassionate way. Rather than a genuine partnership with parents, their role is seen as being to reinforce the school's behaviour policy into which they have had limited input.

In comparison, policy and practice that focusses on building community and relationships has the potential to strengthen the bonds and ties (the *social capital*) and the *cultural capital* of the community; foster empathy, compassion and care for others; create a sense of belonging and connectedness; sees student wellbeing and high-quality learning (relevant, *culturally responsive* curriculum, high quality inclusive pedagogy and the right balance of challenge and support for student learning) as the necessary conditions to promote positive behaviour (rather than vice-versa) (see Figure 12.3); and recognises the important role that school leadership plays in creating the conditions to empower the school community.

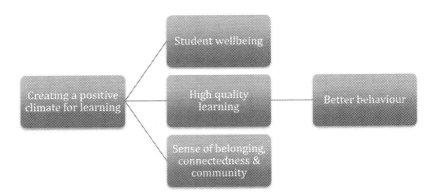

Figure 12.3 A representation of the relationship between wellbeing, learning and behaviour.

Socially Just and Culturally Responsive Leadership 231

This needs to be paralleled by a strong rejection of international and national policies that serve to marginalise communities, families and C&YP and which have led in the USA and beyond to a 'test and punish,' 'no excuses' agenda and to the experience of a 'narrowly defined, scripted curriculum and a hostile, compliance-orientated climate' (p. 3) that ultimately results in exclusionary practices for many C&YP (L. Darling-Hammond, Cook-Harvey, Flook, Gardner, & Melnick, 2018).

A focus on teacher professionalism and 'systemness'

Building teacher capacity through professional development is essential for the creation of equitable learning communities (R. G. Smith & Brazer, 2016). A necessary condition in reducing exclusionary practices is a transformation in how teachers perceive and enact their role. Crucial to this is the education they receive when being inducted into the profession and their continuous professional learning thereafter, including that of prospective and actual headteachers.

Pantić and Florian (2015) envision the role of teacher educators as being concerned with preparing teachers as change agents for inclusion and social justice, working collaboratively with other agents (across professions) to meet student needs, concerned not solely with the implementation of policy, but with the transformation of the system. Key elements are a sense of purpose, pedagogical competence and capacity to work collaboratively with others, autonomy and reflexivity.

If there is one message that should emerge loud and clear from this book, it is the complexity of the issues facing schools in achieving a *climate for learning* and creating *equitable* and *inclusive* school communities. There is no single way of understanding the nature of the challenge or 'one-size-fits-all' solution, whether it be *nurture, trauma-informed practice, restorative practice, pupil participation* or *parental/community engagement* – it is how the extensive range of variables under discussion interact with each other (as illustrated in Figure 12.1) that will enable and empower the school community to meet the needs of C&YP respectfully and with care and compassion.

There are implications for the continuous professional development of teachers, ensuring that they become familiar with emerging approaches such as *trauma-informed practice* and have a deep understanding of *inclusive practice, social justice* and *children' rights* (and the criticality to hold fads, 'flavour of the month' and 'snake-oil' practices at arm's length); for prospective and substantive middle-leaders and school principals/headteachers in developing their understanding of *leadership for social justice*, of *shared, collaborative* and *distributive* forms of leadership and of the importance of *building community* and *partnership working*; and for teacher educators, ensuring that they have the necessary knowledge, understanding and skill to facilitate all of the above. However, as exemplified well in the previous chapter, teacher continuous professional development (CPD) does not just take the form of formal in-service

232 *Empowering the School Community*

Additional Suggested Reading

Leadership for Increasingly Diverse Schools

Routledge, 2015. George Theoharis and Martin Scanlan (Editors)

This edited book draws from a range of perspectives on inclusive leadership as it pertains to intersectionality, disability, poverty, race, gender and gender identity, and religion, amongst other things, including an exploration of family and community engagement. It is largely authored in the USA and reflects the concerns about equity within the USA.

Excellence through Equity: Five Principles of Courageous Leadership to Guide every Student

ASCD, 2016. Alan Blankstein & Pedro Noguerra (Editors)

This edited book draws from a wide range of respected contributors, such as Michael Fullan and Andy Hargreaves but, once again, with a focus largely on the USA education system. The book is organised under the five principles of courageous leadership (see Table 12.2) with exemplifications provided of *Excellence through Equity* in action.

Creating Capacity for Learning and Equity in Schools

Routledge, 2016. Mary Hooper and Victoria Bernhardt

This book draws on theories of *instructional, adaptive* and *transformational leadership* to build capacity within the system focussed on student learning, continuous improvement and engaged community as a means of creating sustainable and equitable school systems. Whilst drawing from theory, it is a much more 'hands-on' book for school leaders with many frameworks, models and reflection points to foster deeper understanding. It serves as a valuable resource for those leading leadership preparation programmes. Once again, it emanates from the USA.

Compassionate Leadership for School Belonging

UCL Press, 2022. Kathryn Riley

Building on her previous work, this newly published book (at the point of writing), draws on the principles of schools as a psychologically safe space; of adults being attentive to the experiences that students bring with them; and the importance of a sense of rootedness to the school within its community, a key theme of this chapter.

---

training, but can be furthered through avenues such as professional enquiry, participation in *professional learning communities* and through opportunities to take on leadership roles.

In conclusion, if the aim of this book to create equitable, inclusive and compassionate schools is to be realised, there is a need to build understanding of how to create empowering, emotionally-safe environments where all members of the school community are valued for who they are and feel a sense of belonging and connectedness to the school. At the systems level, it requires a coalition of hearts and minds, of policies that reach across borders and are not time-limited by political expediencies (e.g., the election cycle) nor bounded by narrow and restricted understandings of the purposes that education serves and associated *neo-liberal* orthodoxies, as argued throughout this book.

Notes

1. See https://professionallearning.education.gov.scot/learn/programmes/into-headship/
2. This study, carried out with colleagues at the University of Strathclyde, is funded by The British Educational Leadership, Management and Administration Society (BELMAS). The initial findings were presented at the European Conference on Educational Research (ECER) in 2021. A 2nd phase of the study is planned.
3. An electronic platform to facilitate online learning and communication in Scottish schools
4. *Bridging social capital*, associated with the work of Robert Putnam, connects people who in normal circumstances would not come into contact with each other, where ties are weak, there is little commonality and trust has not been established to any degree.

References

Adams, M., & Bell, L. A. (Eds.). (2016). *Teaching for diversity and social justice*. London: Routledge.

Adams, M., Hopkins, L. E., & Shlasko, D. (2016). Classism. In M. Adams, & L. A. Bell (Eds.), *Teaching for diversity and social justice* (pp. 213–253). London: Routledge.

Adams, M., & Zúñiga, X. (2016). Core concepts for social justice education. In M. Adams, & L. A. Bell (Eds.), *Teaching for diversity and social justice* (3rd ed., pp. 95–129). London: Routledge.

Addison, D., Casimir, A. E., Mims, L. C., Kaler-Jones, C., & Simmons, D. (2021). Beyond deep breathing: A new vision for equitable, culturally responsive, and trauma-informed mindfulness practice. *Middle School Journal, 52*(3), 4–14.

Ainscow, M., Booth, T., & Dyson, A. (2006a). *Improving schools, developing inclusion*. London: Routledge.

Ainscow, M., Booth, T., & Dyson, A. (2006b). Inclusion and the standards agenda: Negotiating policy pressures in England. *International Journal of Inclusive Education, 10*(4–5), 295–308.

Ainscow, M., Chapman, C., Dyson, A., Gunter, H., Hall, D., Kerr, K., & West, M. (2010). Social inequality: Can schools narrow the gap? In K. Kerr & M. West (Eds.), *Insight paper* (Vol. 2). Macclesfield, UK: BERA.

Ainscow, M., Dyson, A., Goldrick, S., & West, M. (2012). Making schools effective for all: Rethinking the task. *School Leadership & Management: Formerly School Organisation, 32*(3), 197–213.

Ainscow, M., & Sandill, A. (2010). Developing inclusive education systems: The role of organisational cultures and leadership. *International Journal of Inclusive Education, 14*(4), 401–416.

Ainscow, M., Slee, R., & Best, M. (2019). Editorial: The Salamanca statement: 25 years on. *International Journal of Inclusive Education, 23*(7–8), 671–676. doi: 10.1080/13603116.2019.1622800.

Allan, J. (2013). Inclusion for all. In T. G. Bryce, W. M. Humes, D. Gillies, & A. Kennedy (Eds.), *Scottish Education: Referendum* (4th ed., pp. 787–795). Edinburgh: Edinburgh University Press.

Allison, J., & Craig, S. (2014). Keeping our difficult kids in school: The impact of the use of the 'Boxall Profile' on the transition and integration of behaviourally – disordered students in primary schools. *Kairaranga, 15*(2), 25–35.

(The) American Psychiatric Association (APA). (2013). *Diagnostic and Statistical Manual of Mental Disorders (DSM–5-TR)*. Retrieved from https://www.psychiatry.org/psychiatrists/practice/dsm

References 235

Anderson, M. (2018). Getting CONSISTENT with consequences (student behavior management). *Educational Leadership, 76*(1), 27–33.

Anderson, J., Boyle, C., Page, A., & Mavropoulou, S. (2020). Inclusive education: An enigma of 'Wicked' proportions. In C. Boyle, J. Anderson, A. Page, & S. Mavropoulou (Eds.), *Inclusive education: Global issues and controversies* (pp. 1–11). Leiden, The Netherlands: Koninklijke Brill NV.

Andrejevic, M., & Selwyn, N. (2019). Facial recognition technology in schools: Critical questions and concerns. *Learning, Media and Technology, 45*(2), 1–14.

Antonovsky, A. (1979). *Health, stress and coping.* San Fransisco, CA: Jossey-Bass.

Apple, M. W., Biesta, G., Bright, D., Giroux, H. A., Heffernan, A., McLaren, P., & Yeatman, A. (2022). Reflections on contemporary challenges and possibilities for democracy and education. *Journal of Educational Administration and History.* doi: 10.1080/00220620.2022.2052029.

Araújo, M. (2005). Disruptive or disrupted? A qualitative study on the construction of indiscipline. *International Journal of Inclusive Education, 9*(3), 241–268.

Archard, D. (2014). *Children: Rights and childhood* (3rd ed.). London: Routledge.

Armstrong, D. (2018). Addressing the wicked problem of behaviour in schools. *International Journal of Inclusive Education, 22*(9), 997–1013. doi: 10.1080/13603116.2017.1413732.

Armstrong, D., & Hallet, F. (2012). Private knowledge, public face: Conceptions of children with SEBD by teachers in the UK – a case study. *Educational & Child Psychology, 29*(4), 77–87.

Arnott, M. (2017). The SERA lecture 2016: "Jigsaw puzzle" of education policy? Nation, state and globalised policy making. *Scottish Educational Review, 49*(2), 3–14.

Association for Supervision and Curriculum Development. (2018). *Educational leadership: Ccassroom management re-imagined.* Alexandria, VA: ASCD.

Atkins, L., & Flint, K. (2015). Nothing changes: Perceptions of vocational education in a coalition era. *International Journal of Training Research, 13*(1), 35–48.

Atkinson, M. B., & Herrick, C. A. (Eds.). (2006). *Child and adolescent mental health: Interdisciplinary systems of care.* Boston, MA: Jones and Bartlett.

Auerbach, S. (2010). Beyond coffee with the principal: Toward leadership for authentic school– family partnerships. *Journal of School Leadership, 20*(6), 728–757.

Bacher-Hicks, A., Billings, S., & Deming, D. (2021). Proving the school-to-prison pipeline: Stricter middle schools raise the risk of adult arrest. *Education Next, 21*(4), 52–57.

Ball, S. J. (2003). The teacher's soul and the terrors of performativity. *Journal of Education Policy, 18*(2), 215–228.

Ball, S. J. (2009). Academies in context: Politics, business and philanthropy and heterarchial governance. *Management in Education, 23*(3), 100–103.

Ball, S. J. (2015). Education, governance and the tyranny of numbers. *Journal of Education Policy, 30*(3), 299–301.

Ball, S. J., & Noddings, N. (2014). OECD and Pisa tests are damaging education worldwide – academics. *The Guardian.*

Bandura, A. (1997). *Self-efficacy in changing societies.* Cambridge: Cambridge University Press.

Bangs, J., MacBeath, J., & Galton, M. (2011). *Re-inventing schools, reforming teaching: From political visions to classroom reality.* London: Routledge.

Barnard, H. (2017). *Poverty in Scotland 2017.* York, UK: Joseph Rowntree Foundation.

236 *References*

Barnhardt, R. (1981). *Culture, community and the curriculum*. Alaska: University of Alaska Fairbanks.

Bartholomay, D. (2022). A time to adapt, not "Return to normal": Lessons in compassion and accessibility from teaching during COVID-19. *Teaching Sociology, 50*(1), 62–72.

Barton, L. (2019). The politics of education for all. In J. Rix, M. Nind, K. Sheehy, K. Simmons, & C. Walsh (Eds.), *Equality, participation and inclusion: Diverse perspectives* (pp. 90–98). London: Routledge.

Bates, A. (2013). Transcending systems thinking in education reform: Implications for policy-makers and school leaders. *Journal of Education Policy, 28*(1), 38–54.

Bates, J., Lewis, S., & Pickard, A. (2019). *Education, policy, practice and the professional* (2nd ed.). London: Bloomsbury.

Beck, A. (2019). Secondary schools in Scotland under reform: The changing nature of governance, policy and curriculum. In A. Beck, S. Capel, M. Leask, & S. Younie (Eds.), *Learning to teach in the secondary school*. London: Routledge.

Beebe, B., Jaffe, J., Markese, S., Buck, K., Chen, H., Cohen, P., & Feldstein, S. (2010). The origins of 12-month attachment: A microanalysis of 4-month mother–infant interaction. *Attachment & Human Development, 12*(1–2), 3–141.

Belger, T. (2021). Williamson plans behaviour survey and urges 'sensible debate' over exclusions. *Schools Week*. Retrieved from https://schoolsweek.co.uk/gavin-williamson-plans-behaviour-survey-and-urges-sensible-exclusion-debate/

Bell, L. A. (2016). Theoretical foundations for social justice education. In M. Adams, & L. A. Bell (Eds.), *Teaching for diversity and social justice* (pp. 3–26). London: Routledge.

Bellis, M. A., Ashton, K., Hughes, K., Ford, K., Bishop, J., & Paranjothy, S. (2015). *Adverse childhood experiences and their impact on health-harming behaviours in the Welsh adult population*. Retrieved from http://www2.nphs.wales.nhs.uk:8080/PRIDDocs.nsf/7c21215d6d0c613e80256f490030c05a/d488a3852491bc1d-80257f370038919e/$FILE/ACE Report FINAL (E).pdf

Bender, P. K., Sømhovd, M., Pons, F., Reinholdt-Dunne, M. L., & Esbjørn, B. H. (2015). The impact of attachment security and emotion dysregulation on anxiety in children and adolescents. *Emotional and Behavioural Difficulties, 20*(2), 189–204.

Bennathan, M. (2013). Responding to children's needs. In M. Bennathan, & M. Boxall (Eds.), *Effective intervention in primary schools: Nurture groups* (2nd ed., pp. 71–94). London: Taylor Francis.

Bennathan, M., & Boxall, M. (2000). *Effective interventions in primary schools: NGs*. London: Fulton.

Bennathan, M., & Boxall, M. (2013). *Effective intervention in primary schools: Nurture groups* (2nd ed.). London: Taylor Francis.

Bennett, T. (2010). *The behaviour guru: Behaviour solutions for teachers*. London: Continuum.

Bennett, H. (2015). Results of the systematic review on nurture groups' effectiveness: How efficient are nurture groups? Under what conditions do nurture groups work Best? *International Journal of Nurture in Education, 1*(1), 3–8.

Bennett, T. (2017). *Creating a culture: How school leaders can optimise behaviour: Independent review of behaviour in schools*. Retrieved from https://assets.publishing.service.gov.uk/government/uploads/system/uploads/attachment_data/file/602487/Tom_Bennett_Independent_Review_of_Behaviour_in_Schools.pdf

References 237

Berlin, I. (1978). *The hedgehog and the fox*. Chicago, IL: Ivan R. Dee Inc. Publishers.

Berryman, M., & Eley, E. (2019). Student belonging: Critical relationships and responsibilities. *International Journal of Inclusive Education, 23*(9), 985–1001. doi: 10.1080/13603116.2019.1602365.

Bevington, T. J. (2015). Appreciative evaluation of restorative approaches in schools. *Pastoral Care in Education, 33*(2), 105–115.

Biesta, G. (2007). Why "what works" Won't work: Evidence-based practice and the democratic deficit in educational research. *Educational Theory, 57*(1), 1–22.

Bilton, K., & Cooper, P. (2012). ADHD and children with social, emotional and behavioural difficulties. In C. Cole, H. Daniels, & J. Visser (Eds.), *The Routledge international companion to emotional and behavioural difficulties [Routledge Handbook]* (pp. 32–39). London: Routedge.

Black, C., Eunson, J., Murray, L., Zubairi, S. S., & Bowen, L. (2016). *Behaviour in Scottish Schools Research 2016*. Scottish Government [on behalf of Ipsos MORI Scotland]. Retrieved from http://www.gov.scot/Publications/2017/11/5792

Blad, E. (2018, 18.12.2018). Here's what the end of Obama-era discipline guidance means for schools, Commentary. *Education Week*. Retrieved from https://www.edweek.org/leadership/heres-what-the-end-of-obama-era-discipline-guidance-means-for-schools/2018/12

Blankstein, A. M., & Noguera, P. (2015). Introduction: Achieving excellence through equity for every student. In A. M. Blankstein, P. Noguera, & L. Kelly (Eds.), *Excellence through equity: Five principles of courageous leadership to guide achievement for every student* (pp. 3–30). Alexandria, VA: ASCD.

Blankstein, A. M., Noguera, P., & Kelly, L. (2015). *Excellence through equity: Five principles of courageous leadership to guide achievement for every student*. Alexandria, VA: ASCD.

Bohart, A. C. (2007). The actualizing person. In M. Cooper, M. O'Hara, P. F. Schmid, & G. Wyatt (Eds.), *The handbook of person-centred psychotherapy and counselling* (pp. 47–63). Hampshire, UK: Palgrave MacMillan.

Booth, T., & Ainscow, M. (1998). *From them to us*. London: Routledge.

Booth, T., & Ainscow, M. (2011). *The index for inclusion: Developing learning and participation in schools* (3rd ed.). Bristol, UK: CSIE.

Botha, J., & Kourkoutas, E. (2016). A community of practice as an inclusive model to support children with social, emotional and behavioural difficulties in school contexts. *International Journal of Inclusive Education, 20*(7), 784–799. doi: 10.1080/13603116.2015.1111448.

Bottrell, D. (2007). Resistance, resilience and social identities: Reframing 'Problem Youth' and the problem of schooling. *Journal of Youth Studies, 10*(5), 597–616.

Boxall, M. (2013). The nurture group in the primary school. In M. Bennathan, & M. Boxall (Eds.), *Effective intervention in primary schools: Nurture groups* (pp. 19–38). London: Taylor Francis.

Boyd, I. (2019, 31st May 2019). Tackling the pupil equity paradox. *Times Educational Supplement Scotland*, pp. 20–23.

Bøyum, S. (2014). Fairness in education – A normative analysis of OECD policy documents. *Journal of Education Policy, 29*(6), 856–870.

Bozarth, G. (2007). Unconditional positive regard. In M. Cooper, M. O'Hara, P. F. Schmid, & G. Wyatt (Eds.), *The handbook of person-centred psychotherapy and counselling* (pp. 182–193). New York: Palgrave Macmillan.

238 *References*

Bradshaw, P. (2011). *Growing up in Scotland: Changes in child cognitive ability in the pre-school years.* Retrieved from https://dera.ioe.ac.uk/3658/13/0117210_Redacted.pdf

Brann-Barrett, M. T. (2011). Same landscape, different lens: Variations in young people's socio-economic experiences and perceptions in their disadvantaged working-class community. *Journal of Youth Studies, 14*(3), 261–278.

Bright, N. G. (2011). 'Non-servile Virtuosi' in insubordinate spaces: School disaffection, refusal and resistance in a former English coalfield. *European Educational Research Journal, 10*(4), 502–515.

Bronfenbrenner, U. (1979). *The ecology of human development: Experiments by nature and design.* Cambridge, MA: Harvard University Press.

Bronfenbrenner, U. (1986). Ecology of the family as a context for human development: Research perspectives. *Developmental Psychology, 22*(6), 723–733.

Bronfenbrenner, U. (1994). Ecological models of human development. *International Encylopedia of Education* (2nd ed., Vol. 3). Oxford: Elsevier.

Bronfenbrenner, U., & Morris, P. A. (2006). The bioecological model of human development. In R. M. Lerner (Ed.), *Handbook of child psychology: Theoretical models of human development* (6th ed., Vol. 1, pp. 793–828). Hoboken, NJ: Wiley.

Brookfield, S. D. (1995). *Becoming a critically refective teacher.* San Fransisco, CA: Jossey-Bass.

Brophy, J. (2010). *Motivating students to learn* (3rd ed.). New York: Routledge.

Brown, E. T. (2015). ADHD: From stereotype to science. *Educational Leadership, 73*(2), 52–26.

Bruner, J. S. (1973). Going beyond the information given. In J. M. Anglin (Ed.), *Beyond the information given: Studies in the psychology of knowing* (pp. 218–238). London: George Allan and Unwin.

Brunila, K. (2011). The projectisation, marketisation and therapisation of education. *European Educational Research Journal, 10*(3), 421–432.

Brussino, O. (2021), Building capacity for inclusive teaching: Policies and practices to prepare all teachers for diversity and inclusion. *OECD education working papers,* No. 256, OECD Publishing, Paris, https://doi.org/10.1787/57fe6a38-en

Burgess, S. (2014). *Understanding the success of London's schools* (Vol. Working Paper No. 14/333). Retrieved from the Centre for Market and Public Organisation, University of Bristol. http://www.bristol.ac.uk/media-library/sites/cmpo/migrated/documents/wp333.pdf

Burns, T., & Gottschalk, F. (eds.) (2019), *Educating 21st century children: Emotional well-being in the digital age,* Educational Research and Innovation, OECD Publishing, Paris, https://doi.org/10.1787/b7f33425-en

Bywaters, P., Bunting, L., & Davidson, G., et al. (2015). *The relationship between poverty, child abuse and neglect: An evidence review.* Retrieved from Joseph Rowntree Foundation, York. https://www.jrf.org.uk/report/relationship-between-poverty-child-abuse-and-neglect-evidence-review

CALA Childhood Practice. (2013). The importance of the early years – DS John Carnochan. Retrieved from https://calachildhoodpractice.wordpress.com/2013/02/24/the-importance-of-the-early-years-d-s-john-carnochan/

Cameron, T. (2021). *Understanding the value of parental engagement in learning at home through pupil voice.* (Master of Education), University of Strathcldye, unpublished.

References 239

Canter, L., & Canter, M. (2001). *Lee Canter's assertive discipline: Positive behavior management for Today's classrooms* (3rd ed.). Los Angeles, CA: Canter and Associates, Inc.

Carleton, R., Nolan, A. D., Murray, C., & Menary, S. (2021). Renfrewshire's nurturing relationships approach: Utilising nurturing approaches to support school staff and pupils during Covid-19. *International Journal of Nurture in Education*, 7(1), 73–84.

Caro, D. H., & Mirazchiyski, P. (2011). Socioeconomic gradients in Eastern European countries: Evidence from PIRLS 2006. *European Educational Research Journal*, 11(1), 96–110.

Causton, J., MacLeod, K., & Pretti-Frontczak, K. (2021). Ready...Set...Success: A formula for leading schools with love. *Educational Leadership*, 79(2), 20–26.

Cefai, C., & Cooper, P. (2011). The introduction of nurture groups in Maltese schools: A method of promoting inclusive education. *British Journal of Special Education*, 38(2), 65–72.

Chafouleas, S. M., Pickens, I., & Gherardi, S. A. (2021). Adverse childhood experiences (ACEs): Translation into action in K12 education settings. *School Mental Health*, 13(2), 213–224.

Chapman, C., & Ainscow, M. (2021). Developing equitable education systems. In C. Chapman, & M. Ainscow (Eds.), *Educational equity: Pathways to success* (pp. 1–19). London: Routledge.

Chavis, D. M., & Lee, K. (2015). What is community anyway? *Stanford Social Innovation Review*. doi: https://doi.org/10.48558/EJJ2-JJ82.

Chester, K. L., Spencer, N. H., Whiting, L., & Brooks, F. M. (2017). Association between experiencing relational bullying and adolescent health-related quality of life. *Journal of School Health*, 7(11), 865–872.

Choudhury, S., Charman, T., & Blakemore, S.-J. (2008). Development of the teenage brain. *Mind, Brain, and Education*, 2(3), 142–147.

Cigman, R. (2007). A question of universality: Inclusive education and the principle of respect. *Journal of Philosophy of Education*, 41(4), 775–793.

Clark, C. (1998). Discipline in schools. *British Journal of Educational Studies*, 46(3), 289–301.

Coffield, F. (2012). Why the McKinsey reports will not improve school systems. *Journal of Education Policy*, 27(1), 131–149. doi: 10.1080/02680939.2011. 623243.

Cohen, C. E., & Barron, I. G. (2021). Trauma-informed high schools: A systematic narrative review of the literature. *School Mental Health*, 13(2), 225–234.

Cole, T. (2015). *Mental health difficulties and children at risk of exclusion from schools in England: A review from an educational perspective of policy, practice and research, 1997 to 2015*. Oxford: University of Oxford.

Cole, T., Daniels, H., & Visser, J. (2013). Introduction to section 1. In J. Visser, H. Daniels, & T. Cole (Eds.), *The Routledge international companion to social, emotional and behavioural difficulties* (pp. 11–14). London: Routledge.

Cole, T., McCluskey, G., Daniels, H., Thompson, I., & Tawell, A. (2019). Factors associated with high and low levels of school exclusions: Comparing the English and wider UK experience. *Emotional and Behavioural Difficulties*, 24(4), 374–390.

Coleman, M. (2020). Leading the change to establish a whole-school nurturing culture. *Emotional and Behavioural Difficulties*, 25(1), 68–79.

240 *References*

Coleman, V., & Osher, D. (2018). Partnering with communities. In D. Osher, D. Moroney, & S. Williamson (Eds.), *Creating safe, equitable, engaging schools: A comprehensive, evidence-based approach to supporting students* (pp. 107–119). Cambridge, MA: Harvard Education Press.

Colley, D. (2009). Nurture groups in secondary schools. *Emotional and Behavioural Difficulties, 14*(4), 291–300.

Colley, D. (2012). Setting up a nurture group in your secondary school. In J. Visser (Ed.), *Transforming troubled lives: Key issues in policy, practice and provision*. London: Routledge.

Colley, D., & Seymour, R. (2021). An evidence based guide to opening a successful secondary school nurture group. *International Journal of Nurture in Education, 7*(1), 56–72.

Colombi, G., Mayo, R. V., Tanyu, M., Osher, D., & Mart, A. (2018). Building and restoring school communities. In D. Osher, D. Moroney, & S. Williamson (Eds.), *Creating safe, equitable, engaging schools: A comprehensive, evidence-based approach to supporting students* (pp. 147–161). Cambridge, MA: Harvard Education Press.

Condly, S. (2006). Resilience in children: A review of literature with implications for. *Education. Urban Education, 41*, 211–236.

Connell, R. (2013). The neoliberal cascade and education: An essay on the market agenda And its consequences. *Critical Studies in Education, 54*(2), 99–112. doi: 10.1080/17508487.2013.776990.

Connor, D. J., & Berman, D. (2019). (Be)longing: A family's desire for authentic inclusion. *International Journal of Inclusive Education, 23*(9), 923–936. doi: 10.1080/13603116.2019.1602361.

Cooke, C., Yeomans, J., & Parkes, J. (2008). The oasis: Nurture group provision for key stage 3 pupils. *Emotional and Behavioural Difficulties, 13*(4), 291–303. doi: 10.1080/13632750802442219.

Cooper, B. S., & Mulvey, J. D. (2015). Connecting education, welfare, and health for American families. *Peabody Journal of Education, 90*(5), 659–676. doi: 10.1080/0161956X.2015.1087776.

Cooper, P. (2004). Nurture groups: The research evidence. In J. Wearmouth, R. C. Richmond, & T. Glynn (Eds.), *Addressing Pupils' behaviour: Responses at district, school and individual levels* (pp. 176–198). London: David Fulton Publishers.

Cooper, P. (2008). Like alligators bobbing for poodles? A critical discussion of education, ADHD and the biopsychosocial perspective. *Journal of Philosophy of Education, 42*(304), 457–474.

Cooper, M., Evans, Y., & Pybis, J. (2016). Interagency collaboration in children and young people's mental health: A systematic review of outcomes, facilitating factors and inhibiting factors. *Child: Care, Health & Development, 42*(3), 325–342.

Cooper, M., O'Hara, M., Schmid, P. F., & Wyatt, G. (Eds.). (2007). *The handbook of person-centred psychotherapy and counselling*. New York: Palgrave Macmillan.

Cooper, P., & Whitebread, D. (2007). The effectiveness of nurture groups on student progress: Evidence from a national research study. *Emotional and Behavioural Difficulties, 12*(3), 171–190. doi: 10.1080/13632750701489915.

Corcoran, T., Claiborne, L., & Whitburn, B. (2019). Paradoxes in inclusive education: A necessary condition of relationality? *International Journal of Inclusive Education, 23*(10), 1003–1016. doi: 10.1080/13603116.2019.1625453.

References 241

Corrigan, P. W. (2006). Mental health stigma as social attribution: Implications for research method and attitude change. *Clinical Psychology: Science and Practice*, 7(1), 48–67.

Couper, S., & Mackie, P. (2016). *'Polishing the Diamonds': Addressing Adverse Childhood Experiences in Scotland*. Retrieved from National Health Service, Scotland https://www.basw.co.uk/resources/polishing-diamonds-addressing-adverse-childhood-experiences-scotland

Couture, C. (2013). The value of nurture groups in addressing emotional and behavioural difficulties and promoting school inclusion. In T. Cole, H. Daniels, & J. Visser (Eds.), *The Routledge international companion to emotional and behavioural difficulties*. London: Routledge.

Cremin, H., Sellman, E., & McCluskey, G. (2012). Interdisciplinary perspectives on restorative justice: Developing insights for education. *British Journal of Educational Studies*, 60(4), 421–437.

Crittenden, P. (2008). *Raising parents: Attachment, parenting and child safety*. Cullompton; Portland: Willan Publishing.

Crozier, G., & Davies, J. (2007). Hard To reach parents or Hard To reach schools? A discussion of home-school relations, with particular reference To Bangladeshi and Pakistani parents. *British Educational Research Journal*, 33(3), 295–313.

Cubeddu, D., & MacKay, T. (2017). The attunement principles: A comparison of nurture group and mainstream settings. *Emotional and Behavioural Difficulties*, 22(3), 261–274.

Cullinane, C., & Montacute, R. (2020). *COVID-19 and social mobility (Vol. Impact brief #1: School shutdown)*. London: Sutton Trust.

Curwin, R. L., Mendler, A. N., & Mendler, B. D. (2008). *Discipline with dignity: New challenges, new solutions*. Alexandria, VA: ASCD.

d'Agnese, V. (2018). *Reclaiming education in the age of PISA: Challenging OECD's educational order*. London: Routledge.

Darling-Hammond, L., & Cook-Harvey, C. M. (2018). Educating the whole child: Improving school climate to support student success. *Learning Policy Institute, Sept 2018*. Retrieved from https://learningpolicyinstitute.org/sites/default/files/product-files/Educating_Whole_Child_REPORT.pdf

Darling-Hammond, L., Cook-Harvey, C. M., Flook, L., Gardner, M., & Melnick, H. (2018). *With the whole child in mind: Insights from the comer school development program*. Alexandria, VA: ASCD.

Darling-Hammond, L., & DePaoli, J. (2020). Why school climate matters and what can be done to improve it. *State Education Standard*, 20(2), 7–11.

Darling-Hammond, S., Fronius, T. A., Sutherland, H., Guckenburg, S., Petrosino, A., & Hurley, N. (2020). Effectiveness of restorative justice in US K-12 schools: A review of quantitative research. *Contemporary School Psychology*, 24(3), 295–308.

Davis, P., & Florian, L. (2004). *Teaching strategies and approaches for pupils with special educational needs: A scoping study*. Research Report RR516. Retrieved from https://dera.ioe.ac.uk/6059/1/RR516.pdf

Davis, J. M., Ravenscroft, J., & Bizas, N. (2015). Transition, inclusion and partnership: Child-, parent- and professional-led approaches in a European research project. *Child Care in Practice*, 21(1), 33–49.

Deci, E. L., Vallerand, R. J., Pelletier, L. G., & Ryan, R. M. (2011). Motivation and education: The self-determination perspective. *Educational Psychologist*, 26(3 & 4), 325–346.

242 *References*

Department for Education and Skills (1978). *Special educational needs: The Warnock report.* London: Her Majesty's Stationery Office.

Dewey, J. (1915). *The school and society* (3rd ed.). Chicago, Illinois: The University of Chicago Press.

DfE & DoH. (2014). *SEND code of practice: 0 to 25 years.* Retrieved from https://www.gov.uk/government/publications/send-code-of-practice-0-to-25

DfE & DoH. (2015). *SEND code of practice: 0 to 25 years: Statutory guidance for organisations which work with and support children and young people who have special educational needs or disabilities.* Retrieved from https://assets.publishing.service.gov.uk/government/uploads/system/uploads/attachment_data/file/398815/SEND_Code_of_Practice_January_2015.pdf

DfE (2011a). *Guide for heads and school staff on behaviour and discipline.* London: UK Government.

DfE. (2011b). *New powers for teachers to improve discipline in schools [Press release].* Retrieved from https://www.gov.uk/government/news/new-powers-for-teachers-to-improve-discipline-in-schools

DfE. (2012). *Pupil behaviour in schools in England: An evaluation (Vol. Research Report DFE-RR218).* Retrieved from https://assets.publishing.service.gov.uk/government/uploads/system/uploads/attachment_data/file/184078/DFE-RR218.pdf

DfE. (2016). *Behaviour and discipline in schools: Advice for headteachers and school staff.* Retrieved from https://www.gov.uk/government/publications/behaviour-and-discipline-in-schools

DfE. (2018a). *Mental health and behaviour in schools.* Retrieved from https://www.gov.uk/government/publications/mental-health-and-behaviour-in-schools–2

DfE. (2018b). *Special educational needs in England: January 2018.* Retrieved from https://assets.publishing.service.gov.uk/government/uploads/system/uploads/attachment_data/file/729208/SEN_2018_Text.pdf

DfE. (2019a). *Help, protection, education: Concluding the Children in Need review.* (DFE-001220-2019). Retrieved from https://www.gov.uk/government/publications/review-of-children-in-need

DfE. (2019b). *Timpson review of school exclusion.* Retrieved from https://assets.publishing.service.gov.uk/government/uploads/system/uploads/attachment_data/file/807862/Timpson_review.pdf

DfE. (2021). *Behaviour management strategies, in-school units and managed moves: Call for evidence.* UK Government. Retrieved from https://www.gov.uk/government/consultations/behaviour-management-strategies-in-school-units-and-managed-moves-call-for-evidence

DfE. (2022a). *Behaviour in schools: Advice for headteachers and school staff.* Retrieved from https://consult.education.gov.uk/school-absence-and-exclusions-team/revised-school-behaviour-and-exclusion-guidance/supporting_documents/Behaviour%20in%20schools%20%20advice%20for%20headteachers%20and%20school%20staff.pdf

DfE. (2022b). *Consultation on revised behaviour in schools guidance and suspension and permanent exclusion guidance.* Retrieved from https://consult.education.gov.uk/school-absence-and-exclusions-team/revised-school-behaviour-and-exclusion-guidance/

DfE. (2022c). *Opportunity for all: Strong schools with great teachers for your child.* Retrieved from https://www.gov.uk/government/publications/opportunity-for-all-strong-schools-with-great-teachers-for-your-child

DfE. (2022d). *Suspension and permanent exclusion from maintained schools, academies and pupil referral units in England, including pupil movement: Guidance for maintained schools, academies, and pupil referral units in England.* Retrieved from https://consult.education.gov.uk/school-absence-and-exclusions-team/revised-school-behaviour-and-exclusion-guidance/supporting_documents/Suspension%20and%20permanent%20exclusion%20guidance.pdf

Dillon, J., & Pratt, S. (2019). An evaluation of the impact of an integrated multi-disciplinary therapeutic team on the mental health and well-being of young people in an educational setting. *Pastoral Care in Education, 37*(2), 126–142. doi: 10.1080/02643944.2019.1618375.

Dolowitz, D. P., & Marsh, D. (2000). Learning from abroad: The role of policy transfer in contemporary policy-making. *An International Journal of Policy and Administration, 13*(1), 5–24.

Done, E. J., & Andrews, M. J. (2020). How inclusion became exclusion: Policy, teachers and inclusive education. *Journal of Education Policy, 35*(4), 447–464. doi: 10.1080/02680939.2018.1552763.

Dorling, D., & Tomlinson, C. (2016). The creation of inequality: Myths of potential and ability. *Journal for Critical Education Policy Studies, 14*(3), 59–79.

Douglass, A., Chickerella, R., & Maroney, M. (2021). Becoming trauma-informed: A case study of early educator professional development and organizational change. *Journal of Early Childhood Teacher Education, 42*(2), 182–202.

Doyle, C. (2004). *Vygotskian-based developmental cognitive curriculum for early years.* Paper presented at the Tapestry Conference, Glasgow.

Dudley-Marling, C., & Dudley-Marling, A. (2015). Inclusive leadership and poverty. In G. Theoharis, & M. Scanlan (Eds.), *Leadership for increasingly diverse schools* (pp. 39–57). London: Routledge.

DuFour, R., & Mattos, M. (2013). How do principals really improve schools? *Eduational Leadership, 70*(7), 34–40.

Dumay, X., & Dupriez, V. (2014). Educational quasi-markets, school effectiveness and social inequalities. *Journal of Education Policy, 29*(4), 510–531.

Dunlop, A.-W., Lee, P., Fee, J., Hughes, A., Grieve, A., & Marwick, H. (2008). *Positive behaviour in the early years.* Retrieved from https://www.gov.scot/publications/positive-behaviour-early-years-perceptions-staff-service-providers-parents-managing/pages/4/

Dunn, J. (1987). Understanding feelings: The early stages. In J. S. Bruner, & H. Weireich-Haster (Eds.), *The child's construction of the world* (pp. 26–40). London: Methuen.

Dunn, J. (2000). Emotion and the development of children's understanding. *European Review, 8*(1), 9–15. doi: 10.1017/S1062798700004518.

Dunn, J. (2004). The beginnings of moral understanding: Development in the second year. In J. Kagen, & S. Lamb (Eds.), *The emergence of morality in young children* (pp. 91–112). Chicago, IL: The University of Chicago Press.

Dunn, J., Maguire, M., & Brown, J. R. (1995). The development of Children's moral sensibility: Individual differences and emotion understanding. *Developmental Psychology, 31*(4), 649–659.

Dweck, C. S. (2000). *Self-theories: Their role in motivation, personality, and development.* Philadelphia, PA: Psychology Press.

Dweck, C. S. (2002). Motivational processes affecting learning. In A. Pollard (Ed.), *Readings for reflective teaching* (pp. 118–120). London: Continuum.

244 *References*

Dweck, C. S. (2006). *Mindset: The new psychology of success.* New York: Random House.

Dweck, C. S., & Elliot, E. S. (1983). Achievement motivation. In E. M. Hetherington (Ed.), *Socialization, personality and social development* (Vol. *IV*, pp. 643–692). New York: Wiley.

Dyer, F., & Gregory, L. (2014). *Mental health difficulties in the youth justice population: Learning from the first six months of the IVY project.* Retrieved from Centre for Youth and Criminal Justice http://www.cycj.org.uk/wp-content/uploads/2014/07/Briefing-Paper-5-final.pdf

Dyson, A., & Kozleski, E. B. (2008). Disproportionality in special education – A transatlantic phenomenon. In L. Florian, & M. J. McLaughlin (Eds.), *Disability classification in education: Issues and perspectives* (pp. 170–190). Thousand Oaks, CA: Corwin Press.

Editor (2020). Pandemic school closures: Risks and opportunities (Editorial). *The Lancet Child and Adolescent Health, 4*(5), 341.

Education Scotland. (2017a). *Nurture, adverse childhood experiences and trauma informed practice: Making the links between these approaches.* Retrieved from https://education.gov.scot/improvement/Documents/inc83-making-the-links-nurture-ACES-and-trauma.pdf

Education Scotland. (2017b). *Scottish Attainment Challenge.* Retrieved from https://education.gov.scot/improvement/Pages/sac1tosac11scottishattain-mentchallenge.aspx

Education Scotland. (2018). *Applying nurture as a whole school approach: A framework to support the self-evaluation of nurturing approaches in schools.* Retrieved from https://education.gov.scot/improvement/documents/inc55applyingnurtu-ringapproaches120617.pdf

Edwards-Groves, C., & Grootenboer, P. (2021). Conceptualising five dimensions of relational trust: Implications for middle leadership. *School Leadership & Management, 41*(3), 260–283.

Engle, R., Lam, D., Meyer, X., & Nix, S. (2012). How does expansive framing promote transfer? Several proposed explanations and a research agenda for investigating them. *Educational Psychologist, 47*(3), 215–231.

Ey, L.-A., Walker, S., & Spears, B. (2019). Young children's thinking about bullying: Personal, social-conventional and moral reasoning perspectives. *Australasian Journal of Early Childhood, 44*(2), 196–210.

Faupel, A. (2013). Understanding and responding to angry emotions in children with emotional and behavioural difficulties. In T. Cole, H. Daniels, & J. Visser (Eds.), *The Routledge international companion to emotional and behavioural difficulties* (eBook ed.). London: Routledge.

Felitti, V., Anda, R., & Nordenberg, D. (1998). Relationship of childhood abuse and household dysfunction to many of the leading causes of death in adults: The adverse childhood experiences (ACE) study. *American Journal of Preventative Medicine, 14*(4), 245–258.

Feniger, Y., & Lefstein, A. (2014). How not to reason with PISA data: An ironic investigation. *Journal of Education Policy, 29*(6), 845–855.

Fenton, P., Ocasio-Stoutenburg, L., & Harry, B. (2017). The power of parent engagement: Sociocultural considerations in the quest for equity. *Theory Into Practice, 56*(3), 214–225. doi: 10.1080/00405841.2017.1355686.

References 245

Feuerstein, R., Rand, Y., Hoffman, F., & Miller, R. (1980). *Instrumental enrichment: An intervention program for cognitive modifiability.* Baltimore, MD: Baltimore University Park Press.

Fielding, M. (2007). Jean Rudduck (1937-2007) 'Carving a new order of experience': A preliminary appreciation of the work of Jean Rudduck in the field of student voice. *Educational Action Research, 15*(3), 323–336.

Finnis, M. (2021). *Restorative practice.* Carmarthen, Wales: Independent Thinking Press.

Florian, L. (2015). Inclusive pedagogy: A transformative approach to individual differences but can it help reduce educational inequalities? *Scottish Educational Review, 47*(1), 5–14.

Florian, L. (2019). On the necessary co-existence of special and inclusive education. *International Journal of Inclusive Education, 23*(7-8), 691–704. doi: 10.1080/13603116.2019.1622801.

Florian, L., Black-Hawkins, K., & Rouse, M. (2017). *Achievement and inclusion in schools.* London: Routledge.

Forbes, J. (2018). Multi-agency working. In K. Bryce, W. M. Humes, D. Gillies, & A. Kennedy (Eds.), *Scottish Education* (5th ed., pp. 748–758). Edinburgh: University of Edinburgh.

Forbes, J., & Watson, C. (2012). Introducing the complexities of inter-professional working. In J. Forbes, & C. Watson (Eds.), *The transformation of children's services: Examining and debating the complexities of inter-professional working* (pp. 3–12). London: Routledge.

Forde, C., & Torrance, D. (2017). Social justice and leadership development. *Professional Development in Education, 43*(1), 106–120. doi: 10.1080/19415257.2015.1131733.

Forde, C., & Torrance, D. (2021). Leadership at all levels: System alignment through empowerment in Scottish education? *School Leadership & Management, 41*(1–2), 22–40.

Forde, C., Torrance, D., & Angelle, P. (2021). Caring practices and social justice leadership: Case studies of school principals in Scotland and USA. *School Leadership & Management, 41*(3), 211–228.

Forde, C., Torrance, D., Mitchell, A., McMahon, M., & Harvie, J. (2022). Education governance and the role of the headteacher: The new policy problem in Scottish education. *Management in Education, 36*(1), 18–24.

Foucault, M. (1991). *Discipline and punish: The birth of the prison.* London: Penguin.

Francis, B., Mills, M., & Lupton, R. (2012). What would a socially just education system look like? *Journal of Education Policy, 27*(5), 577–585.

Francis, K., & Osher, D. (2018). The centrality of cutlural competence and responsiveness. In D. Osher, D. Moroney, & S. Williamson (Eds.), *Creating safe, equitable, engaging schools: A comprehensive, evidence-based approach to supporting students* (pp. 79–94). Cambridge, MA: Harvard Education Press.

Freeman, T. (2017, February 10). Child poverty bill published by Scottish Government, News item. *Holyrood.* Retrieved from https://www.holyrood.com/news/view,child-poverty-bill-published-by-scottish-government_13077.htm

Frisen, A., Hasselblad, T., & Holmqvist, K. (2012). What actually makes bullying stop? Reports from former victims. *Journal of Adolescence, 35*(4), 981–990.

Fullan, M. (2008). *The six secrets of change.* San Francisco, CA: Jossey-Bass.

246 *References*

Fullan, M. (2016). The path to equity: Whole system change. In A. M. Blankstein, & P. Noguera (Eds.), *Excellence through equity: Five principles of courageous leadership to guide achievement for every student* (pp. 45–54). Alexandria, VA: ASCD.

Fullan, M. (2020). Learning and the pandemic: What's next? *Prospects, 49*(1-2), 25–28.

Fullan, M. (2021). The right drivers for whole system success. *CSE Learning Education Series, 1.* https://michaelfullan.ca/wp-content/uploads/2021/03/Fullan-CSE-Leading-Education-Series-01-2021R2-compressed.pdf

Furlong, V. J. (1991). Disaffected pupils: Reconstructing the sociological perspective. *British Journal of Sociology of Education, 12*(3), 293–307. doi: 10.1080/0142569910120302.

Gambrill, E. (2014). The diagnostic and statistical manual of mental disorders as a major form of dehumanization in the modern world. *Research on Social Work Practice, 24,* 13–36. doi: 10.1177/1049731513499411.

Gardner, H. (1999). *Intelligence reframed: Multiple intelligences for the 21st century.* New York: Basic Books.

Garner, J., & Thomas, M. (2011). The role and contribution of nurture groups in secondary schools: Perceptions of children, parents and staff. *Emotional and Behavioural Difficulties, 16*(2), 207–224. doi: 10.1080/13632752.2011.569410.

Garwood, J. D., & Van Loan, C. L. (2019). Pre-service educators' dispositions toward inclusive practices for students with emotional and behavioural difficulties. *International Journal of Inclusive Education, 23*(12), 1332–1347. doi: 10.1080/13603116.2018.1447614.

Gatherer, W. (2013). Scottish Teachers. In T. G. K. Bryce, W. H. Humes, D. Gillies, & A. Kennedy (Eds.), *Scottish Education: Fourth edition: Referendum.* Edinburgh: Edinburgh University Press.

Gerhardt, S. (2004). *Why love matters: How affection shapes a baby's brain.* London: Routledge.

Gerhardt, S. (2013). How affection shapes a young child's brain: Neurotransmitters, attachment and resilience. In T. Cole, H. Daniels, & J. Visser (Eds.), *The Routledge international companion to emotional and behavioural difficulties [Routledge Handbook].* London: Routledge.

Gewirtz, S., Maguire, M., Neumann, E., & Towers, E. (2021). What's wrong with 'deliverology'? Performance measurement, accountability and quality improvement in English secondary education. *Journal of Education Policy, 36*(4), 504–529. doi: 10.1080/02680939.2019.1706103.

Giddens, A. (2006). *Sociology.* Cambridge, MA: Polity Press.

Giddens, A., & Sutton, P. W. (2017). *Sociology* (8th ed.). Cambridge, MA: Polity Press.

Gillibrand, R., Lam, V., & O'Donnell, V. L. (2011). *Developmental psychology.* London: Pearson.

Glatter, R. (2012). Persistent preoccupations: The rise and rise of school autonomy and accountability in England. *Education Management Administration and Leadership, 40*(5), 559–575.

Goffman, E. (1963). *Stigma: Notes on the management of spoiled identity.* New York: Prentice-Hall.

Goksoy, S. (2016). Analysis of the relationship between shared leadership and distributed leadership. *Eurasian Journal of Educational Research, 16*(65), 295–312.

References   247

Gomendio, M. (2017), *Empowering and enabling teachers to improve equity and outcomes for all*, International Summit on the Teaching Profession. OECD Publishing, Paris, https://doi.org/10.1787/9789264273238-en

Goodall, J. (2013). Parental engagement to support children's learning: A six point model. *School Leadership & Management, 33*(2), 133–150. doi: 10.1080/13632434.2012.724668.

Goodall, C. (2018). Inclusion is A feeling, not A place: A qualitative study exploring autistic young people's conceptualisations of inclusion. *International Journal of Inclusive Education, 24*(12), 1285–1310. doi: 10.1080/13603116.2018.1523475.

Goodall, J. (2021). Parental engagement and deficit discourses: Absolving the system and solving parents. *Educational Review (Birmingham), 73*(1), 98–110.

Goodall, J., & Montgomery, C. (2014). Parental involvement to parental engagement: A continuum. *Educational Review, 66*(4), 399–410. doi: 10.1080/00131911.2013.781576.

Gorski, P. (2008). The myth of the "culture of poverty." *Educational Leadership, 65*(7), 32–36.

Gough, A. (2016). *Secure Care in Scotland: Looking ahead: Key messages and call for action*. Retrieved from Centre for Youth and Criminal Justice http://www.cycj.org.uk/wp-content/uploads/2016/10/Secure-Care-in-Scotland-Looking-Ahead.pdf

Gow, L., & McPherson, L. (1980). *Tell them from me*. Aberdeen: Aberdeen University Press.

Graham, L. J. (2008). From ABCs to ADHD: The role of schooling in The construction of behaviour disorder and production of disorderly objects. *International Journal of Inclusive Education, 12*(1), 7–33.

Graham, L. J., & Tancredi, H. (2019). In search of a middle ground: The dangers and affordances of diagnosis in relation to attention deficit hyperactivity disorder and developmental language disorder. *Emotional and Behavioural Difficulties, 24*(3), 287–300. doi: 10.1080/13632752.2019.1609248.

Grantham, R., & Primrose, F. (2017). Investigating the fidelity and effectiveness of nurture groups in the secondary school context. *Emotional and Behavioural Difficulties, 22*(3), 219–236.

Greaves, E., Macmillan, L., & Sibieta, L. (2014). *Lessons from London schools for attainment gaps and social mobility*. Retrieved from Social Mobility and Poverty Commission https://ifs.org.uk/publications/7243

Green, T. L. (2017). From positivism to critical theory: School-community relations toward community equity literacy. *International Journal of Qualitative Studies in Education, 30*(4), 370–387.

Greenwood, A. (2020). *Understanding, nurturing and working effectively with vulnerable children in schools: 'Why Can't you hear me?* London: Routledge.

Gregory, A., Ward-Seidel, A., & Carter, K. (2021). Twelve indicators of restorative practices implementation: A framework for educational leaders. *Journal of Educational and Psychological Consultation, 31*(2), 147–179.

GTCS. (2012). *The statement for review of professional standards*. Retrieved from https://www.gtcs.org.uk/professional-standards/archive-2012-professional-standards/

GTCS. (2021). *Professional standards for Scotland's teachers*. Retrieved from http://www.gtcs.org.uk/professional-standards/professional-standards-for-teachers.aspx

248 *References*

Gümüş, S., Arar, K., & Oplatka, I. (2021). Review of international research on school leadership for social justice, equity and diversity. *Journal of Educational Administration and History*, *53*(1), 81–99.

Hacking, I. (1999). *The social construction of what?* Cambridge, MA: Harvard University Press.

Hallinger, P., & Heck, R. (2012). Collaborative leadership and school improvement: Understanding the impact on school capacity and student learning. *School Leadership & Management*, *30*(2), 95–110.

Hamill, P., Boyd, B., & Grieve, A. (2002). *Inclusion: Principles into practice: Development of an integrated support system for young people (SEBD) in XXXX*. University of Strathclyde: Glasgow.

Hansen, J. H. (2012). Limits to inclusion. *International Journal of Inclusive Education*, *16*(1), 89–98.

Hardiman, R., Jackson, B. W., & Griffin, P. (2013). Conceptual foundations. In M. Adams, W. J. Blumenfeld, C. Casteñeda, H. W. Hackman, M. L. Peters & X. Zúñiga (Eds.), *Readings for diversity and social justice* (3rd ed., pp. 26–35). New York: Routledge.

Hardy, I., & Woodcock, S. (2015). Inclusive education policies: Discourses of difference, diversity and deficit. *International Journal of Inclusive Education*, *19*(2), 141–164.

Hargreaves, A., & Fullan, M. (2012). *Professional capital: Transforming teaching in every school*. London: Routledge.

Hargreaves, A., & Shirley, D. (2009). *The fourth way: The inspiring future for educational change*. Thousand Oaks, CA: Corwin.

Harper, L. (2015). The voices and hearts of youth. In A. M. Blankstein, P. Noguera, & L. Kelly (Eds.), *Excellence through equity: Five principles of courageous leadership to guide achievement for every student* (pp. 73–96)). Alexandria, VA: ASCD.

Harris, A., & Goodall, J. (2008). Do parents know they matter? Engaging all parents in learning. *Educational Research and Reviews*, *50*(3), 277–289. doi: 10.1080/00131880802309424.

Harris, A., & Jones, M. (2020). COVID 19 – School leadership in disruptive times. *School Leadership & Management*, *40*(4), 243–247. doi: 10.1080/13632434.2020.1811479.

Hart, R. A. (1992). Children's participation: From tokenism to citizenship *innocenti essay no. 4*. Florence: International Child Development Centre.

Hart, C., Drummond, M. J., & McIntyre, D. (2007). Learning without limits: Constructing a pedagogy free from determinist beliefs about ability. In L. Florian (Ed.), *The SAGE handbook of special education* (pp. 449–514). London: SAGE.

Hayden, C. (2013). Youth offending and emotional and behavioural difficulties. In T. Cole, H. Daniels, & J. Visser (Eds.), *The Routledge international companion to emotional and behavioural difficulties [Routledge handbook]*. London: Routledge.

Head, G. (2007). *Better learning, better behaviour (policy and practice in education)*. Edinburgh: Dunedin Academic Press.

Head, G. (2014). Identity, relationships and behaviour. In M. Carroll & M. McCulloch (Eds.), *Understanding teaching and learning in the primary classroom* (pp. 89–101). London: SAGE.

Hearn, J. (2012). *Theories of power*. Basingstoke, UK: Palgrave Macmillan.

Hedegaard-Soerensen, L., & Grumloese, S. P. (2020). Exclusion: The downside of neoliberal education policy. *International Journal of Inclusive Education*, *24*(6), 631–644. doi: 10.1080/13603116.2018.1478002.

References 249

Henderson, N. (2013). Havens of resilience. *Educational Leadership, 71*(1), 22–27.

Hesse, E., & Main, M. (2016). Disorganized infant, child, and adult attachment: Collapse in behavioral and attentional strategies. *Journal of the American Psychoanalytic Association, 48*(4), 1097–1127.

Heubeck, B. G., & Lauth, G. (2014). Parent training for behavioral difficulties during the transition to school: Promises and challenges for prevention and early intervention. In P. Garner, J. M. Kauffman, & J. Elliot (Eds.), *The SAGE handbook of emotional and behavioral difficulties* (pp. 317–334). London: SAGE.

Hibbin, R., & Warin, J. (2020). A language focused approach to supporting children with social, emotional and behavioural difficulties (SEBD. *Education 3-13, 48*(3), 316–331.

Higham, R. (2013). School autonomy, government control and a changing landscape. In P. Earley (Ed.), *Exploring the school leadership landscape; Changing demands, changing realities.* London: Bloomsbury.

Hjörne, E., & Säljö, R. (2013). Institutional labeling and pupil careers: Negotiating identities of children who do not fit in. In T. Cole, H. Daniels, & J. Visser (Eds.), *The Routledge international companion to emotional and behavioural difficulties [Routledge handbook]* (pp. 40–47). London: Routledge.

Hodgson, A., & Spours, K. (2016). Restrictive and expansive policy learning – Challenges and strategies for knowledge exchange in upper secondary education across the four countries of the UK. *Journal of Education Policy, 31*(5), 511–525.

Holloway, J., & Brass, J. (2018). Making accountable teachers: The terrors and pleasures of performativity. *Journal of Education Policy, 33*(3), 361–382.

Hollweck, T., Reimer, K., & Bouchard, K. (2019). A missing piece: Embedding restorative justice and relational pedagogy into the teacher education classroom. *The New Educator, 15*(3), 246–267. doi: 10.1080/1547688X.2019.1626678.

Hooper, M. A., & Bernhardt, V. (2016). *Creating capacity for learning and equity in schools: Instructional, adaptive, and transformational leadership.* London: Routledge.

Hornby, G., & Evans, B. (2014). Including students with significant social, emotional and behavioral difficulties in mainstream school settings. In P. Garner, J. M. Kauffman, & J. Elliot (Eds.), *The SAGE handbook of emotional and behavioral difficulteis* (2nd ed., pp. 235–347). London: SAGE.

Hughes, N. K., & Schlösser, A. (2014). The effectiveness of nurture groups: A systematic review. *Emotional and Behavioural Difficulties, 19*(4), 386–409.

Humes, W. (2020). Re-shaping the policy landscape in Scottish education, 2016–20: The limitations of structural reform. *Scottish Educational Review, 52*(2). https://www.scotedreview.org.uk/media/microsites/scottish-educational-review/documents/Humes_Re-shaping-the-policy-landscape.pdf

Humphrey, N., Lendrum, A., & Wigelsworth, M. (2010). *Research Brief DFE-RB049 October 2010: Social and emotional aspects of learning (SEAL) programme in secondary schools: national evaluation.* (DFE-RB049 October 2010). Retrieved from https://assets.publishing.service.gov.uk/government/uploads/system/uploads/attachment_data/file/197925/DFE-RB049.pdf

Hyman, S. E. (2010). The diagnosis of mental disorders: The problem of reification. *Annual Review of Clinical Psychology, 6*(155–179). doi: 10.1146/annurev.clinpsy

Jung, L. A., & Smith, D. (2018). Tear down your behavior chart! (impact on vulnerable learners). *Educational Leadership, 76*(1), 12–18.

250 *References*

Kalil, A., & Ryan, R. (2020). Parenting practices and socioeconomic gaps in childhood outcomes. *The Future of Children, 30*(1 Spring 2020), 29–54.

Kauffman, J. M. (2005). How do we prevent the prevention of emotional and behavioural difficulties in educaton? In P. Clough, P. Garner, J. Pardeck, & F. Yuen (Eds.), *Handbook of emotional and behavioural difficulties* (pp. 429–440). London: SAGE publications.

Kellett, M. (2011). *Rethinking children and research: Attitudes in contemporary society*. London: Continuum.

Khon, A. (1999). *Punished with rewards: The trouble with gold St*rs, incentive plans, A's, praise, and other bribes*. New York: Houghton Mifflin Company.

Khon, A. (2001). *Beyond discipline: From compliance to community*. Upper Saddle River, NJ: Merrill Education. Association of Supervision and Curriculum Development.

Khon, A. (2005). Unconditional teaching. *Educational Leadership, 63*(1), 20–24.

Khon, A. (2008). Why self-discipline is overrated: The (troubling) theory and practice of control from within. *Phi Delta Kappan, 90*(3), 168–217.

Kidson, M., & Norris, E. (2014). *Implementing the London challenge*. London: Institute for Government (supported by Joseph Rowntree Foundation). Retrieved from https://www.instituteforgovernment.org.uk/sites/default/files/publications/ Implementing%20the%20London%20Challenge%20-%20final_0.pdf

Killen, M., & Rutland, A. (2013). *Children and social exclusion: Morality, prejudice and group identity*. Oxford: John Wiley & Sons Ltd.

Kinsella, W. (2020). Organising inclusive schools. *International Journal of Inclusive Education, 24*(12), 1340–1356. doi: 10.1080/13603116.2018.1516820.

Kohn, A. (2001). *Beyond discipline: From compliance to community*. Upper Saddle River, NJ: Merrill Education/Prentice-Hall.

Kolar, K. (2011). Resilience: Revisiting the concept and its utility for social research. *International Journal of Mental Health Addiction, 9*, 421–433.

Korpershoek, H., Canrinus, E. T., Fokkens-Bruinsma, M., & de Boer, H. (2020). The relationships between school belonging and students' motivational, social-emotional, behavioural, and academic outcomes in secondary education: A meta-analytic review. *Research Papers in Education, 35*(6), 641–680. doi: 10.1080/02671522.2019.1615116.

Koslouski, J. B., & Stark, K. (2021). Promoting learning for students experiencing adversity and trauma: The everyday, yet profound, actions of teachers. *The Elementary School Journal, 121*(3), 430–453.

Kourmoulaki, A. (2013). Nurture groups in a Scottish secondary school: Purpose, features, value and areas for development. *Emotional and Behavioural Difficulties, 18*(1), 60–76.

Kovač, V. B., & Vaala, B. L. (2021). Educational inclusion and belonging: A conceptual analysis and implications for practice. *International Journal of Inclusive Education, 25*(10), 1205–1219. doi: 10.1080/13603116.2019.1603330.

Lacey, R. E., Howe, L. D., Kelly-Irving, M., Bartley, M., & Kelly, Y. (2020). The clustering of adverse childhood experiences in the Avon longitudinal study of parents and children: Are gender and poverty important? *Journal of Interpersonal Violence, 37*(5-6), 2218–2241. doi: 886260520935096.

Landrum, T. J., Wiley, A. L., Tankersley, M., & Kauffman, J. M. (2014). Is EBD 'Special', and is 'Special Education' an appropriate response? In P. Garner, M. Kauffman, & J. Elliot (Eds.), *The SAGE handbook of emotional and behavioral difficulties* (2nd ed., pp. 69–81)). London: SAGE.

References 251

Lang, R. (2007). *The Development and Critique of the Social Model of Disability.* Retrieved from http://citeseerx.ist.psu.edu/viewdoc/download?doi=10.1.1.502.9898&rep=rep1&type=pdf

Langager, S. (2014). Children and youth in behavioural and emotional difficulties, skyrocketing diagnosis and inclusion/exclusion processes in school tendencies in Denmark. *Emotional and Behavioural Difficulties, 19*(3), 284–295. doi: 10.1080/13632752.2014.883785.

Larsen, T. C., Holloway, J., & Hamre, B. (2019). How is an inclusive agenda possible in an excluding education system? Revisiting the Danish dilemma. *International Journal of Inclusive Education, 23*(10), 1049–1064. doi: 10.1080/13603116.2019.1626497.

Lauchlan, F., & Boyle, C. (2007). Is the use of labels in special education helpful? *Support for Learning, 22*(1), 36–42.

Lave, J., & Wenger, E. (1991). *Situated learning: Legitimate peripheral participation.* Cambridge: Cambridge University Press.

Lave, J., & Wenger, E. (2006). Legitimate peripheral participation in communities of practice. In R. McCormick, & C. Paetcher (Eds.), *Learning and knowledge* (pp. 21–35). London: Paul Chapman Publishing.

Leach, T., & Lewis, E. (2013). Children's experiences during circle- time: A call for research-informed debate.. *Pastoral Care in Education, 31*(1), 43–52. doi: 10.1080/02643944.2012.702781.

Learoyd-Smith, S., & Daniels, H. (2014). Social contexts, cultures and environments. In P. Garner, J. M. Kauffman, & J. Elliot (Eds.), *The SAGE handbook of emotional and behavioural difficulties* (2nd ed., pp. 145–163). London: SAGE.

Lee, J. (2020). Mental health effects of school closures during COVID-19. *The Lancet Child and Adolescent Health, 4*(6), 421. doi: 10.1016/S2352-4642(20)30109-7.

Lester, L., Waters, S., & Cross, D. (2013). The relationship between school connectedness and mental health during the transition to secondary school: A path analysis. *Australian Journal of Guidance and Counselling, 23*(2), 157–171.

Lingard, B., & Sellar, S. (2014). Representing your country: Scotland, PISA and new specialities of educational governance. *Scottish Educational Review, 46*(1), 5–10.

Littlecott, H. J., Moore, G. F., & Murphy, S. M. (2018). Student health and well-being in secondary schools: The role of school support staff alongside teaching staff. *Pastoral Care in Education, 36*(4), 297–312. doi: 10.1080/02643944.2018.1528624.

Liu, L., & Xie, A. (2017). Muddling through school life: An ethnographic study of the subculture of 'deviant' students in China. *International Studies in Sociology of Education, 26*(2), 151–170.

Lopes, J. A. (2014). International perspectives in EBD: Critical issues. In P. Garner, J. M. Kauffman, & J. Elliot (Eds.), *The SAGE handbook of emotional and behavioral difficulties* (2nd ed., pp. 9–20). London: SAGE.

Lopez, I. (2017). *Keeping it real and relevant: Building authentic relationships in your diverse classroom.* Alexandria, VA: ASCD.

Lord, P., Rennie, C., Smith, R., Gildea, A., Tang, S., Miani, G., & Bradley, C. (2020). *Randomised controlled trial evaluation of families connect.* Retrieved from NFER https://www.nfer.ac.uk/randomised-controlled-trial-evaluation-of-families-connect/

252 References

Loreman, T. (2009). Straight talk about inclusive education outcomes in Alberta. *CASS Connections*. Retrieved from https://concordia.ab.ca/wp-content/uploads/2017/04/CASS-connections-article.pdf

Lyons, R. (2017). A pilot study of the effectiveness of a nurture group in a secondary special school. *International Journal of Nurture in Education, 3*(1), 6–17.

Lyons-Ruth, K. (2007). The interface between attachment and intersubjectivity: Perspective from the longitudinal study of disorganized attachment. *Psychoanalytic Inquiry, 26*(4), 595–616.

MacAllister, J. (2017). *Reclaiming discipline for education*. London: Routledge.

MacBeath, J. (2006). Leadership as distributed: A matter of practice. *School Leadership & Management, 25*(4), 349–366.

MacBeath, J. (2013). Leading learning in a world of change Leadership for 21st Century learning, Centre for Educational Research and Innovation (pp. 83–106). Paris: OECD Publishing.

MacBeath, J. (2020). Leadership is for learning—a critique of current misconceptions around leadership for learning. *Zeitschrift Für Erziehungswissenschaft, 23*(5), 903–923.

MacBeath, J., Gray, J. M., Cullen, J., Frost, D., Steward, S., & Swaffield, S. (2007). *Schools on the edge: Responding to challenging circumstances*. London: Chapman Publications.

Machlin, L., McLaughlin, K. A., & Sheridan, M. A. (2019). Brain structure mediates the association between socioeconomic status and attention-deficit/hyperactivity disorder. *Developmental Science, 23*(1), e12844.

MacKay, T. (2015). Future directions for nurture in education: Developing a model and a research agenda. *International Journal of Nurture in Education, 1*, 33–40.

Macleod, G. (2006a). *Are we nearly there yet? Curriculum, relationships and disaffected pupils*. Paper presented at the European Conference of Educational Research 'Transforming Knowledge'(13–16th Sept), Geneva.

Macleod, G. (2006b). Bad, mad or sad: Constructions of young people in trouble and implications for interventions. *Emotional and Behavioural Difficulties, 11*(3), 155–167.

Macleod, G. (2013). How children and young people with emotional and behavioural difficulties see themselves. In T. Cole, H. Daniels, & J. Visser (Eds.), *The Routledge international companion to emotional and behavioural difficulties [Routledge handbook]* (pp. 68–74). London: Routledge.

Macleod, G., MacAllister, J., & Pirrie, A. (2012). Towards a broader understanding of authority in student-teacher relationships. *Oxford Review of Education, 38*(4), 493–508.

Macleod, G., Pirrie, A., McCluskey, G., & Cullen, M. A. (2013). Parents of excluded pupils: Customers, partners, problems? *Educational Review, 65*(4), 387–401. doi: 10.1080/00131911.2012.679915.

Macleod, G., Fyfe, I., Nicol, R., Sangster, P., & Obeng, H. (2018). Compliance through care and commitment: Why young people do as adults ask. *Cambridge Journal of Education, 48*(5), 607–623. doi: 10.1080/0305764X.2017.1386160.

Madsen, K. B., Ersbøll, A. K., Olsen, J., Parner, E., & Obel, C. (2015). Geographic analysis of the variation in the incidence of ADHD in a country with free access to healthcare: A Danish cohort study. *International Journal of Health Geographics, 14*(1), 24–24.

Main, M., Kaplan, N., & Cassidy, J. (1985). Security in infancy, childhood, and adulthood: A move to the level of representation. In I. Bretherton, & E. E. Waters (Eds.), *Growing points of attachment theory and research (Monographs of the society for research in child development) (Vol. 50, nos. 1–2, pp. 66-104)*. Chicago, IL: University of Chicago Press for the Society for Research in Child Development.

Main, M., & Solomon, J. (1990). Procedures for identifying infants as disorganized/disoriented during the Ainsworth strange situation. In M. T. Greenberg, D. Cichetti, & E. M. Cummings (Eds.), *Attachment in the preschool years: Theory, research and intervention* (pp. 121–160). Chicago, IL: University of Chicago Press.

Marryat, L., & Frank, J. (2019). Factors associated with adverse childhood experiences in Scottish children: A prospective cohort study. *BMJ Paediatrics Open, 3*(1), e000340. doi: 10.1136/bmjpo-2018-000340.

Marryat, L., Thompson, L., Minnis, H., & Wilson, P. (2017). Primary schools and the amplification of social differences in child mental health: A population-based cohort study. *Journal of Epidemiology & Community Health Education Journal, 72*(1), 1–7. doi: 10.1136/jech-2017-208995.

Maslow, A. H. (1943). A theory of human motivation. *Psychological Review, 50*(4), 370–396.

Maslow, A. H. (1970). *Motivation and personality* (2nd ed.). London: Harper and Row.

Mathews, P., & Ehren, M. (2017). Accountability and improvement in self-improving school systems. In P. Earley, & T. Greany (Eds.), *School leadership and education systems reform* (pp. 44–55). London: Bloomsbury.

Mayall, B. (2015). The sociology of childhood and children's rights. In W. Vandenhole, E. Desmet, D. Reynaert, & S. Lembrechts (Eds.), *Routledge international handbook of children's rights studies* (pp. 77–93). London: Routledge.

Mayes, E. (2020). Student voice in school reform? Desiring simultaneous critique and affirmation. *Discourse: Studies in the Cultural Politics of Education, 41*(3), 454–470. doi: 10.1080/01596306.2018.1492517.

Mays, D., Franke, S., Metzner, F., Boyle, C., Jindal-Snape, D., Schneider, L., & Wichmann, M. (2018). School belonging and successful transition practice. In K.-A. Allen, & C. Boyle (Eds.), *Pathways to school belonging* (pp. 167–187). Leiden, The Netherlands: Brill Academic Publishers.

McAra, L., & McVie, S. (2010). Youth crime and justice: Key messages from the Edinburgh study of youth transitions and crime. *Criminology and Criminal Justice, 10*(2), 179–209.

McCluskey, G. (2006). Exclusion from school – What does it mean to pupils? *CREID Breifing Paper* (Vol. 1): Edinburgh Centre for Inclusion and Diversity, University of Edinburgh.

McCluskey, G. (2011). *Swimming pools, Flash mobs and Disruption in Schools; False Hopes or Promising Futures?* Paper presented at the Restorative Approaches to Conflict in Schools seminar series, Edinburgh. Retrieved from https://www. educ.cam.ac.uk/research/programmes/restorativeapproaches/seminarfour/ MccluskeySeminar4.pdf

McCluskey, G., Cole, T., Daniels, H., Thompson, I., & Tawell, A. (2019). Exclusion from school in Scotland and across the UK: Contrasts and questions. *British Educational Research Journal, 45*(6), 1140–1159. doi: 10.1002/berj.3555.

McCluskey, G., & Lloyd, G. (2019). Not much I can do, he's got ADHD. In R. Arshad, T. Wrigley, & L. Pratt (Eds.), *Social justice re-examined: Dilemmas and solutions for the classroom teacher* (2nd ed., pp. 162–172). London: Trentham Books Ltd.

McCluskey, G., Riddell, S., Weedon, E., & Fordyce, M. (2016). Exclusion from school and recognition of difference. *Discourse: Studies in the Cultural Politics of Education, 37*(4), 529–539. doi: 10.1080/01596306.2015.1073015.

McCluskey, G., Riestenberg, N., & Thorsborne, M. (2019). *Getting more out of restorative practice in schools: Practical approaches to improve school wellbeing and strengthen community engagement.* London: Jessica King Publishers.

McGrath, H. (2014). Directions in teaching social skills to students with specific EBDs. In P. Garner, J. M. Kauffman, & J. Elliot (Eds.), *The SAGE handbook of emotional and behavioral difficulties* (2nd ed., pp. 303–334). London: SAGE.

McKendrick, J., Mooney, G., Dickie, J., & Kelly, P. (Eds.). (2011). *Poverty in Scotland 2011: Towards a more equal Scotland?* London: Child Poverty Action Group.

McKendrick, J. (2018). *Local contributions to tackling poverty and inequality in Scotland.* Retrieved from the Scottish Poverty and Inequality Research Unit. https://researchonline.gcu.ac.uk/en/publications/local-contributions-to-tackling-poverty-and-inequality-in-scotlan

McKendrick, J., Asenova, D., McCann, C., Reynolds, R., Egan, J., Hastings, A., & Sinclair, S. (2016). Conceptualising austerity in Scotland as a risk shift: Ideas and implications. *Scottish Affairs, 25*(4), 451–478.

McKibben, S. (2021). Carla Shalaby on radically inclusive discipline. *Educational Leadership, 79*(2), 14–19.

McKinney, S., Hall, S., Lowden, K., McClung, M., & Cameron, L. (2012). The relationship between poverty and deprivation, educational attainment and positive school leaver destinations in Glasgow secondary schools. *Scottish Educational Review, 44*(1), 33–45.

McKinney, S., & Head, G. (2021). *The effects of COVID-19 lockdowns on children's education.* Retrieved from https://blog.eera-ecer.de/author/prof-mckinney-and-dr-head/

McMahon, S. E. (2012). Doctors diagnose, teachers label: The unexpected in pre-service teachers' talk about labelling children with ADHD. *International Journal of Inclusive Education, 16*(3), 249–294.

Messiou, K. (2012a). Collaborating with children in exploring marginalisation: An approach to inclusive education. *International Journal of Inclusive Education, 16*(12), 1311–1322.

Messiou, K. (2012b). *Confronting marginalisation in education: A framework for promoting inclusion.* London: Routledge.

Messiou, K. (2019). Understanding marginalisation through dialogue: A strategy for promoting the inclusion of all students in schools. *Educational Review, 71*(3), 306–317.

Milner, H. R., Cunningham, H. B., Delale-O'Connor, L., & Kestenberg, E. G. (2018). Are the kids really out of control? (Confronting inequity). *Educational Leadership, 76*(1), 86–87.

Minow, M. (1990). *Making all the difference: Inclusion, exclusion and American law.* Ithaca: Cornell University Press.

Moldavsky, M., Groenewald, C., Owen, V., & Sayal, K. (2013). Teachers' recognition of children with ADHD: Role of subtype and gender. *Child and Adolescent Mental Health, 18*(1), 18–23.

Moore, A. (2007). *Teaching and learning: Pedagogy, curriculum and culture.* London: Routledge.

Moore, A., & Clarke, M. (2016). 'Cruel optimism': Teacher attachment to professionalism in an era of performativity. *Journal of Education Policy, 31*(5), 666–677.

Moore, B., & Woodcock, S. (2017). Resilience to bullying: Towards an alternative to the anti-bullying approach. *Educational Psychology in Practice*, *33*(1), 65–80. doi: 10.1080/02667363.2016.1233488.

Moses, L., Rylak, D., Reader, T., Hertz, C., & Ogden, M. (2020). Educators' perspectives on supporting student agency. *Theory Into Practice*, *59*(2), 213–222.

Mowat, J. G. (2007). *Using support groups to improve behaviour*. London: SAGE Publications.

Mowat, J. G. (2009). The inclusion of pupils perceived as having SEBD in mainstream schools: A focus upon learning. *Support for Learning*, *24*(4), 159–169.

Mowat, J. G. (2010a). 'He comes to talk to me about things': Supporting pupils experiencing social and emotional behavioural difficulties — A focus upon interpersonal relationships. *Pastoral Care in Education*, *28*(3), 163–180.

Mowat, J. G. (2010b). Towards the development of self-regulation in pupils experiencing social and emotional behavioural difficulties. *Emotional and Behavioural Difficulties*, *15*(3), 189–206.

Mowat, J. G. (2011). The development of intrapersonal intelligence in pupils experiencing social, emotional and behavioural difficulties. *Educational Psychology in Practice*, *27*(3), 227–253.

Mowat, J. G. (2015a). Inclusion – That word!' examining some of the tensions in supporting pupils experiencing social, emotional and behavioural difficulties/needs. *Emotional and Behavioural Difficulties*, *20*(2), 153–172. doi: 10.1080/13632752.2014.927965.

Mowat, J. G. (2015b). Towards a new conceptualisation of marginalisation. *European Educational Research Journal*, *14*(5), 454–476. doi: 10.1177/1474904115589864.

Mowat, J. G. (2018a). Closing the attainment gap – A realistic proposition or an elusive pipe-dream? *Journal of Education Policy*, *33*(2), 299–321. doi: 10.1080/02680939.2017.1352033.

Mowat, J. G. (2018b). Closing the gap': Systems leadership is no leadership at all without A moral compass – A Scottish perspective. *School Leadership & Management*, *39*(1), 48–75. doi: 10.1080/13632434.2018.1447457.

Mowat, J. G. (2019a). Exploring the impact of social inequality and poverty on the mental health and wellbeing and attainment of children and young people in Scotland. *Improving Schools*, *22*(3), 204–223. doi: 10.1177/1365480219835323.

Mowat, J. G. (2019b). Supporting the socio-emotional aspects of the primary-secondary transition for pupils with social, emotional and behavioural needs: Affordances and constraints. *Improving Schools*, *22*(1), 4–28. doi: 10.11771/1542305018817850.

Mowat, J. G. (2019c). Supporting the transition from primary to secondary school for pupils with social, emotional and behavioural needs:A focus on the socio-emotional aspects of transfer for an adolescent boy. *Emotional and Behavioural Difficulties*, *24*(1), 50–69. doi: 10.1080/13632752.2018.1564498.

Mowat, J. G. (2020a). Interrogating the relationship between poverty, attainment and mental health and wellbeing: The importance of social networks and support – A Scottish case study. *Cambridge Journal of Education*, *50*(3), 345–370. doi: 10.1080/0305764X.2019.1702624.

Mowat, J. G. (2020b). New directions in headship education in Scotland. In L. Becket (Ed.), *Research-informed teacher learning: Critical perspectives on theory, research and practice*. London: Routledge.

256 References

Mowat, J. G. (in press-a). Establishing the medium to long-term impact of covid-19 constraints on the socio-emotional wellbeing of impoverished children and young people (and those who are otherwise disadvantaged) during, and in the aftermath of, covid-19. In M. Proyer, F. Dovigo, W. Veck, & E. A. Seitigen (Eds.), *Education in an altered world: Pandemic, crises and young people vulnerable to educational exclusion*. London: Bloomsbury.

Mowat, J. G. (in press-b). Working collaboratively with the school community to build inclusion for all. In R. Slee (Ed.), *International encyclopedia of education researching disability studies & inclusive education* (3rd ed.). Oxford: Elsevier.

Mowat, J. G., & McMahon, M. (2018). Interrogating the concept of 'leadership at all levels': A Scottish perspective. *Professional Development in Education, 45*(2), 173–189. doi: 10.1080/19415257.2018.1511452.

Mowat, J. G. (2008). *Teaching for understanding within the affective field*. (PhD), University of Glasgow, Glasgow.

Mulholland, M., & O'Connor, U. (2016). Collaborative classroom practice for inclusion: Perspectives of classroom teachers and learning support/resource teachers. *International Journal of Inclusive Education, 20*(10), 1070–1083. doi: 10.1080/13603116.2016.1145266.

Mullet, J. H. (2014). Restorative discipline: From getting even to getting well. *Children & Schools, 36*(3), 157–162.

Mundschenk, N., & Simpson, R. (2014). Defining emotional or behavioral disorders: The quest for affirmation. In P. Garner, J. M. Kauffman, & J. Elliot (Eds.), *SAGE handbook of emotional and behavioral difficulties* (2nd ed., pp. 43–54). London: SAGE.

Munn, P., & Lloyd, G. (2005). Exclusion and excluded pupils. *British Educational Research Journal, 31*(2), 205–251.

Munn, P., Lloyd, G., & Cullen, M. A. (2000). *Alternatives to exclusion from school*. London: Chapman Publications.

Munn, P., Sharp, S., Lloyd, G., Macleod, G., McCluskey, G., Brown, J., & Hamilton, L. (2009). *Behaviour in Scottish schools*. Edinburgh, UK: Scottish Government.

Murphy, D., & Raffe, D. (2015). The governance of Scottish comprehensive education. In D. Murphy, L. Croxford, C. Howieson, & D. Raffe (Eds.), *Everyone's future: Lessons from fifty years of Scottish comprehensive schooling* (pp. 139–161). London: Trentham.

Music, G. (2017). *Nurturing natures: Attachment and children's emotional, sociocultural and brain development* (2nd ed.). London: Routledge.

Narvaez, D. (2015). Understanding flourishing: Evolutionary baselines and morality. *Journal of Moral Education, 44*(3), 253–262.

National Audit Office (2019). *Support for pupils with special educational needs and disabilities in England*. London: UK Government.

Newman, B. M., & Newman, P. R. (2016). *Theories of human development* (2nd ed.). London: Psychology Press.

Newton, D. P. (2014). *Thinking with feeling: Fostering productive thought in the classroom*. London: Routledge.

NHS Health Scotland. (2020). *Evaluation of the cost of the school day programme (2018–19)*, Summary report. Retrieved from http://www.healthscotland.scot/media/2936/cost-of-the-school-day-evaluation-full-report.pdf

NHS Scotland. (2018). *Child poverty*. Retrieved from http://www.healthscotland.scot/health-inequalities/fundamental-causes/poverty/child-poverty

Noddings, N. (1988). An ethic of caring and its implications for instructional arrangements. *American Journal of Education, 96*(2), 215–230.

Noddings, N. (2010). Moral education and caring. *Theory and Research in Education, 8*(2), 145–151. doi: 10.1177/1477878510368617.

Nolan, A., Hannah, E. F. S., Lakin, E., & Topping, K. J. (2021). Whole-school nurturing approaches: A systematic analysis of impact. *Educational & Child Psychology, 38*(1), 10–23.

Norwich, B. (2013). *Addressing tensions and dilemmas in inclusive education: Living with uncertainty.* London: Routledge.

Norwich, B. (2021). *Labelling students with special educational needs categories: Revisiting continuing theoretical and ethical issues.* Paper presented at the ECER Conference (6th-10th Sept), online.

O'Donovan, R., Berman, N., & Wierenga, A. (2015). How schools can move beyond exclusion. *International Journal of Inclusive Education, 19*(6), 645–658. doi: 10.1080/13603116.2014.961686.

Oatley, K., & Jenkins, K. M. (1996). *Understanding emotions.* Oxford: Blackwell.

OECD (2009). *Creating effective teaching and learning environments: First results from TALIS.* Paris: OECD Publishing. www.oecd.org/edu/talis/firstresults

OECD (2012). *Equity and quality in education: Supporting disadvantaged students and schools,* OECD Publishing, Paris, https://doi.org/10.1787/9789264130852-en

OECD (2013). "Leading learning in a world of change," in *Leadership for 21st century learning,* OECD Publishing, Paris, https://doi.org/10.1787/9789264205406-5-en

OECD (2016), *PISA 2015 results (Volume i): Excellence and equity in education,* PISA, OECD Publishing, Paris, https://doi.org/10.1787/9789264266490-en

OECD (2017), *PISA 2015 results (Volume III): Students' well-being,* PISA, OECD Publishing, Paris, https://doi.org/10.1787/9789264273856-en

OECD (2018), *Equity in education: Breaking down barriers to social mobility,* PISA, OECD Publishing, Paris. https://doi.org/10.1787/9789264073234-en

OECD (2019), *How's life in the digital age?: Opportunities and risks of the digital transformation for people's well-being,* OECD Publishing, Paris. https://doi.org/10.1787/9789264311800-en

OECD (2020), "Coronavirus special edition: Back to school," *Trends shaping education spotlights,* No. 21, OECD Publishing, Paris, https://doi.org/10.1787/339780fd-en

OECD (2021), *Scotland's curriculum for excellence: Into the future,* Implementing Education Policies, OECD Publishing, Paris. https://doi.org/10.1787/bf624417-en

OECD (2022). *Trends shaping education 2022,* OECD Publishing, Paris, https://doi.org/10.1787/6ae8771a-en

OFSTED (2021). *The annual report of her Majesty's chief inspector of education.* London: Children's Services and Skills 2020/21.

Oliver, M., & Barnes, C. (2012). *The new politics of disablement* (2nd ed.). Basingstoke: Palgrave Macmillan.

Oliver, C., Mooney, A., & Stratham, J. (2010). *Integrated working: A review of the evidence.* London: Institute of Education.

Olsson, C. A., Bond, L., Burns, J. M., Vella-Brodrick, D. A., & Sawyer, S. M. (2003). Adolescent resilience: A concept analysis. *Journal of Adolescence, 26*(1), 1–11.

258 References

Oplatka, I., & Gamerman, O. (2021). Compassion in urban teaching: Process, arenas, and factors. *Urban Education (Beverly Hills, Calif.), 56*(2), 319–343.

Orben, A., Tomova, L., & Blakemore, S.-J. (2020). The effects of social deprivation on adolescent development and mental health. *The Lancet: Child and Adolescent Mental Health, 4*(8), 634–640.

Orsati, F. T., & Causton-Theoharis, J. (2013). Challenging control: Inclusive teachers' and teaching assistants' discourse on students with challenging behaviour. *International Journal of Inclusive Education, 17*(5), 507–525.

Osher, D. (2018). Building readiness and capacity. In D. Osher, D. Moroney, & S. Williamson (Eds.), *Creating safe, equitable, engaging schools: A comprehensive, evidence-based approach to supporting students* (pp. 15–24). Cambridge, MA: Harvard Education Press.

Ostiguy, B. J., Peters, M. L., & Shalsko, D. (2016). Ableism. In M. Adams, & L. A. Bell (Eds.), *Teaching for diversity and social justice* (pp. 299–337). London: Routledge.

Owen, D. (2019). *OFSTED: schools, early years, further education and skills: What is off-rolling, and how does OFSTED look at it on inspection?* Retrieved from https://educationinspection.blog.gov.uk/2019/05/10/what-is-off-rolling-and-how-does-ofsted-look-at-it-on-inspection/

Pantić, N., & Florian, L. (2015). Developing teachers as agents of inclusion and social justice. *Education Inquiry, 6*(3), 333–351.

Parker, C., Paget, A., Ford, T., & Gwernan-Jones, R. (2016). '.He was excluded for the kind of behaviour that we thought He needed support with...' a qualitative analysis of the experiences and perspectives of parents whose children have been excluded from school. *Emotional and Behavioural Difficulties, 21*(1), 133–151. doi: 10.1080/13632752.2015.1120070.

Parkes, A., Riddell, J., Wight, D., & Buston, K. (2017). *Growing up in Scotland: Father-child relationships and child socio-emotional wellbeing.* York, UK: Joseph Rowntree Foundation.

Parsons, C. (2016). Ethnicity, gender, deprivation and low educational attainment in England: Political arithmetic, ideological stances and the deficient society. *Education, Citizenship and Social Justice, 11*(2), 160–183.

Paterson, L. (2020). Schools, policy and social change: Scottish Secondary education in the second half of the twentieth century. *Research Papers in Education.* https://www.tandfonline.com/doi/full/10.1080/02671522.2020.1849370

Pavlidis, G. T., & Giannouli, V. (2014). Linking ADHD-dsylexia and specific learning difficulties. In P. Garner, J. M. Kauffman, & J. Elliot (Eds.), *The SAGE handbook of emotional and behavioral difficulties* (pp. 221–235). London: SAGE.

Percival, J. (2017). The historical and philosophical foundations of conservative educational policy. *FORUM, 59*(2), 273–280.

Perkins, D. (1992). *Smart schools: Better thinking and learning for every child.* New York: The Free Press.

Perkins, D., & Salomon, G. (1989). Are cognitive skills context bound? *Educational Researcher, Jan-Feb,* 16–25.

Perkins, D., & Salomon, G. (2012). Knowledge to go: A motivational and dispositional view of transfer. *Educational Psychologist, 47*(3), 248–258.

Perry, B. L., Aronsona, B., & Pescosolido, B. A. (2021). Pandemic precarity: COVID-19 is exposing and exacerbating inequalities in the American heartland. *PNAS, 118*(8), e2020685118. https://doi.org/10.1073/pnas.2020685118

References 259

Petrou, A., Angelides, P., & Leigh, J. (2009). Beyond the difference: From the margins to inclusion. *International Journal of Inclusive Education, 13*(5), 439–448.

Phillips, D. C., & Soltis, J. F. (2004). *Perspectives on learning* (4th ed.). New York: Teachers College Press.

Pihl, J., Holm, G., Riitaoja, A.-L., Ingvar, J., Carlson, K., & Carlson, M. (2018). Nordic discourses on marginalisation through education. *Education Inquiry, 9*(1), 22–39.

Pirrie, A., & Rafanell, I. (2020). Re-conceptualising authority relations in education: A micro-situational approach. *Critical Studies in Education, 61*(1), 101–114.

Place, M., & Elliott, J. (2014). The importance of the 'E' in 'EBD'. In P. Garner, J. M. Kauffman, & J. Elliot (Eds.), *The SAGE handbook of emotional and behavioral difficulties* (2nd ed., pp. 83–93). London: SAGE.

Pluim, G., Nazir, J., & Wallace, J. (2021). Curriculum integration and the semicentennial of Basil Bernstein's classification and framing of educational knowledge. *Canadian Journal of Science, Mathematics and Technology Education, 20*(4), 715–735.

Poed, S., Cologon, K., & Jackson, R. (2020). Gatekeeping and restrictive practices by Australian mainstream schools: Results of a national survey. *International Journal of Inclusive Education, 26*(8), 766–779. doi: 10.1080/13603116.2020.1726512.

Polesel, J., Rice, S., & Dulfer, N. (2014). The impact of high-stakes testing on curriculum and pedagogy: A teacher perspective from Australia. *Journal of Education Policy, 29*(5), 640–657.

Policy First. (2012). *Breaking down barriers: How we can ensure no child's educational success is limited by their socio-economic background.* From Her Majesty's Government https://assets.publishing.service.gov.uk/government/uploads/system/uploads/attachment_data/file/61964/opening-doors-breaking-barriers.pdf

Pope, D., & Miles, S. (2022). A caring climate that promotes belonging and engagement. *Phi Delta Kappan, 103*(5), 8–12.

Porter, L. (2006). *Behaviour in schools. Theory and practice for teachers* (2nd ed.). Buckingham, England: Open University Press.

Price, H. B. (2008). *Mobilizing the community to help students succeed.* Alexandria, VA: ASCD.

Priestley, M., & Humes, W. M. (2010). The development of Scotland's curriculum for excellence: Amnesia and déjà vu. *Oxford Review of Education, 36*(3), 345–361.

Priestley, M., & Minty, S. (2013). Curriculum for excellence: 'A brilliant idea, but...' *Scottish Educational Review, 45*(1), 39–52.

Prince, E. J., & Hadwin, J. (2013). The role of a sense of school belonging in understanding the effectiveness of inclusion of children with special educational needs. *International Journal of Inclusive Education, 17*(3), 238–262.

Pritchard, A., & Woolard, J. (2010). *Psychology for the classroom: Constructivism and social learning.* London; New York: Routledge.

Public Health Scotland. (2017). *Tackling the attainment gap by preventing and responding to adverse childhood experiences (ACEs).* Retrieved from http://www.healthscotland.scot/publications/tackling-the-attainment-gap-by-preventing-and-responding-to-adverse-childhood-experiences

Public Health Scotland. (2022). *Ensuring our future: Addressing the impact of COVID-19 on children, young people and their families: Discussion paper.* Edinburgh: Author.

260 References

Putnam, R. D. (2001). *Bowling alone: The collapse and revival of American community.* New York: Touchstone.

Putnam, R. D. (2015). *Our kids, the American dream in crisis (Reprint Edition).* New York: Simon and Schuster.

Qvortrup, A., & Qvortrup, L. (2018). Inclusion: Dimensions of inclusion in education. *International Journal of Inclusive Education, 22*(7), 803–817. doi: 10.1080/13603116.2017.1412506.

Razer, M., Friedman, V. J., & Warshofsky, B. (2013). Schools as agents of social exclusion and inclusion. *International Journal of Inclusive Education, 17*(11), 1152–1170.

Reay, D. (2012). What would a socially just education system look like? Saving the minnows from the pike. *Journal of Education Policy, 27*(5), 587–599.

Reay, D. (2018). *Miseducation: Inequality, education and the working classes.* Bristol: Policy Press.

Reimer, K. (2019). Relationships of control and relationships of engagement: How educator intentions intersect with student experiences of restorative justice. *Journal of Peace Education, 16*(1), 49–77. doi: 10.1080/17400201.2018.1472070.

Reimer, K. (2020). "Here, It's like you don't have to leave the classroom to solve a problem": How restorative justice in schools contributes to students' individual and collective sense of coherence. *Social Justice Research, 33*(4), 406–427.

Reimer, K., & Pangrazio, L. (2020). Educating on the margins: Young people's insights into effective alternative education. *International Journal of Inclusive Education, 24*(5), 479–495. doi: 10.1080/13603116.2018.1467977.

Render, G. F., Padilla, J. M., & Krank, H. M. (1989). Assertive discipline: A critical review and analysis. *Teachers College Record, 90*, 607–630.

Reynaert, D., Desmet, E., Lembrechts, S., & Vandenhole, W. (2015). Introduction: A critical approach to children's rights. In W. Vandenhole, E. Desmet, D. Reynaert, & S. Lembrechts (Eds.), *Routledge international handbook of Children's rights studies* (pp. 1–23). London: Routledge.

Richters, J. E., & Cicchetti, D. (2008). Mark Twain meets DSM-III-r: Conduct disorder, development, and the concept of harmful dysfunction. *Development and Psychopathology, 5*(102), 5–29.

Riddell, S. (2016). Widening access to Scottish higher education: Unresolved issues and future challenges. *Scottish Educational Review, 48*(1), 3–12.

Riddell, S., & Carmichael, D. (2019). The biggest extension of rights in Europe? Needs, rights and children with additional support needs in Scotland. *International Journal of Inclusive Education, 23*(5), 473–490. doi: 10.1080/13603116.2019. 1580925.

Riddell, S., & McCluskey, G. (2012). Policy and provision for children with social, emotional and behavioural difficulties in Scotland: Intersections of gender and deprivation. In C. Cole, H. Daniels, & J. Visser (Eds.), *The Routledge international companion to emotional and behavioural difficulties [Routledge handbook]* (pp. 57–67). London: Routledge.

Riddick, B. (2012). Labelling learners with SEND: The good, the bad and the ugly. In D. Armstrong, & G. Squires (Eds.), *Contemporary issues in special educational needs* (pp. 25–34). Maindenhead: Open University Press.

Ridge, T. (2011). The everyday costs of poverty in childhood: A review of qualitative research exploring the lives and experiences of low-income children in the UK. *Children and Society, 25*(1), 73–84.

References   261

Riestenberg, N. (2012). *Circle in the square: Building community and repairing harm in school.* Minnesota: Living Justice Press.

Riley, K. A. (2017). *Place, belonging and school leadership: Researching to make the difference.* London: Bloomsbury Academic.

Riley, K. A., & Rustique-Forrester, E. (2002). *Working with disaffected students.* London: Chapman Publications.

Ringarp, J., & Rothland, M. (2010). Is the grass always greener...? The effect of the PISA results on education debates in Sweden and Germany. *European Educational Research Journal, 9*(3), 422–430.

Rix, J., Nind, M., Sheehy, K., Simmons, K., & Walsh, C. (Eds.). (2010). *Equality, participation and inclusion: Diverse perspectives.* London: David Fulton.

Rix, J., Sheehy, K., Fletcher-Campbell, F., Crisp, M., & Harper, A. (2013). Exploring provision for children identified with special educational needs: An international review of policy And practice. *European Journal of Special Needs Education, 28*(4), 375–391.

Robertson, J. (2017). Rethinking learner and teacher roles: Incorporating student voice and agency into teaching practice. *Journal of Initial Teacher Inquiry, 3,* 41–44.

Robertson, L., & McHardy, F. (2021). *The poverty-related attainment dap: A review of the evidence.* Retrieved from https://www.povertyalliance.org/wp-content/uploads/2021/02/The-Poverty-related-Attainment-Gap-A-Review-of-the-Evidence-2.pdf

Robinson, M. (2014). *The feeling child: Laying the foundations of confidence and resilience.* London: Routledge.

Rogers, B. (2002). What changes and what stays the same in behaviour management? In B. Rogers (Ed.), *Teacher leadership and behaviour management* (pp. 4–19). London: Paul Chapman.

Rogers, B. (2011). *Behaviour management: A whole school approach.* London: Paul Chapman.

Rothstein-Fisch, C., & Trumbull, E. (2008). *Managing diverse classrooms.* Alexandria, VA: ASCD.

Rudduck, J., & Fielding, M. (2006). Student voice and the perils of popularity. *Educational Review (Birmingham), 58*(2), 219–231.

Rudduck, J., & Flutter, J. (2000). Pupil participation and pupil perspective: 'carving a new order of experience'. *Cambridge Journal of Education, 30*(1), 75–89.

Rutter, M. (2012). Resilience: Causal pathways and social ecology. In M. Ungar (Ed.), *The social ecology of resilience: A handbook of theory and practice* (pp. 33–42). New York: Springer.

Sahlberg, P. (2020). *Five things not to do when schools re-open.* Retrieved from https://www.shankerinstitute.org/blog/five-things-not-do-when-schools-re-open

Sanders, P. (2007). Introduction to the theory of person-centred therapy. In M. Cooper, M. O'Hara, P. F. Schmid, & G. Wyatt (Eds.), *The handbook of person-centred psychotherapy and counselling.* New York: Palgrave Macmillan.

Save the Children (2021). *"Dropped into a cave": How families with young children experienced lockdown.* Retrieved from https://www.savethechildren.org.uk/content/dam/gb/reports/dropped-into-a-cave-compressed.pdf

Save the Children/UNICEF. (2021). *Impact of COVID-19 on children living in poverty: A Technical note.* Retrieved from https://data.unicef.org/resources/impact-of-covid-19-on-children-living-in-poverty/

262   References

Scanfeld, V., Davis, L., Weintraub, L., & Dotoli, V. (2018). The power of COMMON language (integrated schoolwide language for classroom management. *Educational Leadership, 76*(1), 54–58.

Scanlan, M., & Johnson, L. (2015). Inclusive leadership on the social frontiers: Family and community engagement. In G. Theoharis, & M. Scanlan (Eds.), *Leadership for increasingly diverse schools* (pp. 162–185). London: Routledge.

Scanlan, M., & Theoharis, G. (2015). Introduction: Intersectionality in educational leadership. In G. Theoharis, & M. Scanlan (Eds.), *Leadership for increasingly diverse schools* (pp. 1–12). London: Routledge.

Schiff, M. (2018). Can restorative justice disrupt the 'school-to-prison pipeline?'. *Contemporary Justice Review, 21*(2), 21–139.

Schleicher, A. (2014), *Equity, excellence and inclusiveness in education: Policy lessons from around the world*, International Summit on the Teaching Profession. Paris: OECD Publishing. https://doi.org/10.1787/9789264214033-en

Schmeichel, B. J., & Baumeister, R. (2004). Self-regulatory strength. In R. Baumeister, & K. D. Vohs (Eds.), *Handbook of self-regulation: Research, theory and applications* (pp. 84–98). London: Guilford Press.

Schore, J. R., & Schore, A. N. (2008). Modern attachment theory: The central role of affect regulation in development and treatment. *Clinical Social Work Journal, 36*(1), 9–20.

Schwan, A., & Shapiro, S. (2011). *How to read Foucault's discipline and punish* (Vol. 55581, How to Read Theory). London: Pluto Press.

Scottish Executive Education Department (2001). *Better behaviour – better learning.* Edinburgh: Her Majesty's Stationery Office.

Scottish Government and the Convention of Local Authorities in Scotland (COSLA). (2018). *"Learning together" Scotland's national action plan on parental involvement, parental engagement, family learning and learning at home 2018 – 2021.* Retrieved from https://www.gov.scot/publications/learning-together-scotlands-national-action-plan-parental-involvement-parental-engagement/pages/14/

Scottish Government. (2013). *Better relationships, better learning, better behaviour.* Retrieved from https://education.gov.scot/education-scotland/scottish-education-system/policy-for-scottish-education/policy-drivers/better-relationships-better-learning-better-behaviour/

Scottish Government. (2014). *Child poverty strategy for scotland: Our approach 2014–2017.* Retrieved from https://www.gov.scot/publications/child-poverty-strategy-scotland-approach-2014-2017/pages/4/

Scottish Government. (2015). *Improving schools in scotland: An OECD perspective.* Retrieved from http://www.oecd.org/education/school/Improving-Schools-in-Scotland-An-OECD-Perspective.pdf

Scottish Government. (2016a). *Fairer Scotland Action Plan.* Retrieved from http://www.gov.scot/FairerScotland

Scottish Government. (2016b). *School Education Statistics.* Retrieved from http://www.gov.scot/Topics/Statistics/Browse/School-Education

Scottish Government. (2017a). *Additional support for learning: Statutory guidance 2017: Statutory guidance to the Education (Additional Support for Learning) (Scotland) Act 2004 as amended.* Retrieved from https://www.gov.scot/publications/supporting-childrens-learning-statutory-guidance-education-additional-support-learning-scotland/

References **263**

Scottish Government. (2017b). *Child Poverty (Scotland) Act 2017*. Retrieved from https://www.legislation.gov.uk/asp/2017/6/contents/enacted

Scottish Government. (2017c). *Education governance: Next steps empowering our teachers, parents and communities to deliver excellence and equity for our children.* Retrieved from http://www.gov.scot/Publications/2017/06/2941

Scottish Government. (2017d). *Included, engaged and involved Part 2: A positive approach to managing school exclusions.* Retrieved from https://education.gov.scot/improvement/self-evaluation/included-engaged-and-involved-part-2/

Scottish Government. (2017e). *Supporting Children's Learning Statutory Guidance on the Education (Additional Support for Learning) Scotland Act 2004 (as amended) Code of Practice (Third Edition) 2017*. Retrieved from http://www.gov.scot/Publications/2017/12/9598

Scottish Government. (2018a). *Developing a positive whole-school ethos and culture – Relationships, Learning and Behaviour.* Retrieved from https://www.gov.scot/publications/developing-positive-whole-school-ethos-culture-relationships-learning-behaviour/pages/1/

Scottish Government. (2018b). *Every child, every chance: The Tackling Child Poverty Delivery Plan 2018-2022.* Retrieved from https://www.gov.scot/Resource/0053/00533606.pdf

Scottish Government (2018c). *School exclusions 2016/2017.* Edinburgh: Scottish Government.

Scottish Government. (2020a). *Achievement of curriculum for excellence levels 2018–2019.* Retrieved from https://www.gov.scot/publications/achievement-curriculum-excellence-cfe-levels-2018-19/

Scottish Government. (2020b). *Achieving excellence and equity: 2021 National Improvement Framework and Improvement Plan.* Retrieved from https://www.gov.scot/publications/2021-national-improvement-framework-improvement-plan/

Scottish Government. (2020c). *Support for learning: All our children and all their potential.* Retrieved from https://www.gov.scot/publications/review-additional-support-learning-implementation/

Scottish Government. (2021a). *Attainment Scotland fund evaluation: Fourth interim report – year 5.* Retrieved from https://www.gov.scot/publications/attainment-scotland-fund-evaluation-fourth-interim-report-year-5/

Scottish Government. (2021b). *Tackling child poverty: Third year progress report (2020–2021).* Retrieved from https://www.gov.scot/publications/tackling-child-poverty-third-year-progress-report-2020-2021/

Scottish Government. (2021c). *Coronavirus (COVID-19): Impact of school building closures – equity audit.* Retrieved from https://www.gov.scot/publications/equity-audit-deepening-understanding-impact-covid-19-school-building-closures-children-socio-economically-disadvantaged-backgrounds-setting-clear-are-as-focus-accelerating-recovery/

Scottish Government. (2021d). *Curriculum for excellence: Scottish Government response to OECD Review.* Retrieved from https://www.gov.scot/publications/oecd-review-of-curriculum-for-excellence-scottish-government-response/

Scottish Government. (2021e). *Education reform: Consulting with children and young people. Edinburgh.* Retrieved from https://www.childrensparliament.org.uk/education-reform/

264 References

Scottish Government. (2021f). *Review of the regional improvement collaboratives*. Retrieved from https://www.gov.scot/publications/review-regional-improvement-collaboratives/documents/

Scottish Government. (2021g). *Summary statistics for attainment and initial leaver destinations, No. 3: 2021 Edition*. Retrieved from https://www.gov.scot/publications/summary-statistics-attainment-initial-leaver-destinations-no-3-2021-edition/

Scottish Government. (2022a). *Putting learners at the centre: Response to the independent advisor on education reform's report*. Retrieved from https://www.gov.scot/publications/putting-learners-at-the-centre-response-to-the-independent-advisor-on-education-reforms-report/pages/a-renewed-vision/

Scottish Government. (2022b). *Putting learners at the centre: Towards a future vision for Scottish education*. Retrieved from https://www.gov.scot/publications/putting-learners-centre-towards-future-vision-scottish-education/

Scottish Teacher Education Committee (STEC) (2014). *National framework for inclusion*. Edinburgh: Author.

Seale, S. (2021, 05.11.2021). Written off/at five': Children in England dumped in unfit 'schools'. *The Guardian*. Retrieved from https://www.theguardian.com/society/2021/nov/05/written-off-at-five-children-in-england-dumped-in-unfit-schools

Sellar, S., & Lingard, B. (2013). The OECD and general governance in education. *Journal of Education Policy, 28*(5), 710–725.

Sellar, S., & Lingard, B. (2018). International large-scale assessments, affective worlds and policy impacts in education. *International Journal of Qualitative Studies in Education, 31*(5), 367–381. doi: 10.1080/09518398.2018.1449982.

Sellgren, K. (2017). *Teaching to the test gives 'hollow understanding'*. Retrieved from https://www.bbc.co.uk/news/education-41580550

Sergiovanni, T. J. (1994). *Building community in schools*. San Fransisco: Jossey-Bass.

Seymour, K., Skattebol, J., & Pook, B. (2020). Compounding education disengagement: COVID-19 lockdown, the digital divide and wrap-around services. *Journal of Children's Services, 15*(4), 243–251. doi: 10.1108/JCS-08-2020-0049.

Shakespeare, T. (2014). *Disability rights and wrongs revisited* (2nd ed.). London: Routledge.

Shum, A., Skripkauskaite, S., Pearcey, S., Waite, P., & Creswell, C. (2021). Report 10: Children and adolescents' mental health: One year in the pandemic *Co-space study: Covid-19: Supporting parents, adolescents and children during epidemics* (Vol. 10). Oxford: University of Oxford.

Sinclair, T. (2005). Mad, bad or sad? Ideology, distorted communication and child abuse prevention. *Journal of Sociology, 41*, 227–246.

Skiba, R. J., & Losen, D. J. (2015). From reaction to prevention: Turning the page on school discipline. *American Educator, 39* (Winter 2015-2016), 4–44.

Skovlund, H. (2014). Inclusive and exclusive aspects of diagnosed children's self-concepts in special needs institutions. *International Journal of Inclusive Education, 18*(4), 392–410.

Slee, R. (2013). The labeling and categorisation of children with emotional and behavioural difficulties: A cautionary consideration. In T. Cole, H. Daniels, & J. Visser (Eds.), *The Routledge international companion to emotional and behavioural difficulties [Routledge handbook]* (pp. 15–21)). London: Routledge.

Slee, R. (2014). Evolving theories of student disengagement: A new job for Durkheim's children? *Oxford Review of Education, 40*(4), 446–465.

Slee, R. (2015). Beyond a psychology of student behaviour. *Emotional and Behavioural Difficulties, 20*(1), 3–19. doi: 10.1080/13632752.2014.947100.

Slee, R. (2018a). Defining the scope of inclusive education. *Think piece prepared for the 2020 Global Education Monitoring Report – Inclusion and Education*. Retrieved from https://unesdoc.unesco.org/ark:/48223/pf0000265773

Slee, R. (2018b). *Inclusive education isn't dead, it just smells funny*. London: Routledge.

Slee, R. (2019). Belonging in an age of exclusion. *International Journal of Inclusive Education, 23*(9), 909–922. doi: 0.1080/13603116.2019.1602366

Slee, R., & Allan, J. (2001). Excluding the included: A reconsideration of inclusive education. *International Studies in Sociology of Education, 11*(2), 173–192.

Smith, C. (2020). *In Focus: Children in poverty in working households*. Retrieved from UK Parliament. https://lordslibrary.parliament.uk/children-in-poverty-in-working-households/

Smith, I. (1998). *Is praise always a good thing?* Dundee: Scottish Consultative Council on the Curriculum.

Smith, M. (2018). Capability and adversity: Reframing the "causes of the causes" for mental health. *Palgrave Communications, 4*(13), 1–5.

Smith, M. (2019). Explaining the emergence of attention deficit hyperactivity disorder: Children, childhood, and historical change. *Movement and Nutrition in Health and Disease, 3*. https://doi.org/10.5283/mnhd.14

Smith, R. G., & Brazer, D. S. (2016). *Striving for equity: District leadership for narrowing opportunity and achievement gaps*. Cambridge, Massachusetts: Harvard Educational Press.

Smyth, J., & Wrigley, T. (2013). *Living on the edge: Rethinking poverty, class and schooling*. Oxford: Peter Lang.

Solomon, Y., & Lewin, C. (2016). Measuring 'progress': Performativity as both driver and constraint in school innovation. *Journal of Education Policy, 31*(2), 226–238.

Sosu, E., & Ellis, S. (2014). *Closing the attainment gap in Scottish education*. York: Joseph Rowntree Foundation.

Spillane, J. P. (2006). *Distributed leadership*. San Fransisco: Jossey-Bass.

Spillane, J. P., & Sun, J. (2020). The school principal and the development of social capital in primary schools: The formative years. *School Leadership & Management, 42*(1), 4–23.

Squires, G. (2012). Historical and socio-political agendas around defining and including children with special educational needs. In D. Armstrong & G. Squires (Eds.), *Contemporary issues in special educational needs* (pp. 9–24). Maindenhead: Open University Press.

Stamou, E., Edwards, A., Daniels, H., & Ferguson, L. (2014). *Young people at-risk of drop-out from education: Recognising and responding to their needs*. Oxford: University of Oxford.

Steiner-Khamsi, G. (2014). Cross-national policy borrowing: Understanding reception and translation. *Asia Pacific Journal of Education, 34*(2), 153–167.

Stoll, L. (2007). School culture and improvement. In M. Preedy, R. Glatter, & C. Wise (Eds.), *Strategic leadership and educational improvement* (pp. 93–108). London: SAGE (in conjunction with Open University.

266 References

Strand, S., & Lindorff, A. (2018). *Ethnic disproportionality in the identification of special educational needs (SEN) in England: Extent, causes and consequences.* Oxford: Univeristy of Oxford.

Swinney, J., MSP,. (2019). Swinney: The moral purpose of Scottish education has never been clearer [Press release]

Teasley, M. T. (2014). Shifting from zero tolerance to restorative justice in schools. *Children & Schools, 36*(3), 131–133.

Tett, L., & Macleod, G. (2020). Enacting home–school partnerships: The roles of headteachers, family-learning practitioners and parents. *Cambridge Journal of Education, 50*(4), 451–468. doi: 10.1080/0305764X.2020.1722062.

Tew, M., & Park, J. (2013). Reducing emotional and behaviour difficulties in students by improving school ethos. In T. Cole, H. Daniels, & J. Visser (Eds.), *The Routledge international companion to emotional and behavioural difficulties* (pp. 193–207). London: Routledge.

The Children's Commissioner. (2022). *Children's Mental Health Services 2020/21.* Retrieved from https://www.childrenscommissioner.gov.uk/wp-content/uploads/2022/02/cco-briefing-mental-health-services-2021-22.pdf

The World Bank. (2019). *The education crisis: Being in school is not the same as learning.* Retrieved from https://www.worldbank.org/en/news/immersive-story/2019/01/22/pass-or-fail-how-can-the-world-do-its-homework

Thomas, G. (2014). What do we mean by EBD? In P. Garner, J. M. Kauffman, & J. Elliot (Eds.), *The SAGE handbook of emotional and behavioral difficulties* (2nd ed., pp. 21–42). London: SAGE.

Thomas, G., & Macnab, N. (2019). Intersectionality, diversity, community and inclusion: Untangling the knots. *International Journal of Inclusive Education, 26*(3), 227–244. doi: 10.1080/13603116.2019.1645892.

Thorn, W., & Vincent-Lancrin, S. (2021). *Schooling during a pandemic: The experience and outcomes of schoolchildren during the first round of COVID-19 lockdowns.* OECD Publishing, Paris, https://doi.org/10.1787/1c78681e-en

Tickle, L., & Ratcliffe, R. (2014, 22.07.2014). Michael Gove: 'Bogeyman' or 'the greatest education secretary ever'? *The Guardian.* Retrieved from https://www.theguardian.com/education/2014/jul/22/michael-gove-legacy-education-secretary

Tomlinson, S. (2015). Is a sociology of special and inclusive education possible? *Educational Review, 67*(3), 273–281. doi: 10.1080/00131911.2015.1021764.

Tomlinson, S. (2016). Special education and minority ethnic young people in England: Continuing issues. *Discourse: Studies in the Cultural Politics of Education, 37*(4), 513–528. doi: 10.1080/01596306.2015.1073013.

Torrance, D. (2013a). Distributed leadership: Challenging five generally held assumptions. *School Leadership & Management: Formerly School Organisation, 33*(4), 354–372.

Torrance, D. (2013b). Distributed leadership: Still in the gift of the headteacher. *Scottish Educational Review, 45*(2), 50–63.

Treanor, M. (2012). Impacts of poverty on children and young people. *Research Briefing.* Edinburgh: Scottish Child Care and Protection Network.

Treanor, M. (2016). The effects of financial vulnerability and mothers' emotional distress on child social, emotional and behavioural well-being: A structural equation model. *Sociology, 50*(4), 673–694.

References 267

Treanor, M. (2017). Can we put the poverty of aspirations myth to bed now? *CRFR research briefing* (Vol. 91). Edinburgh: Centre for Research on Families and Relationships, University of Edinburgh.

Treanor, M. (2019). ACEs – Repackaging old problems in shiny new (Emperor's) clothes. Professor Morag Treanor.

Treanor, M. (2020a). *Child poverty: Aspiring to survive.* Cambridge, England: Polity Press.

Treanor, M. (2020b). How covid-19 crisis measures reveal the conflation between poverty and adversity. *Scottish Affairs, 29*(4), 475–492.

Trevarthen, C. (2006). Stepping away from the mirror: Pride and shame in adventures of companionship. In C. S. Carter, L. Ahnert, K. E. Grossman, S. B. Hardy, M. E. Lamb, S. W. Porges, & N. Sachser (Eds.), *Attachment and bonding: A new synthesis. Dahlem workshop report* (Vol. 92, pp. 55–84). Cambridge, MA: MIT Press.

Trevarthen, C. (2011). Innate moral feelings, moral laws and cooperative cultural practice. In J. J. Sanguineti, A. A. Acerbi, & J. A. Lombo (Eds.), *Moral behavior and free will: A neurobiological and philosophical approach* (pp. 385–420). Morolo, Italy: IF Press.

Trevarthen, C., & Delafield-Butt, J. T. (2015). The infant's creative vitality, in projects of self-discovery and shared meaning: How they anticipate school, and make it fruitful. In S. Robson, & S. F. Quinn (Eds.), *International handbook of young children's thinking and understanding* (pp. 3–18). Abingdon, Oxfordshire & New York: Routledge.

Trevarthen, C., & Delafield-Butt, J. T. (2016). Intersubjectivity in the imagination and feelings of the infant: Implications for education in the early years. In E. J. White, & C. Dalli (Eds.), *Under-three year olds in policy and practice* (6th ed., pp. 17–39). New York: Springer.

Tsovoka, D., & Tarr, J. (2012). *Diverse perspectives on inclusive school communities.* Abiingdon, Oxford, England: Routledge.

UNESCO. (1990). *World declaration on education for all and framework for action to meet basic learning needs.* Retrieved from https://unesdoc.unesco.org/ark:/48223/pf0000127583

UNESCO. (1994, 7–10 June). *The Salamanca statement and framework for action.* Paper presented at the World conference on special needs education: Access and quality, Salamanca, Spain. Retrieved from https://unesdoc.unesco.org/ark:/48223/pf0000098427

UNESCO. (2009). *Policy guidelines on inclusion in education.* Retrieved from https://unesdoc.unesco.org/ark:/48223/pf0000177849

UNESCO. (2020). *Leading SDG 4 – Education 2030* [Press release]. Retrieved from https://en.unesco.org/themes/education2030-sdg4

UNESCO, UNICEF & The World Bank. (2020). *What have we learnt? Findings from a survey of ministries of education on national responses to COVID-19.* Retrieved from https://data.unicef.org/resources/national-education-responses-to-covid19/

Ungar, M., Mehdi, G., & Jörg, R. (2013). Annual research review: What is resilience within the social ecology of human development? *Journal of Child Psychology and Psychiatry, 54*(4), 348–366.

UNICEF Data. (2020a). *How COVID-19 is changing the world: A statistical perspective* (Vol 1). Retrieved from https://data.unicef.org/resources/how-covid-19-is-changing-the-world-a-statistical-perspective/

268 *References*

UNICEF Data. (2020b). *How COVID-19 is changing the world: a statistical perspective* (Vol. 2). Retrieved from https://data.unicef.org/resources/how-covid-19-is-changing-the-world-a-statistical-perspective-volume-2/

UNICEF Office of Global Insight & Policy. (2020). COVID-19, global governance and the impact on children: In conversation with public health expert Devi Sridhar. https://www.unicef.org/globalinsight/stories/covid-19-global-governance-and-impact-children

UNICEF Office of Research – Innocenti. (2016). Fairness for children: A league table of inequality in child well-being in rich countries. *UNICEF Innocenti Report Card 13*. Retrieved from https://www.unicef-irc.org/publications/pdf/RC13_eng.pdf

UNICEF Office of Research – Innocenti. (2017). Building the future children and the sustainable development goals in rich countries *Innocenti Report Card 14* (Vol. 14). Retrieved from https://www.unicef-irc.org/publications/890-building-the-future-children-and-the-sustainable-development-goals-in-rich-countries.html

UNICEF & International Telecommunication Union. (2020). *How many children and young people have internet access at home? Estimating digital connectivity during the COVID-19 pandemic.* Retrieved from https://data.unicef.org/resources/children-and-young-people-internet-access-at-home-during-covid19/

UNICEF, & UN Women and Plan International. (2020). *A new era for girls: Taking stock of 25 years of progress.* Retrieved from https://data.unicef.org/resources/a-new-era-for-girls-taking-stock-of-25-years-of-progress/

UNICEF. (1989). *United Nations Convention on the Rights of the Child.* Retrieved from https://www.unicef.org.uk/what-we-do/un-convention-child-rights/

UNICEF. (2019a). *Children and the sustainable development goals.* Retrieved from https://www.unicef.org/sdgs

UNICEF. (2019b). *Every child learns: UNICEF Education Strategy 2019-2030.* Retrieved from https://www.unicef.org/media/59856/file/UNICEF-education-strategy-2019-2030.pdf

UNICEF (2020a). *Children with disabilities: Ensuring their inclusion in covid-19 response strategies and evidence generation.* New York: UNICEF.

UNICEF (2020b). *Protecting children from violence in the time of COVID-19: Disruptions in prevention and response services.* New York: UNICEF.

UNICEF. (2021a). *COVID-19 and school closures: One year of education disruption.* Retrieved from https://data.unicef.org/resources/one-year-of-covid-19-and-school-closures/

UNICEF. (2021b). *The state of the world's children 2021. On my mind: Promoting, protecing and caring for children's mental health* (Executive Summary). Retrieved from https://www.unicef.org/reports/state-worlds-children-2021

Vaandering, D. (2014). Implementing restorative justice practice in schools: What pedagogy reveals. *Journal of Peace Education, 11*(1), 64–80.

Vandekinderen, C., Roets, G., Van Keer, H., & Roose, R. (2018). Tackling social inequality and exclusion in education: From human capital to capabilities. *International Journal of Inclusive Education, 22*(1), 1–20. doi: 10.1080/13603116.2017.1362044

Van Lancker, W. V., & Parolin, Z. (2020). COVID-19, school closures, and child poverty: A social crisis in the making (Comment). *The Lancet Public Health 2020, 5*(5), 243–244.

Vaswani, N., & Brown, A. (2022). *The views of school pupils on the use of restorative justice in Scotland*. Retrieved from the Children and Young People's Centre for Justice, University of Strathclyde https://www.cycj.org.uk/wp-content/uploads/2022/03/RJ-Research-Child-Report.pdf

Velez, G., Hahn, M., Recchia, H., & Wainryb, C. (2020). Rethinking responses to youth rebellion: Recent growth and development of restorative practices in schools. *Current Opinion in Psychology, 35*, 36–40.

Vincent-Lancrin, S., Cobo Romaní, C., & Reimers, F. (eds.) (2022), *How learning continued during the COVID-19 pandemic: Global lessons from initiatives to support learners and teachers*, OECD Publishing, Paris, https://doi.org/10.1787/bbeca162-en

Visser, J., & Zenib, J. (2009). ADHD: A scientific fact or a factual opinion? A critique of the veracity of attention deficit hyperactivity disorder. *Emotional and Behavioural Difficulties, 14*(2), 127–140.

Wall, S., Ainsworth, M. D. S., Blehar, M. C., & Waters, E. (2014). *Patterns of attachment: A psychological study of the strange situation*. Hove, East Sussex, UK: Psychology Press.

Walsh, G. M. (2020). the arrival of the ACES movement in Scotland: Policy entrepreneurship and critical activist responses. *Scottish Affairs, 29*(4), 456–474.

Walsh, D., McCartney, G., Smith, M., & Armour, G. (2019a). Relationship between childhood socioeconomic position and adverse childhood experiences (ACEs): A systematic review. *Journal of Epidemiology and Community Health, 73*(12), 1087–1093.

Walsh, D., McCartney, G., Smith, M., & Armour, G. (2019b). Contextualising ACEs: the relationship between childhood socioeconomic position and adverse childhood experiences. Retrieved from https://www.scotpho.org.uk/media/1883/david-walsh-phins-2019.pdf

Wang, G., Zhang, Y., Zhao, J., Zhang, J., & Jiang, F. (2020). Mitigate the effects of home confinement on children during the COVID-19 outbreak (correspondence). *The Lancet, 395*(March 21, 2020), 945–946.

Ward, S., Bynner, C., & Bianchi, V. (2021). Building a capabilities framework with learners from high-poverty neighbourhoods. In C. Chapman, & M. Ainscow (Eds.), *Educational equity: Pathways to success* (pp. 134–156). London: Routledge.

Warin, J. (2017). Creating a whole school ethos of care. *Emotional and Behavioural Difficulties, 22*(3), 188–199.

Waterhouse, J., & Møller, J. (2009). Shared leadership (Principle 4. In J. MacBeath, & N. Dempster (Eds.), *Connecting leadership and learning: Principles for practice*. London: Routledge.

Watson, C. (2005). Classrooms as learning communities: A review of research. *London Review of Education, 3*(13), 47–64.

Webber, L. (2017). A school's journey in creating a relational environment which supports attachment and emotional security. *Emotional and Behavioural Difficulties, 22*(4), 317–331.

Wenger, E. (1998). *Communities of practice: Learning, meaning and identity*. Cambridge: Cambridge University Press.

Wenger, E., McDermott, R., & Snyder, W. (2002). *Cultivating communities of practice*. Boston, Massachusetts: Harvard University Business School Press.

270 *References*

Wheeler, L. (2010). Critique of the article by Visser and Jehan (2009): ADHD: A scientific fact or a factual opinion? A critique of the veracity of attention deficit hyperactivity disorder. *Emotional and Behavioural Difficulties*, 15(3), 257–268.

White, D. (2021, Friday, October 2021). Strictest head teacher Katharine Birbalsingh says children are born with sin. *The Times*. Retrieved from https://www.thetimes.co.uk/article/strictest-head-teacher-katharine-birbalsingh-says-children-are-born-with-sin-kdndtxlsf

White, J. (2018). *Children's social circumstances and educational outcomes*. Edinburgh: National Health Service.

Wienen, A. W., Sluiter, M. N., Thoutenhoofd, E., de Jonge, P., & Batstra, L. (2019). The advantages of an ADHD classification from the perspective of teachers. *European Journal of Special Needs Education*, 34(5), 649–662. doi: 10.1080/08856257.2019.1580838.

Wilkinson, R., & Pickett, K. (2010). *The spirit level: Why equality is better for everyone*. London: Penguin Books.

Wilkinson, R., & Pickett, K. (2018). *The inner level: How more equal societies reduce stress, restore sanity and improve everyone's wellbeing*. UK: Penguin Random House.

Wilson, R. L., & Wilson, R. (2015). *Understanding emotional development: Providing insight into human lives*. London: Routledge.

Wilson-Ali, N., Barratt-Pugh, C., & Knaus, M. (2019). Multiple perspectives on attachment theory: Investigating educators' knowledge and understanding. *Australasian Journal of Early Childhood*, 44(3), 215–229.

Winter, A. L. (2018). Relational equality in education: What, how, and why? *Oxford Review of Education*, 44(3), 338–352.

Wiske, M. S. (1998). *Teaching for understanding: Linking research with practice*. San Francisco, CA: Jossey-Bass.

Wolff, J., Lamb, E., & Zur-Szpiro, E. (2015). *A philosophical review of poverty*. Retrieved from the Joseph Rowntree Foundation https://www.jrf.org.uk/report/philosophical-review-poverty

World Health Organisation. (2016). *Growing up unequal: Gender and socioeconomic differences in young people's health and well-being: Health behaviour in school-aged children (HBSC) study: International report from the 2013/2014 survey* (Vol. Health Policy for Children and Adolescents, no. 7). Retrieved from https://apps.who.int/iris/handle/10665/326320

World Health Organisation. (2020). *Mental health and psychosocial considerations during the COVID-19 outbreak*. Retrieved from https://www.who.int/docs/default-source/coronaviruse/mental-health-considerations.pdf

Wright, A. (2009). Every child matters: Discourses of challenging behaviour. *Pastoral Care in Education*, 27(4), 279–290.

Wrong, D. (1979). *Power: Its forms, bases and uses*. London: Blackwell.

Yeager, D., Scott, & Dweck, C. S. (2012). Mindsets that promote resilience: When students believe that personal characteristics can be developed. *Educational Psychologist*, 47(4), 302–314.

Young, E. L., Caldarella, P., Richardson, M. J., & Young, R. (2012). *Positive behaviour support in secondary schools: A practical guide*. London: The Guilford Press.

Zachar, P. (2000). Psychiatric disorders are not natural kinds. *Philosophy, Psychiatry and Pscyhology*, 7(3), 167–194.

Zachar, P. (2015). Psychiatric disorders: Natural kinds made by the world or practical kinds made by us? *World Psychiatry*, 14(3), 288–290.

Index

Note: *Italicized* and bold page numbers refer to figures and tables, respectively; page numbers followed by "b" refer to boxes, those by "n" refer to notes and those by "c" refer to charts.

0–25 Education, Health and Care (EHC) Plan 37

ableism 35, 76
absolute poverty 59, 60
abuse 163
academics obsession 192
Academies programme 11, 18, 19
accelerated disablement **84**
acceptability, cultural competence 227
accessibility, cultural competence 227
accountability 2–4, 11, 12, 14, 17, 19, 21, 22, 62, 67, 75, 77, 120, 122, 126, 133, 171, 219
ACEs *see Adverse Childhood Experiences* (ACE)
action schema 108
Adams, M. 46, 49
AD *see Assertive Discipline* (AD)
adaptive leadership 214
Addison, D. 166b
Additional Support Needs (ASN) 37, 53, 62, 84, 151
ADHD *see Attention Deficit Hyperactivity Disorder* (ADHD)
Adult Attachment Interview 98
adulthood 29, 30, 56, 57, 74, 103; *Attention Deficit Hyperactivity Disorder* in 89–90; economic security 99
Adverse Childhood Experiences (ACE) 56–58, 163; and deprivation, relationship between 164–165; unsupported, effects of 164–165
affectional bonds 97

affective domain 174
affirmative restorative justice 181, 184, 187
affordability, cultural competence 227
Africa: disproportionality in special education 34
agency 106, 108, 115, 208, 216, 226, 230; developmental theory 117–118; relationship with autonomy and control 194–196, *195*, **195**, **197**; school discipline policy, implications for 117–118; and social exclusion 51
Ainscow, M. 27, *27*, 30, 34, 219
Ainsworth, M. D. S. 98
ALSPAC *see Avon Longitudinal Study of Parents and Children* (ALSPAC)
alter-ego 3, 138
American Psychiatric Association (APA) 76, 88
American Psychological Association 133
Anda, R. 57, 163
Anderson, M. 134
anxiety 87, 101, 103
APA *see American Psychiatric Association* (APA)
Apple, M. W. 214
Applied Behaviour Analysis 105, 135, 153n2
appropriateness, cultural competence 227
Arar, K. 220
Archard, D. 29–30
Areas of Deprivation, ACEs 64
Areas of Multiple Deprivation 2, 61, 64n5

272 *Index*

Armour, G. 57
Armstrong, D. 34, 134–136
Asia: disproportionality in special education 34
ASN *see Additional Support Needs* (ASN)
Assertive Discipline (AD) 105, 115, 122, 134–138, 142, 144
assessment 12, 13, 16, 19, 29, 36, 93
Atkinson, M. B. 170
attachment theory 97–102, 117, 159; contemporary conceptualisations 101–102; cultural considerations for 101; dynamic maturational theory of attachment and adaptation 101; emotional regulation 99–100; infant, intentionality of 100; intersubjectivity 100–101; maternal sensitivity 99–100; nature of 97–98; parental states of mind and child attachment styles, correlation between 98, **99**; philosophical basis 97; reflections on 102; *Strange Situation* 98; *see also* attunement
attainment 33–35, 38, 45, 55, 58, 148, 149, 226; educational 206; poverty-related 20, 21, 60–63, *61, 63*
Attention Deficit Hyperactivity Disorder (ADHD) 77, 87–94; biomedical perspective, critiques of 90–91; biopsychosocial perspective of 92–93; as complex, normative syndrome 89; controversy around medication 89; heritability of 90, 95n3; impact on childhood and adulthood 89–90; neurological explanations 90; science and controversies around classification 91–92; situated nature of the construct 92; synthesis of 93–94; variability in prevalence rates 89
attunement 99–100, 102, 156, 157, 160, 162
Auerbach, S. 209
Australia: schools exclusions and criminal justice system 74
authenticity 203
authoritarian approaches to school discipline 134–140; *Assertive Discipline* 136; critique of 137–139; nature of 136–137; philosophical underpinnings 136; *Schoolwide Positive Behaviour Support* 136

authority 123–126; coercive 123, **124**, 125, 126, 137, 138, 140; competent 123, 125–127, **125**; by inducement 123, **124**, 125; legitimate 123, 125–127, **125**, 137; personal 123, 125, **125**, 126; as situated 126–127
autonomous school systems 19, 194
autonomy 4, 6, 17, 21, 137, 142, 152, 181, 193, 203, 216, 219, 226, 231; developmental theory 117–118; in developmental theory 117–118; relationship with agency and control 194–196, *195*, **195**, **197**; school discipline and 118–127; school discipline policy, implications for 117–118; teacher 19, 20
availability 227
Avon Longitudinal Study of Parents and Children (ALSPAC) 164

Bandura, A. 105–107, 117, 136
Bangs, J. 18
Barber, M. 18
Batstra, L. 77, 91
Behavioural, Emotional and Social Difficulties (BESD) 83
Behaviour and Discipline in Schools 141, 142
Behaviour and Discipline in Schools: Advice for headteachers 75
Behaviour in schools: Advice for headteachers and school staff 144
Behaviour in Scottish Schools Surveys (2006) 145
behaviourism 102–103, 105, 107, 110, 117, 135, 147
behaviourist theory 103
behaviour management 3, 94, 113; environmental theory 102–107; orthodoxies, challenging 5–6, 115–131, 132–153, 229–230, restorative justice/practice 181, 184, 187; *see also* climate for learning
Bell, L. A. 46, 48–49, 217
BELMAS *see British Educational Leadership, Management and Administration Society* (BELMAS)
Bender, P. K. 99–100
Bennett, H. 161
Bennett, T. 117, 140–143
Berlin, I. 41
Berman, D. 71, 78

Bernhardt, V. 22, 214, 219, 220, 228, 232
Berryman, M. 70, 71
BESD *see Behavioural, Emotional and Social Difficulties* (BESD)
Best, M. 29, 30
Better Behaviour-Better Learning 146, 149c
Better Relationships, Better Learning, Better Behaviour 150c
better learning, better behaviour, relationship between 147–148
big data 10, 16, 22
Bilton, K. 82
bioecological model 109
bioecological theory 108, 110, 117
biological theory: attachment theory 97–102
biopsychosocial 5; perspective of ADHD 92–93
Black-Hawkins, K. 6
Blair, J. 18
blame culture 12, 46, 65
Blankstein, A. M. 218, 219, 232
Booth, T. 27, *27*
Bo Peep theory of transfer 174
boundaries 157, 165, 205, 220; around inclusion 39; distinguish childhood from adulthood 29; fluid 118; geographic 191; social 41; between the state, private and third sector 19; between the state and private sector 10; static 39
bounded learning 176
Bowlby, J. 97
Boxall profile 159, 161
Bøyum, S. 16
Braille 34
Brazer, D. S. 216, 219
'Bridging Cultures' project 229
British Educational Leadership, Management and Administration Society (BELMAS) 233n2
Bronfenbrenner, U. 96, 108, 109
Brookfield, S. D. 174
Brown, E. T. 91
Bruner, J. S. 107
building infrastructure 226
Building Schools for the Future 18
bullying: behaviours 73; cyberbullying 73; definition of 73; restorative justice/practice 179–180, 205, student voice 205; *see also* prejudice

Bunting, L. 165
Bywaters, P. 165

Caldarella, P. 136
Canada: restorative justice 181, 182, **183**
Canter, L. 136, 137, 147
Canter, M. 136, 137, 147
capacity, definition of 214
capacity building 213–217, *215*, 224; to promote social justice at district level 216–217; in staff, students and families 185
capital: cultural 51, 207–208, 210, 225–229; economic 51, 207–208, 225; social 51, 207–208, 210, 211, 225–229, 233n4
Care Experienced (previously *Looked After and Accommodated*) 61, 62, 64n6
Carnahan, J. 152
Casimir, A. E. 166b
Causton, J. 155
CD *see Conduct Disorder* (CD)
Center for Disease Control and Prevention 88
CfE *see Curriculum for Excellence* (CfE)
Chafouleas, S. M. 165
chaotic/disorganised pattern of attachment 158
chaotic systems 109
Chapman, C. 219
Charlotte-Mecklenburg Schools 133
Chavis, D. M. 192
child: as unit and agent of change 137; from the behaviour, separating 180
childhood poverty: adverse childhood experiences 57–58; disproportionality in 57; and education 58; nature of the problem 55; in Scotland 59–60
childhood, understandings of 29–30, 117–118
Child Poverty Strategy 60
Children in Need Review 144
children's learning, understanding of 156
children's rights 231; *see also United Nations Convention on the Rights of the Child* (UNCRC)
childhood psychopathology 87
Child Poverty Action Group 59
children: attachment styles and parental states of mind, correlation between 98, **99**; *Attention Deficit*

274   *Index*

Hyperactivity Disorder 89–90; rights 29–31, 136, 149, 152, 167, 200, 202, 205; separating the child from the behaviour 180
Children and Families Act 2014 37
Children and Young People's Centre for Justice, University of Strathclyde 188n2
Children and Young People (Scotland) Act 2020 167
chronosystem 109
Cigman, R. 28
City Challenge 18
Clark, C. 119
classical conditioning (Pavlov) 103–105, *103*
'classic' nurture group 158–159, 161–162
classroom climate 31, 94, 116, 149, 178; *see also* school climate
classroom, safe base 156–157
Clinton administration (1993–2001) 133
Clydebank 48
Cobo Romaní, C. 14
Code of Practice 27
Code of Practice 2014 37
coercive authority 123, **124**, 125, 126, 137, 138, 140
cognitive developmental stage theory 156
cognitive social-historical theory 107
coherence: comprehensible 180, **181**; curriculum 20, manageable 180, **181**; meaningful 180, **181**; restorative practice as 180–184, SEN(D) 33
Cole, T. 33–34, 75, 86
Coleman, V. 192, 228
collaborative leadership 216
collective individualism 10
Colley, D. 159, **160**
Colombi, G. 177, 186
Comer School Development Program 23
commodification: of education 10; of public services 9
communication 28, 100, 141; authentic 177; barriers to effective 210; and behaviour 158; language as means of 157; and school ethos 146
community: building *see* community building; communities of practice 106, 191, 218, 225; engagement 228, 231; and schools 191–193, *192 (see also* school community)

community building: through nurture and trauma-informed practice 6, 154–171; through participative and collaborative school cultures 203–211; through restorative justice/ practice 6, 173–187
communities of practice 191, 218, 225; legitimate participation in 106; social structure of 106
Community of Practice 225
compassion 155
compassionate discipline 155
competence 193, 196; cultural 227; pedagogical 231; socioemotional 214; technical 214
competent authority 123, 125, **125**, 127
competition 9–11, 16–17, 19, 36, 58, 67, 133, 193
competitive meritocracy 19
compliance 22, 77, 122, **124**, 142–143, 187, 194, **195**, 196, **197**, 229–230
conditioned response 102, 103
conditioned stimulus 103
Conduct Disorder (CD) 87–89, 95n1
congruence 53, 58, 69, 155, 174, **175**, 176, 179, 226–227
Connell, R. 10
Connolly, B. 48
Connor, D. J. 71, 77
constrained behaviour 194
context responsive leadership 221
contingencies 105, 194
continuous professional development (CPD) 231–232
continuum of practice 206–207
control: relationship with agency and autonomy 194–196, *195*, **195**, **197**
Convention on the Rights of the Child 13
Cook-Harvey, C. M. 16, 210
Cooper, M. 170
Cooper, P. 82, 86, 92–93, 127, 160
Co-ordinated Support Plan (CSP) 37, 38, 84, 168
courageous leadership, principles of 218, **218**
Cowley, S. 127
CPD *see* continuous professional development (CPD)
Cremin, H. 179

Index 275

criminal justice system: school discipline policies and 133; school exclusions and 74, 148

crisis: restorative justice/practice 176, 187; in school discipline 119–120, SEN(D) and 55–56

Crisp, M. 33

critical disability studies 26, 39

Crittenden, P. 101

Cross-Party Group for Children and Young People 205

Crozier, G. 210

CSP *see Co-ordinated Support Plan* (CSP)

Cubeddu, D. 160

cultural capital 51, 207–208, 210, 225–229

cultural competence 227

cultural considerations, in attachment theory 101

culturally responsive leadership 211; school community through, empowering 6

culturally responsive learning environments 227

culturally responsive school leadership 227–229, *228*

cultural responsiveness 227, *228*

cultural tools 107, 157

culture, creation of 144, 214

Cunningham, H. B. 134

curriculum 12, 26, 29, 34, 36, 71, 72, 81, 94, 155, 159, 193, 231; culturally responsive 230; national 17, 19, 20, 61; reforms of 18

Curriculum for Excellence (CfE) 20, 61, 151

cyberbullying 73

d'Agnese, V. 9–12, 23

Daniels, H. 33–34, 75, 86, 110

Darling-Hammond, L. 16, 23, 210

data-informed system 145–146

Davidson, G. 165

Davies, J. 210

Davis, L. 134

Deci, E. L. 193

deficit perspectives on parents and families 208–211, *209*

degree 40; of control 194

de Jonge, P. 77, 91

Delafield-Butt, J. T. 101

Delale-O'Connor, L. 134

deliverology 18, 21

Delivery Unit 18

demographics, school exclusions and 74

Denmark: Attention Deficit Hyperactivity Disorder 89; labelling 77; schools, as agents of exclusion 67

dependency 156, 196

dependent behaviour 194

depressive disorders 87

deprivation and ACEs, relationship between 164–165

Developing a Positive Whole-School Ethos and Culture: Relationships, Learning and Behaviour 149, 151c

developmental stage theory 172n1

developmental theory 5; agency 117–118; autonomy 117–118; power 117–118

Developmental Strands 159, 161

'deviant' student and school disaffection, relationship between 127–130

Dewey, J. 107, **121**

Diagnostic and Statistical Manual of Mental Disorders (DSM) 76, 84, 88

Diagnostic Profile 159, 161

digital inclusion 222

dilemma of difference 32

disability: as form of oppression 34–35; as social construct 34–35

disablism 35

discipline: compassionate 155; as form of coercive control 137–138; as objectification 122; as surveillance 120, 122

Discipline with Dignity 135

Discipline Task Force 146

dispositions 174

discrimination 33–35, 54, 57, 59, 72, 217, 219

disordered behaviours 85

disordered people 85

disproportionality: in childhood poverty 57; in special education 33–34

distributive leadership 216, 221, 231

DMM *see* dynamic maturational theory of attachment and adaptation (DMM)

Dotoli, V. 134

down regulation 87

DSM *see Diagnostic and Statistical Manual of Mental Disorders* (DSM)

Dudley-Marling, A. 62

Dudley-Marling, C. 62

276 *Index*

Dumay, X. 11
Dupriez, V. 11
Durkheim, D. É. 120, **121**, 132, 137
Dweck, C. S. 31
dynamic maturational theory of attachment and adaptation (DMM) 101
dynamics 51
Dyson, A. 27, *27*

early years, positive behaviour in 147, *150*
Ebbsfleet Academy 143
EBD *see* Emotional and Behavioural Difficulties (EBD)
ecological perspective on marginalisation 52
economic capital 51, 207–208, 225
economic inequality 58
economic prosperity: drive for **15**
eco-system 109–110, 117
Education (Additional Support for Learning) (Scotland) Act (2004) 37
educational inequality 133, 213
Educational Leadership 133–134
Education Endowment Foundation 142, 153n1
Education For All movement 13, 25
Education Reform Act 1988 17
Education Scotland 2016 37, 147, 184, 187
education system, transformation of 36
Edwards-Groves, C. 217
EHC *see* 0–25 Education, Health and Care (EHC) Plan
Eley, E. 70, 71
Elliot, E. S. 31
Emotional and Behavioural Difficulties (EBD) 81–85; definitions 82–83; explanations for 86–94; 'extreme, chronic condition' 85–86; key concerns **84**; needs 85; presentation of 86–94; round pegs in square holes 86; terminology 82–83
emotional containment 164–165
emotional regulation 99–100
emotions, nature and function of 87
empathy 69, 100, 108b, 155, 160, 176, 177, 230
empowerment 21; school culture 225–229
empowering the school community: collaboration 191–212, pupil

participation and parental engagement, 189–212; socially just and culturally responsive leadership, 213–233
encouragement of desired responses **104**
England: *Behaviour and Discipline in Schools* 141, *142*; *Behaviour and Discipline in Schools: Advice for headteachers* 75; behaviour management 113; *Building Schools for the Future* 18; bullying 73; Chief Inspector for Schools 66; Department for Education (DfE) 141, 142, 144, 146; disproportionate rates of school exclusion in 75; Education Endowment Foundation 142, 153n1; Education Reform Act 1988 17; excellence and social justice, drive for 17–19; GCSEs (General Certificate of Secondary Education) reforms 18; *Initial Teacher Training* 143; *London Challenge* 18, 21; marginalisation 46; *National Challenge* 18; *National Literacy and Numeracy strategies* 18; *National Union of Teachers* survey (2016) 18; New Labour 17, 18, 139; NHS 145; *Pupil Premium Grant* 18; restorative practice 179; school discipline policies 113, 132, 139–145; SEAL 147; SEMHN 3; *Suspension and Permanent Exclusion* 75; University Technical Colleges 71; *see also* United Kingdom (UK)
England, school discipline policies in 139–145; culture, creation of 142–143; new trajectory 140–142, *142*; *Social and Emotional Aspects of Learning* (SEAL) *Programme* 139–140, 147; subsequent developments 144–145
Engle, R. 176
English policy context, disparity between rhetoric and reality in 37
entity mindset 175
environmental theory: behaviourism 102–103; classical conditioning (Pavlov) 103, *103*; operant conditioning 103–104, **104**; social learning theory 105–107
epistemological governance 11
epistemology 93

equality 63, 67, 139, 219; relational 69; *see also* inequality

equity 27, 45, 213, 214, 217, 218, 219, 228, 229, 232; challenge of 222; excellence and 22; in Scottish education 20–21

eradication of childhood poverty 60

Ersbøll, A. K. 89

Esbjørn, B. H. 99–100

essentialist bias 39

ethic of caring 217

ethnicity 26, 33, 34, 57, 191, 210; *see also* race

Every Child, Every Chance 60

Every Child Learns 12–13, 18

evidence-based practice 118

excellence 35, 218; drive for 15–19, **15**

exclusion 2, 3, 132, 202; and inclusion, dialectic and dynamic relationship between 38–41; as inclusion 77–78; school 65–80; social 5, 45, 50–51, 72, 79, 80

exclusionary mindsets 76

exosystem 109

expansive learning 176

external control 198

externalising behaviours 83

externalising disorders 83, 87–89

external regulation **194**

extrinsic motivation 196; types of 193–194, **194**

factory model of schooling 86

Fairer Scotland 60

Family Connects programme 208

Felitti, V. 57, 163

Fenton, P. 211

Fielding, M. 203

financial vulnerability 209

Finnis, M. 178, 184–185, 198

Fletcher-Campbell, F. 33

flexible consistency in approach 179

Flook, L. 16, 210

Florian, L. 6, 31–34, 198, **200**, 201, 231

flourishing 194

focus for enquiry 199–201, **200**, **201**

Forde, C. 226

formal schemata 107

Foucault, M. 36, 120, 122, 204

fragmentation 33; systemic 181

Framework for Belonging **201**

Framework For Participation 200, **202**

Framework for Promoting Inclusion **201**

Francis, B. 219, 220

Francis, K. 227

Frank, J. 164

Free Schools programme 11, 19

Frost, J. 70

Fullan, M. 22, 192, 214, 219, 221, 225

Furlong, V. J. 81, 127–129, 137, 143

Gambrill, E. 92

Gardner, M. 16, 210

Garner, J. 159, **160**

gemeinschaft 191

General Teaching Council for Scotland (GTCS) 32, 38, 151, 225

gender 26, 134

Gerhardt, S. 164

Getting it Right for Every Child (GIRFEC) 148–149, 151, 160, 167, 168

Gewirtz, S. 22

Gillibrand, R. 101, 104

GIRFEC *see Getting it Right for Every Child* (GIRFEC)

Glasgow City Council 160

Global Education and Monitoring Report (UNESCO) 25, 41

globalisation: impact on educational policy 9–12

goals for understanding 3

Goffman, E. 131n2

Golden Rules 69

Golden Time 69

Goodall, J. 206, 207, 209, 210

good health 13

Gove, M. 127, 140

Graham, L. J. 91–93

Green, T. L. 209

Greenwood, A. 158, 164

Gregory, A. 185, 187

Grootenboer, P. 217

groupthink 20

Growing up in Scotland 59

Grumloese, S. P. 68, 69

Gümüş, S. 220

Hacking, I. 39

Hamre, B. 67

Hansen, J. H. 39–40

'hard to reach parents,' narrative of 208–211, *209*

Hardy, I. 33

Hargreaves, A. 22, 131n3, 219

Harper, A. 33

Harper, L. 211

278 *Index*

Harris, A. 207, 221, 225
Hart, C. 31
Hart, R. A. 204, *204*
Head, G. 135, 142, 147, 185, 221
headline measures 18
Hearn, J. 123
Hedegaard-Soerensen, L. 68, 69
Herrick, C. A. 170
Hertz, C. 116
hidden injuries of schooling 127–130,
    137, 143; production of **129**
hierarchy of needs 118
high transfer 174, **175**
Hirst, P. **121**
holistic needs of children 22–23
Holloway, J. 67
Hollweck, T. 185–186
Hooper, M. A. 22, 214, 220, 228, 232
household adversities 163
Hughes, N. K. 161
humanism 115, 154–155
humanistic approaches 108, 134, 143,
    186, 191: *see also* nurture; relational
    approaches; restorative justice/
    practice; trauma-informed practice
Hyman, S. E. 92

ICEA *see International Council of
    Education Advisors* (ICEA)
IDEA *see* Individuals with Disabilities
    Education Act (IDEA)
identified regulation **194**
identity 106; safety, cultural
    competence 227
IDM *see* Individual, Deficit, Medical
    (IDM) model
imbalances of power, restorative
    practice and 179–180
*Included, Engaged and Involved Part 2:
    A positive approach to preventing and
    managing school exclusions* 75, 148,
    149c
inclusion 3, 199, 202, 213, 217, 219,
    225, 229, 231; arenas of 40–41,
    40; challenge of 222–223; degrees
    of 40, **40**; dialectic and dynamic
    relationship between 38–41;
    exclusion as 77–78; levels of 40, **40**;
    limitations of 28; and performativity,
    conflict between 35–36; and
    SEN(D), tension between 31–32;
    typology of 27–28, *27*; wicked
    problem 27–28; wicked proportions
    26–27; *see also* inclusive education

inclusive education 4, 25–42; and
    children's rights 29–31; *see also*
    inclusion
inclusive pedagogy 29, 30, 41, 86, 173,
    199, 219, 230
inclusive school communities, building
    219
inclusive teaching 29
incoherence 33, 182
income 14, 21, 46, 56, 60, 66, 181;
    gaps 55; inequality 55; low 59;
    maximisation 10
inconsistency 33, 68, 96, 98, 145, 157
incremental mindset 31
Index for Inclusion 34
indiscipline 2, 96, 120, 129, 133, 138,
    146, 152
individual 22
Individual, Deficit, Medical (IDM)
    model 34
Individualised Educational Programme
    168
individualistic culture of the school 229
Individuals with Disabilities Education
    Act (IDEA) 84
inequality 1, 2, 13, 14, 25, 33, 38, 56,
    76, 166, 206, 220, 227; economic
    58; educational 133, 213; income
    55; social 11, 45, 58, 163; socio-
    economic 165; structural 16, 46, *48*,
    57, 68; *see also* equality
infant, intentionality of 100
influence 123–126
infrastructural governance 11
inhibition of undesired responses **104**
Initial Teacher Training 143
insecure attachment 99, 102, 156, 157,
    163–164
insecure-avoidant attachment 98
insecure–disorganised attachment 98
insecure-resistant/ambivalent
    attachment 98, 157
insecure resistant attachment 157
instructional leadership 214
Instrumental Enrichment 108
integrated regulation 193, 194, **194**
intelligence 31
intentionality 101, 117; of infant 100
interdisciplinary working 169; barriers
    to 170–171, **170–171**; facilitators
    170–171, **170–171**
internalisation 210
internalised feelings 97
internalising behaviours 83

internalising disorders 87
internal working (or mental) model 82, 97, 99, 100, 108, 157
International Council of Education Advisors (ICEA) 20
internalised behaviour 193
intersectionality 54, 61–62
intersubjectivity 100–102, 117
Into Headship 222, 224–225
intrinsic motivation 193, 194, 196
introjected regulation **194**

Johnson, L. 210–211, 229
joint enterprise 218, **218**, 225
Jones, M. 221, 225
Jung, L. A. 134

Kaler-Jones, C. 166b
Kant, I. 120, **121**, 132, 137
Kestenberg, E. G. 134
Khon, A. 69, 119, 138, 193
Killen, M. 128
Korpershoek, H. 31
Kourmoulaki, A. 176
Kovač, V. B. 71

labelling 31, 39, 49, 76–77, 84, 88, 91, 92, 173
Lacey, R. E. 164
Ladder of Participation 204, *204*
Lam, D. 176
Landrum, T. J. 85, 86
Langager, S. 77
language 71; adopted by teachers 135; basic 66; of caring 135; of dignity 122; of 'offender' 176; of SEN(D) 32; soft 138; symbolic system of 107; of 'victim' 176
Larsen, T. C. 67
Lave, J. 117, 191
law of effect 104
law of exercise 104
laying the foundations 185
leadership: adaptive 214; collaborative 216; context responsive 221; culturally responsive 227–229; distributive 216, 221, 231; instructional 214; positional 216; relational 217; shared 216, 228; social justice *see* social justice leadership; transformational 215
lead professional 168
learning, better 147–148
Learning Together 208

Learoyd-Smith, S. 110
Lee, K. 192
legitimacy 49, 50, 52, 86, 106, 123, 127
legitimate authority 123, **125**, 125–127, 137
levels of inclusion 40, **40**
limitations of behaviourism 105; inclusion 28, 40; the social model of disability 35
Lingard, B. 11, 12, 16
Lloyd, G. 51, 90
London Challenge 18, 21
looping effect 39, *39*
Lopes, J. A. 85, 88
Loreman, T. 29
Losen, D. J. 133
low transfer 174, **175**
Lupton, R. 219
Lyons-Ruth, K. 100–102

MacAllister, J. 119, 120, 123, 132, 133, 135, 141, 184, 185, 191, 229
MacBeath, J. 14, 18, 216
Machlin, L. 89
MacKay, T. 160, *161*, 163
Macleod, G. 78, 123, 126, 209, *209*
MacLeod, K. 155
MacMurray, J. **121**
macrosystem 4, 9–23, 109
Madsen, K. B. 89
Main, M. 98, 99
mainstreaming 33, 79
maltreatment 164
'manage-and-discipline' approach to school control 134
managerialism 10
marginalisation 2, 3, 5, 16, 22, 33, 36, 39–41, 45–55, *50*, 63, 65, 67, 68, 71, 77, 79, 91, 143, 199, 200, 202, 210, 211, 217, 220, 227, 231; as affective state 51–52; ecological perspective of 52, *54*; as enduring, pervasive, global problem 45–46; as fluid and dynamic concept 49–50; as form of social construction 49–50; manifestation of 49; new conceptualisation of 52–55, *54*; as normative concept 50; oppression and 46–47; as reflective of an 'ideal' 51–52; and social exclusion, relationship between 50–51; social justice and 46–47; as subjective, situated and contextualised experience 47–49; understanding of 51

280 *Index*

marginalised group 48, 49, 51, 211
market 10; competition 11, 19; quasi-market 11, 19
marketisation 9, 10, 16, 17
Marryat, L. 164
Mart, A. 177
Maslow, A.: *Theory of Motivation* 156, 212n1
mastery-goal orientation 31
material deprivation 56, 59
maternal deprivation 97
maternal sensitivity 99–100
Mayo, R. V. 177
McCartney, G. 57
McCluskey, G. 33–34, 75, 76, 90, 179
McGrath, H. 64n3
McKinney, S. 221
McLaughlin, K. A. 89
Mead, G. H. 131n2
mediation 107; misappropriation of social justice 220; peer 178–179; unequal power relations, 179
medicalisation of normality 76
medical model 34–35, 38; *see also* Individual, Deficit, Medical (IDM) model
Melnick, H. 16, 210
Mental Health Foundation 205
mesosystem 109
Messiou, K. 6, *50*, 77, 198–200, **200**, **201**, 203, 212n2
Meyer, X. 176
micro-aggressions 217
microsystem 109
Mills, M. 219
Milner, H. R. 134
Mims, L. C. 166b
Minchin, T. 80n2
mindset: entity 31; exclusionary 76; incremental 31
modelling of behaviour 106, 107, 136, 174, 228
Moldavsky, M. 89
Montgomery, C. 206, 210
Morris, P. A. 109
Moses, L. 116
Mosley, J. 69
motivation 174; extrinsic 193–194, **194**, 196; intrinsic 193, 194, 196; *see also* self-determination theory
Mowat, J. G. **15**, 42n5, 45, *53*, 54, *54*, 77, 108, *201*, 212n2
Muir Review of the Scottish Education system 20, 205

Multi-Academy Trusts 19
multi-agency working 169; barriers to 170–171, **170–171**; facilitators 170–171, **170–171**; governance 170; management 170; processes 170; resources for 170
Mundschenk, N. 84
Munn, P. 51
mutual accountability 22
mutual engagement 218, **218**
My World Triangle 168

naive knowledge 174
named person 168
National Audit Report 37
National Challenge 18
National Framework for Inclusion 37–38
National Improvement Framework (NIF) 20–21, 150
National Literacy and Numeracy strategies 18
National Union of Teachers survey (2016) 18
neglect 163
neo-liberalism 4, 7, 22, 23, 25, 219, 220, 226, 233; relentless and insidious march of 10–11
Netherlands, the: *Attention Deficit Hyperactivity Disorder* 91–92; labelling 77; prejudice 72
net-widening **84**
neuroscience 159
neutral stimulus 103
Newman, B. M. 102, *103*, 104
Newman, P. R. 102, *103*, 104
new trajectory 140–142
NIF *see National Improvement Framework* (NIF)
Nind, M. 33
Nix, S. 176
Noble, T. 64n3
No Child Left Behind 16, 133
Noguera, P. 218, 219
Nolan, A. 162, 163
Nordenberg, D. 57, 163
Northern Ireland 17
Norwich, B. 28, 29, 32, 34, 38–39, 41
nurture 117, 118, 231; in action 158–160; behaviour and 158; children's learning, understanding of 156; classroom 156–157; community building through 6,

154–171; critique of 162–163; and development of wellbeing 157; impact of 161–162, **162**; language and 157; principles of 156–158; secondary 159, **160**; transitions 158; variant models of 159; as whole-school approach 160–162, *161*; *see also* trauma-informed practice

Obama, B. 16, 24n3; administration (2009–2017) 133
Obel, C. 89
objectified being 204
O'Connor, L. 134
ODD *see Oppositional Defiance Disorder* (ODD)
OECD *see* Organisation for Economic Cooperation and Development (OECD)
off-rolling 75, 144
OFSTED (Office for Standards in Education, Children's Services and Skills) 139, 142
Ogden, M. 116
Olsen, J. 89
ontology 93
OOSCI *see Out-of-School Children Initiative* (OOSCI)
operant conditioning: mechanisms of **104**; reinforcement, role of 104–105; trial-and-error learning 103–104
Oplatka, I. 220
Oppositional Defiance Disorder (ODD) 87, 89, 95n1
oppression: components of **47**, 48–49; definition of 46; disability as form of 34–35; and marginalisation 46–47
Organisation for Economic Cooperation and Development (OECD) 4, 9, 10, 14, 20–22, 27, 226; cyberbullying 73; discipline as objectification 122; Emotional and Behavioural Difficulties, definition of 82; policy documentation, excellence and social justice in 15; on poverty measurement 56; role in the globalisation of educational policy 11–12; on school climate 155; standardised tests 36; *Trends Shaping Education 2022* 14
Osher, D. 177, 192, 214, 227, 228
Out-of-School Children Initiative (OOSCI) 13

over-representation of specific groups 83–85
Oxford Co-Space Longitudinal survey 66

PACE (Playfulness, Acceptance, Curiosity and Empathy) framework 160
pandemic: impact on children and young people 1, 25, 65–66; socio-emotional and psychological impact of 65–66; global 13–14
Pantić, N. 231
parental engagement 226, 231; continuum of practice 206–207; deficit perspectives on parents and families 208–211, *209*; economic, social and cultural capital and 207–208; 'hard to reach parents,' narrative of 208–211, *209*; and parental involvement, conflation of 206, *207*; school community through, empowering 6
parental involvement and parental engagement, conflation of 206, *207*
parental states of mind and child attachment styles, correlation between 98, **99**
Parner, E. 89
Parsons, C. 34
participation 27, 34; legitimate 106; pupil 6, 191–211, 231
participative and collaborative school cultures, community building through 203–211; parental engagement 206–211; pupil voice and participation 203–205, *204*
partnership working 13, 110, 231
participative approaches to school discipline 196, *197*
participative school cultures 220–223; *see also* parental engagement; pupil voice, and participation; school culture
PBIS *see Positive Behaviour Interventions and Supports* (PBIS)
PBS *see Positive Behaviour Support* (PBS)
pedagogy 5, 21, 23, 33, 34, 36, 67, 71, 78, 81, 91, 92, 94, 125, 154, 174, 186, 227, 231; inclusive 29, 30, 41, 86, 173, 199, 219, 230; relational 185

282   *Index*

peer mediation 178, 179; flexible consistency 179
Percival, J. 139
performativity 10, 11, 21, 60, 67, 77; and inclusion, conflict between 35–36
Perkins, D. 111n1, 174, 175; *Teaching for Understanding Framework* 3–4, 111n1
personal authority 123, 125, **125**, 126
person-centred therapy/therapeutic practice 154, 180
person–environment interaction: bioecolgical theory 110; bioecological theory 108; cognitive social-historical theory 107; eco-system 109–110; sociocultural theory 107–108
Peters, R. S. **121**
Piaget, J. 156, 172n1
Pickett, K. 46
PIRLS *see* Progress in International Reading Literacy Study (PIRLS)
Pirrie, A. 123, 126
PISA *see* Programme for International Student Assessment (PISA)
'place makers,' school leaders as 201–203
policy borrowing 4, 14, 15, 23, 174
policy context 4; in England 17–19, 139; in Scotland 19–21; in the USA 16–17
policy context pertaining to school discipline: in England 139–145; in Scotland 145–151; in the USA 133–134
policy context, disparity between rhetoric and reality in: English policy context 37; Scottish policy context 37–38
policy documents, comparison between 149–151, *149–151*
Pons, F. 99–100
Porter, L. 115, 135, 153n2
positional leadership 216
positive behaviour 3, 69, 70, 75, 117, 136, 143, 146, 147, **197**, 211, 226, 230; in early years 147, *150*
Positive Behaviour in the Early Years 147, 150c
Positive Behaviour Interventions and Supports (PBIS) 204
Positive Behaviour Support (PBS) 134–136

positive discipline 3, 135, 147, 167
positive whole-school ethos and culture, developing 149, 198–199
post-traumatic stress 52
poverty 22, 45, 49, 52; absolute 59, 60; and ACEs 164; of aspiration 56–57; definition of 55–56; as dynamic 56; impact on children and young people 5, 55–63; as insidious 56; measurement of 55–56; persistent 56; and relationships 58–59; relative 56, 59, 60; severe 57; social and relational aspects of 51; stigma of 58
power 123–126, 134, 205; as authority 137; definition of 123; developmental theory 117–118; by inducement 138; as manipulation 136, 137; relations, unequal 203; school discipline policy, implications for 117–118
power for 134
powerful collective responsibility 22
power over 123, 135
power to 123, 135
power with 135
practice: associated with neo-liberalism 22; and behaviour management 132–152; building community through 6; child-rearing 101; communities of 106, 191; continuum of 206–207; evidence-based 118; exclusionary 3, 27, 77, 79; exclusionary disciplinary 36; exclusionary teaching 36; inclusive 26, 39, 42, 51, 67, 75, 78–79, 231; promoting positive behaviour 3; restorative 117–118, 173–188, 231; social 40; transformational 49; trauma-informed 6, 154–172, 231
prejudice 46, 51, 72–73, 82, 85, 174, 193, 227, 228
Pretti-Frontczak, K. 155
Price, H. B. 229
a principled approach to education and society 28
professional learning communities 232
Professional Standards 38, 225; *see also* General Teaching Council for Scotland (GTCS)
Programme for International Student Assessment (PISA) 11, 12, 16, 24n2
Progress in International Reading Literacy Study (PIRLS) 24n2
psychological developmental theory 159
psychopathology 52

punishment 16, 104, **104**, 119–120, 138, 187, 196, **197**
Pupil Equity Fund 62
pupil participation 141, 231; school community through, empowering 6, 191–211; *see also* school community
Pupil Premium Grant 18
Pupil Referral Units 139
pupil voice, and participation 203–205, *204*; *see also* pupil participation; school community
Putnam, R. D. 49, 225, 233n4

quasi-market 11, 19
quality education 13
Qvortrup, A. 28, 40
Qvortrup, L. 28, 40

RA *see* restorative approaches (RA)
race 26, 76, 134; *see also* ethnicity
Race to the Top 16, 133
Rafanell, I. 126
Rashford, M. 108
rationale for action 199–201, **200**, **201**
reactive *vs.* proactive approaches to school discipline 196
Reader, T. 116
Reay, D. 220
reflective self-functioning 99
reflexes 105
reflex responses 105
Regional Improvement Collaboratives (RICs) 21
regular classrooms 33
Reimer, K. 180, 181, 185, 187
Reimers, F. 14
reinforcement: of behaviour 70, 104–105, 136 (*see also* behaviourism and operant conditioning); of learning 176
Reinholdt-Dunne, M. L. 99–100
relatedness 192, 193, 196; inner-relatedness 81; social 70
relational approach 1, 3, 5–6, 113, 152, 154, 155, 157, 161, 166, 167, 171, 173, 176, 177, 186, 191, 196, *197*, 211, 226, 230
relational approaches *see* humanistic approaches; nurture; restorative justice/practice; trauma-informed practice
relational leadership 217
relational pedagogy 185
relational school 154

relational trust 210, 217, 221, 223–224, 226, 227
relationship 146–147; between ACE 164–165; with agency and control 194–196, **195**, *195*, **197**; with autonomy and control 194–196; better 147–148; better learning and better behaviour 147–148; 'deviant' student and school disaffection 127–130; dialectic and dynamic exclusion 38–41; and poverty 58–59; social exclusion and marginalisation 50–51; working 170
relationships 70, 73; between adults and children 193; between teachers and students 58–59, 86, 126, 145, **160**; family 97; school-family-child 63; with staff and peers 66
relative poverty 56, 59, 60
relativity 51
religious beliefs 26
Renfrewshire 160
repression 128, 164
resilience 5, 52, 53, *54*, 58, 64n3, 83, 148, 165, 224, 225
Resilience Matrix 168
responsive to need 196, *197*
restorative approaches (RA) 184–185; *see also* restorative justice/practice
restorative circles 178, 181
restorative conferencing 178, 180
restorative conversations 173, 174, 178–180, 187
restorative justice (RJ): affirmative 181, 184, 187; community building through 6, 173–187; recent developments within the field 186; restorative practice *versus* 177; 'sticky-problem' of transfer 173–176, *175*, **175**; teacher educators, role of 185–186; transformative 181, 184, 187
restorative practice (RP) 117, 118, 146, 187, 205, 231; in action 178; as coherence 180–184, **181**, **183**; community building through 6, 173–187; flexible consistency in approach 179; framework for 185, *186*; and imbalances of power 179–180; recent developments within the field 186; restorative justice *versus* 177; and school discipline 178–179; in schools 177–178; separating the child from the behaviour 180; 'sticky-problem'

284 *Index*

of transfer 173–176, *175*, **175**;
transformative 177; as understood by
C&YP 178
restorative questions 178
Richardson, M. J. 136
RICs *see Regional Improvement
Collaboratives* (RICs)
Riestenberg, N. 179, 180
Rights Respecting Schools movement 205
Rights, Support and Wellbeing Team
147
Riley, K. A. 6, 36, 68, 128, 192–193,
198–201, **200**, **201**, 203, 211, 212n2
Rix, J. 33
RJ *see* restorative justice (RJ)
Robertson, J. 116
Rogers, C. 69, 119, 154,180; *see also*
person-centred therapy/therapeutic
practice; unconditional positive
regard
Rogers, B. 135
role models 106, 159, 162; *see also*
Bandura, A.
Rothstein-Fisch, C. 210, 229
Rouse, M. 6
RP *see* restorative practice (RP)
Rudduck, J. 203
Russell, B. 123
Rustique-Forrester, E. 68
Rutland, A. 128
Ryan, R. M. 193
Rylak, D. 116

SAC *see Scottish Attainment Challenge*
(SAC)
safe haven 97
Sahlberg, P. 221, 225
Salamanca Agreement see Salamanca
Statement and Framework
Salamanca Statement and Framework
30, 67
Salomon, G. 174, 175
Sandill, A. 219
Save the Children 55, 66, 208
scaffolding 107, 157, 158
Scanfeld, V. 134
Scanlan, M. 210–211, 213, 218,
229, 232
schema: action 108; mental 87
Schiff, M. 176, 179
Schleicher, A. 27
Schlösser, A. 161
school climate 116, 155, 231;
authoritative 149; and *RP* 178; and

social capital 226; *see also* classroom
climate; climate for learning; school
ethos
school community 6, 226–229;
building through parental
engagement 206–211; building
through pupil voice and participation
203–205; empowering 6, 211,
226–229, *228*
school community during lockdown,
supporting 222–225
school culture 198–199; empowering
225–229; rationale for action and
focus for enquiry 199–201, **200**, **201**
school disaffection 2, 5, 65–81; and
'deviant' student, relationship
between 127–130
school discipline: authoritarian
approaches to 134–139; as coercive
control 137; crisis in 119–120;
as objectification 122; reactive
vs. proactive approaches to 196;
restorative practice and 178–179; as
surveillance 120, 122; theoretical
perspectives on 120
school discipline policies 113, 132–152;
in England 139; new trajectory
140–142, *142*; power, agency and
autonomy, implications of 117–118;
in Scotland 145–151; in USA
133–134
school ethos 58, 75, 81, 85, 141,
146–147, 150–151, 155, 177, 201,
229
school leaders: as 'place makers,' role of
201–203
school leadership 81, 161, 184, 201,
213, 221–222, 227–229
schools: autonomous systems 19;
climate for learning 193–198;
community and 191–193, *192* (*see
also* school community); disaffection
5; governance 19; restorative practice
in 177–178
schools, as places of belonging
or exclusion 65–80; agents of
exclusion 67; as 'a stubborn foe'
68–69; bullying behaviours 73;
conundrum 74–76; and criminal
justice system 74; and demographics
74; disproportionate rates 75–76;
exclusionary mindsets 76; hierarchies
67; impact on children and families
74; labelling 76–78; prejudice

72–73; stigmatisation 76–78; student disaffection 71–72; unconditional positive regard 69–70

school-to-prison pipeline **84**, 133, 179

Schoolwide Positive Behaviour Support (SWPBS) 136–138

Schore, A. N. 101

Schore, J. R. 101

Scotland: *Additional Support Needs* 62; agenda of empowerment 21; *Areas of Multiple Deprivation* 61; *Attention Deficit Hyperactivity Disorder* 89; *Behaviour in Scottish Schools Surveys* (2006) 145; behaviour management 113; *Care Experienced* (previously *Looked After and Accommodated*) 61, 62, 64n6; Child Poverty Act 60; *Child Poverty Strategy* 60; Children and Young People (Scotland) Act 2020 167; Children (Equal Protection from Assault) (Scotland) Act 2019 131n1; *Curriculum for Excellence* 20, 61; *Discipline Task Force* 146; disproportionate rates of school exclusion in 75, 76; education policy 19–20, as devolved 17; *Education Scotland* 20, 147, 184, 187; equity in education 20–21; *Every Child, Every Chance* 60; *Fairer Scotland* 60; *Growing up in Scotland* 59; *Included, Engaged and Involved Part 2: A positive approach to preventing and managing school exclusions* 75; General Teaching Council for Scotland (GTCS) 38, 42, 151, 225; intersectionality 61–62; *Learning Together* 208; Mental Health Foundation Peer Education Programme 169; *Muir Review* of the Scottish Education system 20; *National Improvement Framework* (NIF) 20–21; over-representation of specific groups 84; poverty-related attainment gap, nature of 60–61, *61*; policy context 19–21; poverty-related attainment gap 60–62, tensions within the system 62–63; *Professional Standards* 225; Public Health Scotland 66; *Pupil Equity Fund* 62; *Regional Improvement Collaboratives* (RICs) 21; restorative justice 181–184, **183**; *Rights, Support and Wellbeing Team* 147; school exclusions 74,

78; *Scottish Attainment Challenge* (SAC) 22, 62, 64n7; *Scottish Child Payment* 60; Scottish Index of Multiple Deprivation (SIMD) 61, 64n5; *Scottish National Standardised Assessments* 21; SEBN 2, 3; staged intervention model 167–168, **168**; statutory guidance 2017 168–169; *Tackling Child Poverty Fund and through* 60

Scotland, childhood poverty in: eradication of 60; flipping the thinking 63; manifestation of 59–60; state of 59; tensions within the system 62–63, *63*

Scotland, school discipline policies in 113, 132, 145–151; behaviour 146–149; comparison between policy documents 149–151, *149–151*; data-informed system 145–146; included, engaged and involved 148–149, *148*; learning 147–149; positive behaviour in the early years 147; positive whole-school ethos and culture, developing 149; relationships 146–149

Scottish Attainment Challenge (SAC) 22, 62, 64n7

Scottish Child Payment 60

Scottish Index of Multiple Deprivation (SIMD) 61, 64n5

Scottish National Standardised Assessments 21

Scottish policy context, disparity between rhetoric and reality in 37–38

SDGs *see* Sustainable Development Goals (SDGs)

SEBD *see Social, Emotional and Behavioural Difficulties* (SEBD)

SEBN *see Social, Emotional and Behavioural Needs* (SEBN)

secure attachment 97–99, 157

secure base 97

segregation 31, 36, 45, 58, 67, 85

self-actualisation 118, 155, 194, 195, 212n2

self-control 119

self-determination theory 119, 193, 226

self-discipline 118, 119, 137

self-efficacy 105, 117

self-regulation 88, 97, 108b, 116, 118, 119, 193

self-responsibility 137, 177

Sellar, S. 11, 12, 16

286 *Index*

SEL *see* social and emotional learning (SEL)
SEMHD *see Social, Emotional and Mental Health Difficulties* (SEMHD)
SEMHN *see Social, Emotional and Mental Health Needs* (SEMHN)
SEN(D) 34, 42n3; and inclusion, tension between 31–32; as rational concept 33
SEND *see Special Educational Needs and Disabilities* (SEND)
senior leaders, changing conceptualisation of role of 223–225
sense of belonging 1, 3, 5, 27, 28, 31, 36, 58, 59, 63, 69–71, 73, 78, 79, 185, 191, 199, 202, 203, 227, 230, 233
SEP *see* socio-economic position (SEP)
Sergiovanni, T. J. 192
SES *see* socio-economic status (SES)
sexual orientation 26
Shakespeare, T. 34–36, 39
Shalaby, C. 155
shame 58, 74, 118
SHANARRI 168; *see also* Getting it Right for Every Child (GIRFEC)
shaping 104
shared leadership 216, 228
shared repertoire 218, **218**
Sheehy, K. 33
Sheridan, M. A. 89
Shirley, D. 219
SIMD *see* Scottish Index of Multiple Deprivation (SIMD)
Simmons, D. 166b
Simmons, K. 33
Simpson, R. 84
situated experience 106
situated learning 106–107, 191
Skiba, R. J. 133
Slee, R. 26, 29–32, 34–36, 38, 51, 67, 68, 70, 76, 84, 91, 127, 129–130, 135, 211
Sluiter, M. N. 77, 91
Smith, D. 134
Smith, M. 57, 90
Smith, R. G. 216
Social and Emotional Aspects of Learning (SEAL) *Programme* 139–140, 147
Social, Emotional and Behavioural Difficulties (SEBD) 59, 62, 78, 82, 84, 147

Social, Emotional and Behavioural Needs (SEBN) 2, 3, 5, 29, 43, 78, 82, 102, 108b, 157, 160, 161
Social, Emotional and Mental Health Difficulties (SEMHD) 83
Social, Emotional and Mental Health Needs (SEMHN) 3, 5, 29, 43, 83, 102, 157, 161, 169
social and emotional learning (SEL) 137, 139–140, 159, 165, 192, 205, 212n3
social capital 51, 207–208, 210, 211, 225–229; bridging 229, 233n4
social constructivism 107–108; compatibility with attachment theory and social learning theory 110; incompatibility with behaviourism 110
social exclusion 5, 43–64, 65–80; agency and 51; dynamics 51; and marginalisation, relationship between 50–51; relativity and 51
social inequality 11, 45, 58, 163
social justice 6, 15–16, **15**, 18, 19, 36, 45–47, 51, 55, 78, 134, 152, 189, 213–214, *215*; capacity building to promote 216–217; drive for 15–19, **15**; leadership for *see* social justice leadership; and marginalisation 46–47
social justice leadership 6, 217–225, 231; conceptualisation of 217; courageous leadership, principles of 218, **218**; equity, challenge of 222; focus on the system 219–220; inclusion, challenge of 222–223; inclusive school communities, building 219; as politically loaded 220; school community during lockdown, supporting 222; school leadership perspective of 221–222; senior leaders, changing conceptualisation of role of 223–225; socially just leaders 213, 217; socially just schooling 218, **218**; systems perspective of 221; tensions and dilemmas in socially just schools 219; in unprecedented times 220–225
social learning theory 105–107, 117
socially just leaders 213, 217; *see also* socially just leadership; socially just schooling

socially just leadership: school community through, empowering 6; *see also* socially just leaders; socially just schooling
socially just schooling 218, **218**; tensions and dilemmas in 219
social mobility 3, 56, 64
social model of disability 34, 35, 38
social norms 35, 52, 70, 77, 105, 107, 109, 143, 186
social self 131n2
social structures 127
social theory of learning 106
sociocultural process 216
sociocultural theory 107–108, 136, 156, 157, 218
socio-economic inequality 165; *see also* economic inequality; income inequality; inequality; social inequality; structural inequality
socio-economic position (SEP) 164
socio-economic status (SES) 33, 45, 67, 73, 106, 134; and ADHD 89, 90
socio-emotional learning 174; *see also Social and Emotional Aspects of Learning* (SEAL)
sociological systems theory 40
solution-focused approaches 115
solution-focused support 169
solution-orientated approaches 117
Sømhovd, M. 99–100
South America: disproportionality in special education 34
space 12, 66, 202–203, 205, 211, 232
Special Educational Needs and Disabilities (SEND) 27, 42n1, 53, 66, 71, 74, 75, 83, 84, 141, 144, 145, 147; *Code of Practice* 83
Special Educational Needs and Disability Regulations (2014) 37
special education, disproportionality in 33–34
Spillane, J. P. 216, 226
stable attachment 102
staged intervention model 167–168, **168**
State of the World Report 66
statutory guidance 2017 168–169
'sticky-problem' of transfer 173–176, *175*, **175**
stigma 59, 74; of poverty 58
stigmatisation 32, 39, 45, 51, 76–77, 79, 84, 143, 173, 205

stimulus 104; conditioned 103; neutral 103; and response, association between 103; unconditioned 103
Stoll, L. 198
Strange Situation 98
structural inequality 16, 46, 57, 68; levels of *48*
student achievement 11, 31, 155, 227; *see also* student attainment; poverty-related attainment gap
student attainment 33–34, 38, 45, 55, 58, 62, 148, 149, 149c–151c, 206, 226; *see also* poverty-related attainment gap
student disaffection 65–80, 127–128, 211
student participation 204; *see also* pupil voice, and participation
student voice 203–205; *see also* pupil voice, and participation
Sun, J. 226
'Super Nanny' 70, 96
Support Groups 108, 108b
Supporting Children's Learning Code of Practice 38
surveillance, discipline as 120, 122, 166
Suspension and Permanent Exclusion 75, 144
sustainability 15
Sustainable Development Goals (SDGs): SDG1 (no poverty) 13; SDG3 (good health and wellbeing) 13; SDG4 (a quality education) 13; SDG10 (reduced inequalities) 13
SWPBS *see Schoolwide Positive Behaviour Support* (SWPBS)
symbolic interactionism 126
symbolic interactionists 131n2
symptoms 230
systemness 214, 231–233
system segmentation **84**
systems perspective of social justice leadership 221

Tackling Child Poverty Fund and through 60
Tancredi, H. 91–93
Tanyu, M. 177
Tawell, A. 33–34, 75
teacher educators, role of 185–186
teacher professionalism 219, 230, 231–233; *see also* teacher autonomy

288 *Index*

teacher autonomy 19–21, 216, 219, 231; tension between accountability and 219
Teaching for Understanding Framework (Perkins) 3–4, 111n1
Tebbit, N. 220
'Tell Them from Me' 128
TESS *see Times Educational Supplement Scotland* (TESS)
Theoharis, G. 213, 218, 232
Tett, L. 209, *209*
theoretical perspectives on school discipline 120–2, **121**
Thomas, M. 159, **160**
Thompson, I. 33–34, 75
Thoutenhoofd, E. 77, 91
tiers of support 185
Times Educational Supplement Scotland (TESS) 116, 116b
Timpson review of school exclusion 144
TIMSS see Trends in International Mathematics and Science Study (TIMSS)
tokenistic reward systems 69–70, 118, 136, 138, 230
Torrance, D. 226
transfer: high 174; of learning 173–176; low 174; of policy 14
transformational leadership 214, 216
transformation of the education system 36
transformative restorative justice 181, 184, 187
transitions 158
trauma-informed practice 134, 150, 163–167, 186, 231; community building through 6, 154–171; critique of 165–166; impact of 165; *see also* nurture
Treanor, M. 56–57, 63, 209
Trends in International Mathematics and Science Study (TIMSS) 24n2
Trends Shaping Education 2022 14
Trevarthen, C. 101, 102, 118
trial-and-error learning 103–104, **104**
Trumbull, E. 210, 229
Trump administration (2017–2021) 133
types of social communities 40

UK *see* United Kingdom (UK)
unconditional positive regard 3, 5, 69–70, 155, 180; *see also* person-centred therapeutic practice/person-centred therapy; Rogers, C.

unconditioned stimulus 103
UNCRC *see* United Nations Convention on the Rights of the Child (UNCRC)
UNESCO 28; *Global Education and Monitoring Report* 25, 40; *Guide for Ensuring Inclusion and Equity in Inclusion* 30; Out-of-School Children Initiative (OOSCI) 13
UNICEF *see* United Nations Children's Fund (UNICEF)
United Kingdom (UK) 3, 4, 42n2; autonomous school system 19; behaviour management 113; crisis in school discipline 119; disproportionality in special education 33; disproportionate rates of school exclusion in 75–76; Education Endowment Foundation 153n1; education policy 17; excellence and social justice, drive for 17; *Family Connects* programme 208; macrosystem 4; multi-agency and interdisciplinary working 171; oppression 47; pandemic on learning, impact of 14; parental engagement 208; poverty 56; *Save the Children* 208; school discipline policies 113, 132, 139–152; Social Mobility Unit 143; *Special Educational Needs and Disabilities* (SEND) 27; *Suspension and Permanent Exclusion* 144; trauma-informed practice 165; unconditional positive regard 70; *see also* policy context; Wales and Northern Ireland.
United Nations Children's Fund (UNICEF) 4, 10, 55; Education Strategy 2019–2030 12; *Every Child Learns* 12–13, 18; sustainability, goals for 60
United Nations Convention on the Rights of the Child (UNCRC) 30, 151, 167, 203
United Nations General Assembly 13
University of Strathclyde 233n2
University Technological Colleges 19
unsupported trauma, effects of 164–165
USA 9, 113, 229, 231, 232; *Attention Deficit Hyperactivity Disorder* 88; authoritarian approaches 6; capacity building to promote social justice at district level 216–217; cultural

responsiveness 227; excellence and social justice, drive for 16–17; Federal Funding 136; macrosystem 4; *No Child Left Behind* 16, 133; policy context 16–17; poverty 56, 57; poverty-related attainment gap 60; *Race to the Top* 16, 133; restorative practice 179; school discipline policies 133–134; trauma-informed high schools 165

Vaala, B. L. 71
Vaandering, D. 178–179
Velez, G. 178
Vincent-Lancrin, S. 14
Visser, J. 86, 91
Vygotsky, L. 96, 107–108; *see also* Zone of Proximal Development

Wales 17; disproportionate rates of school exclusion in 75
Walsh, C. 33
Walsh, D. 57, 165, 166
Warin, J. 176
Warnock report 31
Watson, C. 70
Webber, L. 160
Weintraub, L. 134
wellbeing 2, 5, 13, 14, 19, 28, 29, 33, 45, 46, 52, 55–63, 70, 71, 73, 74, 145, 160, 166b, 169, 177–179, 192, 202, 217, 220, 223, 229, 230; development, nurture and 157; emotional 100; nurture and

157; psychological 66, 82; pupil 147–149; relationship with learning and behaviour *230*; socio-emotional 65, 75
Wenger, E. 117, 191
Wheeler, L. 91
Whitebread, D. 160
whole provision 22
wicked problem 27–28
wicked proportions 26–27
Wienen, A. W. 77, 91, 92
Wilkinson, R. 46
Williamson, G. 144
Wilson, J. **121**, 132, 137
Woodcock, S. 33
working relationships 170
working with (relationship) 228
World Bank 13
Wrong, D. 123, 125, 126, 136–138, 140

Young, E. L. 136
Young, R. 136

Zachar, P. 39
Zenib, J. 91
zero-tolerance approaches 117, 132–134, 136, 143, 144, 153n1, 177, 220, 229
Zone of Proximal Development 107; *see also* Vygotsky, L.
Zúñiga, X. 46, 49

Printed in the United States
by Baker & Taylor Publisher Services